MOTHERS AND OTHERS

Mothers and Others

THE EVOLUTIONARY ORIGINS OF MUTUAL UNDERSTANDING

Sarah Blaffer Hrdy

The Belknap Press *of* Harvard University Press   Cambridge, Massachusetts·London, England   2009

Library of Congress Cataloging-in-Publication Data

Hrdy, Sarah Blaffer, 1946-

Mothers and others : the evolutionary origins of mutual
understanding / Sarah Blaffer Hrdy.

     p. cm.

Includes bibliographical references and index.

ISBN 978-0-674-03299-6 (alk. paper)

     1. Mother and child.   2. Parental behavior in animals.

3. Child rearing--Psychological aspects.   4. Behavior evolution.

I. Title.

BF723.M55H73 2009

155.7--dc22   2008052936

For my children
and my children's children

CONTENTS

The leading problem in sociobiology today is explaining
why we have prosocial emotions.

—H. Gintis (2001)

Which is why we need to keep in mind that

. . . the causal chain of adaptive evolution begins with development.

—M. J. West-Eberhard (2003)

1

APES ON A PLANE

However selfish . . . man may be supposed, there are evidently some
principles in his nature which interest him in the fortunes of others.

—Adam Smith (1759)

Each year 1.6 billion passengers fly to destinations
around the world. Patiently we line up to be checked and patted down by
someone we've never seen before. We file on board an aluminum cylinder
and cram our bodies into narrow seats, elbow to elbow, accommodating
one another for as long as the flight takes.

With nods and resigned smiles, passengers make eye contact and
then yield to latecomers pushing past. When a young man wearing a
backpack hits me with it as he reaches up to cram his excess paraphernalia
into an overhead compartment, instead of grimacing or baring my
teeth, I smile (weakly), disguising my irritation. Most people on board
ignore the crying baby, or pretend to. A few of us are even inclined to signal
the mother with a sideways nod and a wry smile that says, "I know

how you must feel." We want her to know that we understand, and that the disturbance she thinks her baby is causing is not nearly as annoying as she imagines, even though we also can intuit, and so can she, that the young man beside her, who avoids looking at her and keeps his eyes determinedly glued to the screen of his laptop, does indeed mind every bit as much as she fears.

Thus does every frequent flier employ on a regular basis peculiarly empathic aptitudes for theorizing about the mental states and intentions of other people, our species' gift for mutual understanding. Cognitively oriented psychologists refer to the ability to think about what someone else knows as having a "theory of mind."[1] They design clever experiments to determine at what age human children acquire this ability and to learn how good at mind reading (or more precisely, attributing mental states to others) nonhuman animals are. Other psychologists prefer the related term "intersubjectivity," which emphasizes the capacity and eagerness to share in the emotional states and experiences of other individuals—and which, in humans at least, emerges at a very early stage of development, providing the foundation for more sophisticated mind reading later on.[2]

Whatever we call it, this heightened interest in and ability to scan faces, and our perpetual quest to understand what others are thinking and intending, to empathize and care about their experiences and goals, help make humans much more adept at cooperating with the people around us than other apes are. Far oftener than any of us are aware, humans intuit the mental experiences of other people, and—the really interesting thing—care about having other people share theirs. Imagine two seat-mates on this plane, one of whom develops a severe migraine in the course of the flight. Even though they don't speak the same language, her new companion helps her, perhaps holding a wet cloth to her head, while the sick woman tries to reassure her that she is feeling better. Humans are often eager to understand others, to be understood, and to cooperate. Passengers crowded together on an aircraft are just one example of how empathy and intersubjectivity are routinely brought to play in human interactions. It happens so often that we take the resulting accommodations for granted. But just imagine if, instead of humans being crammed and annoyed aboard this airplane, it were some other species of ape.

At moments like this, it is probably just as well that mind reading in humans remains an imperfect art, given the oddity of my sociobiological musings. I cannot keep from wondering what would happen if my fellow human passengers suddenly morphed into another species of ape. What if I were traveling with a planeload of chimpanzees? Any one of us would be lucky to disembark with all ten fingers and toes still attached, with the baby still breathing and unmaimed. Bloody earlobes and other appendages would litter the aisles. Compressing so many highly impulsive strangers into a tight space would be a recipe for mayhem.

Once acquired, the habit of comparing humans with other primates is hard to shake. My mind flits back to one of the earliest accounts of the behavior of Hanuman langurs, a type of Asian monkey that, as a young woman, I went to India to study. T. H. Hughes was a British functionary and amateur naturalist who had been sent out to the subcontinent to help govern the Raj. "In April 1882, when encamped at the village of Singpur in the Sohagpur district of Rewa state . . . My attention was attracted to a restless gathering of 'Hanumans,'" wrote Hughes. As he watched, a fight broke out between two males, one of them traveling with a group of females, the other presumably a stranger. "I saw their arms and teeth going viciously, and then the throat of one of the aggressors was ripped right open and he lay dying." At that point Hughes surmised that "the tide of victory would have been in [the stranger's favor] had the odds against him not been reinforced by the advance of two females . . . Each flung herself upon him, and though he fought his enemies gallantly, one of the females succeeded in seizing him in the most sacred portion of his person, depriving him of his most essential appendages."[3]

Descriptions of missing digits, ripped ears, and the occasional castration are scattered throughout the field accounts of langur and red colobus monkeys, of Madagascar lemurs, and of our own close relatives among the Great Apes. Even among famously peaceful bonobos, a type of chimpanzee so rare and difficult to access in the wild that most observations come from zoos, veterinarians sometimes have to be called in following altercations to stitch back on a scrotum or penis. This is not to say that humans don't display similar propensities toward jealousy, indignation, rage, xenophobia, or homicidal violence. But compared with our nearest ape relations, humans are more adept at forestalling outright mayhem. Our first impulse is usually to get along. We do not automatically attack a stranger, and face-to-face killings are a much harder sell for humans than for chimpanzees. With 1.6 billion airline passengers annually compressed and manhandled, no dismemberments have been reported yet. The goal of this book will be to explain the early origins of the mutual understanding, giving impulses, mind reading, and other hypersocial tendencies that make this possible.

"WIRED" TO COOPERATE

From a tender age and without special training, modern humans identify with the plights of others and, without being asked, volunteer to help and share, even with strangers. In these respects, our line of apes is in a class by itself. Think back to the tsunami in Indonesia or to hurricane Katrina. Confronted with images of the victims, donor after donor offered the same reason for giving: Helping was the only thing that made them feel better. People had a gut-level response to seeing anguished faces and hearing moaning recitals of survivors who had lost family members—wrenching cues broadcast around the world. This ability to identify with others and vicariously experience their suffering is not simply learned: It is part of us. Neuroscientists using brain scans to monitor neural activity in people asked to watch someone else do something like eating an apple, or asked just to imagine someone else eating an apple, find that the areas of the brain responsible for distinguishing ourselves from others are activated, as are areas of the brain actually responsible for controlling the muscles relevant to apple-eating. Tests in which people are requested to imagine others in an emotional situation produce similar results.[4] It is a quirk of mind that serves humans well in all sorts of social circumstances, not just acts of compassion but also hospitality, gift-giving, and good manners—norms that no culture is without.

Reflexively altruistic impulses are consistent with findings by neuroscientists who use magnetic resonance imaging (MRI) to monitor brain activity among experimentally paired strangers engaged in a variant of a famous game known as the Prisoner's Dilemma. In this situation, two players earn rewards either by cooperating or defecting. If neither player defects and both continue to cooperate over sequential games, both gain more than they would have without playing at all. But if one player opts out while his partner cooperates, the defector wins even more and his

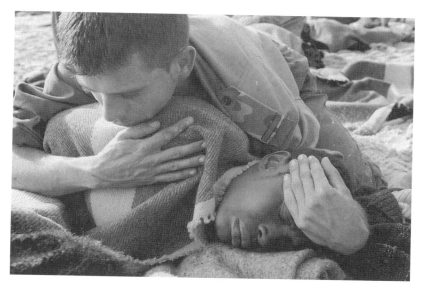

Compassion is not necessarily confined to group members. The Spanish soldier shown here is using his own body's warmth to revive an African refugee who was rescued while attempting to cross by boat from Morocco to Spain. (R. Perales/AP)

partner gets nothing. If both defect, they lose out entirely. Such experiments yield a remarkable result. Even when players are told by the experimenters that this is going to be a one-shot game, so that each player has only one chance to cooperate or defect, with no possibility of cooperating again to mutual advantage, 42 percent of randomly selected strangers nevertheless opt to behave cooperatively.[5]

Such generosity at first seems irrational, especially to economists who are accustomed to celebrating individualism and economic models that assume self-interested "rational actors," or to a sociobiologist like me who has devoted much of her professional life researching competition between primate males for access to fertile females, between females in the same group for resources, and even between offspring in the same family for access to nourishment and care. When considered in the context of how humankind managed to survive vast stretches of time and dramatic fluctuations in climate during the Pleistocene, in the period from around 1.8 million years ago until about 12,000 BCE, such generous tendencies turn out to be "better than rational" because people had to rely so much on time-tested relationships with others.[6]

Among people living in small, widely dispersed bands of intercon-
nected families likely to interact again and again, prosocial impulses—
meaning tendencies to voluntarily do things that benefit others—are
likely to be reciprocated or rewarded. The generous person's well-being
and that of his or her family depended more on maintaining the web
of social relationships that sustained them through good times and bad
than on the immediate outcome of a particular transaction. The people
you treat generously this year, with the loan of a tool or gift of food,
are the same people you depend on next year when your waterholes dry
up or game in your home range disappears.[7] Over their lifetimes people
would encounter and re-encounter their neighbors, not necessarily often, but again and again. Failures to reciprocate would result in loss of
allies or, worse still, social exclusion.[8]

Jump ahead thousands of years to the laboratories where researchers
administer such experiments today. As shown by research subjects who
cooperate even when there is no possibility for the favor to be reciprocated, "one-shot deals" are not an eventuality that human brains were
designed to register. Right from an early age, even before they can talk,
people find that helping others is inherently rewarding, and they learn to
be sensitive to who is helpful and who is not.[9] Regions of the brain activated by helping are the same as those activated when people process
other pleasurable rewards.[10]

Anyone who assumes that babies are just little egotists who enter
the world needing to be socialized so they can learn to care about others
and become good citizens is overlooking other propensities every bit
as species-typical. Humans are born predisposed to care how they relate
to others. A growing body of research is persuading neuroscientists that
Baruch Spinoza's seventeenth-century proposal better captures the full
range of tensions humans grow up with. "The endeavor to live in a shared,
peaceful agreement with others is an extension of the endeavor to pre-
serve oneself." Emerging evidence is drawing psychologists and economists alike to conclude that "our brains are wired to cooperate with others" as well as to reward or punish others for mutual cooperation.[11]

Perhaps not surprisingly, helpful urges are activated most readily
when people deal with each other face-to-face. Specialized regions of the
human brain, huge areas of the frontal and parietotemporal cortex, are
given over to interpreting other people's vocalizations and facial expres-

sions. Right from the first days of life, every healthy human being is avidly monitoring those nearby, learning to recognize, interpret, and even imitate their expressions. An innate capacity for empathizing with others becomes apparent within the first six months.[12] By early adulthood most of us will have become experts at reading other people's intentions. So attuned are we to the inner thoughts and feelings of those around us that even professionals trained *not* to respond emotionally to the distress of others find it difficult not to be moved. Therapists face particular challenges in this respect. Empathy, the stock-in-trade of psychotherapists because it really does produce better results, turns out to be their worst nightmare as well.[13] People who deal day-in-and-day-out with the troubles of others face such occupational hazards as "vicarious traumatization" and "compassion fatigue," or face the threat of "catching" a client's depression.[14]

New discoveries by evolutionarily minded psychologists, economists, and neuroscientists are propelling the cooperative side of human nature to center stage. New findings about how irrational, how emotional, how caring, and even how selfless human decisions can be are transforming disciplines long grounded in the premise that the world is a competitive place where to be a rational actor means being a selfish one. Researchers from diverse fields are converging on the realization that while humans can indeed be very selfish, in terms of empathic responses to others and our eagerness to help and share with them, humans are also quite unusual, notably different from other apes.[15]

"Without prosocial emotions," two theoretical economists opined recently, "we would all be sociopaths, and human society would not exist, however strong the institutions of contract, governmental law enforcement and reputation."[16] Coming from practitioners of the dismal science, this is revolutionary stuff. For evolutionists, it requires either special pleading or else new ways of thinking about how our species evolved and what being human means.

WHAT IT MEANS TO BE EMOTIONALLY MODERN

Time and again, anthropologists have drawn lines in the sand dividing humans from other animals, only to see new discoveries blur the boundaries. We drew up these lists of uniquely human attributes without realizing how much more they revealed about our ignorance of other animals than about the special attributes of our species. By the middle of the twentieth century, Man the Toolmaker had lost pride of place as Japanese and British researchers watched wild chimpanzees tailor twigs to fish for termites.[17] By now, every one of the Great Apes is known to select, prepare, and use tools, crafting natural objects into sponges, umbrellas, nutcrackers—even sharpening sticks for jabbing prey.[18] Furthermore, Great Apes have unquestionably been using tools for a long time. Archaeologists trace the special stone mortars that chimpanzees in west Africa use for nut cracking back in time at least 4,300 years.[19]

Great Apes employ tools in a wide range of contexts, and do so spontaneously, inventively, and sometimes with apparent foresight. In a recent article in *Science* magazine titled "Apes Save Tools for Future Use," Nicholas Mulcahy and Josep Call describe orangutan and bonobo subjects who were trained to use particular tools to solve a problem and earn a reward, and then were permitted to select particular tools to bring with them for tasks they would be asked to perform an hour later. They chose the tools likely to be most useful. Such experiments have led primatologists (and even comparative psychologists working with smart birds like corvids) to credit nonhuman animals with some ability to plan ahead.[20]

Arguably, Great Apes have been making and using tools since they last shared common ancestors with humans and with each other, and they transmitted this technological expertise along with various behaviors (like grooming protocol or greeting ceremonies) from one generation to another so that different populations have different repertories. Other apes also store memories much as we do, and in terms of spatial cognition or traits such as their ability to remember ordered symbols that briefly flash up on a computer screen, specially trained chimpanzees test better than graduate students.[21] In general, the basic cognitive machinery for dealing with their physical worlds is remarkably similar in humans and other apes.[22]

What about locomotion as the distinguishing trait? A key criterion of humanness, upright walking on two legs, bit the dust with the discovery of a fossilized trail of bipedal footprints left in volcano ash by australopithecines—apes with brains no bigger than a chimpanzee's—some four million years ago. Fossilized footprints together with fossilized skeletal remains made it clear that these long-armed, small-brained, extraordinarily chimplike creatures were walking upright millions of years before the emergence of the genus *Homo*.[23]

Bipedality is not what makes us human, and as clever as we think we are, the really big differences between chimpanzees and humans do not lie in the realm of basic spatial cognition or memory.[24] Apart from language, where humankind's uniqueness has never been in serious dispute, the last outstanding distinction between us and other apes involves a curious packet of hypersocial attributes that allow us to monitor the mental states and feelings of others, as scientists at the Max Planck Institute of Evolutionary Anthropology have recently suggested.

This institute is the premier place for studying psychological traits possessed by humans and other apes. Part of its ambitiously interdisciplinary research project is housed in a large building in the heart of the historic German city of Leipzig. Its offices and laboratories are filled with psychologists, behavioral ecologists, primatologists, and geneticists, who in a technical tour de force were recently able to extract DNA from extinct Neanderthals and compare it with that from modern humans. Research on children's cognitive development goes on here as well. The other branch of the institute is located a short distance away, in a sprawling zoological garden that is home to social groups of gorillas, chimpanzees, bonobos, and orangutans. Special laboratories enable scientists to conduct experiments on ape cognition, including recent experiments showing that bonobos and orangutans can plan ahead. All five species— human children and the four Great Apes—are being studied simultaneously using comparable methods, with spectacular results.

In 2005 Michael Tomasello, the American-born leader of the Max Planck team, proposed a new dividing line between humans and nonhuman apes. "We propose," he and his colleagues announced, "that the crucial difference between human cognition and that of other species is the ability to participate with others in collaborative activities with shared goals and intentions."[25] For the moment, this trait, along with our extralarge brains and capacity for language, marks the new dividing line separating our natures from those of other apes. Accordingly, "human beings, and only human beings, are biologically adapted for participating in collaborative activities involving shared goals and socially coordinated action plans."[26] Only among humans do we find large-scale cooperative endeavors involving people who are not necessarily close kin. Only hu-

During the dry season in central Brazil, Kayapó men wade into the shallow currents of the Xingu River where they release a fish poison by beating bundles of a plant called *timbo*. Stunned or suffocated by the timbo sap, fish float to the surface and are easily gathered by women and children who wade in with baskets at the water's edge. Such high-value food sources were out of reach of our prehominin ancestors but became accessible once hominins with stone-age technologies began to understand one another's goals well enough to coordinate complex activities. (Joan Bamberger)

mans, for example, can fan out around an encampment, gather building materials, consciously register the mental blueprint someone else has in mind, and chip in to help construct a shelter.

Humans "are the world's experts at mind reading," far more "biologically adapted" to collaborate with others than any other ape, Tomasello stresses. To him, these aptitudes are nearly synonymous with our special ability to perceive what others know, intend, and desire.[27] Human infants are not just social creatures, as other primates are; they are "ultrasocial."[28] Unlike chimpanzees and other apes, almost all humans are naturally eager to collaborate with others. They may prefer engaging with familiar kin, but they also easily coordinate with nonkin, even strangers. Given opportunities, humans develop these proclivities into complex enterprises, such as collaboratively tracking and hunting prey, processing food, playing cooperative games, building shelters, or designing spacecraft that reach the moon.[29]

At some point in the course of their evolution, our ancestors became more deeply interested in monitoring the intentions of others and eager to share their inner feelings and thoughts as well as their mental states. This interest laid the groundwork for the peculiarly cooperative natures that would distinguish these hominins from other bipedal apes and rendered apes in the line leading to the genus *Homo* what I think of as emotionally modern.[30] My goal in writing this book is to understand how such other-regarding tendencies could have evolved in creatures as self-serving as apes are.

The fact that humans are better equipped to cooperate than other apes does not mean that men do not compete with one another for status or for access to mates, or that women are not also fiercely competitive in the domains that matter to them, striving for desirable mates, local clout, and access to resources for themselves and their children. Such status quests are primate-wide propensities, and, under pressure, conflict boils over into violence. Nevertheless, as Tomasello emphasizes, people's peculiar eagerness to read and share the feelings and concerns of others, their quest for intersubjective engagement and mutual understanding, provides the underpinning for behaving in a more prosocial way. It is what makes humans so much more desirable as travel companions than other apes are. So where did this human questing for intersubjective engagement come from?

TO CARE AND TO SHARE IS TO SURVIVE

The benefits to humans of their other-regarding tendencies have never been in doubt. This mutual understanding provided the foundation for the evolution of cooperative behaviors. Before returning to the perplexing question about origins so central to this book, namely, "How on Darwin's earth did the stage for such cooperation get set?" I briefly want to remind readers why (once the initial propensities had evolved) being eager to share and willing to cooperate were so critical during the long stretch of time when our ancestors lived as hunters and gatherers. That done, we can return to the question of origins, and ask how mind reading, empathy, and the other underpinnings for higher levels of cooperation became so well developed in one particular line of apes. Still later developments, having to do with the evolution of our unique intelligence, language, and other critical components of human-level cooperation, are beyond the scope of this book. So let's start with sharing, a quintessentially human trait.

During the voyage of the *Beagle* when the young Charles Darwin first encountered the "savages" living in Tierra del Fuego, he was amazed to realize that "some of the Fuegians plainly showed that they had a fair notion of barter . . . I gave one man a large nail (a most valuable present) without making any signs for a return; but he immediately picked out two fish, and handed them up on the point of his spear."[31] Why would sharing with others, even strangers, be so automatic? And why, in culture after culture, do people everywhere devise elaborate customs for the public presentation, consumption, and exchange of goods?

Gift exchange cycles like the famous "kula ring" of Melanesia, where participants travel hundreds of miles by canoe to circulate valuables, extend across the Pacific region and can be found in New Zealand, Samoa, and the Trobriand Islands. In New Caledonia, giant yams are publicly displayed in the Pilu Pilu ceremonies, while among the Kwakiutl, Haida, or Tsimshian peoples along the resource-rich coast of northwest North America as well as among the Koryak or Chuckchee peoples of Siberia, quantities of possessions are publicly shared and destroyed in elaborate potlatch ceremonies. As I write these words, I am reminding myself to update the long lists of recipients to whom we send cards and boxes of fresh walnuts each Christmas—my own tribe's custom for staying in touch with distant kin and as-if kin, the creation of which is a specialty of the human species. The point is not merely to share but to establish and maintain social networks, as Marcel Mauss argued in one of anthropology's early classics, *Essai sur le don* (*The Gift*). This is why dopamine-related neural pleasure centers in human brains are stimulated when someone acts generously or responds to a generous act.[32]

One of the earliest in-depth studies of traditional exchange networks was undertaken by the anthropologist Polly Wiessner, who has done extensive fieldwork in Africa and New Guinea. She began her Kalahari research in the 1970s among the San-speaking Ju/'hoansi people, also known as the !Kung or Bushmen, who at that time still lived as mobile gatherers and hunters belonging to one of the most venerable human groups on earth. Genetic comparisons of mitochondrial DNA across extant human populations indicate that ancestors of this relatively isolated population of Khoisian people, along with those of some other

No matter how skilled the hunter, locating and killing prey is a risky enterprise, with unpredictable outcomes. A man can go hunting every day and still come home empty-handed for weeks in a row. A hunter like this Ju/'hoansi man can afford to fail because he can count on a share of fruits, nuts, and tubers gathered by women, and also because other men may have better luck that day. Inherently less of a gamble, gathering still depends on the vagaries of rainfall and fruiting cycles as well as which other creatures get to a particular food source first. (Peabody Museum/Marshall Expedition image 2001.29.363)

remnant foragers in Central Africa, split off from humankind's founding population at a very early date. Both men and women carry the mitochondrial DNA characteristic of the deepest roots of the African phylogenetic tree from which all modern humans descend.[33]

As among our earliest Pleistocene ancestors, Ju/'hoansi women gathered and the men hunted, with communities sharing the fruits of their labors. Over the next thirty years, Wiessner followed the lives of group members even after they were displaced from their traditional foraging grounds. Today, their descendants eke out a living by gardening and herding when they can, subsisting on government handouts or "lying out the hunger"—patiently suffering—when they can't. When they still roamed across the semi-arid Kalahari, with no way to store food, these people understood that their most important resources were their reputations and the stored goodwill of others.

The sporadic success and frequent failures of big-game hunters is a chronic challenge for hungry families among traditional hunter-gatherers. One particularly detailed case study of South American foragers suggests that roughly 27 percent of the time a family would fall short of the 1,000 calories of food per person per day needed to maintain body weight. With sharing, however, a person can take advantage of someone else's good fortune to tide him through lean times. Without it, perpetually hungry people would fall below the minimum number of calories they needed. The researchers calculated that once every 17 years, caloric deficits for nonsharers would fall below 50 percent of what was needed 21 days in a row, a recipe for starvation. By pooling their risk, the proportion of days people suffered from such caloric shortfalls fell from 27 percent to only 3 percent.[34]

For those who store social obligations rather than food, unspoken contracts—beginning with the most fundamental one between the group's gatherers and its hunters, and extending to kin and as-if kin in other groups—tide them over from shortfall to shortfall. Time-honored relationships enable people to forage over wider areas and to reconnect with trusted exchange partners without fear of being killed by local inhabitants who have the advantage of being more familiar with the terrain.[35] When a waterhole dries up in one place, when the game moves away, or, perhaps most dreaded of all, when a conflict erupts and the group must split up, people can cash in on old debts and generous reputations built up over time through participation in well-greased networks of exchange.

The particular exchange networks that Wiessner studied among the Ju/'hoansi are called *hxaro*. Some 69 percent of the items every Bushman used—knives, arrows, and other utensils; beads and clothes—were transitory possessions, fleetingly treasured before being passed on in a chronically circulating traffic of objects. A gift received one year was passed on the next.[36] In contrast to our own society where regifting is regarded as gauche, among the Ju/'hoansi it was *not* passing things on—valuing an object more than a relationship, or hoarding a treasure—that was socially unacceptable. As Wiessner put it, "The circulation of gifts in the Kalahari gives partners information that they 'hold each other in their hearts' and can be called on in times of need."[37] A distinctive feature of human social relations was this "release from proximity." It meant that even people who had moved far away and been out of contact for many years could meet as fondly remembered friends years later.[38] Anticipation of goodwill helps explain the 2008 finding by psychologists at the University of British Columbia and Harvard Business School that spending money on *other* people had a more positive impact on the happiness of their study subjects than spending the same amount of money on themselves.[39]

In her detailed study of nearly a thousand *hxaro* partnerships over thirty years, Wiessner learned that the typical adult had anywhere from 2 to 42 exchange relationships, with an average of 16. Like any prudently diversified stock portfolio, partnerships were balanced so as to include individuals of both sexes and all ages, people skilled in different domains and distributed across space. Approximately 18 percent resided in the partner's own camp, 24 percent in nearby camps, 21 percent in a camp at least 16 kilometers away, and 33 percent in more distant camps, between 51 and 200 kilometers away.[40]

Just under half of the partnerships were maintained with people as closely related as first cousins, but almost as many were with more distant kin.[41] Partnerships could be acquired at birth, when parents named a new baby after a future gift-giver (much as Christians designate godparents), or they could be passed on as a heritable legacy when one of the partners died. Since meat of large animals was always shared, people often sought to be connected with skilled hunters. This is why the best hunters tended to have very far-flung assortments of *hxaro* contacts, as did their wives.

Contacts were built up over the course of a life well-lived by individuals perpetually alert to new opportunities. When a parent died, his or her children or stepchildren inherited the deceased person's exchange partners as well as kinship networks, and gifts were often given at that time to reinforce the continuity, since to give, share, and reciprocate was to survive.[42] Multiple systems for identifying kin linked people in different ways, increasing the number of people to whom an individual was related. One kinship system was based on marriage and blood ties, while another involved the name one was given, which automatically forged a tie to others with the same name. These manufactured or fictive kin were also referred to as mother, father, brother, or sister.

Such dual systems function to spread the web of kinship widely, and since the second system can be revised over the course of an individual's lifetime, it becomes feasible for a namesake to bring even distant kin into a closer relationship when useful.[43] Every human society depends on some system of exchange and mutual aid, but foragers have elevated exchange to a core value and an elaborate art form. People construct vast and intricate terminologies to identify kin and as-if kin, in order to expand the potential for relationships based on trust. Depending on the situation, these can be activated and kept going by reciprocal exchange or left dormant until needed.

Marriages that Ju/'hoansi partners arranged for their children provided new opportunities to cast the net wider still. At marriage, band members offer gifts to the newlyweds that are then recycled among in-laws. A wife taken by force would be far less valuable than the same woman freely given by in-laws properly compensated and ready to reciprocate. Under conditions of high child mortality, a kinless woman would make a less advantageous mate than one whose family support system was intact, because children without maternal grandmothers and other kin to help nurture them would be less likely to survive. Kinship ties, together with the terminologies and relationships based on the exchange of goods and services that are used to reify them, increase the number of people that one could call upon, share with, count on to reciprocate, go to live with when in need, and elicit help from in rearing one's young.[44] The advantage of casting the net of kinship as widely as possible is presumably why foraging people are far more likely to trace relatedness through both mother and father, as opposed to only one or the other line, as is more typical in the matrilineal or patrilineal descent systems that prevail in nonforaging societies.[45]

Archaeological evidence suggests that unilineal—and perhaps especially patrilineal—inheritance systems began to emerge when foragers in habitats rich with marine resources began living more sedentary lives at higher population densities, as they did in coastal South Africa from at least 4,300 years ago. As with most primates, population densities of Paleolithic foragers would have varied across their range, from very low (with less than one person per square mile) to somewhat higher.[46]

Consider one of the most successful, widespread, and long-lived of all hominins, *Homo erectus,* which first emerged around 1.8 million years ago. Some members of this highly variable (or polytypic) species must

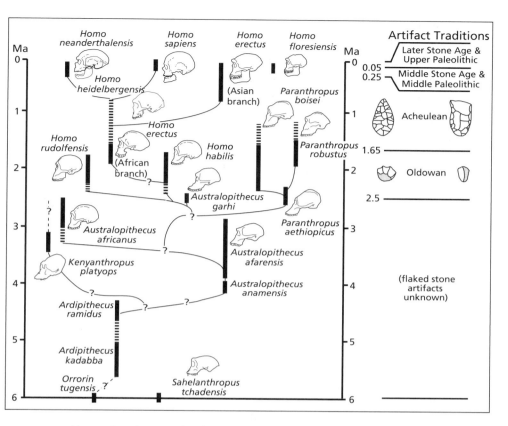

Many systematists now place *Homo erectus* along with all the other bipedal apes into the tribe Hominini. This new term "hominin" replaces the older term "hominid" because in the new classification other apes such as chimpanzees fall, along with humans, into the family Hominidae, as in "We are all hominids now." The fossil hominins depicted in this family tree include *Australopithecus, Homo habilis, Homo erectus,* and *Homo heidelbergensis,* but there are many others, not shown, and no doubt still others not yet discovered. As illustrated here, modern humans probably all descended from an African branch of *Homo erectus* (also called *Homo ergaster*) that evolved around 1.8 million years ago. This diagram, originally prepared by evolutionary anthropologist Richard Klein, is adapted here from Henry McHenry (2009).

have migrated out of Africa early on. Fossils from an archaic form of *Homo erectus* are being unearthed at the Dmanisi site in the Republic of Georgia, with other remnants uncovered in Java, China, and Spain. Indeed, many paleontologists believe that the miniaturized hominins from the island of Flores off Indonesia were similarly left over from one of these early Pleistocene diasporas. As far as we know, all of these early-dispersing populations eventually died out. However, a branch of *Homo erectus* remained in tropical Africa and continued to evolve there. All humans today descend from this enduring African branch of *Homo erectus,* which some paleontologists regard as a separate species, *Homo ergaster.* Whatever we call them, these larger-brained African hominins were our ancestors, giving rise around 200,000 years ago to even-larger-brained *Homo sapiens.* Sometime afterward, between 100,000 and 50,000 years ago, these anatomically modern humans spread out of Africa, and *Homo sapiens* began its extraordinary expansion around the world.[47]

So here we have a footloose hominin that managed to persist—albeit initially just barely—for 1.6 million years, eight times longer than *Homo sapiens* has been on this earth. Yet there were probably never very many of them. Unlike the case of other large mammals traversing savannas and mixed woodland-savanna habitats a million years ago, it takes tremendous effort and considerable luck to find even a single skull belonging to the African branch of *Homo erectus.* My guess is that one reason for the scarcity of such finds is that the creatures themselves *were* scarce. It was probably not until 80,000 or so years ago in Africa, and perhaps 50,000 years ago in Europe, that human populations began to expand. Prior to that, Paleolithic populations would have been small and dispersed. In total, they would have numbered in the tens of thousands, and the resources they needed would often have been widely distributed as well as unpredictable.[48] When vegetable food or game were available, luck, skill, and the effort expended to harvest them would have mattered more than fighting for them.

Without kin and as-if kin to help protect and especially to help provision them, few Pleistocene children could have survived into adulthood. The fact that children depend so much on food acquired by others is one reason why those seeking human universals would do well to begin with sharing. Nevertheless, in Darwinian circles these days the most widely invoked explanation for how humans became so hypersocial is to stress how helpful within-group cooperation is when defending against or wiping out competing groups. We are told again and again that "the human ability to generate in-group amity often goes hand in hand with out-group enmity."[49] Such generalizations are probably accurate enough for humans where groups are in competition with one another for resources, but how much sense would it have made for our Pleistocene ancestors eking out a living in the woodland and savannas of tropical Africa to fight with neighboring groups rather than just moving?

Small bands of hunter-gatherers, numbering 25 or so individuals, under conditions of chronic climatic fluctuation, widely dispersed over large areas, unable to fall back on staple foods like sweet potatoes or manioc as some modern foragers in New Guinea or South America do today, would have suffered from high rates of mortality, particularly child mortality, due to starvation as well as predation and disease. Recurring population crashes and bottlenecks were likely, resulting in difficulty recruiting sufficient numbers. Far from being competitors for resources, nearby members of their own species would have been more valuable as potential sharing partners. When conflicts did loom, moving on would have been more practical as well as less risky than fighting.[50]

Nevertheless, from the early days of evolutionary anthropology to today's textbooks in evolutionary psychology, the tendency has been to devote more space to aggression and our "killer instincts" or to emphasize "demonic" chimpanzeelike tendencies for males to join with other males in their group to hunt neighboring groups and intimidate, beat, torture, and kill them.[51] No doubt our Pleistocene ancestors experienced jealousy, competed for reputation, and harbored grudges or desires for retribution that occasionally escalated into mayhem. Homicides among hunter-gatherers are well documented, often crimes of passion involving women. But such killings tend to involve individuals who know each other rather than warfare between adjacent groups. In spite of abundant evidence documenting intergroup conflict over the past 10,000 to 15,000 years, there is no evidence of warfare in the Pleistocene. Such absence of evidence is not evidence of absence, but it helps to explain why many of those who actually study hunter-gatherers are skeptical about projecting the bellicose behavior of post-Neolithic peoples back onto roaming kin-based bands of hunter-gatherers, and why some anthropologists refer to the Pleistocene as the "period of Paleolithic warlessness."[52]

I am not about to argue that competition is unimportant. We are primates, after all. But what worries me is that by focusing on intergroup competition, we have been led to overlook factors such as childrearing that are at least as important (in my opinion, even more important) for explaining the early origins of humankind's peculiarly hypersocial tendencies. We have underestimated just how important shared care and provisioning of offspring by group members other than parents have been in shaping prosocial impulses.

I am assuming that prior to the Neolithic, when around 12,000 or so years ago people began to settle down and produce rather than just gather food, band-level societies would have gone to the same lengths to avoid outright conflicts and to maintain harmonious relations as do the African hunter-gatherers studied by twentieth and twenty-first century ethnographers. Acutely aware of how divisive and potentially dangerous status-striving and self-aggrandizing tendencies can be, hunter-gatherers almost everywhere are known for being fiercely egalitarian and going to great lengths to downplay competition and forestall ruptures in the social fabric, for reflexively shunning, humiliating, even ostracizing or executing those who behave in stingy, boastful, or antisocial ways.[53]

When murder does occur, group members intervene and customs are invoked that help keep violent apelike instincts from escalating and to prevent homicides from spiraling into wider blood feuds or intergroup fighting.[54] People living in band-level gathering and hunting societies behave as if they understand that their survival and that of their children depend on others, that without kin and as-if kin to help keep children safe and fed, their communities cannot survive. Maintaining social contacts and exchanging goods and services, even with those who are not particularly close relatives, is something humans are emotionally and temperamentally peculiarly well equipped to do, especially when compared with other apes.

Yet textbooks in fields like evolutionary psychology devote far more space to aggression, or to how men and women competed for or appealed to mates, than they do to how much early humans shared with one another to jointly rear offspring.[55] Even when human hypersociality is noted, explanations tend to emphasize between-group competition rather than how difficult it was to ensure the survival to breeding age of costly, slow-maturing children. Yet as this book will make clear, without shared care and provisioning, all that inter- and intragroup strategizing and strife would have been—evolutionarily speaking—just so many grunts and contortions signifying nothing.

PAN-HUMAN COMPARISONS

The Great Apes known as common chimpanzees (*Pan troglodytes*) lack the giving impulses typical of people. Reflexively xenophobic, either sex is more likely to attack than to tolerate a stranger of the same sex. However, members of another Great Ape species, bonobos (*Pan paniscus,* sometimes called pygmy chimpanzees), are more tolerant and relaxed around conspecifics. Bonobos are temperamentally more similar to humans in this respect than common chimpanzees are. Genetically, however, neither species of chimpanzee is closer to humans than the other is. Humans shared a common ancestor with these other two apes six or so million years ago.

Although genetically equidistant from humans, the two species of the genus *Pan* diverged from each other only in the past two million years. No one knows whether bonobos derived from a more chimpanzee-like ancestor or the other way around. Yet because *Pan troglodytes* has been intensively studied for much longer than *Pan paniscus,* and also because their dominance-oriented and aggressive behavior, including murderous raids on neighboring groups, more nearly conforms to widely accepted stereotypes about human nature, there is a bias toward viewing common chimpanzees as the template for the genus, while dismissing bonobos as some eccentric offshoot. As a result, the violence-prone temperament assigned to male *Pan troglodytes* is routinely projected back onto our Paleolithic ancestors.[56]

Even though no one knows whether common chimpanzees or bonobos provide the better model for reconstructing particular traits among our hominin ancestors, if I had to bet on which species made the more plausible candidate for reconstructing a line of apes with the potential to evolve extensive sharing, particularly care and provisioning of young by group members other than parents (known as alloparents),* I would bet on bonobos. Based on laboratory experiments, bonobos appear to be more gregarious, and bonobo females in particular are temperamentally better suited to tolerate others and to learn to coordinate their behavior with them.[57] In the wild as well as in captivity, bonobos tend to be more peaceful and sociable than common chimpanzees. Thus far, bonobos have not been observed to stalk or kill neighbors, although we know too little to say they never do. What we do know is that when bonobo communities meet at the border of their home ranges or when strange males try to immigrate into a group, the responses vary with the circumstances. Individuals may exhibit hostility or they may intermingle peaceably. Males and females may even consort with one another.[58] Opportunistic copulations with strangers are facilitated because female bonobos are nearly continuously sexually receptive and exhibit red sexual swellings during most days of their estrous cycles, with no specific visual advertisement at ovulation.[59]

Both in captivity and in the wild, bonobos share more readily than chimpanzees do, and when begged by youngsters, group members of both sexes may provide food to the offspring of their female friends.[60] In general, bonobos seem more eager to cooperate and may be more adept at reconciliation after conflict.[61] They nimbly and routinely combine vocalizations, facial expressions, and gestures for effective, flexible communication.[62] Yet bonobos rarely exhibit the spontaneous giving impulses commonly observed in very young human children.

Among people, these giving impulses, combined with chimpanzees' and the other Great Apes' rudimentary capacity for attributing mental states and feelings to others, lead humans of all ages to routinely seek out opportunities to engage with other individuals. The kind of interindividual tolerance so typical of humans suggests that even before people had language to discuss things, prehuman or early human apes were equipped with the capacity to identify with others and engage with them in ways that avoided fights.[63] These hominins were already emotionally

---

* An alloparent (from the Greek "allo-" for "other than") refers to any group member *other than* the parents who helps them rear their young. Since it is often impossible to assign paternity, I often opt for "allomother," a term which might or might not include the father.

different from other apes. This is where the homology between humans and "demonic" chimpanzees breaks down. In what follows I will argue that as long as a million and a half years ago, the African ancestors of *Homo sapiens* were already emotionally very different from the ancestors of any other extant ape, already more like the sort of ape one would prefer to travel with in a confined space.

GIVING IMPULSES

A human child is born eager to connect with others. In a gathering and hunting society, that child also would become accustomed to being cared for and fed by others in a nurturing environment.[64] Before Ju/'hoansi children are a year old and able to talk, they are already socialized to share with their mother and with other people as well. Among the first words a child learns are *na* ("Give it to me") and *i* ("Here, take this").[65] Polly Wiessner recalls an old woman cutting off a strand of ostrich egg-shell beads from around her grandchild's neck, washing the beads off, and then placing them in the child's hand to present (however grudgingly) to a relative. After the lesson of giving was accomplished, the child was given new beads. This routine was repeated until, by about age nine, children themselves initiated giving. By adolescence, a fully socialized donor expands his or her *hxaro* contacts further and further afield. The fearful prospect of disrupting the fabric of relationships that sustained the lives of our ancestors acted as a perpetual lid, constraining conflict.

Among nonhuman apes, however, sharing is uncommon, neither spontaneous nor reciprocal. An alpha male chimpanzee grasping the carcass of a monkey he just killed may allow a sexually receptive female or close male associate to rip off a piece, but this is more like "tolerated theft" than a real gift.[66] Rarely have fieldworkers seen a wild chimpanzee extend a preferred section of meat, even to his best ally. Yet humans routinely offer preferred foods to others—the best hospitality we can possibly provide. A mother chimpanzee or orangutan will tolerate her youngster taking a desirable scrap of the food she is eating, but she rarely takes the initiative in offering it. If a *Pan troglodytes* mother does extend her hand with a tidbit, she will most likely proffer a stem or some other unpalatable plant part that she herself does not particularly want to eat.

Although bonobos may be more tolerant about food sharing than

These photos were extracted from a video made in the middle of the twentieth century by the pioneering human ethologist Irenäus Eibl-Eibesfeldt. He traveled around the world with a specially designed camera whose right-angle lens could be aimed in one direction while recording images from another. This allowed him to compile a precious archive of candid photographs illustrating infant care in traditional societies such as the !Xo, G/wi San, and Himba of southern Africa, the Eipo of West Papua, the Trobrianders of Papua New Guinea, and the Yanomamo of Venezuela. Picking up where Darwin left off in his 1872 classic *The Expression of Emotions in Animals and Man*, Eibl-Eibesfeldt sought to demonstrate the universality of human facial expressions, gestures, and emotions. Here, a Yanomamo toddler goes over to her playmate, carrying two large leaves, and sits down beside the other girl. Unnoticed by her friend (second frame), the little girl swipes one of the leaves and hides it behind her. But when her playmate spontaneously presents her with the other leaf as a "gift" (third frame), she returns the "stolen" leaf, as if aware that generosity must be reciprocated. Such is the power of gift-giving, right from an early age, even before language and terms to describe the giving impulse develop. (I. Eibl-Eibesfeldt/Human Ethology Archives)

common chimpanzees, no one would mistake their behavior for gift-giving. The majority of sharing involves plant foods rather than meat and usually occurs between two adult females or an adult female and an infant—her own or the infant of one of her female allies or associates. Instead of being offered some delectable treat, infants merely have license to take food in the possession of allomothers. When an adult bonobo shares food with another adult, almost invariably the offer is in reaction to begging gestures similar to those infants make.[67] Not long ago, at a bonobo study site in the Congo called Lamoko, researchers watched as females gathered to feed on the corpse of a duiker. Among common chimpanzees, males are dominant over females and control access to meat; but among bonobos, females are dominant to males and control the flow of food. On this particular occasion, all three infants present could pick at the carcass and were also permitted to casually take pieces of meat from the hands and mouths of adults, but this is as generous as things got.[68]

Where gift-giving does occur in the animal world, it tends to be a highly ritualized, instinctive affair, as when a male scorpion fly offers prey to a prospective mate as a "nuptial gift" to induce the female to mate with him, or when male bowerbirds or flightless cormorants bring some eye-catching object to a fertile female to use in decorating her nest. Cases of nonhuman animals voluntarily offering a preferred food in the true spirit of gift-giving are rare, except in species which, like humans, also have deep evolutionary histories of what I call cooperative breeding, where there is shared care and provisioning of young.[69]

Among the higher primates, humans stand out for their chronic readiness to exchange small favors and give gifts. Donors often take the initiative, actually seeking opportunities and expending inordinate thought and effort to select "just the right gift," the one most likely to suit the occasion or to impress or appeal to the recipient. Humans spontaneously notice and keep track of the smallest detail about their exchanges.[70] Custom, language, and personal experiences shape the specifics, but the urge to share is hard-wired, and neurophysiologists are getting to the point where they can actually monitor, if still only crudely, the pleasure humans derive from being generous, helping, and sharing.[71]

This should not come as a surprise. As early as a million years ago,

A four-and-a-half-year-old Himba girl urges her cousin to have a bite of her snack. Young children are eager to give and readily learn to share, even though they sometimes may need some prodding. (I. Eibl-Eibesfeldt/Human Ethology Archives)

archaeologists tell us, hominins were transferring materials between distant sites. By the Middle Stone Age (50,000 to 130,000 years ago), the type and quantity of such transfers indicates the existence of long-distance exchange networks.[72] We can say with considerable confidence that the sharing of material objects, and with it a degree of intersubjectivity that would make such sharing a satisfying activity, go far back in time. Yet as universal and presumably ancient in the hominin line as sharing appears to be, a comparable giving impulse is not present in other apes. Whereas competitiveness and aggression are fairly easy to understand, generosity is both less common and more interesting, but from an evolutionary perspective far harder to explain.

HOW COULD HUMANS BECOME SUCH COOPERATIVE APES?

The archaeological record over the past 10,000 years, and especially the historical record of the past few millennia, abounds with ruined abodes, smashed skulls, and skeletons penetrated by arrowheads. Beautifully colored murals from ancient Mexico and other locales depict the grisly torture of captured enemies, fearsome and totally convincing war propaganda from the distant past. Such evidence renders a bloody-awful record bloody clear. Yet selfish genes and violent predispositions notwithstanding, it takes high population densities, competition for the same resources, long-standing conflicts of interest, and major provocations (often filtered through virulent ideologies and rabble-rousing propaganda) to persuade human apes that neighboring people are sufficiently alien, evil, and potentially dangerous to warrant face-to-face killing and the risks associated with trying to wipe out another group.[73]

One of the most dangerous things that could ever happen to a common chimpanzee would be to find himself suddenly introduced to another group of chimpanzees. A stranger risks immediate attack by the group's same-sex members. Now think back to Christopher Columbus's arrival in the Bahamian Islands, his first landfall in the New World. To greet his ship, out came Arawak islanders, swimming and paddling canoes, unarmed and eager to greet the newcomers. Lacking a common language, they proceeded to proffer food and water, as well as gifts of parrots, balls of cotton, and fishing spears made from cane. Something similar may have happened to Captain Cook on his arrival in the Hawaiian islands. "The very instant I leaped ashore," wrote Cook, the local people "brought me a great many small pigs and gave us without regarding whether they got anything in return."[74]

European sailors were amazed by such spontaneous generosity, although Christopher Columbus simply found the Arawak naive. Columbus's description of first contact parallels those of Westerners with the Bushmen and other pre-Neolithic peoples: "When you ask for something they have, they never say no. To the contrary, they offer to share with anyone." But Columbus, himself the product of Europe's long post-Neolithic traditions, had different ideas: "They do not bear arms, and do not know them, for I showed them a sword . . . and [they] cut themselves out of ignorance," the explorer noted in his log. "They would make fine servants . . . With fifty men we could subjugate them all and make them do whatever we want."

Examples abound of individuals from highly stratified, dominance-oriented, aggressive societies expanding at the expense of people from more egalitarian and group-oriented traditions, people who stockpile social obligations rather than amass things. Alas, it is far easier to imagine the Arawak becoming more like Columbus than the other way around. Only with more reliable food sources from unusually rich coastal or freshwater habitats or with food surpluses from horticulture or herding would higher population densities and increasingly stratified societies become possible, along with the need to protect such resources. As groups grow larger, less personalized, and more formally organized, they would also be prone to shift from occasional violent disagreements between individuals to the groupwide aggression that we mistakenly take for granted as representative of humankind's naturally warlike state.[75]

Although it is unclear just how much fighting and mayhem went on among our Pleistocene ancestors (it probably varied a lot with local circumstances) or just when organized warfare first appeared, what is clear is that once local conditions promote the emergence of warlike societies, that way of life (as well as the genes of those who excel at it) will spread.[76] Altruists eager to cooperate fare poorly in encounters with egocentric marauders.[77] So this is the puzzle: How was it possible that the more empathic and generous types of hunter-gatherers developed, much less ever flourished, in ancient African landscapes occupied by highly self-centered apes?

This is a profoundly relevant question. Were it not for the peculiar combination of empathy and mind reading, we would not have evolved to be humans at all. This poor teeming planet of ours would be under the thrall of one of the other ten or so branches of the genus *Homo,* populated by some alternate variation on the themes of bipedal hunting apes with large brains, elaborate tool kits, and an omnivorous diet who entered the fray over the preceding two million years. Without the capacity to put ourselves cognitively and emotionally in someone else's shoes, to feel what they feel, to be interested in their fears and motives, longings, griefs, vanities, and other details of their existence, without this mixture of curiosity about and emotional identification with others, a combination that adds up to mutual understanding and sometimes even compassion, *Homo sapiens* would never have evolved at all.[78] The niches humans occupy would have been filled by very different apes. This is where intersubjectivity comes in. But what was the impetus? Given the ecological circumstances of early hominin populations, do we really want to rely on out-group hostility and reflexively genocidal urges as the explanation of choice for the emergence of peculiarly prosocial natures?

According to the best available genetic reconstructions of our own species, the founding population of anatomically modern humans who left Africa some time after 100,000 years ago numbered 10,000 or fewer breeding adults, a rag-tag bunch preoccupied with keeping themselves and their slow-maturing children alive. The chimpanzee genome today is more diverse than that of humans probably because these once highly successful and widespread creatures descended from a more diverse and numerous founding stock than modern humans did.[79] These days, chimpanzees are in far more immediate danger of extinction than are humans, but 50,000 to 70,000 years ago the situation was reversed. Only barely, by the skin of their teeth, did the original population of *Homo sapiens* avoid the same fate—extinction—suffered by all the other hominins.

Apart from periodic increases in unusually rich locales, most Pleistocene humans lived at low population densities.[80] The emergence of human mind reading and gift-giving almost certainly preceded the geographic spread of a species whose numbers did not begin to really expand until the past 70,000 years. With increasing population density (made possible only, I would argue, because they were already good at cooperating), growing pressure on resources, and social stratification, there is little doubt that groups with greater internal cohesion would prevail over less cooperative groups. But what was the *initial* payoff? How could hypersocial apes evolve in the first place?

As Tomasello argues, the capacity to be far more interested in and responsive to others' mental states was the critical trait that emerged and set the ancestors of humans apart from other nonhuman apes. Capacities for learning from each other and sophisticated cooperation that flowed from enhanced mind reading led to unprecedented advances in the realm of culture and, with cumulative cultural knowledge, in technology—gradual advances that eventually took on a life of their own. As a consequence, humans were able to prosper, develop networks of exchange to survive where otherwise they could not, and eventually to spread around the globe. The rest is history—as well as our species' best hope for having a future. But recognizing this unusual human capacity for caring about what others think, feel, and intend begs the question: How did it happen that cognitive and emotional traits with such obvious benefits for enhancing survival came to characterize only this single surviving line of apes? How could natural selection ever have favored the peculiarly empathic qualities that over the course of human evolution have served our species of emotionally modern humans so well?

Natural selection has no way to foresee eventual benefits. Future payoffs cannot be used to explain the initial impetus, that is, the origin of mind reading. I don't doubt (as book after book describing "human nature and the origins of war" remind us) that "a high level of fellow feeling makes us better able to unite to destroy outsiders."[81] But if hypersociality helps one group beat out another, would not in-group cooperation in the service of out-group competition have served other apes (for example, warring communities of chimpanzees) just as well? Indeed, we already know that chimpanzees perform best on tests requiring a rudimentary theory of mind when they are in competitive situations.[82]

When I confided these theoretical difficulties to Polly Wiessner, she acknowledged worrying about the same problem. This expert on hunter-gatherer social relations, who as it happens was raised in Vermont, proceeded to recount the following anecdote about a lost tourist asking directions from a local: "If I were aiming to go there," replied the crotchety New Englander, "I would not start out from here."[83] There it was, my problem in a nutshell. Starting out with an ape as self-centered and competitive as a chimpanzee, how could natural selection ever have favored the aptitudes and quirks of mind that underpin the high levels of cooperation found in humans? How could Mother Nature concoct such a hypersocial ape starting with such an impulsively selfish one? The answer, as we will see, is that she didn't start from there.

THIS BOOK

Mothers and Others is about the emergence of a particular mode of child-rearing known as "cooperative breeding" and its psychological implications for apes in the line leading to *Homo sapiens*. As defined by sociobiologists and discussed in a rich empirical and theoretical literature, "cooperative breeding" refers to any species with alloparental assistance in both the care and provisioning of young. I will propose that a long, long time ago, at some unknown point in our evolutionary history but before the evolution of 1,350 cc sapient brains (the hallmark of *anatomically* modern humans) and before such distinctively human traits as language (the hallmark of *behaviorally* modern humans), there emerged in Africa a line of apes that began to be interested in the mental and subjective lives—the thoughts and feelings—of others, interested in understanding them. These apes were markedly different from the common ancestors they shared with chimpanzees, and in this respect they were already *emotionally* modern.

As in all apes, the successful rearing of their young was a challenge. Mortality rates from predation, accidents, disease, and starvation were staggeringly high and weighed most heavily on the young, especially children just after weaning. Of the five or so offspring a woman might bear in her lifetime, more than half—and sometimes all—were likely to die before puberty. Unlike mothers among other African apes, who nurtured infants on their own, these early hominin mothers relied on groupmates to help protect, care for, and provision their unusually slow-maturing children and keep them on the survivable side of starvation.

Cooperative breeding does not mean that group members are necessarily or always cooperative. Indeed, as we will see, competition and coercion can be rampant. But in the case of early hominins, alloparental care and provisioning set the stage for infants to develop in new ways. They were born into the world on vastly different terms from other apes. It takes on the order of 13 million calories to rear a modern human from birth to maturity, and the young of these early hominins would also have been very costly. Unlike other ape youngsters, they would have depended on nutritional subsidies from caregivers long after they were weaned.[84]

Years before a mother's previous children were self-sufficient, she would give birth to another infant, and the care these dependent youngsters required would be far in excess of what a foraging mother by herself could regularly supply. Both before birth and especially afterward, the mother needed help from others; and even more importantly, her infant would need to be able to monitor and assess the intentions of both his mother and these others and to attract their attentions and elicit their assistance in ways no ape had ever needed to do before. For only by eliciting nurture from others as well as his mother could one of these little humans hope to stay safe and fed and to survive.

No one has a machine to go back in time to observe what child-rearing in the Pleistocene was like or to record the consequences of novel developmental trajectories. But what we do have is evidence from a diverse array of primates and other animals that is relevant to understanding why other group members would begin to help and how cooperative breeding evolves. We also have a growing body of information about contemporary gathering-hunting people, revealing for the first time how many others have to pitch in if a nomadic foraging mother is going to rear her offspring to breeding age. To reconstruct the deep history of Pleistocene family life and the development of youngsters dependent on both mothers and an array of others, I will be drawing on information, much of it quite new, from comparative primatology and the ethnographic study of childhood in foraging societies, along with cognitive psychology, neuroendocrinology, and the flourishing new field of comparative infant development as well as from paleontology, sociobiology, and human behavioral ecology. Published 150 years after Darwin's *Origin of Species,* this book, like the far greater one that inspired it, is written as "one long argument." As evidence-based and consistent with evolutionary theory as I can make it, this book is an attempt to reconstruct long-ago events detailing the emergence of emotionally modern humans, step by Darwinian step.

Before turning to a detailed examination of the cooperative breeding hypothesis that I favor, let's begin by considering some of the main alternative hypotheses that have been proposed to explain why intersubjectivity evolved in the line leading to *Homo sapiens.*

2

WHY US AND NOT THEM?

Had humanity not been the interested party,
we would have been the fifth great ape.

—Richard Leakey (2005)

I sat gazing at a chimpanzee who sat on the other side of a fence, gazing at
me. As a psychoanalyst, I have been taught to analyze the countertransfer-
ence, which means that I try to formulate how this animal is making me
feel. So I sat there and tried my very hardest to do that. I felt . . . something
missing, I could not connect. I was reminded of the experience one
sometimes get when relating to a child with autism . . . It was as if this
chimp was not at home, mentally speaking.

—Peter Hobson (2004)

Are humans just another ape, or an utterly different
ape? No one can map the DNA of a chimpanzee, watch a bonobo strid-
ing upright on two legs or concentrating and excelling at object manipulations, or look a gorilla or orangutan in the eye and fail to be impressed by how similar we are to them. From Darwin onward, scientists
have traced the anthropoid origins of emotions, ranging from satisfaction, loyalty, and joy to embarrassment, anxiety, shame, anger, and dis-
gust.[1] Thus when the paleontologist Richard Leakey looks deeply into
the eyes of a chimpanzee, he sees a kindred creature. And well might a
psychiatrist like Peter Hobson wonder, "What is he thinking?" But when
our hairy cousin returns that gaze, the film in his camera seems different. Thus, whereas Leakey the paleontologist emphasizes the profound

homologies between humans and other apes, Hobson the psychiatrist is more struck by differences between two closely related species.[2] Both are right.

Primatologists familiar with chimpanzee behavior will be quick to point out that Hobson's simian acquaintance scarcely knew him from Adam. Had Hobson actually had a prior relationship with that chimpanzee, the eyes returning his gaze might well have seemed less blank.[3] Certainly there are circumstances when chimpanzees sense how someone else feels. Chimpanzees yawn when someone else does, just the way humans do, and they seem to understand what to do when another ape seeks help, paying special attention to licking the inaccessible places, for example, when tending a fellow chimpanzee that has been wounded by a leopard. Apes seem especially helpful toward offspring or younger siblings.[4] When it occurs, empathetic-seeming behavior by apes makes a huge impression. Audiences are riveted when the renowned ethologist Frans de Waal tells the story of Kuni the captive bonobo who picked up a stunned starling. After a concerned keeper urged the ape to let the bird go, the bonobo made abortive attempts to get it to fly before climbing high in a tree where he "carefully unfolded its wings and spread them wide open" as he threw the bird up into the air.[5] But as de Waal himself stresses, we have to be cautious about interpreting what we see.

Yes, human-reared chimpanzees test surprisingly well at simple cooperation, like helping someone else extract something.[6] But in spite of their rudimentary understanding of what someone else is trying to do, these apes' capacity for attributing separate mental states to others (or else the extent to which they care to do so) seems limited. Furthermore, such intersubjective capacities as they can muster emerge more readily in competitive than in cooperative situations.

Consider one recent experiment. A psychologist placed food in various places, some items in full view of a dominant chimpanzee, others out of his sight, while a subordinate in an adjacent cage was allowed to watch. When both were released into the cage with the food, the subordinate took advantage of his advance knowledge to bypass food in plain sight and make a beeline for the hidden treats.[7] When tested in a noncompetitive situation, however, chimpanzees seem less concerned about others, especially if they do not have a previous relationship. Compared with human children, chimpanzees have excellent spatial memory and are very good at discriminating quantities, but they test far less well on social learning or reading nonverbal cues having to do with hidden rewards or intentions.[8]

The strongest evidence for chimpanzees' lack of regard for others comes from experiments by the UCLA primatologist Joan Silk. As a Stanford undergraduate, Silk went to the Gombe Stream Reserve of Tanzania to study mother-infant behavior among chimpanzees. Subsequently, she became known for her work on macaques, baboons, and humans. But she never forgot her early experiences with chimpanzees. She knew that they sometimes engage in collective activities like hunting, and they share food under special circumstances, console a victim of aggression with a hug, or stay near a dying relative. Still, the extremely analytical Silk was skeptical of claims about chimpanzee empathy. She thought up a clever experiment to test just how eager they would be to help when given an opportunity to do so at no particular cost to themselves. Silk and her team deliberately opted to use individuals who were familiar with one another but not close relations.

Her subjects were trained to obtain edible rewards by pulling on one of two ropes. If the chimpanzee pulled the first rope, food was delivered to his own cage. If instead the chimpanzee selected the other rope, food was delivered to both the puller's cage and the cage adjacent to him. Did it make any difference to the chimpanzee in charge whether or not the adjacent cage was occupied by another animal, also eager to be fed? The chimpanzees behaved as if they couldn't care less whether or not their neighbor got something to eat. However, when researchers at Max Planck subsequently performed similar experiments using chimpanzees with prior relationships, they found that individuals who knew each other not only cooperated in obtaining food but kept track of "reputations." These captive chimpanzees exhibited a preference for collaborating with others who had demonstrated that they were good at rope-pulling.[9]

Additional experiments were set up at Max Planck to explicitly test Silk's conclusions. They seemed to confirm that the chimpanzees were "almost totally self-regarding."[10] Whether or not another chimpanzee also got a reward, or failed to, was just not that important to the chimpanzee subjects in these experiments. Like Silk's original paper, which was titled "Chimpanzees Are Indifferent to the Welfare of Unrelated Group Members," the new Max Planck work was titled "What's in It for

Me? Self-Regard Precludes Altruism and Spite in Chimpanzees." Both stressed the absence of spontaneous impulses to give or care about what others receive.

Undeniably, chimpanzees, especially when they reach out a hand to beg, embrace, or kiss another, pat another on the back, comfort, or even assist a fellow group member, seem eerily like us. We are still in the early days of comparing and contrasting the cooperative tendencies of other apes with those found in humans, and the results continue to be difficult to interpret. This is why some researchers characterize chimpanzees as by nature "highly cooperative creatures," while others focus on the fact that cooperation among chimpanzees has been documented only among specially trained chimpanzees or chimpanzees who have opportunistically learned how to cooperate under captive conditions or have been observed only when food is not involved.[11]

In my opinion, there is little question that human children are less self-centered, more spontaneously cooperative, and more strongly inclined to share than chimpanzees are. But then again, children are exposed right from birth to the same sort of human models that the captive chimpanzees who do better on tests of cooperation are exposed to. Nevertheless, the experiments by Silk's team as well as those from Max Planck and elsewhere seem to consistently show that chimpanzees—even those reared by humans—are just not terribly interested in understanding what someone else wants or intends. Unless specially trained, chimpanzees pay attention to what others know when they are competing, not when they are cooperating. By contrast, humans pay attention to others in both spheres.

Talented researchers who often disagree continue to probe chimpanzee-human similarities and differences. Some of them may end up softening their conclusions about chimpanzee indifference. But what I do not expect to change is the contrast between the natural readiness of most people to help an unrelated travel companion (though under contemporary conditions this may be becoming less common!), and the absence of such giving impulses in apes living under natural conditions. Compared with other primates, humans are born far more eager to share the mental and affective states of others.

So far as most psychiatrists are concerned, caring about someone else's mental as well as their physical state (whether they might be hungry, for example) is integral to human nature. The absence of such impulses to give and share feelings (as among children who are autistic) is taken as an indicator of pathology. If humans show a compassionate interest in someone else's mental state, it is taken for granted that these capacities are useful and in an evolutionary sense were adaptive.[12] No doubt, once acquired, such traits did aid the survival of group-living animals. But the premise that intersubjectivity must have been adaptive in the environments in which humans evolved is only convincing until someone asks: So how did other, comparably defenseless, savanna-dwelling primates like baboons, patas monkeys, or vervets manage to evade the lions that stalked *them*? If intersubjectivity was so useful for maintaining cohesive social groups, defending one's in-group from violent neighbors, or wiping out competitors, why didn't other social primates (those "demonic" neighbor-stalking chimpanzees in particular) evolve such gifts as well? Why us and not them?

LOGICALLY, LANGUAGE COMES LATER

The first time I ever considered the question "Why humans and not other apes?" the answer seemed obvious. Surely, I thought to myself, it is our innate capacity to learn language, our unique ability to use words to express what is on our own and on others' minds, which explains why humans can empathize with others through articulating their feelings and sharing their mental states, and which renders them capable of such effective cooperation. This is the view held by such eminent experts on chimpanzees as Jane Goodall. "What makes us human," she remarked recently, "is an ability to ask questions, a consequence of our sophisticated spoken language . . . Once you can discuss something and talk about it in the abstract and take lessons from the past and plan for the future—that is what makes the difference." But on further reflection, I find the focus on language unsatisfactory.[13]

Unquestionably, the uniquely human capacity for language enhances our ability to connect with others and exponentially increases the complexity of the information we can convey. But language is not just about conveying information, as in warning others to "Look out!" An animal alarm call does that. Even vervets (which are Old World monkeys, after all, not even apes) have specific calls that alert conspecifics to danger and also inform them whether the threat is from the air and likely to be a predatory bird, as opposed to something scary on the ground, like a snake. Honeybees convey surprisingly precise information about the location of food (how far away and in what direction) by the type and duration of their ritualized "dance" movements. Animals have all kinds of ways of communicating information about their environment or state of arousal to other members of their species and to other species as well.[14]

The open-ended qualities of language go beyond signaling. The impetus for language has to do with wanting to "tell" someone else what is on our minds and learn what is on theirs. The desire to psychologically connect with others had to evolve *before* language. Only subsequently do the two sets of attributes coevolve. As Hobson puts it, "Before language, there was something else—more basic . . . and with unequalled power in its formative potential."[15] If we are looking for sources of human empathy, these emotion-laden quirks of mind had to evolve before the words came along to articulate them. Even before humans began actually speaking to one another in a behaviorally modern way, their immediate hominin ancestors already differed from other apes in their eagerness to share one another's mental states and inner feelings. In this sense, these creatures were already emotionally modern long before they became anatomically or behaviorally modern and were routinely using speech to converse with one another. The ancestors of people who acquired language were already far more interested in others' intentions and needs than chimpanzees are. What we need to explain is why.

EMPATHIC GLIMMERINGS AS OLD AS MAMMALS

All sorts of animals are sensitive to those around them. Mice have emotional reactions to the pain of other mice. They respond to the writhing of groupmates by becoming more sensitive to pain themselves.[16] The suffering of others is contagious, as well it should be. What is painful or alarming to another creature could well be dangerous to oneself. This is why fear is a particularly contagious emotion.

Many kinds of animals, whether cold-blooded or warm-blooded, winged or scaled, may tend others and be sensitive to their well-being. Most such cases involve parents. Male fish sense the presence of eggs they are likely to have fertilized and fan the eggs with their tail to keep clean water circulating about them. Mother squid ensnare their own ballooning egg masses with long tentacles so as to brood them under the protective shadow of a mother's body. Even mother crocodiles or rattlesnakes will linger protectively near newly hatched or live-birthed young until babies are mobile enough to fend for themselves.[17] Wherever parental care evolved, it marked a watershed in the way animals perceived other individuals, with profound implications for the way vertebrate brains were structured.

Nowhere have these cognitive and neurological transformations been more revolutionary than among mammals. Mammal mothers fall in a class by themselves. One has only to recall a mother dog returning to her litter again and again, nosing each pup, alert to distress, sensing their needs, suckling babies, keeping them warm. The postpartum human mother who checks her baby every 15 minutes to be sure he is still breathing follows in this venerable tradition of compulsive concern.

Lactating mothers date back to the end of the Triassic, around 220 million years ago. This is when babies began to be born so helpless that mothers needed to be attuned to the smell, sounds, and slightest perturbations in the condition of vulnerable young that had to be kept both warm and fed. Since any nearby newborns were likely to have issued from their own bodies, it was adaptive for mothers to perceive all neonates as attractive.[18] Mothers who had just undergone the hormonal transformations of pregnancy were especially susceptible.

Superacute hearing was just one of many ways that selection operated on mother mammals to render them responsive to others. New modes of hearing, sensitivity to touch and odors, along with new ways of distinguishing one's own young from others coevolved with cognitive frameworks for processing information about others.[19] My favorite example dates back to the age of dinosaurs. Confronted with the special challenge of signaling distress to their mothers without attracting lizards and other reptiles who might eat them, early mammals evolved the ability to emit high-frequency sounds. To this day, mammals can still detect sounds at higher frequencies than reptiles can, and a mouse pup that has strayed from its mother's nest will attract her attention by emitting ultrasonic squeaks that almost no one else can hear.[20]

So, while their mothers were evolving to be more sensitive to others,

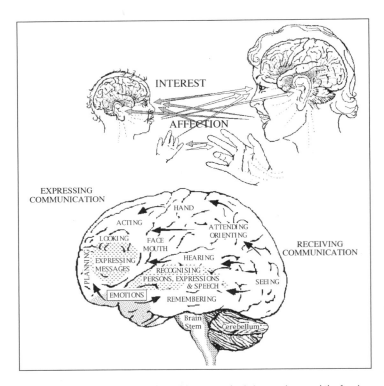

INTEREST

AFFECTION

EXPRESSING
COMMUNICATION

HAND

ACTING

ATTENDING
ORIENTING

LOOKING   FACE
            MOUTH

RECEIVING
COMMUNICATION

EXPRESSING
MESSAGES

HEARING

RECOGNISING
PERSONS, EXPRESSIONS
& SPEECH

SEEING

EMOTIONS   REMEMBERING

PLANNING

Brain
Stem   Cerebellum

Humans have brains specially adapted for sympathetic interactions and the forging of relationships. At birth, an enormous amount of brain tissue, especially in the neocortex, is already allocated to processing faces, facial expressions, gestures, and vocalizations of others. The processing of this information is also motivated and stimulated by older subcortical sections of the brain that are related to the emotions and memories of earlier interactions. (Trevarthen 2005)

baby mammals were evolving too. Natural selection favored babies who were sensitive to their mother's body warmth and smells, able to squirm close to her and latch onto her teats, and capable of signaling effectively (and safely) when separated. It is no accident that the first regions of the neocortex to form in utero are those that eventually represent and control sucking actions by the mouth and tongue. Once a baby is born, wriggles close to his mother, and locates a nipple, he will need to wrap his lips around it, latch tight, and suck so as to stay fed and, just as importantly, to further stimulate his mother's nurturing impulses. The tugging at her nipples stimulates the production of prolactin along with a surge of the neuropeptide oxytocin, with its pleasurable and soothing effects.[21]

Stimulating and conditioning its mother, making sure that she becomes addicted to nurturing, is actually a mammalian baby's first critical, if unconscious, mission. The neocortex, which first evolved among mammals and overlays older, reptilian portions of the brain, serves as the control center of the nervous system.[22] The neocortex equips baby mammals to form attachments to their mothers and helps get their mothers to bond with them. In time, the baby's neocortex will expand and develop into the main decision-making area of the brain. But it will also continue to equip grown-up mammals to bond with babies and to form multifaceted relationships with others.[23]

This requirement for mothers to bond with babies, and babies with mothers, meant that mammals' brains were designed for the formation of relationships in ways that the brains of other animals are not. The need for mothers to anticipate the needs of offspring is integral to several of the hypotheses that have been proposed to explain the evolution of mind reading. Prime among these is the "mind-reading mums" hypothesis. An important alternative hypothesis centers on the need of competitive social creatures to manipulate others, known as the "Machiavellian intelligence hypothesis." Both merit serious consideration.

THE MIND-READING MUMS HYPOTHESIS

The first social bonds ever forged were between a mother and her offspring. Her need to look out for vulnerable young remains the most widely accepted explanation for why, in most mammalian species, females are more affiliative and socially responsive than males are, even though there are important exceptions, as we will see in the next chapter. Such differences in sex roles are especially well documented in Old World monkeys.[24] Among langur monkeys, for example, females at every life phase are more attracted to infants than males are. Even females far too young to be mothers respond to infantile vocalizations, and they eagerly approach, attempt to touch, hold, inspect, and carry infants. More than 99 percent of all attempts to take babies involve females.[25] Except in extreme situations, and then only briefly to rescue (or maul) them, male langurs never carry babies.[26] Not only do more responsive mothers make better mothers, but among some monkeys, such as savanna baboons, the more affiliative a female is and the more social contacts she maintains, the higher the probability that her offspring will survive.[27]

Although less clear-cut and also far more difficult to interpret due to the myriad ways behavior gets shaped by cultural expectations, sex differences in caretaking have also been observed in humans. In Western society, little girls are expected to be more socially responsive and affiliative than little boys are. Whether because of such social expectations or because of innate differences, girls seem more likely than boys to form secure relationships with their care providers, and girls more readily form secure attachments to allomothers, according to recent research done in Germany.[28] As early as two years of age, little girls are more likely to comfort others in distress than little boys are.[29] It's not that little boys do not comfort others, for they do. Rather, it usually takes stronger signals of distress to elicit their sympathy.[30]

Childhood differences in sensitivity to others, and particularly to their signs of distress, persist into adulthood and have been documented in new parents. The Canadian psychologist Alison Fleming has been one of the pioneers in this area. She and her colleagues found that it takes more urgent-sounding cries to get a father to respond to a fretting newborn than it does a mother.[31] Women also seem to be more sensitive than men are (that is, quicker and more accurate) when reading facial expressions.[32]

Impressed by such reports, the New Zealand psychiatrist Raewyn Brockway proposed that highly intuitive moms not only perceive what irks their babies—a skill that enhances their ability to care for them—but are also better equipped to guide immatures as they acquire survival-enhancing skills. Mind reading is advantageous to mothers, Brockway argues, because "good teaching utilizes an empathic awareness of the infant's point of view, both physical and psychological." Over the course of human evolution there would have been selection for "smarter, more efficient mothering or different kinds of learning, or perhaps, most critically, in different kinds of teaching. Even the simplest components of our current theory-of-mind capacities would have been useful for promoting the survival of offspring."[33]

Sensible as it seems to argue that women evolved to be more intuitive and empathetic than men because mothers need to be more sensitive to the needs of their infants, by itself this argument cannot account for intersubjective aptitudes that appear to be uniquely human. All sorts of mammals enter the world helpless and vulnerable, none more so than baby apes. Possibly their mothers become conditioned to associate specific responses with calmer outcomes, or they may have some conscious sense of what their babies are and are not capable of and what they need. In any event, all Great Ape mothers in the wild are both extremely wary of their surroundings and extraordinarily responsive to the slightest sign of discomfort in their infants, swiftly adjusting them and holding them close.

Chimpanzee, orangutan, and gorilla mothers are more single-mindedly devoted than human mothers are, and for a much longer period of time. Their offspring would benefit from having gifted teachers sensitive to their pedagogical needs, just as human children do.[34] As Brockway readily acknowledges, even chimpanzee mothers will model appropriate skills, and in doing so display sensitivity to the limitations and learning needs of apprentices practicing important subsistence tasks. Yet apes do not teach or learn from others nearly so readily as humans do, and typically not at all.

For example, in many areas of Africa, fat-rich kernels from cracked nuts are a very important food for both humans and other apes. During seasons when nuts are available, a typical chimpanzee will average around 3,450 calories per day from this resource. But it takes years of trial and mostly error to master the technique of nut-cracking. The faster they learn this skill, the better fed young chimpanzees and young humans will be.[35] Well-nourished youngsters can also be weaned sooner without the risk of starvation, leaving mothers more time to keep themselves fed. Earlier weaning and better nutrition for the mother translate into a shorter interval between the last birth and the next conception. Over a lifetime, such cumulative advantages contribute to higher maternal reproductive success. Over generations, quicker mastery of foraging techniques will mean evolutionary advantages for that lineage.

So why haven't chimpanzees been selected to develop the same sort of mind-reading skills that pay off in more efficient learning among humans? If mind-reading human mothers respond more flexibly to infant needs and are better equipped to rear and tutor offspring, why haven't other apes spent 6 million years evolving and refining their intersubjective aptitudes? A lovely hypothesis for mind reading still leaves us grap-

(Top) A child growing up in a gathering and hunting society watches attentively as his mother cracks mongongo nuts, a staple food among the !Kung. Learning just how to strike the extremely hard shells is a skill that can take years to master. (Bottom) During some seasons, chimpanzees as well spend hours cracking open the hard outer shells of palm oil and coula nuts by hammering them against a stone "anvil." Like their modern human counterparts, chimpanzee mothers patiently model how to hold the stone "hammer" or position a nut on the anvil, even allowing a grabby little apprentice to take tools or nuts right out of their hands. Although chimpanzee mothers do not actively teach, they remain sensitive to their infants' struggles. In the best pedagogical tradition, mothers may even allow a frustrated apprentice to take some of her own already extracted nut meats, a well-timed and encouraging reward. (Top: I. DeVore/AnthroPhoto. Bottom: © Tetsuro Matsuzawa)

pling with the question: Why us and not them? The next hypothesis, currently the most widely cited of the alternative explanations for mind reading, suffers from the same limitation.

THE MACHIAVELLIAN INTELLIGENCE HYPOTHESIS

The craftiness of a subordinate chimpanzee able to take advantage of inside information about what another chimpanzee knows is often explained with reference to Machiavellian intelligence. The hypothesis derives its name from Niccolò Machiavelli, whose advice to a sixteenth-century Italian prince has become associated with ruthless political manipulation (much as Karl Rove's advice did for a recent generation of American politicians). Most thoroughly developed by Andrew Whiten and Richard Byrne at St. Andrews University in Scotland, the Machiavellian intelligence hypothesis posits a 70-million-year legacy of extreme sociality combined with a universal primate urge to strive for status.

Higher primates possess a general social intelligence that equips them to differentiate probable kin from nonkin, assess the strengths and weaknesses of different individuals, keep track of past social interactions in order to predict who is currently dominant to whom or who is likely to reciprocate and who will not.[36] To cope with social complexity, monkeys and apes alike have to be what the primatologist Alexander Harcourt terms "consummate social tacticians."[37] Baboons, rhesus monkeys, and chimpanzees all keep track of the intricate and fluctuating status of other group members so as to select and maintain advantageous allies when competing with their fellows. Apes are if anything even more sophisticated than monkeys at gauging status fluctuations and assessing competitive intentions, combining typically primate social intelligence with a rudimentary theory of mind.[38]

Together with its corollary, the social intelligence hypothesis, the Machiavellian intelligence hypothesis has become the explanation of choice for why some higher primates excel at problem-solving tests involving what others can see or know—the better to manipulate or deceive them—and for why they have larger brains for their body size than do other mammals.[39] Indisputably, Machiavellian intelligence does a fine job of accounting for why a chimpanzee subordinate might disguise the fact that he has located some preferred food, enabling him to circle back later and enjoy the fruits of his deception once the dominant animal is out of the way.[40] The same Machiavellian intelligence that renders primates adept at forging complex political alliances and deceiving others may also have helped chimpanzees coordinate joint activities like hunting. A band of males will fan out so that one or more males block any escape route that their prey, say a colobus monkey, might take. Then one of the males climbs up after the targeted prey. Even though it's not clear just how conscious or actually coordinated this behavior is, the hunters *act* as if they know what other animals will do and anticipate what the consequences are likely to be. Their actions have the earmarks of what we would call planning.[41]

Just as the need for empathizing and responding to the needs of vulnerable young helps to explain the development of specific areas in mammalian brains, so too the need for greater Machiavellian intelligence can help to explain the expansion of the neocortex. These planning portions of the brain were useful in assisting the common ancestors of humans and other apes to predict what others would do in competitive or predatory contexts.[42] But here's the problem. We still have to explain why humans are so much better than chimpanzees at conceptualizing what others are thinking, why we are born innately eager to interpret their motives, feelings, and intentions as well as to care about their affective states and moods—in short, why humans are so well equipped for mutual understanding.[43] Chimpanzees, after all, are at least as socially competitive as humans are. Attacks from conspecifics (both infanticide and deaths due to lethal raids by bands of males from neighboring groups) are major sources of mortality.[44] Male and female chimpanzees are even less abashed about striving for dominance status than men and women are.

And like humans, chimpanzees have a lust for meat, and they cooperate in rudimentary ways when hunting or making raids on other groups. Surely, chimpanzees would benefit from being able to outwit quarry or psych out competitors every bit as much as our ancestors did. So why didn't selection favor even greater and more Machiavellian intelligence in *Pan troglodytes*? If social intelligence evolved to help individuals wipe out their neighbors, surely chimpanzees needed it as much, or more, than humans did.

Such questions are so obvious that some readers are probably wondering why no one asked them before. The main reason is that we were laboring under a wrong starting assumption about the capacities of so-cial cognition in the common ancestor of humans and other apes. Most, perhaps all, researchers assumed that the ability of newborns to seek out faces, fixate on them (on eyes especially), gaze deeply into those eyes, and process information about the expressions observed there were uniquely human and acquired after our hominin ancestors split off from the long-ago common ancestor of humans and other apes. Because we took for granted that human infants' capacity for interpreting and imitating faces was unique, we presumed that it was a recent human acquisition absent in other apes.[45] Certainly scientists were aware of selection pressures fa-voring Machiavellian intelligence in other apes, but we assumed that nonhuman apes lacked the neural underpinnings to seek out, read, and imitate others' facial expressions—initial steps toward mind reading.

Mistakenly, we thought baby chimpanzees did not look into or imi-tate faces the way human babies did. As long as we assumed that only human newborns possessed the basic neural apparatus for assessing con-specific facial expressions, empathizing with what others were experienc-ing, and thereby reading their intentions, there seemed little need to ask why other apes never evolved better capacities for mind attribution. We simply took for granted that they lacked the basic equipment. All this started to change around the beginning of the twenty-first century, when revolutionary discoveries about what other apes are actually capable of forced reconsideration of the question of why humans are so much more inclined than other apes toward intersubjective engagement.

MONKEY SEE, MONKEY FEELS WHAT
IT WOULD BE LIKE TO DO

In 1996 an Italian neuroscientist who was part of a team carrying out routine studies on how particular motor skills are reflected in brain activity noticed something odd. The neurons that fired when a macaque grabbed a raisin also fired when the monkey simply watched the researcher pick up and eat a raisin.[46] Neuroscientists quickly christened this new class of brain structures "mirror neurons" because the same areas of the brain that would be activated by doing something are also activated just by watching someone else do the same thing. The seren-dipitous discovery of mirror neurons led to an explosion of speculation and new research into "the neural underpinnings of embodied simulation" to learn how the brain reacts when we watch someone else do something.

Researchers hypothesize that mirror neurons allow creatures to vicariously experience what another individual is doing. By mentally going through the same motions, the mimic gains a better understanding of what the actor being copied is intending to do.[47] Thus, the discovery of mirror neurons generated enormous excitement among developmental psychologists and clinical psychologists as well as among neuroscientists. From the outset, researchers suspected that mirror neurons play a role in empathy as well as imitation. This was consistent with at least one theoretical model for how human infants first learn that other individuals have mental states and minds of their own. In this model, the developmental psychologist Andrew Meltzoff sought to integrate what neuroscientists were learning about neural structures with older theories about how babies observe, imitate, and learn.

Years before, Meltzoff together with Keith Moore reported that some human babies as young as 12 hours old possess the innate ability to imitate others. Hard as it was to believe when first reported back in 1977, and in spite of continuing debate over whether the responses by very young babies are actually imitation, indisputably some babies exhibited a complex responsiveness to others much earlier than previously assumed. Meltzoff's findings have been replicated in more than 13 different labs, not to mention in the homes of curious parents who can't resist making funny faces at their babies. My own babies are grown, but Meltzoff's tongue protrusion test remains one of my favorite ways to while away time at airports. Caught in the right mood, a baby will often respond to tongue protrusions by sticking out her tongue. After repeating his experiments with even younger newborns, Meltzoff quipped, "You can't get much younger than 42 minutes old." Meltzoff was convinced that he had documented that "a primitive capacity to imitate is part of the normal child's biological endowment."[48]

It has been known for a long time that humans, including babies, are fascinated by faces. Today we realize that a special region of the brain and special cells register and process information about faces.[49] Right from birth, human babies seek out any nearby face, and when they encounter their mother's face, they may gaze deep into her eyes as she

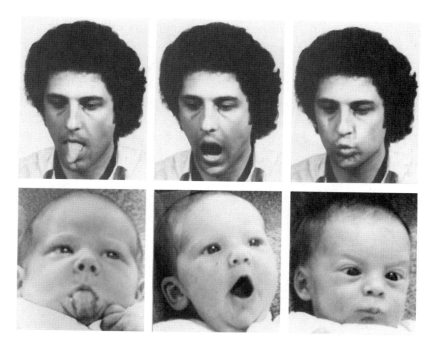

Like many readers of *Science* magazine back in 1977, I was astounded by two juxta-posed strips of photos. In the strip on top, a young and goofy-looking Meltzoff was photographed sticking out his tongue, opening his mouth, and pursing his lips. Just below, with eyes fixated on Meltzoff's face, an alert newborn performed an approximation of each expression. (Meltzoff and Moore 1977:75)

returns their gaze. In an inspired set of experiments, Meltzoff demonstrated that some of these very new babies were not just looking for faces but seeking to engage and perhaps also identify with them. To Meltzoff, early imitation implies that "seeing others as *like me* is our birthright."[50]

When Meltzoff's observations were originally made, most of us still took for granted that mutual gazing along with this early capacity of newborn babies to imitate what they saw was uniquely human as well as universal. This was consistent with the limited evidence we then had for other apes. Hypothesizing that a baby who first observed and then imitated someone else was mentally making an analogy between himself and that someone else, Meltzoff proposed "that infants' connection to others emerges from the fact that the bodily movement patterns they see others perform are coded as like the ones they themselves perform."[51]

Babies everywhere are fascinated by faces. Here a Himba mother in Namibia gazes into the face of her three-to-four-month-old baby, first making eye contact, then kissing him on the lips. Seconds later, the mother scrunched up her face to copy the baby's snorts and smiles as she touched him with her nose. The fascinated baby smiled back with flashing eyebrows and little snorts, occasionally sticking his tongue out. Even after the mother became distracted by conversation with other people, the pair would occasionally resume their mutual gaze. (Video by I. Eibl-Eibesfeldt/Human Ethology Archives, with summary of image context by Niko Larsen)

Once memories of such experiences are stored away, they become the basis for future assessments about both self and others, and the relationship between them. In Meltzoff's words: "Empathy and role-taking and all manner of putting yourself in someone else's shoes emotionally and cognitively seem to rest on the connection between self and other."

As soon as mirror neurons were discovered, Meltzoff began to wonder if they might help explain the unusually well-developed abilities for making connections with and imitating others that he had documented in human infants. He hypothesized that "the neuro-cognitive machinery of imitation lies at the origins of empathy and developing a theory of mind."[52] Combine mirror neurons with mutual gazing and imitation, and, for Meltzoff, mind reading follows. Convinced that he was on the right track, Meltzoff lapsed into poetic metaphor: "Through understanding the acts of others, we come to know their souls."[53] The mention of souls leaves little doubt that developmental psychologists at the beginning of the twenty-first century still assumed they were dealing with exclusively human capacities. Eyes, long celebrated by poets as "windows" into the human soul, played a big role in such assumptions. But what is distinctive about human eyes that allows this unique depth of insight?

THE EYES HAVE IT

Post a photograph of two staring eyes above the coffeemaker in an office lounge and you are likely to discover—as a team of British psychologists did in 2006—that people pouring themselves a cup will be more likely to deposit the recommended payment (in that instance, fifty pence).[54] Humans are not unusual in this respect. From time immemorial, staring eyes possessed this special salience. Vertebrates with brains no bigger than an iguana's or a wild turkey's can sense if someone is looking at them. I can personally vouch for this after trying to sneak up on the wild turkeys at our farm in northern California. Somehow, they always know how to stay just out of view, not necessarily farther away, but just below some obscuring ridge so I cannot see them. Like many animals, Old World monkeys and apes find it unnerving to be stared at (though, curiously, this is not true for New World monkeys such as marmosets or tamarins).[55]

Like other apes, humans also perceive direct stares as threatening. But meanings conveyed by long looks can also be quite variable. Human eyes convey extra information about what an individual is feeling, looking at, and intending. True, other apes also focus, squint, and blink, and their eyes register patterns involving light and color the same way human eyes do. Other primates like baboons call attention to their eyes by lowering pale lids and "flashing" their brows upward in arches of great significance much like humans do. But humans communicate with their eyes more; many humans emphasize the direction of their gaze with a conspicuous white surround highlighting exactly where the pupils are pointed.[56] The direction of such people's gaze is thus easier to read than it is in other apes, whose gaze direction is obscured by a dark surrounding matrix. Only a sliver of white is ever—and then only occasionally—visible when an orangutan or chimpanzee glances sideways.

It is this ratio of white to dark that magnifies intensity and lends emotional meaning to facial expressions, generating the psychological response to eyes that are open wide in fear or surprise.[57] It is the flash of white that jolts our amygdalae when we notice another person startle. It would be pointless for a marauding chimpanzee on patrol (even assuming that a chimp could talk or carry a gun) to tell his comrades, John Wayne–style, "Don't shoot 'til you see the whites of their eyes." No matter how close the enemy came, defenders would be unlikely ever to see any whites of eyes unless their enemies were human beings. This difference suggests that eyes capable of communicating information about intentions may have evolved in collaborative rather than competitive contexts. Information thus conveyed was beneficial to the signaler as well as the receiver.[58]

Such differences are one reason why it was taken for granted that humans were the only apes that engaged in mutual gazing, imitated facial expressions, and used eyes to attribute mental states to others. This view fit with Meltzoff's ideas about the importance of imitation in empathy. Our supposed uniqueness in these respects was also consistent with Tomasello's proposal that "human beings, and only human beings, are biologically adapted for participating in collaborative activities involving shared goals and socially coordinated action plans." It followed that human babies would be born with special physical attributes and aptitudes for reading mental states and intentions, and communicating their own. What a lovely conceptual package—as long as it lasted. If only other apes would stick to their side of the Rubicon!

Over the past decade or so primate psychologists have documented mutual gazing in both monkeys and apes, and have observed one monkey following the gaze of another. They also now recognize that nonhuman apes (chimpanzees, for example) will sometimes signal by pointing with a hand or finger—especially if they were reared in close association with human role models.[59] Even if mirror neurons turn out to be important for understanding how individuals come to empathize with others, by themselves mirror neurons could scarcely be sufficient to explain the development of human-caliber empathy, since other primates possess mirror neurons as well.

Then in a stunning reversal of something behavioral scientists had long taken for granted, comparative psychologists discovered that chimpanzee newborns sometimes fixate on eyes, seek out faces, gaze into others' eyes, and even engage in Meltzoffian-style imitation of facial expressions. The neural equipment that supposedly allowed humans to read intentions and minds is right there in baby chimpanzees and possibly other primates as well.

ONCE WE LEARNED THAT OTHER APES BOTH GAZE AND IMITATE . . .

Years ago, Darwin noted that it is not incorrect ideas that impede scientific progress but "false facts." In the case of the wrong hypotheses, other researchers "take a salutary pleasure in proving their falseness," and they are soon corrected. But when wrong facts get enshrined in the literature, they "often long endure."[60] The problem for those of us thinking about comparative infant development in apes was that for many years we wrongly assumed that face-to-face gazing and imitation did not occur in other apes. This turns out to have been an error, albeit one that in retrospect is understandable.

Systematically monitoring the visual gaze of a nonhuman ape is no easy task. Not only are ape mothers extraordinarily protective, but throughout the first months of life baby chimpanzees mostly sleep or suck on their mother's nipples, and they rarely fuss or fidget. Baby apes are actively alert to the world around them for only about 10 percent of each day.[61] In spite of such difficulties, in 1991 the psychologist Hanus Papousek undertook the first-ever comparative study of mother-infant eye gazing in humans, captive gorillas, and bonobos. Based on what he was able to see, Papousek reported that "eye-to-eye gaze for prosocial purposes was unique to humans."[62] Since this discovery was pretty much what psychologists had expected, Papousek's initial finding went unchallenged for another decade. As late as 2002 (and in some circles to this day) it was taken for granted that the long, loving, reciprocated "extended mutual gaze" was "a human-specific adaptation . . . essential for developing a rich understanding of others' mental states, often called 'a theory of mind.'"[63] But, once again, closer scrutiny of other apes under more empathetic conditions compelled scientists to rethink the differences between other apes and us.

The psychologist Kim Bard, currently director of the Centre of the Study of Emotion at the University of Portsmouth in England, was among the first to challenge the conventional wisdom. She began to systematically study mutual gazing in chimpanzees at a time when most of the rest of us still assumed such behavior did not occur. She learned that chimpanzee mothers spend about 12 minutes of every hour looking at their newborns. Half of the time the mother seemed to peer directly into her baby's face. Some mother chimpanzees looked at their babies even longer. Occasionally mothers would use one hand to turn their infant's head toward their own face while continuing to gaze. Approximately ten times an hour the infant peered back.[64]

In addition to their mother's face, some babies looked into the eyes of their human keepers. The chimpanzee babies most prone to extended eye-to-eye contact with humans were the ones who had been separated from their mothers and were especially eager to reestablish *any* kind of contact. Since the chimpanzee babies who had been seeking eye contact in her studies also tended to be reared by mothers who themselves had spent a lot of time in close association with humans, Bard proposed that eye gaze in chimpanzees was "culturally" regulated and depended on circumstances.[65] That is, chimpanzees were adopting some of the interpersonal styles of the people they spent time with. The more exposure to human caretakers young apes had, the closer their sociocognitive responses came to those of human children in realms like intention-reading, give-and-take games involving objects, or engagement with others about their responses to objects.[66]

Bard's suspicions about the importance of rearing context were strengthened by what her colleagues in Japan were learning.[67] To this day the prize for the most intimate and expressive gazing goes to a baby chimpanzee named Ayumu. He was born in 2000 to a female chimpanzee named Ai, who had been born in Africa in 1977 and brought to Japan. From 1978 onward, Ai worked closely with the psychologist Tetsuro Matsuzawa at the Primate Research Institute at the University of Kyoto. Abandoning conventional laboratory protocols, Matsuzawa (who referred to his star chimpanzee pupil as his "partner" rather than his research subject) treated the chimpanzees he studied as friends. In the process, he pioneered a more intuitive approach for probing the perceptual and cognitive abilities of our closest primate relatives.

In addition to the usual greetings and reassurances that any good psychologist would provide his animal subjects, Matsuzawa's collaboration with Ai was punctuated by hugging, cuddling, mutual grooming, and scratching as well as long bouts of just hanging out together. The gentle and debonair lab director spent hours with a brush, patiently combing the hairs down Ai's back. Over a 30-year-long relationship, Ai has learned to trust Matsuzawa as a close associate who behaves more calmly, benevolently, and predictably than any of the more impulsive members of her own species.

So completely did Matsuzawa gain Ai's trust that in 2000 when she gave birth for the first time, she rewarded her human friend with unprecedented access to her newborn, access denied even her closest chimpanzee relations. Over the years, Matsuzawa's methods were used with other chimpanzees as well, leading the Kyoto team to dogma-shattering insights into the sensibilities and capabilities of *Pan troglodytes*. Chimpanzees raised by both their mothers and human others not only proved to be far more engaging as newborns than anyone had previously realized but mastered an impressive array of cognitive tasks. With special training, four-year-old Ayumu and his peers were actually better than university students at memorizing number sequences and then rapidly punching them onto a computer screen.[68]

Prior to Matsuzawa, scientists seeking to observe or film a baby chimpanzee face-to-face had to first remove the baby from its mother and rear it under highly artificial conditions. Never before had anyone other than the mother been allowed such privileged access to a newborn chimpanzee actually being reared by its own mother. Days after Ayumu's birth, Matsuzawa became the first person to observe and film the ephemeral "fairy" smiles that flit across the pale pink face of a newborn chimpanzee during Rapid Eye Movement sleep. Prior to that moment, neonatal smiles (which thanks to Matsuzawa we now know begin in utero) had been presumed to be uniquely human.[69]

Born smiling, chimpanzees keep right on doing so. Two months after Ayumu's birth, Matsuzawa and his team videotaped the baby chimpanzee's wildly enthusiastic (and infectious) "social" smiles in response to photographs affixed above the lens that portrayed either his mother's face or the face of his mother's very responsive human friend, Matsuzawa, who had become the baby's trusted friend as well. Baby Ayumu's response to his mother was the same gleeful greeting that Ai reserved for Matsuzawa himself, only there was no camera behind Matsuzawa's eyes

When Matsuzawa looked into his face, Ayumu returned his gaze, with eyes light-
ing up, radiating infectious glee. It would be impossible for another ape, chimpanzee, or human not to respond. Just watching Matsuzawa's videos, my own coun-
tertransference was complete. Needless to say, I smiled back. (Nancy Enslin/
T. Matsuzawa)

to film it. In line with Peter Hobson's assessment of how much relationships matter for the development of social cognition in children, Matsuzawa showed that early relationships matter for chimpanzees as well.

INTERACTIVE FOUNDATIONS WITH A NEW DIMENSION

Could a baby chimpanzee, gazing into someone else's face and interacting with others, also identify with—perhaps even empathize with—others
sufficiently to imitate the expressions on their faces the way human babies do? Neural equipment dedicated to registering eye gaze is built into
the brains of most vertebrates, but it is especially well developed in humans. Within days of birth, human newborns seek out eyes and will look
longer at any face if there are eyes there looking back. Soon after, babies
spontaneously smile or laugh on making contact. By six months of age,
little humans not only are attracted to eye gaze but also begin to evaluate just what the person observed is gazing at.[70] A direct gaze produces
stronger neurological responses than an averted one.[71] Visually engaging

eyes and face-to-face gazing play a key role in the mind reading and imitation process among infants. It has even been suggested that gazing's importance may help explain why children born blind are prone to difficulties developing connections with others.[72]

As if Ayumu's revelations were not enough, another little chimpanzee was born at Matsuzawa's institute, and unfortunately, as not infrequently happens with apes artificially reared in captivity, the mother failed to care for her. Within 24 hours of birth, the keepers transferred the newborn to an incubator for bottle-feeding. Masako Myowa, one of the students working with Matsuzawa, saw in this tragic separation an opportunity to find out just what the imitative capacities of a baby chimpanzee actually are. Myowa already knew that apes readily learn to use tools and solve problems by first watching others and then imitating the way others solve the same problem.[73] Indeed, chimpanzees reared by people may be even better at imitating what people do than human babies are.[74] From watching Matsuzawa with Ai, Myowa understood how important the relationship between subject and investigator could be, and also (in line with Bard's research) realized that human-reared chimpanzee newborns were likely to react to human facial expressions. Chimpanzees reared by humans were probably going to be even more prone to respond to facial expressions than those raised by their own mothers. Thus, Myowa reasoned, if other apes possess any capacity to respond to or imitate facial expressions, the little female she was rearing would be a good prospect to prove it.

Myowa's hunch paid off, resulting in an astonishing series of photographs. Literally aping Meltzoff and Moore's famous experiment, the photos chronicled a wide-eyed baby chimpanzee responding to the funny faces Myowa made by sticking out her tongue, opening her mouth, protruding her lips, and to all appearances enjoying this process very much. Myowa's little apprentice turned out to be even more persistent in responding to mouth movements than human babies are.[75]

At least that's how the little chimpanzee behaved at first. By 12 weeks after birth, however, the baby who had previously seemed so responsive and eager to imitate Myowa lost all interest in doing so. She had begun to respond at about five weeks and continued through eleven weeks, and then bam! Myowa contorted her face in all sorts of odd configurations, but got no response. The game had lost its appeal. In subsequent experiments, other baby chimpanzees followed the same course.[76] Then in 2006, a team of cognitive neuroscientists claimed to have demonstrated that newborn monkeys (rhesus macaques) also imitate facial expressions. But once again, the urge to do so faded by day seven.[77] Even though other primates are turning out to be far better at reading intentions than primatologists initially realized, early flickerings of empathic interest—what might even be termed tentative quests for intersubjective engagement—fade away instead of developing and intensifying as they do in human children.[78]

In 1996, following the same format used by Meltzoff in 1977, Masako Myowa showed that a human-reared female chimp between 5 and 11 weeks of age would respond to a human experimenter who stuck out her tongue, opened her mouth, or protruded her lips by doing likewise. (M. Myowa-Yamakoshi)

The documentation of facial imitation in nonhuman primates leaves many questions unanswered. Were the little macaques separated from their mothers really imitating the experimenters or just desperate to engage somebody, anybody, by making contact any way they could? Even though chimpanzee and human newborns stick out their tongues in response to someone else doing so, is this really what we mean by intentional imitation?[79] Are the responses seen in very new babies really continuous with the more self-conscious and elaborate imitation human children exhibit at older ages? Recent findings by the psychologist Susan Jones suggest they may not be.

Jones studied how willing 162 infants aged 6 to 20 months would be to imitate as their parents put a hand on their heads, stuck out their tongues, tapped on a table, wiggled their fingers, clapped their hands, or made funny little "eh, eh" noises. Overall, children younger than 12 months seemed to her less involved in "behavioral matching" than in responding to novel and interesting stimuli in their environment. It took most of the first two years, she determined, for true imitative ability to develop. Rather than a single "competency" present at birth, Jones proposed that this more self-conscious imitative capacity only emerges over time as children acquire an understanding about their body parts and what they can do.[80] In other words, the responsiveness that is present at birth in humans—and also, we now know, in chimpanzees (and perhaps macaques)—is not the same imitative capacity apparent in human infants later on. By the second year of life, the human child has developed a sense of self and begun to combine it with new understanding about bodily competencies in ways that other apes never do.

Interpreting such experiments is fraught with difficulties. For one thing, we lack anything like a complete understanding of what the neurological differences between chimpanzees and humans actually are. Nor can we be sure that the common ancestors of both chimpanzees and humans possessed the requisite neural basis for early processing of facial expressions, but my guess is that they did.

Both ape and human newborns exhibit a powerful urge to connect with and engage others. Almost all spontaneously stick out their tongues, and some percentage of human and chimpanzee neonates are more prone to do so if they see someone else do it. Apes raised by humans may be especially susceptible, but humans (also of course raised by humans) are prone to develop such traits even further. Over time, human infants become increasingly sophisticated at learning not just what attracts attention but what appeals to others, which may be what is happening with imitation. All the same, if chimpanzees are less prone to imitate and learn from others by observing, if they are not as good at mind reading as children are, the difference cannot be attributed to a lack of the basic brain equipment.

For example, consider dogs and why they do not copy their masters' facial expressions. These domesticated descendants of wolves happen to be unusually good at reading human cues, perhaps even more sensitive to human cues like pointing to where a treat is hidden than many chimpanzees are.[81] Nevertheless, dogs are no good at imitating a protruding tongue or other weird facial expressions, and this surprises no one. Dogs descend from cooperatively breeding wild ancestors, after all, and subsequently coevolved with humans and became dependent on bipedal alloparents for provisioning. But the basic neuromuscular underpinnings for this sort of facial imitation are simply not present in canines.

We now know that some other primates possess mirror neurons and also look into the faces of those near to them, engage in deep mutual gazes, and imitate what they see there. They may even experience rudimentary empathy for the travails and suffering of others and (so long as it does not require giving up desirable food) voluntarily help others or share food with them. Since we've learned that such capacities are present (even if not always employed or expanded upon), we are confronted with a conundrum that until recently scientists did not even realize we had. We are challenged to explain why prosocial impulses became so much more developed in the line leading to the genus *Homo*. Why us and not them?

A BIZARRE DIGRESSION

Neither in humans nor any other ape does the initial impetus to connect need to be learned. Rudimentary wiring for intersubjective engagement seems to be there. But by seven weeks little humans up the ante, vocalizing with vowel sounds, and by ten weeks begin to laugh. Children spontaneously seek to engage others and do not need to be coached or bribed to do so.[82] Although it is frequently assumed that such smiling and other facial expressions occur only in response to social stimuli or else must be learned, even babies born blind, who have never seen anyone make faces, start to smile around six weeks of age in response to touch, bouncing, or the sounds of a familiar voice.[83] It seems possible then that even in a social vacuum human babies would spontaneously practice smiling and other means of social engagement. The closest demonstration of this point is an appalling experiment that I came across while trolling through the old psychological literature on smiling.

Back in the 1930s, an American psychologist named Wayne Dennis and his wife managed to adopt one-month-old twin girls through the Social Services Department of the University of Virginia Hospital and then proceeded to rear the babies in virtual isolation, out of sight of one another, visited only by the experimenter/adoptive parents. Whenever the Dennises were in the same room with the babies, they made every effort to keep their faces blank and deliberately refrained from giving the babies expressive templates to imitate. For their first 26 weeks, no one ever smiled or spoke to either Del or Ray, as the babies were called. Yet the normal onset of smiling in the socially deprived twins was only slightly delayed. From the fifteenth week onward the babies almost invariably greeted the still-faced experimenters "with a smile and a vocalization" whenever one of them opened the door and entered the room. Only after the twins were six months old did the psychologists decide to return the infants' smiles and speak to them.[84]

I was unable to learn anything about what became of these unfortunate children. After wrestling with myself over the advisability of including this story together with all its ethical and scientific lapses, I decided that it was in some ways instructive. Although the experiment is (mercifully) unlikely to be repeated, the observations are consistent with the premise that, like the fairy smiles of newborn chimpanzees and humans, social smiles and laughter emerge spontaneously, although social smiles (unlike neonatal smiles?) are triggered by some stimulus in the environment (including even a nonresponsive blank-faced caretaker entering the room). More conclusive work on this subject will require the kind of ingenuity, empathy for other apes, and patience so beautifully demonstrated by Matsuzawa and his colleagues, scientists keenly aware that it is no less cruel or distorting of natural inclinations to separate a nonhuman primate baby from an attachment figure than to rear human babies in isolation.

RESOLVING THE PUZZLE

Even at this early stage in our understanding of what baby humans and other apes do spontaneously and what they do in response to social invitations from others, the revelations coming out of Kyoto and elsewhere demonstrate beyond question that other apes have the rudimentary neural equipment to seek out eyes and faces, and they register information about the expressions they see there sufficiently for at least some baby apes to imitate them. Nevertheless, after a while nonhuman ape babies seem no longer interested in this activity and differ from humans in this respect. Human infants either continue to develop and perfect imitative abilities or else (like chimpanzees) abandon the early imitative game and begin to develop a different repertoire of imitative properties.

Like early hominins, the ancestors of these laboratory chimpanzees would have benefited from being able to engage, imitate, and learn from others. After all, the common ancestors of chimpanzees and humans probably hunted in groups. They also bore offspring who would have benefited from being able to learn faster from mothers sensitive to their struggles. Ancestral apes would surely have benefited from being better at guessing what someone else intended—from being better able to read the mental states of apprentices as well as of social competitors or potential allies. Yet as they grow up, other apes remain mired in their immediate desires and needs, leaving us to ponder why Mother Nature did not favor better and better mind readers among the ancestors of modern chimpanzees as well as among our own. How did it happen that eagerness to enter into the mental and emotional states of others and engage them developed in one line of apes but not the other?

The fact that other apes are born with the equipment to engage and imitate others but soon lose interest in doing so leaves unresolved much about the original "Why us and not them?" question. What was it about the rearing conditions of infants in the genus *Homo* that led to the evolution of more persistent and sophisticated monitoring of group members, of seeking out and gazing into the faces of others, reading their expressions, and gleaning information about their mental states? And what was the payoff? How did such gifts enhance the survival of their possessors? Right from birth, humans develop (as the psychiatrist Daniel Stern likes to say) "in a soup of other people's feelings and desires."[85] So just what were the special ingredients in that soup?

Of the handful of psychologists who actually spend time pondering what life was like for youngsters millions of years ago, most take for granted that early hominin infants were cared for in the same way as chimpanzees, gorillas, orangutans, and bonobos are today—that is, exclusively by their mothers. This has been a fundamental tenet of "attachment theorists," as we will see in Chapter 3. Until recently, it is certainly what I believed as well. However, in the next chapter I explain why—in spite of the many similarities—chimpanzees and other nonhuman apes are not the appropriate prototypes to use when reconstructing early hominin childcare.

In the next two chapters I review the many different ways that infant primates are cared for, and I contrast observed infant care among wild Great Apes with the childcare practices of people still living as nomadic hunters and gatherers. These observations make clear that infants in foraging societies confront challenges unlike those faced by any other apes.

I will argue that this was probably the case among our hominin ancestors as well, although the existence of such different modes of childcare and their implications for answering the question "Why us and not them?" have long been overlooked. So what were the main differences in the ways hominin and other ape infants were reared?

3

WHY IT TAKES A VILLAGE

Every family has secrets. The secret that concerns us here has to do with the taxonomic subfamily Homininae, our bipedal ape ancestors, and dates back millions of years. Fossilized fragments are all that is left of the skeletons in this closet. Yet each of the six billion living descendants from a single hominin line from this subfamily is heir to an ancient legacy endowing them with a penchant for cooperation rarely expressed in other members of the family Hominidae. No other ape, nor any gorilla, chimpanzee, or bonobo, is anything near as good as humans at guessing what others want, or as eager to understand *why* they might want what they want. Humans alone exhibit spontaneous impulses to share with others and are routinely eager to help.

Much has been written about the large-brained bipeds who buried their dead in elaborate graves, envisioned what stone tools should look like before they crafted them, and left pictographs on cave walls. Remains of anatomically modern people with skulls and bones indistinguishable from those of people today do not appear in the paleontological record before 200,000 years ago. Based on genetic evidence, all humans on earth today descend from a common ancestor that lived in Africa between 50,000 and 150,000 years before the present, and these were the first anatomically modern people who began to think symbolically and use language, possibly a language containing some of the click sounds that can still be heard today among San and Hadza-speakers.[1]

From an evolutionary perspective, anatomically and behaviorally modern humans are remarkably recent. However, I am convinced that *emotionally modern humans* date back much further. By emotionally modern I mean bipedal apes born with giving impulses and empathic, intersubjective aptitudes profoundly different from those we see in chimpanzees today—people preadapted to get along with one another even when crowded together on an airplane. Such hominins, I suspect, emerged in Africa hundreds of thousands of years before inventive, symbol-generating, and talkative humans did.

In Chapter 2, I explained that other primates possess neural machinery for imitation and at least a rudimentary capacity to identify with others. The common ancestor of modern humans and chimpanzees presumably also had every incentive to evolve a sophisticated theory of mind and would have benefited from ever-shrewder and more Machiavellian intelligence or from enhanced pedagogical capacities, yet natural selection never favored their acquisition. What happened, then, in the line leading to the genus *Homo* to favor evolution of these traits? In this chapter and the next I hypothesize that novel rearing conditions among a line of early hominins meant that youngsters grew up depending on a wider range of caretakers than just their mothers, and this dependence produced selection pressures that favored individuals who were better at decoding the mental states of others, and figuring out who would help and who would hurt.

It is often asserted that early hominins were selected for a better mind-reading capacity because it would prepare youngsters to acquire culture, or because it would make humans better at coordinating complex activities.[2] Sounds good—except that natural selection, lacking foresight, does not work that way. Blindly groping along with no particular end in view, Mother Nature pays no heed to future benefits such as being better able to generate culture or coordinate large-scale activities. Directional selection favoring improved mind reading required immediate payoffs. Individuals a little bit better at interpreting someone else's mental state and engaging with them emotionally had to have a better chance than groupmates of surviving and reproducing in the here-and-now. What other apes apparently lacked was an environment in which the components of mind reading and sharing could first develop and then be subjected to selective pressures that favored their possessors.

So what sort of environment would provide already clever and manipulative, highly social (but also highly selfish) apes the opportunity, first, to develop intersubjective abilities right from a formative early age and, then, to benefit from them? In what sort of environment would natural selection actually favor those who were just a little bit more inclined to share? In this chapter I will summarize evidence for thinking that hominin infants must have been reared differently from any other ape. By possibly as early as 1.8 million years ago, hominin youngsters were being cared for and provisioned by a range of individuals in addition to their mothers, and these rearing conditions set the stage for the emergence of an emotionally more modern ape. Long before our ancestors evolved into big-brained, anatomically modern humans, early hominins were being reared by alloparents as well as parents. Once outed, this long-hidden secret in our family closet requires us to consider exactly what roles these hitherto unacknowledged benefactors played.

It was the end of the twentieth century before evolutionary anthropologists like myself began to consider just how hard it would have been for foragers to rear surviving children, and then to piece together disparate strands of evidence indicating that the help of group members in addition to the genetic parents was absolutely essential for the survival of infants (birth to weaning) and children (weaning to nutritional independence) in the Pleistocene. The need for alloparental succor transformed the selection pressures that shaped our species, and in doing so altered the way infants developed and then the way humans evolved. Like protagonists in a Dickens novel (think of the convict Magwitch and what his anonymous legacy did for Pip's "great expectations"), these secret benefactors—whose identities we had never even considered before—

completely transformed human prospects, including our own lives. But to tell this story, I need to begin at the beginning, with mothers.

MOTHER-CENTERED BEGINNINGS

Let me be clear. None of the family secrets revealed here challenges the central importance of mothers. With the emergence of the first mammals some 200 million years ago, babies were born dependent on nurture from one other individual—their mother, who kept them safe, warm, and milk-fed. Bonds between mother and infant were fundamental to the evolution of the ways creatures like ourselves smell, hear, remember, sense the nearness of, and feel comforted by those close to us. Absent mammals and minus mothers, we would not be groping for terms to express affiliative emotions or need a word like "love" to describe the ties that bind one intimate to another.

Of all the attachments mammalian babies form, none is more powerful than that between baby primates and their mothers.[3] The emotional ties that bind ape mothers to their infants and infants to their mothers are unusually long-lasting. Under natural conditions, an orangutan, chimpanzee, or gorilla baby nurses for four to seven years and at the outset is inseparable from his mother, remaining in intimate front-to-front contact 100 percent of the day and night. The earliest a wild chimpanzee mother has ever been observed to voluntarily let a baby out of her grasp is three and a half months.[4] Among wild orangutans, half a year elapses, five months at the very least, before a mother allows any other individual, even her own older offspring, to hold her baby.[5] A baby ape's earliest education about the world comes from his relationship with this utterly significant other, his compulsively possessive, highly reliable and responsive mother. His or her mother was every ape's first and only source of warmth, locomotion, provisioning, and safety, as well as, for months on end with only an occasional glance at others, the sum total of each infant's social world. Few if any baby apes would have had opportunities to engage and imitate others, much less benefit when they did.

In fact, this continuous-care-and-contact mothering characterizes only about half of the roughly 276 species of living primates, though it includes all four nonhuman Great Apes and many species of Old World monkeys such as the very-well-studied and much-written-about rhesus

Mothers in roughly half of the species in the order Primates remain in continuous contact with their babies for the first weeks or months of life. This orangutan mother will not be out of touch with her baby even for an instant until five to six months after his birth, and the baby will continue to nurse until around age seven. (Tim Laman)

macaques and savanna baboons.[6] The constant care provided exclusively by mothers in these species is due largely to the possessiveness of mothers, not to lack of interest from would-be babysitters. In all primates, other group members (most often subadult females) are attracted to and eager to touch and hold new babies. The mother herself is the limiting factor who determines whether or not they succeed, and in the case of wild apes, the mother is adamant that they will not. Of all continuous-care-and-contact primate mothers, none are more intransigently possessive than Great Apes—a fact, alas, known all too well to poachers. The way to capture a baby gorilla or orangutan is, first, shoot the mother.

Like many mammals, a Great Ape female near the end of pregnancy grows restless.[7] An orangutan mother-to-be builds and rebuilds her sleeping nest, moves about, anxiously checks and rechecks her environs. Prior to birth, the near-term chimpanzee female moves away from group-mates and seeks seclusion. Minutes after birth, possibly while the mother is still consuming the placenta, the tiny, spidery newborn ape on the ground beside her will catch hold of her hairy belly and pull himself aboard, or else the mother herself will pick the newborn up.

The neonate clings to his mother as if his life depends on it, which it does. In the forests and savannas where primates evolved, separation means early death from either predation or starvation. Yet despite their Velcro-like grasp, a newborn chimpanzee or gorilla's finger-and-toe-hold can be tenuous. Newborns are so poorly coordinated that they can grip tight for only minutes at a stretch, so a mother needs to constantly reach down to readjust her baby or help him gain access to a nipple. Often a mother will walk three-legged or, if climbing vertically, prop the baby up using one or both thighs. Hours or days after birth when the mother rejoins her community, she holds her newborn close, rebuffing every attempt to touch him, wrapping her arms about him and turning her broad, hairy back on would-be nursemaids, folding her body over the baby, foiling access. The awkwardness of this enterprise notwithstanding, ape mothers are unfailingly responsive to infant needs. At the slightest signal of discomfort, the mother reaches down to reposition her burden. As one observer of wild orangutans, Carel van Schaik, put it, the mother responds to every wriggle, every whimper "with the attentiveness of a private nurse and the patience of an angel."[8]

Many mammalian mothers can be surprisingly selective about which babies they care for. A mother mouse or prairie dog may cull her litter, shoving aside a runt; a lioness whose cubs are too weak to walk may abandon the entire litter "with no attempt to nudge them to their feet, carry them or otherwise help."[9] Some mammals (and this includes humans) even discriminate against healthy babies, if they happen to be born the "wrong" sex. But not Great Ape or most primate mothers. No matter how deformed, scrawny, odd, or burdensome, there is no baby that a wild ape mother won't keep. Babies born blind, limbless, or afflicted with cerebral palsy—newborns that a hunter-gatherer mother would likely abandon at birth—are picked up and held close. If her baby is too incapacitated to hold on, the mother may walk bipedally or tripedally so as to support the baby with one hand.[10]

The primatologist Sarah Turner, who is studying a population of Japanese macaques known for its high prevalence of birth defects, observed a particularly extreme case, a newborn with neither hands nor legs. And yet, as she wrote to me, "His mother carries him everywhere and holds him up to nurse when he can't reach her nipple."[11] Had local people not fed these monkeys (it was a free-ranging but provisioned and

Monkey and ape mothers rarely discriminate based on a baby's particular attributes, as some human mothers do. Except perhaps for those born very prematurely, babies are cared for (and carried) almost no matter what. Even if her baby dies, the mother will continue to carry the desiccated corpse about for days, as this langur mother is doing. (S. B. Hrdy/AnthroPhoto)

also protected, largely predator-free population), the mother would not have been able to constantly assist her handicapped infant to stay aboard and still remain fed and safe herself. But there is no question that she would have tried.

Maternal devotion in the human case is more complicated. A woman undergoes the same endocrinological transformations during pregnancy as other apes. At birth, her cortisol levels and heartbeat reflect just how sensitive to infant cues she has become.[12] But whereas the nonhuman ape mother undiscriminatingly accepts any infant born to her without taking into account physical attributes, the human mother's devotion is more conditional. A newborn perceived as defective may be drowned, buried alive, or simply wrapped in leaves and left in the bush within hours of birth.[13] "Defective" may mean anything from having too many toes to too few. It may mean being born with a deformed limb or at a very low birthweight, coming too soon after the birth of an older sibling, or having some culturally arbitrary or other affliction such as having too much or too little hair, or being born the wrong sex.

Humans last shared a shaggy, arboreal common ancestor with compulsively possessive orangutan mothers 14 million years ago, with gorillas closer to 8 million. We shared a common ancestor with continuous-care-and-contact chimpanzee and bonobo mothers a mere 6 million years ago or so.[14] At some point in the intervening eons hominin mothers lost the hair that other ape babies cling to. The best available estimate (based on genetic evidence indicating when our ancestors exchanged a type of body louse that lives in fur for one that lives in pubic hair) suggests that hominins started to lose much of their body hair by 3.3 million years ago.[15] This meant that a newborn whose inexperienced first-time mother did not immediately pick him up would not have had the option of grabbing a scraggly foothold until his mother began to respond to him. With hair loss, mothers and babies alike probably could have used help more than ever.

Although human infants are born with the same grasping reflex that other apes have, they lose it shortly after birth. Furthermore, unlike any other ape, a mother in a hunter-gatherer society examines her baby right after birth and, depending on its specific attributes and her own social circumstances (especially how much social support she is likely to have), makes a conscious decision to either keep the baby or let it die. In most traditional hunter-gatherer societies, abandonment is rare, and almost always undertaken with regret. It is an act no woman wants to recall, a topic ethnographers must tiptoe around gingerly. Typically, interviewers will broach the subject indirectly, asking other women rather than the mother herself.[16] Back when the !Kung still lived as nomadic hunter-gatherers, the rate of abandonment was about one in one hundred live births. Higher rates were reported among people with strong sex preferences, as among the pre-missionized Eipo horticulturalists of highland New Guinea. Forty-one percent of live births in this group resulted in abandonment, and in the vast majority of cases the abandoned babies were newborn daughters whose mothers hoped to reduce the time until a son might be born.[17]

Once a baby has nursed at his mother's breast and lactation is under way, a woman's hormonal and neurological responses to this stimulation, combined with visual, auditory, tactile, and olfactory cues, produce a powerful emotional attachment to her baby. Once she passes this tipping point, a mother's passionate desire to keep her baby safe usually overrides other (including conscious) considerations. This is why if a mother is going to abandon her infant, she usually does so immediately, before her milk comes in and before mother-infant bonding is past the point of no return.

A STRIKING DEPARTURE FROM OTHER APES

Human babies resemble other ape babies in their powerful desire to be held close, and as with all apes, nothing suits them better than warm and continuous contact with a responsive mother. But humans enter the world on vastly different terms. They are born to a hairless mother whose commitment to her infant is contingent on far more than her own prior experience or physical condition. Her commitment depends as well on her assessment of her baby's particular attributes and on how much social support she anticipates receiving.[18] Near-term women are just as restless and alert to conceivable sources of harm to their baby as other apes would be. They are just as vigilant right before and right after birth, and prone to postpartum anxiety. Even in a modern context, with their infant sleeping soundly in a crib inside a walled, well-heated nursery, new mothers compulsively check again and again to be sure that their baby is still breathing, still safe, still comfortable. I vividly recall my own spontaneous fantasies after bringing a new baby home from the hospital, imagining the most implausible dangers. Years later I was astonished to learn from Yale psychiatrist James Leckman that such anxious, obsessively compulsive fantasies are typical of most new mothers.[19]

Women are just as prone as other apes to worry about the well-being of new babies. But what hunter-gatherer mothers do not do postpartum is refuse to let anyone else come near or hold their baby. This is an important difference. A brief survey of caretaking practices across traditional hunting and gathering peoples—the closest proxies for Pleistocene hominins we have—reveals that even though nomadic foragers differ in where and how they make a living, babies are universally treated with warm indulgence. Hunter-gatherers are no different from apes in this respect. Babies are never left alone and are constantly held by someone, but that someone is not invariably the mother.[20] Human mothers are just as hypervigilant; they are just not so hyperpossessive. From the outset a human mother will allow other group members (typically relatives) to take and hold her baby.

The first systematic study of infant care among hunter-gatherers by

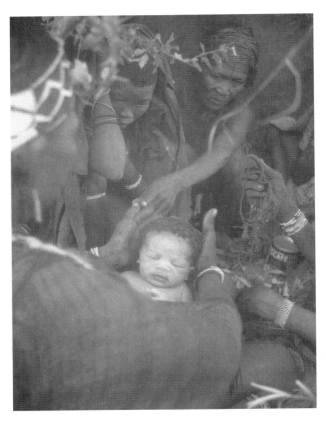

In this extraordinary portrait, members of a Ju/'hoansi (!Kung) band cluster about a newborn. The photograph, by the late Marjorie Shostak, was taken just after the mother gave birth alone in "the bush" and then returned to camp a short distance away. She handed the baby to her mother, who gently massaged the baby and "shaped" its skull with her palms in the customary way. (Marjorie Shostak/Anthro-Photo)

the anthropologist Mel Konner described how !Kung infants were carried long distances across the veldt on their mother's back or else held in a sling vertically at their mother's side, in "continuous skin-to-skin contact"—a description that invited comparisons with other apes, leading Konner himself and the rest of us to overlook what was really a striking difference between humans and other apes, the amount of time that infants were held by others as well.[21] In fact, !Kung infants did spend more time in direct, intimate contact with their mothers than is typical

Iconic images of mothers traveling long distances with their babies carried at their sides in a leather sling produced the impression that mothers were the exclusive caretakers of babies. Because the pioneering field observations among the !Kung were extremely influential, this image was extrapolated to hunter-gatherers generally. (Richard Lee/AnthroPhoto)

of foraging peoples generally, and far more time in contact with their mothers than is typical of infants in farming or postindustrial societies. But even !Kung infants were held by others some 25 percent of the time— a big difference from other apes, among whom new infants are *never* held by anyone other than their mother.[22]

Hunter-gatherers vary a lot in how they make their living, depending on local terrain and what kind of game and wild plants are available.[23] But in all locations, even with the invention of devices like slings, carrying infants is energetically costly, by some estimates even more costly than lactation, which takes about 500 calories per day to sustain.[24] It is not surprising that mothers allow other group members to hold their babies. A quick survey of available ethnography indicates how widespread shared care is among foraging peoples. "From their position on the mother's hip," writes Konner, babies among the !Kung San

> have available to them [the mother's] entire social world . . . When the mother is standing, the infant's face is just at the eye-level of desperately maternal 11- to 12-year-old girls who frequently approach and initiate brief, intense, face-to-face

interactions including smiling and vocalization. When not in the sling [babies] are passed from hand to hand around a fire for similar interactions with one adult or child after another. They are kissed on their faces, bellies, genitals, sung to, bounced, entertained, encouraged, even addressed at length in conversational tones long before they can understand words. Throughout the first year there is rarely any dearth of such attention and love.[25]

"The Hadza child's first year of life," writes the ethologist Nick Blurton Jones, "appears not to differ greatly from that of the !Kung infant . . . The mother is the principal caretaker . . . Suckling is frequent, and often, but by no means always 'on demand.'" As with other apes, the baby is in continuous contact with someone, frequently the mother, but is also held by grandmothers, great-aunts, older siblings, fathers, and even visitors from neighboring groups.[26] Other group members are so attracted by this new addition to the community that Hadza newborns are held by alloparents 85 percent of the time in the first days right after birth. Thereafter, mothers take over more of the care.[27]

Infant sharing is even more common among Central African foragers. In nomadic communities composed of 25–30 Aka or Efe, mothers share their babies with group members immediately after birth and then keep right on sharing. Among the Mbuti, "the mother emerges and presents the child to the camp," whereupon "she hands the [baby] to a few of her closest friends and family, not just for them to look at him but for them to hold him close to their bodies."[28] Over the first days of his life, all females in the vicinity "attempt to comfort a distressed or fussy infant."[29] Among the Aka, the mother's mother typically takes the neonate right after birth, washes him in a stream, wraps him in cloth, and holds him until the placenta is delivered. Among the Efe, other women cluster around a woman in labor, several of them acting as midwives.[30]

Both Efe and Aka women pass the infant around after birth, and regardless of whether they are actually lactating, they may comfort the newborn by allowing him to suck on their nipples. Over the next 48 hours or so, before the mother's own milk comes in, the baby will also be nursed—as often as two or three times a day—by one or more lactating allomothers.[31] If a lactating woman does not currently reside in camp, a wet nurse may be temporarily recruited from another village.[32] Although

Because nut groves where women collect food were often miles from camp, !Kung women carried their infants with them. This way, if babies wanted to nurse, they could. In a hot, arid world without pasteurized milk or baby bottles, breast milk was often the only way to keep babies safely hydrated. The harsh Kalahari conditions were probably one reason why !Kung infants spent relatively more time than do Aka or Efe infants in direct contact with their mothers. (Peabody Museum/Marshall Expedition image 2001.29.410)

shared suckling is not observed among wild apes, it occurs at least occasionally in 87 percent of typical foraging societies documented in the Human Relations Area Files.[33]

Around the world, wherever traditional ways of life persist—that is, in communities where mothers have not yet begun to live in compartmentalized families and started to worry about not exposing their babies to germs—shared care is the rule. Far from Africa, the Agta in the Philippines still live as foragers and are famous for women's participation in hunting. A newborn Agta will be "eagerly passed from person to person until all in attendance have had an opportunity to snuggle, nuzzle, sniff, and admire the newborn . . . Thereafter he enjoys constant cuddling, carrying, loving, sniffing, and affectionate genital stimulation."[34] Similarly, among Ongee foragers on the Andaman Islands off the eastern coast of India, and among Trobriand Islanders in the Pacific, infants are routinely shared and are suckled by lactating allomothers.

Focusing on the best-studied hunter-gatherer societies, we find a continuum, with people like the !Kung engaging in comparatively little infant-sharing and people like the Efe doing a lot of it. The Hadza fall somewhere in between, with babies under four years of age held by their mothers 69 percent of the time and held by allomothers, mostly relatives, the rest of the time.[35] These proportions are reversed among the Efe, where allomothers hold babies 60 percent of the time during daylight—more than their own lactating mothers do. But even in the Efe case, where babies pass from caretaker to caretaker on average eight times an hour, mothers hold babies more than any other single individual. And as is true for all apes, !Kung, Efe, and Aka infants spend their nights nestled next to their mothers.

Even with such extensive babysitting at their disposal, Aka and Efe mothers are rarely far away from their infants and are available to breast-feed on demand as often as several times per hour.[36] No wonder babies are emotionally most strongly attached to their mothers. But with all these commonalities, what stands out and contrasts with other apes is that these mothers trust others and allow them to take their infants shortly after birth.

So why are postpartum women so much more tolerant of group members than other apes living in the wild? Humans' large neocortex is an obvious possibility. Not only do human mothers need more help getting big-brained babies through narrow birth canals but they are better able to evaluate the costs and benefits of their own behavior.[37] Conscious awareness that they will need help rearing their babies renders human mothers more discriminating. Mothers also understand how beneficial it is for a baby to be introduced to a community of others. By sharing her baby, the mother sends a clear signal that both she and her offspring will be counting on help from the clan. By exposing alloparents to the sight, sound, and smell of her alluring little charge, the mother lays the groundwork for emotional ties binding her baby to potential caretakers and vice versa.

But other factors are involved as well. If human mothers exhibit greater postpartum tolerance of others, it must be because they are more confident of the benign intentions of those around them. Their trust is sufficient to override the compulsive hypervigilance universally found in new ape mothers. In Chapter 8, I examine *why* postpartum women should be more trusting and tolerant of groupmates than other apes are.

BORN IN A NEW MILIEU

Efe babies average 14 different caretakers in the first days of life.[38] Male caregivers are usually fathers, brothers, or cousins, less often grandfathers or uncles. Females are typically older sisters, aunts, or grandmothers. Cousins are less frequently involved, possibly because they have their own younger siblings to care for.[39] More distant relations also help out—sometimes orphans fostered in from elsewhere, possibly acting as *au pairs* in exchange for their board. Babies soon become powerfully bonded to their mothers, but right from birth they are introduced to a range of alloparents who also become familiar to them.

The Efe are an extreme case, but in general hunter-gatherer babies are exposed to, cared for, stimulated, and entertained by a wider cast of characters than other apes are. Perhaps even more remarkably, they are also provisioned by alloparents, who comfort and distract their charges by offering a breast or mouth-to-mouth kisses laced with the juice of ripe berries or sugary ground powder from baobab pods.[40] Sweetened saliva adds an extra and exciting dimension to the pleasurable sensations of kissing. As young as three to four months, babies receive premasticated mouthfuls of food from allomothers, who push these delicacies in with their tongues. In a particularly detailed study of allomaternal care, Barry Hewlett and his colleagues found that 15 of 20 three-month-old Aka infants were being provisioned in this way.[41] From an early age, food sharing becomes a highlight of relations with allomothers—the *amuse bouche* to the decades of alloparental provisioning to follow.

Sharing food with immatures still too young to obtain or process

An Efe infant is born into an ever-expanding social world, passed between mother and allomother, and among allomothers, in the days just after birth. (Steve Winn/ AnthroPhoto)

food for themselves has been a critical but often-overlooked chapter of the human story. Alloparental provisioning has been well-studied in birds, however, where males are almost as likely to provide for young as females are. In other cooperatively breeding mammals like wild dogs, wolves, or meerkats, not only do alloparents of both sexes routinely bring back food to the den but lactating mothers also suckle another female's young. Yet no other immatures depend on others to provision them for years the way that human children do.

Among chimpanzees, who also grow up slowly, infants are provisioned insofar as they are permitted to grab food from their mothers. A youngster as old as two years has been observed to push pouted lips into his mother's face until she delivers a lipfull of shared food right into his mouth.[42] But only among humans is maternal and alloparental generosity initiated from the first months and then sustained for years. Premasticated mouthfuls of baby food are followed by finger foods, which are followed by nuts and cooked roots, collected and often laboriously processed by grandmothers and great-aunts—and most delectably of all, honey or meat brought in by the father, the child's uncle, or other hunt-

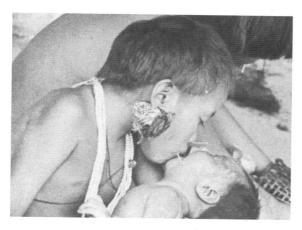

(Top) This eight-year-old Yanomamo allomother hugs and gently rocks a three-month-old baby, as she kisses him on the mouth, transferring sweet saliva. (Bottom) This Himba grandmother delivers food in mouth-to-mouth transfer, only to have the baby playfully return the favor. Early ethologist Eibl-Eibesfeldt referred to such behaviors as "kiss-feeding" after similar behaviors seen in birds and some other primates. (I. Eibl-Eibesfeldt/Human Ethology Archives)

ers. Everyone receives a share of the highly prized meat. I agree with Daniel Stern's remark that "we grow up in a soup of other people's feelings and desires," but I doubt that Dr. Stern intended for his metaphor about edible milieus to apply quite so literally.[43]

Even though no other ape shares care and provisioning of young as spontaneously or as routinely as humans do, shared care and provisioning is found in some other primates. But before turning to these cases, I need to explain how a fixation with mother-only care initially led evolutionists to overlook alternative modes of infant care.

WHAT ATTACHMENT THEORISTS OVERLOOKED

Within the field of developmental psychology, the most influential evolutionist since Darwin was unquestionably John Bowlby. Back in the middle of the last century, this kindly, evolutionarily-minded psychiatrist set about situating the emotional needs of developing infants within what he termed humankind's "environment of evolutionary adaptedness." Attachment theory, arguably evolutionary theory's most important contribution to human well-being, has grown out of Bowlby's insights into the need of primate infants to feel secure and to forge emotional attachments to a primary caretaker. What follows here and in the next chapter is meant to correct an underlying assumption about the universality of exclusive maternal care in primates, not to challenge Bowlby's fundamental insights.

Back in my mother's day, anyone with a college-level course in psychology would have been at least subliminally aware of the behaviorist John Watson's famous (now infamous) admonition to be ashamed of "the mawkish, sentimental way you have been handling your child."[44] Watson warned that it was ill-advised to pick up a crying baby. It would spoil the child and condition him to cry more. Far better to let the baby cry it out. From the late 1960s onward, however, with the spread of attachment theory, such attitudes changed.

Unlike Watson, who viewed crying as perverse, Bowlby viewed it as natural, shaped by Darwinian selection during humankind's 70-million-year primate heritage. Far from being spoiled egotists, babies were responding adaptively, in ways that would have kept their ancestors safe from predation by hyenas and leopards and from other hazards of their ancestral environments. In words that to my sociobiologically conditioned ears still sound remarkably fresh today, Bowlby wrote: "When he is born, an infant is far from being a *tabula rasa*. On the contrary he is equipped with a number of behavioral systems ready to be activated but each system is already biased so that it is activated by stimuli falling within one or more broad ranges."[45]

Little humans are born preprogrammed to look for eyes, follow their gaze, seek out faces, especially "prettier" feminine faces (though babies routinely settle for less), and quickly memorize their mother's voice and smell, seeking to maintain contact with her and in time forge a powerful emotional attachment to this all-important other.[46] Forget the behaviorists. Post-Bowlby, babies are viewed as well within their rights to cry when left alone.

The rise of attachment theory in the postindustrial West not only ushered in more humane treatment of babies, it also led to practical benefits for parents. A baby confident of a rapid response by a mother committed to his well-being is likely to become a child who will be quicker to soothe and adapt to new situations, and likely to grow up to feel confident about human relations generally. In a complete reversal of Watsonian logic, over the long haul babies with more responsive mothers are going to cry and cling to their parents less, not more.

Today, the main outlines of attachment theory are widely accepted. Developmental psychologists have fanned out around the world to test its major tenets among babies in Africa, Europe, Japan, and Israel, as well as Central, South, and North America.[47] The *Handbook of Attachment Theory* published in 1999 runs 925 pages, weighs in at just under four pounds, and already has a new edition in the works. It summarizes hundreds of studies, most of them from Western societies, elucidating how and why a baby's felt need for a "warm, intimate, and continuous" relationship turns out to be as addictive as opium. It also lays out compelling evidence for how and why the infant's confidence in his or her caretakers contributes to emotional security and sets up expectations (or "internal working models") about the social world that lay the groundwork for subsequent relationships.

By the late 1990s, however, an explosion of new information concerning the demography and behavior of other apes along with new information about childcare among hunter-gatherers and other traditional peoples began to call into question the applicability of Bowlby's homology between maternal behavior in humans and our closest ape relations. For Bowlby, the continuous-care-and-contact mothering so readily apparent among the nonhuman Great Apes was not only appealing and consistent with Western presumptions about how "good mothers" ought to behave, it fit with his assumptions about the homologies between infant needs in human and nonhuman primates. What Bowlby overlooked was the many alternative modes of infant care found among primates.

In his classic 1969 book *Attachment,* Bowlby singled out chimpanzees, gorillas, and two species of catarrhine Old World monkeys—baboons and rhesus macaques—as *the* primate templates for how our African savanna-dwelling ancestors must have cared for babies. Bowlby specifically chose them because, as he put it, "All four species, and especially baboon and gorilla, are adapted to a terrestrial existence." Among primates who traveled and spent a lot of time feeding on the ground, a baby would need to be continuously held by his mother, Bowlby reasoned, in order to be safe from predators.

The discipline of primatology was still fairly new, and these four species did happen to be among the first ones studied. Furthermore, experimental studies of captive chimpanzees and rhesus monkeys supplemented information from the wild. Nevertheless, Bowlby's choice was probably also influenced by an additional criterion that he may not have been conscious of. Each of these species conformed to preconceived Western ideals of how a mother *should* care for her infant.[48] Mothers belonging to primate species that also spent a lot of time on the ground but happened not to remain in continuous tactile contact with their babies went unremarked.

The continuous contact between mother and infant that seemed so self-evident and so natural to Bowlby, as well as to Darwin, in fact characterizes only a slim majority (if that) of the living primates. Exclusively maternal infant care is scarcely the whole story. It leaves out the other 40 to 50 percent of some 276 species. These include such notably terrestrial African savanna-dwelling catarrhine Old World monkeys as vervet monkeys and patas monkeys, as well as various semiterrestrial north African and Southeast Asian species of macaques.[49] Mothers in these species freely allow other group members to hold their babies, presumably saving energy and sparing themselves the awkwardness of carrying new babies while they feed. Detailed studies of infant-sharing species only became available later, but preliminary observations of infant sharing in some species were known, albeit accorded little significance by early attachment theorists.[50]

When Bowlby's 1969 classic *Attachment* was republished in paperback, the cover photo of an Amazonian Indian emphasized the then-prevailing assumption of continuous skin-to-skin contact between mothers and their infants in nomadic hunter-gatherer societies. (Basic Books/Perseus Book Group)

To correct the record, join me on a brief tour of how mothers among this overlooked half of the primate order deal with infants in the period after birth. Three points will emerge. First, *there is no one, universal pattern of infant care among primates.* Second, far from being a hardwired primate-wide trait, *continuous-care-and-contact mothering is a last resort for primate mothers who lack safe and available alternatives.* Third, and perhaps most important so far as primates are concerned, *there is nothing evolutionarily out of the ordinary about mothers cutting corners or relying on shared care.*

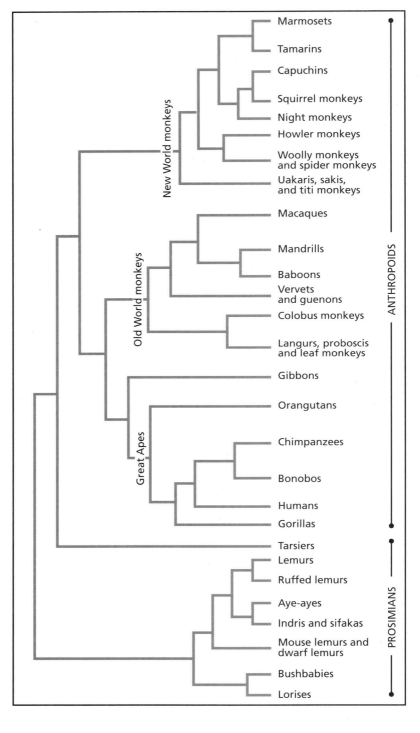

Marmosets
Tamarins
Capuchins
Squirrel monkeys
Night monkeys
Howler monkeys
Woolly monkeys
and spider monkeys
Uakaris, sakis,
and titi monkeys

New World monkeys

Macaques
Mandrills
Baboons
Vervets
and guenons
Colobus monkeys
Langurs, proboscis
and leaf monkeys

Old World monkeys

Gibbons
Orangutans
Chimpanzees
Bonobos
Humans
Gorillas

Great Apes

Tarsiers
Lemurs
Ruffed lemurs
Aye-ayes
Indris and sifakas
Mouse lemurs and
dwarf lemurs
Bushbabies
Lorises

ANTHROPOIDS

PROSIMIANS

A simple guide to the prosimians, monkeys, and apes mentioned in the text. For additional detail I recommend Noel Rowe's *Pictorial Guide to the Living Primates*.

Our survey of maternal shortcuts begins with prosimians. Of all extant primates, the ones that most closely resemble ancient primates from the fossil record of 50 million years ago are lemurs, lorises, and bushbabies. It is assumed that their now-extinct primate precursors gave birth to multiple young, like many prosimians today. If so, mothers probably left them in nests when they went off to forage, just as some of their modern lemur descendants do. Among mouse lemurs, dwarf lemurs, and bush-babies (or "galagos"), mothers nonchalantly leave entire litters in their sleeping nests while they forage. "Stay put, see you later."

Among the ruffed lemurs of Madagascar, one of the few primates that can actually be said to have a nesting instinct, pregnant females close to parturition build nests specifically for use as nurseries. These mothers share care of their infants (often twins) with the father and per-haps another lactating mother. When the mother goes off to forage, one of these allomothers stays behind, and if the babies get hungry before their mother returns, a lactating co-mother may suckle them.[51] Galago and mouse lemur babies may similarly be co-suckled as well as kept warm by allomothers who are usually aunts, sometimes grandmothers.[52]

With neither nests nor allomothers, some prosimians simply stash babies as best they can, the way bamboo lemur and many lorisid mothers do. Parking babies this way is risky. Indian slender loris mothers often hedge their bets by hiding one twin in one spot and the other someplace else. If a predator stumbles on one, the mother still has an heir to spare.[53] Monkey mothers with singleton young are understandably more cau-tious. Nevertheless, in a pinch, woolly spider monkeys (the rare and en-dangered Brazilian muriquis) may park older babies. In one rare instance when a mother's own mother was available (unusual because muriqui mothers typically leave home before breeding), the maternal grand-mother carried her grandson for extended periods.[54]

Pretty clearly, leaving a baby with someone else is preferable to park-ing it, as long as a caregiver is available, willing, competent, and well-disposed and the mother trusts him or her to return the infant un-harmed. Not surprisingly, the best primate caregiver on offer will often be the father. In most mammals, fathers would not be anywhere nearby. But primates are unusual. Instead of decamping after they mate, fathers in most species in the order Primates remain year-round in the same social group as the mothers of their offspring (about which much more in Chapter 5).

Nowhere in mammaldom do fathers behave in a more exemplary fashion than among two types of New World monkeys, the sixteen monogamously mating titi monkey species belonging to the genus *Callicebus,* and the various wide-eyed species of night monkeys in the genus *Aotus.* These fathers not only carry babies about but provide them with food.[55] New mothers are followed everywhere by a mate whose top priority in all the world, day in and day out, is to remain nearby and carry her baby whenever it is not nursing. Human mothers can only fantasize about such an unlikely state of affairs. *Callicebus* and *Aotus* dads are so attentive that infant titi or night monkeys form their primary attachment to the father. While a night monkey baby is more likely to beg food from his dad than his mom, a titi baby becomes more upset (as measured by vocalizations and elevated adrenocortical activity) if the father is removed than if the infant is separated from his mother.[56] I know of no other mammals whose babies are routinely more attached to their fathers than to their mothers.

By the end of the first week, a titi monkey mother's daytime contact with her baby is down to just four or five bouts of suckling per day. Her mate carries the baby 90 percent of daytime—with a little help from an older sibling, if there is one. Nevertheless (do some things never change?), mom still does diaper duty, licking her baby's genitalia clean during the brief periods when the baby is back on board to nurse. Even after the baby starts to move about, around six months of age, the father will be more eager than the mother either to play or to share food, typically fruit and insects. Meanwhile, the no-nonsense titi monkey mom concentrates on her own feeding, preparing herself to gestate and then breastfeed their next baby.

A titi male's mate is rarely out of his sight, making him the likeliest sire of any baby born to these typically monogamous primates. This differs from the usual situation where a primate male's paternity is less certain. But even without the certainty of paternity, males sometimes help, as among the Barbary macaques of North Africa. When in estrus, female *Macaca sylvanus* eagerly solicit and mate promiscuously with just about

This titi monkey baby spends most of his day riding on his father's back. His older sister (in front) also occasionally helps out. When researchers at the University of California-Davis briefly removed a parent, the baby was more distressed by separation from his father than from his mother. (Mike Nelson/California National Primate Research Center)

every male in their multimale troop. Yet after babies are born, right from day one, males take turns carrying them around.[57] Such care by possible or would-be fathers is neither so exclusive nor so costly as the attention lavished on young by the single-minded titi monkey male. Yet without this extra care from males, Barbary macaque infants could not survive the harsh winters of the Atlas Mountains where they evolved.[58] To ensure that at least some of his offspring survive, a male *Macaca sylvanus* errs on the conservative side of the uncertainty that surrounds paternity in this species. The risk to a male's posterity from caring for another male's offspring is outweighed by the still graver risk of dying childless.

In an overwhelming majority of primates, males remain year-round in the same social group as females with whom they have mated, but their assistance is typically limited to generalized protection of the troop from predation or from marauding males likely to kill infants, since in many populations infanticide by alien males is the major source of infant mortality.[59] In extreme emergencies, probable fathers may snatch an infant out of harm's way or, if the mother should die, adopt a weaned orphan. Nevertheless, as far as direct care is concerned, most primate mothers have to rely on other adult females or on juveniles or subadults eager to practice their mothering skills, rather than on male caregivers. So in which species do mothers voluntarily share access to young infants?

Old World monkeys are divided into two subfamilies, the cercopithecines and colobines. Most cercopithecine Old World monkeys, including such well-known species as rhesus macaques and savanna baboons, exhibit quintessentially continuous-care-and-contact mothering. Interested allomothers might be allowed to briefly touch, but not take, a new infant. Relatively few cercopithecine monkeys behave like Barbary macaque mothers, who freely hand over their newborns to others. Among colobine Old World monkeys, however, this pattern is reversed. Infant-sharing occurs in most of them. In only a few species (such as the Central African red colobus monkeys) do mothers refuse access.

Aside from humans, few primate mothers are more willing to share their newborns than the beautiful gray Hanuman langurs that I studied in India. I originally chose this species because I was interested in finding out why males among these colobine monkeys were sometimes killing infants. Subsequently, even though I knew a bit about shared care from having watched babysitting behavior among African patas monkeys, I was surprised to find how big a role infant sharing played in langur lives.

Throughout life, a female langur remains in the same group in which she is born, in the company of her mother, maternal grandmother, aunts, and other kin. On average, females in this highly matrilocal group are related as closely as first or second cousins.[60] Since dominance relations between females in the same group are relatively flexible and relaxed, mothers do not need to worry (as they do among more rigidly hierarchical rhesus macaques or baboons) that an allomother will harm an infant or prevent the mother from retrieving it—which, when it happens, may end with the baby starving to death. Baby langurs are passed among their cousins and older siblings, held briefly by aunts or grandmother, and may be off their mothers for up to half a day as early as their first day of life. Yet babies are always safely retrieved by the mother. Young and inexperienced females are the most eager to hold babies.[61] Yet, like most

Although it is often assumed that continuous contact with the mother would be essential for infant survival among primates that spend time on the ground, langur monkeys are the most terrestrial of the colobines and are also inveterate infant-sharers. The female langur on the left is taking the infant (who resists the transfer) from the allomother on the right. (S. B. Hrdy/AnthroPhoto)

other primates (titi and night monkeys being important exceptions), a baby Hanuman langur's primary attachment remains to his mother.

Family daycare is found across the far-flung colobine subfamily, among black-and-white colobus monkeys of Africa, dusky leaf monkeys of Thailand and Malaysia, ebony langurs of Java and Bali, silver leaf monkeys of Burma and Borneo, and purple-faced leaf monkeys of Sri Lanka, to name just a few. Only a handful of colobine mothers refuse to let others hold new babies, and the exceptions are revealing. They include species like the red colobus monkeys of Central Africa (*Procolobus badius*) among whom babies are three or four months old before their mothers let them approach another female.[62] The reason these mothers are so possessive is that they do not ordinarily have close matrilineal kin nearby when they give birth. Like chimpanzees or gorillas, red colobus females leave their natal troops and move to another troop before reproducing.[63] Not having kin that she can trust constrains a mother's childcare options. These options are further constrained by the fact that the mother is usually the only one providing her baby with food. Other than humans, the most important exceptions to this primate rule are found among fairly distant primate relations rather than among our fellow apes. These cooperatively breeding monkeys are worth considering in some detail.

FULL-FLEDGED COOPERATIVE BREEDERS
(DAYCARE PLUS SNACKS)

Alloparental care of infants is widespread across the order Primates. However, only in some 20 percent of species do alloparents ever *provision* as well as care for young, and for the most part this provisioning does not amount to much.[64] As mentioned above, some prosimian co-mothers will suckle one another's young, as will New World monkeys in the genus *Cebus,* among whom a lactating female may provide a brief pick-me-up to another female's older but still suckling three-to-six-month-old infant when that infant approaches her and clamps onto her nipple.[65] In addition to such suckling, cebus monkeys occasionally allow someone else's infant to take food. Even though meat is not a big component of *Cebus* diets, all species in this genus are avid hunters, and allomothers may permit older infants to scrounge bits of baby squirrel or coatis that they have caught. This tolerated scrounging of highly desired items goes beyond the rare instances of tolerated taking of food seen in bonobos. Among capuchin monkeys (*Cebus capucinus*) as many as one fifth of all instances of food sharing involved food actively offered by an older monkey to an immature.[66]

More extensive provisioning is of course commonly observed in titi and night monkeys, but since the provisioner is almost always the mother's monogamously mated partner, this behavior qualifies as biparental care rather than cooperative breeding. So far the only nonhuman primates among whom alloparents frequently bring food to the young of others, doing so regularly, spontaneously, and voluntarily, fall into four genera (*Callithrix, Leontopithecus, Saquinus,* and *Callimico*) belonging to the family Callitrichidae—mostly marmosets and tamarins. Even though roughly a fifth of all primates exhibit some degree of shared care and provisioning, these marmosets and tamarins, along with humans, are the only ones I consider to be "full-fledged cooperative breeders."[67]

Famous for breeding fast and for their rapid colonization of new habitats, some 39 species of Callitrichidae are currently deployed across

Central and South America. Babies in these species, typically twins, are carried most of the day by one or more adult males. Usually, only the group's most dominant female breeds, although groups with two breeding females have been observed. Males attempt to defend access to breeding females, but females have their own predilections and may copulate with several partners.

Since a male marmoset or tamarin is no bigger than his mate, it is hard for him to exercise much control over her. Instead of expending energy growing weaponry and duking it out tooth-and-claw in a vain effort to defend exclusive sexual access to his mate, males compete for paternity by other means—specifically, by ejaculating more sperm than a competitor does. Relative to their body size, callitrichid testicles are enormous. There can be as much as a 45 percent difference in size between one male's testes and another's.[68] Energy conserved by avoiding direct competition can be channeled into caretaking. This also means that in the absence of DNA testing, it is impossible to know who the father is.

The usual uncertainty surrounding primate paternity is complicated in the callitrichid case because they are among the mammals (like ground squirrels, prairie dogs, dwarf mongooses, wild dogs, and various cats, including lions) where the same clutch or litter can have multiple progenitors. Twins can have different fathers. Trickier still, marmosets are among the only mammals in the world thought to have chimeric germ lines.

The phrase "germ line" refers to the inherited material that comes from the eggs or sperm ("germ cells") and is passed on to offspring. Animals that have genetically distinct cells from two different germ lines are known as *chimeras,* named for a mythical Greek beast that was part lion, part goat, part serpent. It has long been known that, owing to a peculiarity of callitrichid placentas, the embryonic membrane enclosing fetal twins fuses so that somatic cells—those that form the nerves, muscles, bones, and so on (as distinct from germ cells)—migrate between twins in utero. But not until 2007 was it reported that germ cells can also travel from one twin to the other. In 2007, Corrina Ross, Jeffrey French, and Guillermo Orti at the University of Nebraska in Omaha discovered this phenomenon in Wied's black tufted-ear marmosets, and it probably occurs in other marmosets as well.[69] This sharing of cells between twins has interesting implications for genetic relatedness among marmoset family members. As French puts it, "There's a male marmoset wandering around the forests of eastern Brazil with sperm in his testes that has alleles from his twin as well as his parents. This is a really twisted pedigree: the male is the uncle of offspring he produces."[70]

Unlike ordinary fraternal twins, who share 50 percent of their genes by common descent, callitrichid brothers can be even closer relatives.[71] It might also mean that offspring are more closely related to their mother than they would be to their own offspring.[72] It is not yet known how chimerism affects body odors and other cues marmosets might use for kin recognition. However, Ross and her colleagues found that mothers pay less attention to infants with chimeric hair and saliva, while fathers actually pay *more* attention to chimeric young, carrying them for significantly longer periods than nonchimeric young. Perhaps fathers, who could also be uncles—or both—are picking up multiple cues of relatedness, so that the chimeric infant serves as a super-stimulus. Alternatively, mothers may simply find chimeric babies less attractive, and dads may be just picking up the slack.

In addition to their possible fathers and "more than fathers," marmoset infants may also be tended by prereproductive groupmates. Typically, helpers are offspring from previous seasons who are close relatives. However, helpers may also be nonkin, wannabe breeders who have entered the group from outside. I return in Chapter 6 to the question of why unrelated group members help.

Given that female callitrichids give birth to twins or triplets as often as twice a year and provision their fast-growing young with unusually rich milk (not your usual dilute primate fare), mothers need all the help they can get.[73] We know that the ancestors of modern callitrichids originally gave birth to singleton young. The likeliest scenario is that twinning and tripleting coevolved along with shared care and unusually high degrees of relatedness between family members.[74] The payoff from all this assistance is a virtually unrivalled reproductive pace. The all-time birth record for any primate is held by a common marmoset female living in a captive colony at the University of Stirling in Scotland. Over a 13-year period, she gave birth 25 times to 64 offspring.[75]

When food is abundant, family groups in the wild expand rapidly, as breeding-age daughters with a sufficient complement of male and female helpers bud off to establish new families that colonize new areas. Not surprisingly, there is a linear correlation between availability of adult male helpers in newly formed groups and the likelihood that infants will survive. In mature groups, the correlation extends to the number of both male and female caregivers.[76] The importance of alloparental help is one reason mothers strive for social dominance and fiercely defend access to this critical resource. The alpha female may drive away rival females or, if a subordinate female in her group (even her own daughter) does conceive and give birth, kill (and perhaps eat) her babies. Among common marmosets, alpha females are most infanticidal when they themselves are in the last stages of pregnancy.[77] To avoid diverting energy to a doomed enterprise, subordinate females typically postpone ovulation until the alpha female dies or until they sense an opportunity to establish their own family someplace else.[78]

Because provisioning is involved, females in cooperatively breeding species compete for more than just childcare. In addition to the heavy lifting, callitrichid helpers respond to noisily begging babies by providing them with beetles, crickets, spiders, frogs, little birds, and other delectable, protein-rich tidbits. They can also be reflexively generous, sometimes volunteering food to immatures even without being begged. Still, there is considerable competition between babies, and handouts are especially sought after and critical for survival around the time of weaning. Too large to be sustained by milk alone, youngsters are still too inexperienced to entirely fend for themselves and are at a disadvantage in competing with full-grown adults.

As early as nine weeks, marmoset and tamarin alloparents deliver food to noisily begging babies. Youngsters continue to be provisioned this way until around nine months old, long after they can move about on their own. In one study of *Saguinus oedipus,* most food was proffered in response to begging, though some was volunteered. At about the same time that alloparents start to find the growing youngsters less appealing, juvenile marmosets and tamarins become more confident, greedier, and pushier in demanding food. Eventually, their table manners disintegrate altogether, and they are more likely to snatch or steal food than wait to have it offered.[79]

Cooperation in feeding young spills over into helpful tolerance in other realms. Tamarins (possibly the most similar to the ancient line of callitrichids that originally gave rise to marmosets) not only cooperate with the mother by carrying her young, they also cooperate with one another when harvesting oversized fruits and legumes. During the rainy season when little fruit is available in the forest, several moustached tamarins will work their canines in concert to strip off the hard husks from pods so they can use nimble fingers to pry them open and get at soft flesh and seeds within. The tamarins share afterward with no sign of antagonism, each taking a palatable portion and moving to a nearby spot to eat it. In *Saguinus mystax* the overall ratio of cooperative to aggressive acts is 52 to 1.[80]

This degree of mutual tolerance provides an excellent environment for youngsters to acquire information about diverse food sources in a relatively short time. Many primates utter special food calls when they encounter a food, recruiting group members to the feeding site. But so far, callitrichids are the only primates known to utter such calls more often when infants are present than when they are not. These staccato calls encourage infants to approach, expose them to palatable food, and invite them to sample new things to eat. As primatologists Lisa Rapaport and Gillian Brown note, the dynamics of cooperatively breeding callitrichids "require coordination with, and tolerance of, other group members" in ways that foster "both a predisposition to pay close attention to others and socially mediated learning."[81]

When tested in laboratory experiments, tamarins and marmosets also turn out to be unusually altruistic, displaying a curiously human-like impulse to give. In experiments where one individual has to perform a task so that an animal in a nearby cage gets food, callitrichids exhibit far greater concern for what their neighbors will receive than do other primates, most notably chimpanzees. Unusual levels of callitrichid altruism were first detected in 2003 during a series of experiments with a colony of tamarins (*Saguinus oedipus*) undertaken by Harvard psychologist Marc Hauser's team. Subsequently, similar giving impulses (without the reciprocal component observed in the Hauser study) were reported from experiments at the University of Wisconsin.[82] When the anthropologist Judith Burkart and her colleagues at the University of Zurich tried to replicate Hauser's findings with a larger, carefully controlled series of experiments using another callitrichid species, common marmosets (*Callithrix jacchus*), they were astounded by how much "unsolicited prosociality" and "other-regarding behavior" these little monkeys exhibited.[83]

A single marmoset was placed in a cage next to another marmoset, but only one of them was in a position to pull a food tray within reach of the other. Both breeding and nonbreeding marmoset males, and breeding females (the same ones who were doing most of the infant care), proved significantly more likely to pull the food within range of the adjacent cage if it was occupied rather than empty. They demonstrated this considerate concern for their neighbor whether the marmoset next door was a relative or not. However, females who were not breeding and not currently in what might be called a "caretaking mode" displayed the least interest in providing food to others. Nonbreeding females were no more likely to place food within range of the cage next door when it was occupied than when it was empty.

Burkart's experiments were specifically designed to facilitate comparisons with the "other-regarding" tests that had produced such dismal results back when Joan Silk and her colleagues showed that chimpanzees were indifferent to the well-being of others, particularly where food is concerned (see Chapter 2). Cooperatively breeding marmosets turned out to be more sensitive to the needs of others than larger-brained and generally much smarter chimpanzees. Apart from humans, callitrichids are the only primates among whom such giving impulses have been reported.

Not only do marmosets spontaneously go out of their way to provide food to others, but, like humans, tamarins keep track of and reciprocate material benefits (as in "We should probably have them over to dinner; they had us over last month"), and reputation seems to matter. The amazing thing about Hauser's early experiments was how adept his tamarins were at remembering exactly which individuals were the helpful ones and which were not. Two separately caged tamarins from different families were given the opportunity to pull a cord that would provide food to the other as well as to himself or herself. But the apparatus was rigged so that half the subjects always delivered food to their neighbor, whereas the other half never did, even though they too pulled the cord. The more likely a tamarin was to provision his neighbor, the greater the probability the unrelated monkey would reciprocate. In what may be the best demonstration to date of reciprocal altruism and the importance of "reputation" in a nonhuman animal, tamarins were more generous to former benefactors, and grudging to the previously "stingy."[84]

Marmosets and tamarins stand out among primates for just how ea-

Groups of golden lion tamarins frequently contain two adult males, often brothers who migrated into the group together. In most cases, there is only one breeding female per group. When she comes into estrus, the most dominant male monopolizes matings, but other males may also copulate with her. If a female dies, another female takes her place. In that case, a father and a son may both share sexual access. All males who have mated with the mother will later help rear her young (typically twins). In the upper left-hand corner, a male is passing infants back to the mother so they can nurse. Younger helpers (like the subadult in the foreground, who is catching a beetle) may be older offspring of the breeding pair or recent immigrants who have not yet begun to breed. (Pen and ink drawing, a treasured gift to the author from the artist Sarah Landry)

ger fathers and alloparents of both sexes are to help mothers rear their young. Males expend so much energy carrying infants that they actually lose weight. To get ready for fatherhood, a callitrichid male whose mate becomes pregnant undergoes a hormonal transformation, gaining up to 15 percent of his body weight in anticipation of the energetic demands infant care will soon impose.[85] Partway through gestation, even before the mother-to-be herself "shows," he will begin to produce prolactin (a hormone best known for stimulating lactation in female mammals, but also known to promote nurturing responses in birds and mammals of both sexes) and bulk up. These prolactin effects are most pronounced in males with prior caretaking experience.[86]

Men have also been known to exhibit these couvade-like (or "male pregnancy") symptoms. We do not know what triggers them in either species. The primate endocrinologist Toni Ziegler has speculated that fetal metabolites in the urine of a tamarin male's pregnant companion may be implicated. Elsewhere among the Callitrichidae, marmoset males have been observed to consume the placenta, ingesting along with this liverlike organ a rich cocktail of steroids in the surrounding fluids. In Chapter 5 we will see how human males as well are transformed both endocrinologically and behaviorally by spending time in intimate association with a pregnant woman or a newborn infant.

COOPERATIVE BREEDING'S DARK SIDE

Like all cooperative breeders, tamarin and marmoset mothers depend on others to help rear their young. Shared care and provisioning clearly enhances maternal reproductive success, but there is also a dark side to such dependence. Not only are dominant females (especially pregnant ones) highly infanticidal, eliminating babies produced by competing breeders, but tamarin mothers short on help may abandon their own young, bailing out at birth by failing to pick up neonates when they fall to the ground or forcing clinging newborns off their bodies, sometimes even chewing on their hands or feet.

It is not that uncommon for mother mammals to abandon ill-fated young, especially if they give birth to litters, and some cull large litters or discriminate against runts that are unlikely to survive. But among monkeys and apes reared in natural settings, abandonment is exceedingly rare. Except for young and inexperienced first-time mothers, who lose a disproportionate number of firstborns due to incompetence and failure to respond appropriately to infant cues, it takes extreme duress to induce a mother monkey or ape to abandon her infant—duress such as being in very poor physical condition or finding herself stalked day after day by a strange male intent on killing her infant. Instead, what stands out about primate mothers is their devotion to their singleton young. By far the most common exceptions to this general primate pattern are found in the family Callitrichidae—and among members of our own species.

Along with humans, marmosets and tamarins are virtually the only primates where mothers have been observed to deliberately harm their own babies or leave newborns to die. Staggeringly high rates of postpartum abandonment, up to 50 percent or more of live births, are reported from breeding colonies of cotton-top tamarins, mostly owing to mothers who give birth to twins or triplets under circumstances in which they have little help. According to one analysis of several decades of data from a large breeding colony, the probability that cotton-top tamarin babies would be abandoned or even viciously rejected rose from an average of 12 percent when the mother had older offspring to help her up to a whopping 57 percent when she had multiple young and was also short on alloparental assistance.[87] Although infanticide is a hazard across the Primate order (having been reported now in several dozen species), observations almost always implicate either strange males or females *other than* the mother, not the mother herself. The high rates of maternal abandonment or infanticide seen among callitrichids and humans are unheard of elsewhere among primates. It would appear that highly contingent maternal commitment, along with a propensity to abandon young when mothers perceive themselves short of alloparental support—typically in the first 72 hours or so after birth—represents the dark side of cooperative breeding.[88]

More than 30 million years have passed since humans last shared a common ancestor with these tiny (rarely more than four pounds), clawed, squirrel-like arboreal creatures. New World monkeys literally inhabit a different world from that of their primate cousins who evolved in Africa. Theirs is a sensory world dominated by smell rather than sight. And of course there is considerably less genetic overlap between humans and New World monkeys than between humans and chimpanzees (where the overlap is greater than 96 percent).[89] Yet in many respects callitrichids may provide better insight into early hominin family lives than do far more closely related species like chimpanzees or cercopithecine monkeys.

What humans have in common with the reproductively hyperburdened Callitrichidae is worth itemizing. In both types of primates, group members are unusually sensitive to the needs of others and are characterized by potent impulses to give. In both groups, a mother produces either multiple young or else sequential, closely spaced offspring whose needs exceed her capacity to provide for them. Thus the mother must rely on others to help care for and provision her young. When prospects for support seem poor, mothers in both groups are more likely to bail out than other primates are. Human and callitrichid mothers stand out for their pronounced ambivalence toward newborns and their extremely contingent maternal commitment. Infants have adapted, as we will see later, with special traits for attracting the attention of potential caregivers. And finally, humans, like their tiny distant relatives, breed unusually fast, and they have a marmosetlike ability to colonize and thrive in novel habitats.

DEMOGRAPHIC IMPLICATIONS OF SHARED CARE

Life history theory is the branch of evolutionary biology devoted to questions such as "How big should an organism grow to be?" "What size babies should it produce?" "How much time and energy should an animal spend on growing before starting to breed, and then how often should it breed?" And so forth. One widely accepted tenet of life history theory is that, across species, those with bigger babies relative to the mother's body size will also tend to exhibit longer intervals between births because the more babies cost the mother to produce, the longer she will need to recoup before reproducing again. Yet humans—like marmosets—provide a paradoxical exception to this rule. Humans, who of all the apes produce the largest, slowest-maturing, and most costly babies, also breed the fastest.[90]

Constrained by bearing costly young that mothers nurture by themselves, gorillas, chimpanzees, and orangutans breed more slowly. Orangutans hold the record, with intervals between births as long as eight years. Across the Great Apes, the average is closer to six years. Once weaned, these offspring provision themselves. But human children, born even more helpless than other apes, also mature more slowly and remain dependent far, far longer. When the anthropologist Hillard Kaplan surveyed the literature from every foraging society for which he could find quantitative data, he calculated that it takes roughly 13 million calories to rear a human baby from birth to nutritional independence at around age 18 or older. The anthropologist Karen Kramer has come up with similar estimates for a Maya horticultural society. Long before her first child was self-sufficient, the Mayan mother typically bore another.[91] Even though human babies are unusually fat at birth (three times fatter than expected for a mammal of their size) and take far longer to become nutritionally independent, hunter-gatherer mothers routinely produce them at three- to four-year intervals, almost twice as fast as the six- to eight-year intervals typical of other apes.[92] Such hyperfertility would have been feasible only if mothers in ancestral populations had been able to count on alloparental assistance.

A simple comparison between primates with and without assistance reveals a clear pattern. In species with shared care (that is, help carrying infants but no provisioning), infants still grow faster and their mothers breed again after shorter intervals.[93] Presumably this is because mothers save energy, are free to forage more efficiently, and are better fed themselves.[94] On average, mothers with help wean their young at an earlier age and conceive again sooner. Provided it was safe to turn their infants over to another group member, mothers with willing caregivers in their group breed faster and consequently produce more offspring who reach reproductive age.

From this broad comparative perspective, some curious demographic patterns in the Primate order start to make sense. One reason that leaf-eating colobine monkeys living in tightly knit kin groups with relatively relaxed female dominance relations breed faster than other monkeys is that they can afford to take advantage of offers by other females to carry their babies. When alloparental baby-carrying includes provisioning as well, benefits from daycare are magnified further. With care by both mothers and others, and with infants buffered from starvation around the time of weaning, such full-fledged cooperative breeding means infants survive in spite of being weaned early.

Mothers in a range of creatures produce costly young, but none more costly than a human infant. Nor does any other animal, even other apes (who also have slow life histories), take anything like so long to mature.[95] Yet humans living under "natural" conditions (by gathering and hunting) breed faster than other apes. Colonizers par excellence, anatomically modern humans spread out of Africa and then migrated around the globe to Europe, Asia, Australia, and eventually to North America, South America, and the Pacific. The only other primates to routinely share both care and provisioning of young in this way and as a consequence to breed faster and to rapidly colonize new habitats are the callitrichids. So how can such broad comparisons inform the way we think about childcare in the genus *Homo*?

Historians of the family like Stephanie Coontz, along with anthropologists, psychologists, and social workers, have long been aware that, across time and in diverse locales, infants born into poverty, at low birthweight or premature, or to a teenage or unmarried mother tend to do better cognitively, emotionally, and physically if they grow up in extended families. Whether alloparental interventions involve older siblings, grandmothers, or other kin, or just a particularly interested mentor, a vast cross-disciplinary literature attests to the fact that mothers with more social support are more responsive to their infants' needs. The greater the risk factors, the more evident do correlations between alloparental support, maternal sensitivity, and child well-being become. As Coontz puts it, "Children do best in societies where childrearing is considered too important to be left entirely to parents."[96]

It is hard to imagine babies at greater risk than those born to desperately poor women in eighteenth-century Europe—an era when depositing infants in foundling homes or abandoning them outright was rampant. Tellingly, the availability of support from matrilineal kin to help the mother and reduce the opportunity costs of caring for her child played a bigger role in the mother's decision to keep rather than abandon her baby than did actual income.[97] Three hundred years later, the perception that social support—in the form of available childcare—is going to be hard to obtain leads women in industrialized nations like Germany and the United States to postpone childbirth or decide against having children altogether.[98]

Evidence from high-risk groups in the United States underscores how much social support matters. The presence of a grandmother in the same household with a teenage mother, or just frequent visits from a grandmother, increases the chance that infants will forge more secure attachments to their young and inexperienced mothers.[99] Babies born to unmarried, low-income teenagers who grow up with a grandmother in the household also tend to test better on cognitive development—perhaps because they have spent less time alone or feel more secure.[100] Similar correlations are reported for low-birthweight infants born to teenage mothers. Having a grandmother on hand early on (typically the maternal grandmother) was correlated with improved health and cognitive outcomes three years later.[101]

Again and again, the mother's perception of social support and the infant's sense of security (perhaps in response to stronger signals of maternal commitment) seem to matter more than any actual improvement in material resources available to the mother-infant pair. In a randomized controlled trial carried out by David Olds and his colleagues at the Prevention Research Center for Family and Child Health at the University of Colorado in Denver, trained nurses were sent to the homes of first-time expectant mothers. They made six or seven visits during pregnancy, followed by 21 visits in the period between birth and the child's second birthday. Modest as such intervention may seem—little more than every so often having another woman offer social support and mentoring—it was correlated with a cascade of beneficial outcomes detectable as long as 15 years later. When matched with similar mothers not visited by nurses, the children of visited mothers grew up emotionally more responsive, were less likely to exhibit emotional vulnerability when exposed to fearful stimuli, learned language sooner, and had higher Mental Development Index scores than children in the control group. Children of visited mothers were also significantly less likely to be abused by their mothers.[102]

Supportive interventions have produced similar outcomes in other cultures. For example, visits to a Brazilian maternity ward resulted in mothers' increased willingness to feed their babies exclusively with breast milk, and mothers who continued to receive visits after they returned home were more likely to continue breastfeeding irrespective of their socioeconomic status.[103] The tougher that times become, and the more that childrearing competence is compromised, the more pronounced the psychological benefits from alloparental support seem to be.

Even though social scientists have long been aware of such correlations, and mothers clearly feel the need for social support, the evolutionary rationale for links between perceived support, maternal decision-making and behavior, and the emotional well-being of children went unexplored. Relevant studies were rarely undertaken with past survival and fitness concerns in mind. The most extensive and methodologically sophisticated psychological studies were almost invariably undertaken in Western countries where people are socially and spatially separated into nuclear families, live in houses with walls and access to modern medicine, and no longer have to worry all the time about eventualities like their children being eaten. Emotional and cognitive benefits to extended families were noted, but there were few opportunities to link alloparental support to actual child survival. Yet from an evolutionary perspective, child survival was the currency that mattered.

We failed to consider the profound impact of older siblings, grandmothers, uncles, or the mother's lovers in worlds where more than half of all infants born would starve, be murdered or eaten, or succumb to accident or disease before they matured. Only at the end of the twentieth century, as findings by human behavioral ecologists and sociobiologists started to come in, did it become clear that in foraging societies with high rates of infant and child mortality—societies like those our ancestors evolved in—support from alloparents not only improved health, social maturation, and mental development, it was *essential* for child survival.

THE PENNY DROPS

By the last quarter of the twentieth century, a handful of human behavioral ecologists and sociobiologists, aware of the occurrence of shared care and cooperative breeding in some other animals, began to entertain suspicions about collateral kin. But only since about 1999 has sufficient evidence been amassed to allow us to consider these disparate findings in an evolutionary perspective and to interpret their impact.

In the mid-1980s a young doctoral candidate in anthropology, now a pediatrician, Paul Turke, became sufficiently impressed by sociobiological research on "helpers at the nest" in monkeys and other animals to want to find out if helpers affected the reproductive success of humans as well. Together with the sociobiologist Laura Betzig, Turke went out to study the relation between family composition and reproductive success among Pacific islanders on Ifaluk atoll. What this husband-wife team discovered was that parents whose firstborn was a daughter actually produced more surviving children than parents whose firstborn was a son because (Turke hypothesized) daughters are more active in caring for younger siblings than sons are in that society.[104]

About this same time, a fellow sociobiologist, Mark Flinn, found a similar correlation between alloparental assistance and maternal reproductive success among Caribbean villagers in Trinidad. Mothers with nonreproductive helpers on hand had higher reproductive success than those without.[105] Daughters proved the most helpful, but having any helper in the household, male or female, was still correlated with increased child survival. Shortly afterward, Kristen Hawkes noticed something odd about grandmothers among the Hadza people she was studying. Her discovery would provide the catalyst for her fellow anthropologists to begin to think in new ways about the evolutionary significance of women past childbearing age.

Hawkes has been a pioneer in the study of foraging strategies among hunter-gatherers, and she had gone out to the eastern rift valley of Tanzania to study one of the last remaining such groups. She and her team were among the first fieldworkers to measure just how much food different members of a Hadza group contributed to the daily diet. Along with James O'Connell, an archaeologist, and the human ethologist Nick Blurton Jones, Hawkes followed Hadza men, women, and children as they foraged, counting and weighing every edible item that each man, woman, and child brought back. Day after day, they trudged along as women collected berries and nuts or hacked at the ground with their digging sticks to pry out starchy tubers from underneath the sun-baked surface. They trotted after men when they went off hunting—or at least when they attempted to, for Hadza men's predilection for reputation-enhancing big game like eland meant that hunters rarely succeeded. Eland weigh 500 kilograms or more and are, relative to the leanness typical of most wild game, deliciously marbled with fat. Yet these most desirable of ungulates are also widely dispersed, elusive, and more difficult to bag than common prey like hares or tortoises. Most days the men came home empty-handed, and it was food gathered by women day to day that kept children fed.

Hawkes and her colleagues also noticed something else. The first gatherers to leave camp in the morning and the last to return in the evening, as well as those who ended up carrying the heaviest loads, were not (as one might expect) young women in their prime. Nor were they the mothers with hungry children waiting back at camp. Rather, the most dedicated food-gatherers were the leathery-faced old women, long past their prime. In a landmark paper titled "Hardworking Hadza Grandmothers," the researchers described great-aunts and grandmothers who, far from taking advantage of their no-longer-child-burdened "golden years" to put their feet up, were working harder than ever.[106]

For children in these foraging groups, having a grandmother or great-aunt helping to feed them was correlated with faster growth rates.[107] In times of food shortage, it was also correlated with a higher likelihood of survival.[108] Turke's reports from Ifaluk atoll, Flinn's from Trinidad, and now these findings from hunter-gatherers in Tanzania all pointed to intriguing parallels among cooperative breeders. Whether older sisters, grandmothers, or great-aunts, in every study it was alloparents willing to help who permitted mothers to produce more children likely to survive. Impressed by these discoveries, I became convinced that humans, like many birds and mammals, must have evolved as cooperative breeders, and by 1999 I was saying so.[109] Since then, the case for cooperative breeding has only grown stronger, as researchers collected and analyzed data from larger populations, including horticultural as well as foraging societies. These bigger sample sizes quickly began to yield highly significant results.

Only a tiny fraction of humanity still lives by gathering plant foods and hunting with spears—or, in a few cases, nets—as people in African forests have done for tens of thousands of years and as the Aka still do.[110] But even as foragers have come to rely at least in part on trade with their settled neighbors, or on occasional employment by them, they continue to rear children in the traditional way, and with good reason. By 2000, the anthropologist Paula Ivey Henry had discovered that among the Efe the number of alloparents a baby had at one year of age was correlated with how likely the child was to be alive at age three.[111] That same year, a reanalysis of old medical records showed that even among settled, horticultural peoples, alloparents were critical for child survival.

Tantalized by findings such as those from the Efe, and by Hawkes's suspicions about the role of Hadza grandmothers, two British anthropologists, Rebecca Sear and Ruth Mace, dusted off records from one of the most ambitious studies ever undertaken on maternal and child health in a traditional society before the introduction of modern medicine. Between 1950 and 1980 researchers from the United Kingdom Medical Research Council had monitored the nutritional status of mothers and the growth rates of their children among Mandinka horticulturalists in The Gambia, West Africa. Of 2,294 children in their sample, 883, nearly 40 percent, died before age five. As Sear and Mace pored over the old records on growth rates and child mortality, they asked themselves questions about family composition that the medical researchers had not thought to analyze before. They already knew that if a mother died before a child was weaned, it was bad news. But this time they asked who else, besides the mother, mattered to a child's survival?

The results from their reanalysis of the Gambian data were stunning. If the child had older siblings (especially sisters) or if the child's maternal grandmother was living nearby and was herself past reproductive age, the child's probability of dying before age five fell from 40 percent to 20 percent.[112] Not surprisingly, mothers were critical for survival during the first two years of life while the baby was still dependent on breast milk. After age two, however, by which time Mandinka children are usually weaned, the presence of a mother no longer had any measurable effect on child growth or survival. Apparently, compensatory care by allomothers was sufficiently good that the physical condition of weanlings was unaffected by the death of their mothers. Thus Mandinka referred to anyone plump as being "fat as an orphan."[113]

From the perspective of a Mandinka child, having an older sister on hand to babysit or a maternal grandmother to provide extra food as well as care was, literally, a lifesaver. Yet the presence of the biological father, paternal grandparents, or an elder brother had no measurable impact on child survival. If paternal loss ushered a stepfather into the picture, however, a child's chances of survival plummeted.[114] Otherwise, as the researchers bluntly put it, "Fathers make absolutely no difference to child anthropometric status or survival"—provided allomothers were on hand.[115]

In later chapters I will consider these findings more broadly, including specific contexts where fathers *do* matter very much, and where a child's older siblings, aunts, uncles, and especially grandmothers may have negative as well as positive impacts on child well-being. But for the moment, my point is simply that for primates generally and for humans there are circumstances when alloparents can be as important, sometimes more important, than parents. Frankly, this was not something social scientists had expected to find, and it became apparent only because the mortality rates among Mandinka children, especially in the months and years right after weaning, were so high.

High as they seem, child mortality rates among Gambian horticulturalists at the middle of the twentieth century were not atypical for African populations before the introduction of modern medicine. They are high compared with rates at the end of the century but are within the range of mortality statistics reported for various wild primates, for nomadic hunters and gatherers, and presumably for our Pleistocene ancestors as well. The best available data for Hadza, Ju/'hoansi, or Aka foragers indicate that 40 to 60 percent of children in these populations—and more in bad times—died before age 15.[116] Given that child survival is the single most important component of maternal reproductive success, if allomaternal involvement reduced mortality by even a small amount, over generations the evolutionary implications would be significant.[117] And if these heretofore unacknowledged benefactors actually managed to cut child mortality in half—as in the Mandinka case—their evolutionary impact would have been enormous.

The recognition that a child's survival depended not just on staying in contact with his mother or provisioning by his father but also on the availability, competence, and intentions of other caregivers in addition to parents is ushering in a new way of thinking about family life among our ancestors. Well might anthropologists and politicians remind us that "it takes a village" to rear children today. What they often leave out, however, is that so far as the particular apes that evolved into *Homo sapiens* are concerned, it always has. Without alloparents, there never would have been a human species.

4

NOVEL DEVELOPMENTS

The truth is that the least-studied phase of human development
remains the phase during which a child is acquiring all that
makes him most distinctively human.

—John Bowlby (1969)

"There is no such thing as a baby," the child psychiatrist David Winnicott liked to say. "There is a baby and someone." The
someone he had in mind was the mother. Winnicott's was an apt sum-
mation from the early years of attachment theory, and it remains an
apt maxim so far as other apes are concerned. But recent research in infant psychology indicates that little humans are casting their nets more
broadly to encompass others as well as mothers, evaluating their intentions and learning from their actions. In the original Bowlbian equation,
infant survival in our "environment of evolutionary adaptedness" depended on the baby's relationship with his mother, which is true as far as
it goes. But that equation is incomplete when applied to babies born in

societies like those of our Pleistocene ancestors. Maternal commitment, and ultimately child survival, entailed a baby plus mother plus others.

No one advocating this expanded equation would dispute that a mother is unusually responsive to her baby and that maternal signals of commitment have a special salience for infants.[1] By two months of age a baby's relationship with his mother is likely to include long, seemingly soul-seeking mutual looks. By the end of two months, increasingly alert babies look even longer, while their eyes squint, their pudgy cheeks bob upward, and the corners of their mouths rise into deliciously appealing social smiles that invite the mother to keep right on loving. But others are being invited to join in as well. By the time the baby is three months old, his smiles and gestures begin to be accentuated by attractive coos and chortles, and by seven months full-fledged babbling is heard.[2] All the while the baby is acutely sensitive to how responsive his mother is, but he is taking note of others as well.

Mothers have no precise equivalent in the way they respond to their babies. But in communities where people live in close quarters, the mutual gazes and rhythmic, playful looks engage others as well as mothers (think of how readily a human infant engages in a game like peek-a-boo). Psychologists refer to the high-pitched patter that adults use when addressing babies as "motherese." However, in contexts where females other than the mother also interact with babies, alloparents as well lapse into high-pitched, melodic tones on the order of "Oooh, are you all right?" (Skeptical? Try talking to a baby, any baby, for a length of time and see what happens to your voice.) Since chimpanzee, orangutan, and other ape infants are rarely out of touch with mothers, they have far less need for this infantile equivalent of sex appeal. Nor do their mothers have the same need for reassuring banter.

In foraging societies, then, just who converses with babies or talks in motherese? Among people like the Aka, where either the mother or a familiar alloparent is in constant tactile contact with a baby, Hewlett reports that mothers spend little if any time talking to their babies in this cooing way.[3] Among the !Kung, alloparents and mothers are about equally likely to offer the infant some object to examine, and equally likely to encourage him or utter some prohibition. But overall, lumping together various interactions with sibs, cousins, fathers, and other adults, nearby caregivers are more likely to speak to babies in motherese and entertain them than their mothers are.[4] These "others" start vocalizing to infants from their first days of life, and keep right on doing it.[5]

Cultures vary tremendously in the significance accorded to babbling, in what people say to babies (and how they say it), and in the rituals they perform. Babies may be swaddled or wear diapers. They may be draped with amulets, dusted with talcum, basted with palm oil, or ceremoniously finger-painted with protective symbols. But regardless of language or custom, the message conveyed by such ministrations is equivalent: You are cared for and will continue to be. Love (and that is a perfectly good word for what we are talking about here) is a message babies are all too eager to receive, and small wonder. How secure an infant feels depends on how responsive the mother is to his physical and emotional needs. Where resources are scarce, there is likely to be a positive correlation between maternal commitment, a child's feeling of attachment to his mother, and the child's nutritional status, since committed mothers pay more attention to keeping their babies fed.[6] But mothers are not the only ones who care.

Even as information from traditional societies with a great deal of alloparental involvement flowed in, such cases continued to be viewed as atypical. Bowlbian stereotypes of continuously available, chimpanzee-like mothers prevailed. Textbooks emphasized continuous-care-and-contact mothering among the !Kung and implied that this was both typical of "the" hunter-gatherer and also optimal for natural human development. By the beginning of the twenty-first century, even as systematic data came in from African societies with high levels of shared care, anthropologists continued to consider shared care as unusual and to refer to societies with high levels of alloparental care as having a "unique child-rearing system."[7] The paradigm shift away from thinking of our Pleistocene ancestors as reared by all-nurturing chimpanzee-like mothers, and toward thinking of them as apes with species-typical shared care, has been slow in coming. Only in the past decade have cooperative breeding's implications for attachment theory begun to be addressed, and its evolutionary implications taken into account.[8]

In this chapter, I describe findings by a small group of often self-consciously iconoclastic developmental psychologists who, long before me, began to consider how infants might form multiple attachments—a first step toward expanding and refining mother-centered models for human evolution. Next I consider how their findings relate to what comparative primatologists and child developmentalists have learned about the probable impact on a helpless ape of growing up dependent on multiple caretakers rather than a single caretaker. What are the psychological implications for an infant when his mother's initial response to him, as well as her availability over time, is contingent not just on her own past experience and physical condition but also on her perceptions about who else is around and willing to help? How does contingent maternal commitment affect an infant's need and desire to understand and engage others? How does dependence on (and even becoming emotionally attached to) multiple others affect an individual's outlook during his lifetime, as well as over the many lifetimes that cumulatively add up to evolutionary change?

THE EXTRA SOMETHING HUMAN BABIES LOOK FOR

As attachment theorists have long assumed, all primate infants evolved to seek contact with a warm and nurturing mother. There is no questioning Bowlby's insight on this point. But unless she was incapacitated, a chimpanzee, orangutan, or gorilla mother's motivation to maintain tactile contact with her baby was nearly as strong as her baby's powerful urge to stay attached to her. Such babies had little occasion to worry about psychological ambivalence on the part of their mothers. Nor did they need to fret about separation from mothers with whom they were in constant contact anyway. Any chimpanzee or orangutan under six months of age who found himself off his mother was very likely an orphan already, a little ape with awful prospects.

At some point in the emergence of the genus *Homo,* however, mothers became more trusting, handing even quite young infants over to others to temporarily hold and carry. A little ape might be separated from his mother for variable amounts of time. A baby thus had far more incentive to monitor his mother's whereabouts and to maintain visual and vocal contact with her, as well as far more motivation to pay attention to her state of mind and also to the willingness of others who might be available to care for him when his mother was disinclined. I propose that such separations, together with the chronic challenges and uncertainties they posed, caused little apes, already endowed with considerable gifts for reading (and even imitating) the facial expressions of others and with the neural equipment for rudimentary mind reading, to devote even more time and attention to interpreting the intentions of others, an activity which in turn would affect the organization of their neural systems.[9]

All primates are born innately predisposed to seek tactile contact with somebody or, in the worst-case scenario (think of Harry Harlow's terrycloth-covered wire "surrogate" mothers), to *something*. But human infants seem to require more than the warm, soft, tactile stimulation that monkeys so obviously seek.[10] Yes, human babies become attached to inanimate objects like security blankets or teddy bears, but primarily as backups when more animated and communicative sources of security are out of reach.[11] By the second or third month, human babies actively seek a higher level of emotional responsiveness, mediated by increasingly long and expressive looks and by high-pitched, soothing queries.[12] When the psychiatrist Ed Tronick asked mothers to don expressionless "still-face" masks, babies who failed to find the emotional responses they sought became apprehensive. When the artificial face looking back at them continued to appear blank, they became distressed.[13]

From about eight months onward, babies become increasingly interested in other people's reactions—the beginnings of what you might call intellectual curiosity. Really, though, it's a more elemental concern having to do with how much value another person ascribes to some object the baby is holding or, perhaps even more importantly, to the baby himself, as in "What does this other person think and feel about me and what I am doing?" Babies don't just register what other people find nice or frightening and allow that to shape their own response, as in the "social contagion" and "social referencing" seen in many primates and other animals as well. Rather, human babies seek to understand what others think or feel about the object they are looking at or handling; they scan the faces of mothers and alloparents not just to predict what they will do (other animals do that) but to gauge their impressions of what they see, to use these caregivers as "curators of meaning."[14] I remember games with my own children much like those described for the !Kung. Infants who up to that time have held objects in an iron-clad grasp will "show" the object to others and then miraculously release it so as to give the object to someone else. For weeks this game, repeated again and again, is a source of interest, excitement, and profound satisfaction.

By six months of age, babies are storing away information about which other individuals are likely to be helpful, as recently demonstrated by Yale University psychologists Kiley Hamlin, Karen Wynn, and Paul Bloom. Six- and ten-month-old infants were given a puppet show in which anthropomorphic shapes either helped or hindered an unknown third party who was trying to climb a steep hill. When the infants subsequently had an opportunity to choose which cartoonlike character they wanted to play with, infants showed a robust preference for the helpful characters. Long before infants have words to describe a concept like helpfulness, they readily discriminate between someone likely to be nice and someone potentially mean, and they act on this knowledge when eliciting assistance.[15] By the time humans really start attending to the intentions, reliability, and effectiveness of others, they are combining this information with assessments of their potential benevolence.

Psychologists like Michael Tomasello refer to "the nine months revolution"—the time when babies' "understanding of other persons as intentional agents like the self" begins to more fully develop.[16] In light of how much alloparental food sharing goes on in traditional societies, it is worth noting that by this age even infants who are still far from being weaned are spending much more time with alloparents and are on the receiving end of kiss-fed treats. One of Bowlby's initial early insights had to do with recognizing that an infant's attachment to his mother is separate from his quest for milk (the "cupboard" theory of love).[17] But this does not mean that interest in and preferences for various caretakers (mother included) are not going to be influenced and conditioned by food rewards. Delectable gifts are factored into a child's perception of who is generous and who is not, right along with assessments about who wants to help and who might hurt.

No doubt having a larger and more complex neocortex than any monkey does, along with attendant cognitive and linguistic gifts, is going to factor into children's sophisticated social assessments and preferences for particular caregivers.[18] But their curiosity about other people's reactions and their quite nuanced evaluations of "character" are traits that have been sharpened by a long evolutionary history of coping with complex early environments and with contingencies that are far less predictable than those with which other baby apes had to cope.[19] As early as their first year of life—far earlier than, until recently, most psychologists would have thought possible—human babies exhibit concern with what someone else not only thinks but *thinks about them.* For example, babies obviously bask in what can only be described as personal pride when they sense they are approved of, and they act shamed or embarrassed when they sense that something they have done is not okay with their caregivers.[20]

If human babies are sensitive to such signals, it follows that they are capable of attributing mental and emotional states to others—that is, they are capable of some level of intersubjective involvement. I am arguing that the most plausible way to explain this difference between humans and other apes is to take into account the vast stretch of time (perhaps as long as two million years) during which babies who were better at gauging the intentions of others and engaging them were also better at eliciting care, and hence more likely to survive into adulthood and reproduce. Children who develop this way are also going to be naturally more responsive to disapproval, social sanctions, and behaviors affecting not just status but reputation.

CONNOISSEURS OF COMMITMENT

All primates are born with a suite of traits that help them stay in touch with their mothers.[21] Taken off his mother, a baby will flail and complain, though under some conditions he readily becomes accustomed to being held by someone else (his father, in the case of a titi monkey). Even among infant-sharing species, babies initially resist leaving their mother and are typically relieved to be returned. When they are not returned, their calls become more and more plaintive—to my maternal ears, unbearably so. After his initial protest at separation, the baby's symptoms of distress escalate as he looks around for his mother and calls loudly so as to bring her back. Young langur monkeys have a specialized, high-pitched, birdlike trill precisely adapted to the rare mishap of prolonged separation. The call really does sound like a bird, presumably so that passing predators will register the caller as a winged creature liable to fly off rather than as helpless prey.

The less accustomed babies are to being consoled by others, the stronger their distress. If not consoled, the baby's desperate searching for its mother will be followed by obvious signs of misery. Eventually, the baby sinks into an energy-saving torpor characterized by all the earmarks of despair.[22] Such evident, palpable suffering is why the most thoughtful pioneers from back in the Harlow era—scientists like Robert Hinde at Cambridge University—have concluded that given what we now know, it is no more ethical to experimentally separate baby monkeys from their mothers than to engage in other forms of animal torture.[23]

Once reunited with his mother, an infant subjected to prolonged separation and attendant despair may respond with what Bowlby termed "detachment," a self-reliant-seeming superficial bravado that presumably would help a luckless infant cope in spite of having an unreliable mother. Self-reliance might even lay the groundwork for forging new, if necessarily less discriminating and less profound, attachments to such substitute caregivers as might present themselves.[24] Indiscriminate attachments by youngsters who approach and make overtures to available adult candidates in an effort to adopt a mother-surrogate are typical of children and monkeys alike.[25] The similarities will be obvious to anyone who has watched heart-breaking videos from research experiments where infant monkeys are separated from their mothers, or has visited orphanages or refugee camps where—because of poverty, war, AIDS, or indifference—children who find themselves with neither parents nor alloparents desperately seek substitutes. Recognizable too will be our own deeply rooted responses to their distress, along with the near-overwhelming impulse to scoop these children up and offer succor. After all, we are primates as well.

Human infants' biologically based drive to seek out and maintain attachments builds on a highly conserved set of behaviors found among all primates.[26] Decades ago, Bowlby's colleague, Mary Ainsworth, pointed out that "there is nothing implicit in attachment theory that suggests that sensitive maternal responsiveness is required for infant attachment formation."[27] Yet human babies still seem to need something more than tactile contact, some extra reassurance of maternal commitment. Throughout the evolutionary history of other apes, the mother was either there and highly motivated to remain in continuous touch with her baby or else she was incapacitated and probably dead. By contrast, the challenges confronted by early human infants have always been more complicated.

Such a legacy helps explain why, even in the first months before a baby's brain is anything like fully developed, months before he is capable of learning a language, a human infant is sensitive to how responsive his caretakers are with a connoisseurship that goes beyond the universal primate need for a secure base. A human baby gravitates toward enlivened eyes, a lively tone, the cadences of a voice that seems to echo his own, ever attentive to the give-and-take and mutual pacing of responses as if he was using the lilt in a mother's murmurings as well as her overall attunement to his own internal state—all the rhythms implicit in the interactions between these two beings—as indicators of commitment. It should come as no surprise then that newborns whose mothers are depressed and less responsive to infant cues exhibit neurological and physiological profiles indicative of stress (as measured by high levels of serotonin and dopamine). Compared with other babies, their brain waves are characterized by more activation in the right frontal lobe (as traced by electroencephalograms), and they are less easily soothed by listening to music (as gauged by delayed heart-rate deceleration).[28]

Bowlby interpreted maternal sensitivity as a sign of a mother's "respect" for her baby. From my perspective, the message sought by an infant born to a species in which maternal commitment is far from guaranteed is more nearly "You will be cared for no matter what." The attention paid by human infants to the rhythms of turn-taking and the give-and-take in their relationship with their mother is exquisitely nuanced.[29] This perpetual testing of maternal responsiveness is different from what goes on in ape babies whose ancestors were never out of tactile contact with their mothers to begin with. Such infants had both less occasion and less need to monitor the whereabouts and intentions of their mothers. Human babies all have "special needs," and in Chapter 9 I consider some of the long-term implications of that vulnerability.

CONSEQUENCES OF TIME OFF MOTHER

According to a classic Bowlbian scenario, absence makes the infantile heart grow if not fonder at least more apprehensive and clingy. The more inconsistently a mother responds, the more insecurely attached her infant will be, rendering him hypervigilant if not outright anxious. The more that hominin mothers worried about such questions as "Shall I ask my mother to hold the baby while I crack these nuts?" or "Should I carry my baby with me on a long trek to gather food, or leave him with auntie?" or "Should I get rid of this child altogether?" the more ambivalent her responses were going to be, and the more natural selection would have favored youngsters temperamentally inclined to keep a watch on facial expressions or body tones that signal states of mind relevant to maternal commitment, and to respond accordingly.

In *Mother Nature: A History of Mothers, Infants and Natural Selection,* I reviewed the selective pressures that ambivalent mothers exert on infants, acknowledging the millions of infants through historical and evolutionary times who were abandoned at birth by their mother either because she lacked social support or because (in her eyes) the baby did not pass muster. Space does not permit revisiting such emotionally charged and sensitive topics as why human infants are born so plump (compared with other apes) and so "adorable" or why human newborns are under special selection pressure to prove that they are "worth rearing."[30] Here, I simply take as given that through evolutionary time human newborns confronted a special challenge in eliciting maternal commitment in the postpartum period, and I focus on the much less drastic situation, asking how babies respond to brief and routine separations from an otherwise committed mother.

Psychologists already know that the more direct physical contact there is between a mother and her infant, the less time each party spends looking into the face of the other or seeking what Bowlby, quoting the novelist George Eliot, referred to as "the eyes of love" ("A child forsaken, waking suddenly . . . seeth only that it cannot see the meeting eyes of love").[31] This observation applies to other apes and holds up across human cultures.[32] In one of the very few controlled experimental studies of mother-infant eye contact, psychologists Manuela Lavelli and Alan Fogel found that human babies out of physical contact with their mothers seek eye contact more. Observing babies between one and three months of age, Lavelli and Fogel found that being out of direct contact with their mother's body (being propped up on a couch nearby, for example) stimulated infants to look for their mother more and, having located her, to look into her face significantly longer.[33]

Among other apes as well, reduction in tactile contact produces a need to reestablish the bond through other means. Recently, Kim Bard and her colleagues found that the more time a mother chimpanzee spent cradling her baby close or grooming him, the less time the two spent looking into each other's faces. The more they are deprived of touch, the harder little apes strive to reestablish contact through visual means.[34]

Under natural conditions, nonhuman ape babies are almost never out of touch with their mothers until they are capable of scampering off and returning on their own initiative. By contrast, in contemporary hunter-gatherer societies babies are taken off their mothers by others many months before they can locomote on their own. Babies passed around in this way would need to exercise a different skill set in order to monitor their mothers' whereabouts. As part of the normal activity of maintaining contact both with their mothers and with sympathetic alloparents, they would find themselves looking for faces, staring at them, and trying to read what they reveal.

Infants separated from their mothers might be comforted, entertained, and provided with edible treats by caregivers, or they might be lugged about nonchalantly and have their treats taken away by envious older sibs. The proximity of adults within earshot would keep a lid on behaviors like teasing but would not put an end to these little threats altogether. Over the first months of life, highly stimulating contacts—emotionally rewarding for the most part, but not always—set the stage for a new kind of ape equipped with differently sensitized neural systems, alert from a very early age to the intentions of others. This novel nervous system would in turn have been exposed to selection pressures that favored the survival of any child born with slightly better aptitudes for enlisting, maintaining, and manipulating alloparental ministrations. In this way, natural selection would lead to the evolution of cognitive tendencies that further encouraged infants to monitor and influence the emotions, mental states, and intentions of others. Traits that helped babies stay connected even when out of physical contact helped these vulnerable infants survive.

STAYING IN TOUCH WITHOUT TOUCH

Primatewide, two conditions cause babies to vocalize more: when they are separated from their mothers and when they are in tactile contact with her but interacting with someone else.[35] During the first three months of life, infant chimpanzees are just as reactive toward alloparents who approach as their human counterparts are. Human and nonhuman ape babies alike respond to stimulation from others with long looks and vocalizations. We can see this in the case of human-reared chimpanzees. For example, one 19-week-old chimpanzee infant was more likely to respond to a strange human than to either its own mother or a familiar human caretaker.[36] However, under natural circumstances a chimpanzee that age would not have opportunities to interact with alloparents, and even if it did, the encounter was unlikely to enhance survival.

All ape babies complain loudly and pitifully in emergency situations that separate them from their mother. But human infants, frequently out of direct contact with their mother's body, required a more nuanced coping repertoire. They needed to find a way to vocalize in nonemergency situations—some new means of maintaining contact and engaging others through sound. The repetitive, rhythmical vocalizations known as babbling provided a particularly elaborate way to accomplish this.

Human babies begin to babble at about seven months.[37] Typically, they pass through this stage as the "milk teeth" first peek through, beginning with two tiny incisors on the bottom gums, then four more on top, eventually twenty in all—sharp little teeth that help babies chew their first other-than-milk foods, whether soft fruit or tubers and meat premasticated by someone else. So far the only other primates observed to pass through a babbling phase (if by babbling we mean repetitive strings of adultlike vocalizations uttered without obvious vocal referents) all belong to the family Callitrichidae. Along with humans, these marmosets and tamarins are among the very few primates who qualify as full-fledged cooperative breeders, with both shared care and provisioning.

Nonhuman primate babbling has been particularly well studied by Chuck Snowdon and Margaret Elowson among tiny, Ewok-like pygmy marmosets from Brazil. Shortly after birth, these *Cebuella pygmaea* babies begin to utter complex streams of vocalizations, stringing together sounds common to the adult repertoire. It is significant that babbling emerges in this species right about the time that caregivers other than the mother take over, because both in captivity and in the wild these distinctive vocalizations serve to attract alloparental attention. Thus Snowdon and Elowson hypothesized that attracting caretakers is actually the *function* of marmoset babbling.[38] In some callitrichids, such vocalizations actually elicit food, leading marmosetologists to label them "chuck" calls in honor of one of their first describers, Chuck Snowdon.[39]

Fed or not, babies keep on babbling even after they make contact with a caretaker, suggesting that babbling plays a role in maintaining as well as establishing relationships with parents and alloparents.[40] If Snowdon and Elowson are correct, it is scarcely surprising that babbling has not been heard among continuous-care-and-contact species like chimpanzees, who indeed may not even possess the physiological apparatus for babbling.[41] Chimpanzee infants simply don't need it. Among humans, however, with their very different caretaking history, babbling is universal.

Recently, the anthropologist Dean Falk sought to explain babbling—as well as motherese—with a somewhat different scenario of Pleistocene caretaking. In Falk's view, these two ways of communicating evolved in the human lineage so that bipedal, newly hairless mothers could reassure infants no longer able to cling to them.[42] In what she called her "putting-the-baby-down hypothesis," Falk proposed that protohuman mothers would need to set their babies on the ground in order to have their own hands free to work. She wrote, "I have a difficult time imagining early hominin mothers *not* setting their babies down frequently in order to free their hands for noncarrying tasks prior to the invention of baby slings."[43] However, apart from prosimians and muriquis, it is very rare for wild primates or people in foraging societies to park babies.[44] Falk was starting from the assumption that our protohuman ancestors resembled naked versions of chimpanzees, lacking hair for babies to cling to but no more likely to take advantage of alloparents' assistance than other apes are.

I agree with Falk that motherese, like infant babbling, is composed of contact-promoting as well as reassuring vocalization. However, in the human case, I suspect the function was different than say the clucking sounds a mother muriqui makes after parking an older infant in the canopy of some tree while she forages nearby unencumbered.[45] Rather, in the hominin case, I suspect that both babbling and motherese evolved in response to the need for babies and mothers to maintain contact while infants were being held by others. Motherese reassured babies of their mothers' whereabouts and intentions, while babbling attracted the attention of mothers and allomothers alike.

Falk is probably right that once language evolved (or coevolved with other human attributes) a baby's imitation of adult sounds provided useful practice for language acquisition.[46] But in my view, the recursive and syntactical elaborations of human language arose long after cooperative breeding evolved, and with it the need for infants to attract attention and maintain relationships with others. The power of babble, I suspect, preceded the gift of gab by more than a million years.[47]

THE CAST WIDENS, THE PLOT THICKENS

Most primates and all apes are born with the same basic need to feel securely attached, but humans need more reassurance still. Why should this be so? Throughout the 1950s and 1960s Bowlby and his followers took continuous-care-and-contact mothering as a given for all primates and paid little attention to emerging information on shared care.[48] When data from the first detailed observations of hunter-gatherer childrearing among the !Kung started to come in, these findings were interpreted through a Bowlbian lens. In time, however, critics of this dominant view began to refer to mother-only caretaking models as "monotropic."[49]

In fairness to Bowlby, he did not remain as dogmatically mother-focused as some critics imply. Prodded by Ainsworth (who was heavily influenced by her field experience in Uganda), he began to mention how much help mothers needed and to acknowledge assistance from various sources. At the opening of a lecture he delivered in 1980, Bowlby noted that "very often it is the other parent [who provides this help]; in many societies, including more often than is realized our own, it comes from a grandmother. Others to be drawn into help are adolescent girls and young women. In most societies throughout the world these facts have been, and still are, taken for granted and the society organized accordingly. Paradoxically it has taken the world's richest societies to ignore these basic facts."[50]

Yet scratch him hard and Bowlby's view of infant development was profoundly mother-centered. Through attachment theory's first half century, research focused on the infant's relationship with this one other person. From an evolutionary perspective, however, mothers were far from the whole story. Even as attachments to individuals other than the mother were gradually taken into account, it usually came about in the context of highly charged and polarized late-twentieth-century debates over daycare.

Studies were specifically designed to compare developmental outcomes between children cared for at home by their mother and children cared for outside the home by unrelated childcare providers in daycare centers of variable quality. The questions asked were how "secure" or "insecure" an infant's attachment to his mother would be; how well-adjusted, compliant, or aggressive an infant would become in early childhood; and so forth. Such studies provided little information about the developmental effects of multiple caretakers per se simply because the studies had been designed to learn whether or not there were any harmful effects from daycare.[51] Hence, results from the first large-scale empirical study of the effects of daycare came as a real surprise to hardline Bowlby disciples who were convinced that babies develop best with full-time care from mothers.

By the end of the twentieth century, officials at the National Institute of Child Health and Human Development (NICHD) were growing increasingly concerned as some 62 percent of U.S. mothers with children under age six worked outside the home, and the majority of these women were going back to work within three or four months of giving birth. Yet in spite of heated debates over daycare, and with some 13 million preschoolers in some form of care by persons other than their mothers, there had never been a large-scale, carefully controlled study of daycare's effects. Beginning in 1991, the NICHD funded a consortium of top psychologists to follow 1,364 children whose families came from ten different locales in the United States and spanned diverse ethnic and economic backgrounds, all using different childcare arrangements.[52]

As the data poured in, it became clear that many factors influenced developmental outcomes for children in daycare. These included the quality of the infant's relationship with the mother at home, how many hours away from home the child spent, child-to-caretaker ratios, and staff turnover at the daycare center. But the key finding was that maternal and alloparental sensitivity and responsiveness to infants' needs were better predictors of developmental outcomes like self-control, respect for others, and social compliance than (within limits) actual time spent away from the mother was. In the case of inattentive or neglectful mothers, children were actually better off in daycare, where their needs were often more routinely or predictably met.

The massive NICHD study was informative on many fronts. But the main message was that it was not the presence of the mother per se that mattered most (though quality of the child's attachment to the mother was invariably important) but how secure infants felt when cared for by familiar and responsive people. Given that mothers are not likely to quit working outside the home, practically speaking the news that rampant daycare was not crippling the nation's children was welcome indeed. However, the results were also discouraging because good, or even adequate, daycare is so rarely available, and it tends to be expensive. Even in the best-equipped daycare centers with trained staff, turnover among caregivers is a persistent problem. It is difficult to find a substitute for familiarity and the sense of trust a child develops in kin or as-if kin with long experience responding to his particular temperament and needs.[53]

The findings about daycare also raised questions about evolutionary models for child development. If Bowlby and the early attachment theorists were right that infants in humankind's "environment of evolutionary adaptedness" were almost entirely cared for by their mothers, why were infants managing to adapt as well as they did to multiple-caretaker contexts? And why were outcomes for children in high-quality daycare centers generally pretty good?

EXPANDING ATTACHMENT THEORY

Prior to the big NICHD study, there had been relatively little systematic research on the effects of multiple caretakers per se, much less studies of multiple attachments. Nevertheless, from the 1970s onward, a handful of psychologists began to ask about the role of infant attachments to individuals other than the mother—and in particular, attachments to fathers. Michael Lamb was among these pioneers. A psychologist, Lamb subscribed to the main outlines of attachment theory, never doubting that a distressed baby would preferentially seek his mother. But Lamb found the mother-centered assumptions implicit in classical attachment theory overly narrow.

Initially, he simply wanted to see more attention paid to involved fathers like himself. Analyzing data from one of the first studies of attachment between infants and "others," Lamb found (as he expected) that babies were attracted by their mother's sensitive and predictable care, her high-pitched motherese, and the satisfying breast she offered,

(Top) Western fathers may attempt to make up for minimal time spent with infants by packing a lot of excitement into relatively brief encounters. (Bottom) Hunter-gatherer fathers spend considerably more time in intimate and often relaxing proximity to children, as this !Kung father is doing. (Top: S. B. Hrdy/AnthroPhoto. Bottom: Peabody Museum/Marshall Expedition image 2001.29.411)

and they became attached to her. But babies in his study also became emotionally attached to their father after comparatively brief periods of exposure. When both mother and father were involved in childcare, babies became attached to both, although they interacted differently with each.[54] With fathers, babies tended to interact in short and intense bouts of vigorous (and exciting) play. (The descriptions reminded me of watching my own husband throw our toddlers up above his head and then catch them in midair—never missing, but all the same definitely exciting and memorable.) Infants became attached to their fathers even though the typical father in the United States was in direct contact with his baby just under an hour a day, substantially less than the amount of face-time fathers spend with babies in most hunter-gatherer societies.[55]

Because hunter-gatherers live in tight-knit groups and spend a lot of time in camp, fathers tend to establish intimate associations with their children. In worlds without computers, television, or iPods, the antics of youngsters are primetime entertainment for adults. The highest average frequency of direct father-infant contact reported anywhere in the world comes from Barry Hewlett's pathbreaking observations of infant care among Aka foragers in Central Africa. Fathers are within arm's reach of their one- to four-month-old babies more than 50 percent of any 24-hour period and are nuzzling, kissing, hugging, or mostly just holding them a whopping 22 percent of the time they spend in camp. Even when Aka parents go on hunting expeditions in the woods, they take quite young infants and their other children along, being careful to remain in constant contact. Almost invariably, fathers in hunter-gatherer societies spend more time with infants than fathers in most Western societies do, and *much* more time than fathers in farming societies. Indeed, in many farming societies fathers never hold their infants at all. All the same, even among hunter-gatherer societies, the Aka were extraordinary.[56]

The empirical study of allomaternal caregiving among humans began by focusing on fathers, but the more psychologists like Lamb compared notes with anthropologists, the more apparent it became that in the nomadic hunter-gatherer context, mother-only or even primarily maternal care was more nearly an impossible ideal projected onto traditional peoples by Western observers than a species-typical universal. By the mid 1980s and early 1990s, a few researchers in the United States, Holland, and Israel were already beginning to question the monotro-

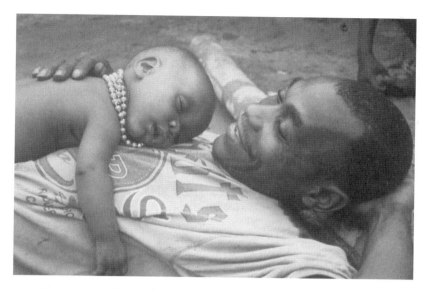

Aka fathers are within earshot of their infants most of the time, often holding them during daytime and sleeping near them at night. However, rather than communicating commitment through focused attention and hyper-stimulating play, as Western fathers tend to do, an Aka father communicates by literally "being there" for children, both in camp and when families go into the forest to hunt. As the anthropologist Barry Hewlett put it in his book on Aka fathering, "The Aka father-child relationship is intimate not because of quality time but because the father knows his child exceptionally well through regular interactions." (Hewlett 1991a)

pic focus of attachment theory and to ask what the effect of multiple caretakers was for the development of infants.[57] A team headed by the Israeli psychologist Abraham Sagi and his Dutch collaborator Marinus van IJzendoorn undertook an ambitious series of studies in Israel and the Netherlands to compare children cared for primarily by mothers with those cared for by both mothers and other adults. Their findings led them to question whether "only a stable relationship with regularly recurring interaction episodes" could produce a harmonious Bowlbian "match" between mothers and their babies.[58]

In line with a great deal of attachment research, van IJzendoorn, Sagi, and their colleagues found that the level of security in the infant's attachment to his mother was a good predictor of "later socioemotional development." However, infants readily formed attachments to other people as well, forging different types of attachments to different individuals. For example, a child might be insecurely attached to his mother but securely attached to an aunt or grandmother.[59] Overall, children seemed to do best when they have three secure relationships—that is, three relationships that send the clear message "You will be cared for no matter what." Such findings led van IJzendoorn and Sagi to conclude that "the most powerful predictor of later socioemotional development involves the quality of the entire attachment network." They termed this their "integration model."[60]

Israeli kibbutzim provided natural laboratories for studying how infants integrated different relationships and for learning more about how a child's sleeping arrangement affected attachment formation. At birth, babies in the kibbutzim were assigned to a particular nursery group. Typically there were two caregivers, called *metapelet* (Hebrew for "caregiver"), for every six infants. Babies were fed and cared for exclusively by their mothers during the first three months, and they continued to be fed by their mothers until at least six months, even after they had begun to spend time in the nursery and were getting to know their *metapelet*. *Metaplot* (the plural of metapelet) were typically well trained and unusually motivated women who had voluntarily chosen a job in childcare. As mothers returned to work for increasingly long hours, *metaplot* gradually took over most daytime care. In these respects, all 37 kibbutzim encompassed in the study were quite similar, but they differed with respect to where babies spent the night. Each baby had his or her own crib in a separate quiet room for daytime naps, but the sample was split between kibbutzim where babies went home late each afternoon and stayed at home for the night with their families and those where babies went home in the late afternoon but then returned to spend the night in a communal nursery, tended by rotating and relatively less familiar night nurses.

Infants who spent the night in communal nurseries tended to be less securely attached to their mothers, and also less securely attached to caretakers generally.[61] It is tempting to interpret the greater sense of security derived from sleeping near the mother in line with the comparative evidence across primates and foraging societies. As Hewlett puts it, "Humans communicate at night and it makes sense that trust and confidence should develop during the night just as it does during the day." Influenced by his time among the Aka, Hewlett now regards co-sleeping as a key cultural variant linked to the frequency and scope of other relationships, such as sharing.[62]

Mother-infant co-sleeping may be as close to a primate universal in childcare as can be found. Even among species with lots of shared care, babies are in contact with their mothers at night. Consider the marmoset. Although babies spend much of their day clinging to their fathers, at night they are on their mothers. Videotaped records also show that mothers are the ones most likely to be awakened by their babies during the night.[63] The existence of this near-universal suggests that human infants who find it distressing to be put alone in a dark room at night, or who find bedtime especially stressful when away from home, are well within what we might call their "primate rights."

MULTIPLE ATTACHMENTS AND THEIR INTEGRATION

So far in this chapter I have focused on how shared care leads to the development of enhanced capacities for mental attribution. In the process, it sets the stage for directional selection favoring infants who possess better abilities to read someone else's intentions, while concurrently promoting intersubjective communication—critical baby steps toward the evolution of emotionally modern humans. It is time now to consider how having relationships with multiple caretakers affects other aspects of cognitive and socioemotional development.

One of the most striking findings from the Israeli study was that infants securely attached to their *metaplot* were also more self-confident and socially sophisticated several years later when they entered kindergarten.[64] This correlation reminded Sagi and van IJzendoorn of an earlier finding by psychological anthropologists working among Gusii agricultural villagers in Kenya. Even though a Gusii child's nutritional status was best predicted by the security of his attachment to his mother, cognitive performance was better predicted by the security of his attachment to other caretakers.[65] As Sagi and van IJzendoorn mulled over their results and began to think more about the findings from the African case, they concluded that "an extended network was the best predictor of later advanced functioning." The strongest predictor of empathy, dominance, independence, and achievement orientation often turned out to be a strong attachment to a nonparental caretaker. They could find no significant associations between socioemotional development and the quality of children's attachments to their parents.[66]

To anyone accustomed to conventional Western wisdom that children develop optimally when cared for by a single sensitive and reliably responsive individual—namely, the mother—these results may at first seem startling, even nonsensical. But on closer consideration, what the results from Israeli, Dutch, and East African studies actually show is not that having a responsive mother does not matter (of course it does) but that infants nurtured by multiple caretakers grow up not only feeling secure but with better-developed and more enhanced capacities to view the world from multiple perspectives. As Lamb suspected early on based on his observations of infants jointly attached to both mother and father, awareness of diverse perspectives from early in life can make a child more empathetic as well as contribute to more sophisticated capacities for attributing mental and emotional states to others.

A greater integration of different perspectives is scarcely guaranteed by all daycare contexts, especially many of the ones available to Western mothers these days.[67] However, several features characteristic of hunter-gatherer societies increase the prospects of a secure caretaking environment. Because forager communities are composed of flexible assemblages of close and more distant blood relations and kin by marriage, all potential caretakers would be familiar. A typical group of 25–35 members will be both culturally homogeneous and very conservative.

In contrast to the spiraling rate of change that characterizes modern societies, the worldview of individuals in a hunter-gatherer group remains remarkably consistent across generations. Individuals might come and go, outsiders might be occasionally "fostered" in, yet day to day a child's extended family and especially the cultural context people were embedded in would remain extremely predictable compared with the fast rate of cultural change children and adults alike encounter in the modern world. Among people like the Aka, Hewlett stresses, childcare customs are vertically transmitted and everyone conforms to the same customs. This results in highly conserved childrearing practices and great consistency among caretakers, further promoting secure attachment to caregivers.[68]

THE WORLD AS A "GIVING" PLACE

A capacity for compassion is characteristically human. Yet its expression in any particular human depends on both heritable propensities and each person's experiences over the course of development. At fourteen months of age, two identical twins having virtually 100 percent of their genes in common will be more alike in how they respond to an experimenter who pretends to pinch her finger on a clipboard and gives an exaggerated "Ooooh" sound than will fraternal twins, who share only half of their genes.[69] But such empathy also has a learned component, which is acquired by learning to look at and experience the world from someone else's perspective.

Psychologists are increasingly struck by how early and eagerly children seek to establish connections with others and how connected to others children feel right from an early age. They are eager to help and to share, not just with their mothers but with various others, even strangers, so long as their mother or a familiar companion is close by and they feel safe. As early as the second year of life, children appear ready, even desperately eager, to comfort someone who seems sad, to help someone in distress.[70] Their interest in how someone else feels toward them, or how others respond to a particular object or game like peek-a-boo, develops even earlier.[71] Perhaps by four months of age, certainly by the end of the first year, babies are sufficiently aware of other people's responses (and to some extent opinions) to seek their approval, often being quite coy in how they solicit praise. Babies may also look embarrassed when someone else's expectations are not met.[72] Such reactions require a sense of self as distinct from but related to others.

Learning about this self occurs in the context of early experiences with other people. Typically, infants become accustomed to trusting and relying on others or else they learn not to. As the evolutionary psychiatrist Randy Nesse once told me, "As soon as we become convinced love is not possible, love becomes impossible." The same is true of trust.[73] Bowlby conceptualized this process as acquiring an "internal working model" for how the world and the people inhabiting that world are likely to work.[74] What is striking about the worldviews of foragers (among people as widely dispersed as the Mbuti of Central Africa, Nayaka foragers of South India, the Batek of Malaysia, Australian Aborigines, and the North American Cree) is that they tend to share a view of their physical environment as a "giving" place occupied by others who are also liable to be well-disposed and generous.[75] They view their physical world as being in line with benevolent social relationships. Thus, the Mbuti refer to the forest as a place that gives "food, shelter and clothing just like their parents." The Nayaka simply say, "The forest is as a parent."[76]

Confidence about one's place in the world does not mean life is necessarily easy. Among our hunter-gatherer ancestors, food was often scarce, predators ever present. Over generations, children would have watched with dismay as half or more of their siblings and cousins died at young ages. Yet by definition, individuals who *did* survive would have done so surrounded by others who cared for and shared with them. This endowed them with a personal confidence notably different from that of many modern people who grow up in environments with more available resources but less caring. People with French and German agricultural ancestors like my own are more likely to have been reared to beware of strangers. Many of us were put to bed with folktales about the world "outside over there," a scary place peopled by impoverished widows, cruel stepmothers, hungry orphans, and unwanted children who lived surrounded by a dangerous forest where malign creatures—wolves and witches—lurked.[77] To an Mbuti child, the forest is not so much dangerous as nurturing—it is a benignly encompassing mother-figure. Such a child is taught to be at least initially (until encountering information to the contrary) curious rather than fearful of outsiders.

Intrigued by the notion that "foragers are, in general, more likely than people with other subsistence modes to develop trusting and confident views of others, the self, and the environment," Barry Hewlett and Michael Lamb teamed up with the German psychologists Birgit Leyendecker and Axel Scholmerich to ascertain whether this was really true. If it was true, they were interested in identifying specific mechanisms, such as patterns of childcare, that underlay the trusting worldviews typical of hunter-gatherers.[78] The team delved deeply into existing cross-cultural reports on infant care and then compared daily experiences of three- to four-month-old infants among Central African Aka foragers, nearby Ngandu farmers, and upper-middle-class Americans living near Washington, D.C., quantifying their different caretaking patterns. How often were babies held? By whom? How long were babies left alone?

Hewlett and his collaborators knew how much foraging societies differ from one another and were well aware of the limitations surrounding this first-of-its-kind study. But what impressed them were the commonalities in the emotional milieu that forager children grow up in. Aka children were nearly continuously held by someone, touched more often, breastfed more frequently (sometimes by more than one individual), and responded to more reliably than were infants among nearby Ngandu farmers or among upper-middle-class American children. Such early experiences, they suggest, help explain why children in foraging societies tend to acquire working models of their world as a "giving place."[79] But even among farmers and postindustrialites, children who were accustomed to multiple caregivers grew up less likely to fear strangers.[80]

Understandably, childcare arrangements shaped by local hazards and subsistence modes vary greatly and have their own effects on childhood outlooks. Savanna foragers who worry about hyenas by night and lions at any time strive never to be left alone, while a peasant mother who is not able to take her child with her to work in a faraway field, and has no other person to leave him with but also does not have to worry about prowling leopards, may leave her swaddled infant hanging from a peg on the back of a door, safe at least from crawling into the fire and out of reach of foraging, omnivorous pigs.[81] Yet beyond actual environmental hazards, the Hewlett survey indicates that the way children interact with their caretakers influences their sense of belonging and shapes how they feel about the environment they live in.

BECOMING EMPATHETIC AND
OTHERWISE EMOTIONALLY MODERN

One of psychology's more robust findings is that children learn to attribute mental states to other people from early experiences interacting with them. To care about others requires a sense of self along with the capacity to conceptualize others as separate selves with their own mental states and feelings.

In a classic 1994 paper entitled "Theory of Mind Is Contagious: You Catch It from Your Sibs," psychologists Josef Perner and colleagues reported that the more brothers and sisters a four-year-old had, the better she did on false-belief tests.[82] Understanding that someone else can hold a view about the world different from one's own is the first step in being able to understand that someone else might think something that you know is not so. The games children play provide excellent opportunities for finding this out. False-belief experiments have become one of my own favorite parlor games for entertaining children (and myself). Ask a two-year-old sitting in his mother's lap to watch while you carefully set a cookie on the table. Next, ask his mother to shut her eyes, and hide the cookie on your lap, under the table. Then ask the two-year-old where his mother (eyes still shut) thinks the cookie is. A child younger than three or four years lacks sufficient "theory of mind" to be able to understand that his mother has a different understanding of the situation than he does. He will almost always tell you that his mother thinks the cookie is under the table (where the cookie actually happens to be), even though she could not see the cookie being put there and thus could not know that. Almost all four-year-olds and a few children as young as three will announce that their mother thinks the cookie is still on the table, where it is not.

Beginning around age three, children are able to interpret the feelings and intentions of others and even to imagine what it is like to be someone else altogether.[83] By age four, children display sensitivity to other people's self-image, beginning to flatter and attempting to ingratiate themselves with them.[84] The more older siblings a child has, engaging (and also perhaps tormenting) her, the better a child does on tests that require her to see the world the way someone else does. On closer examination, however, it turns out that it is not so much the *number* of siblings that matters as the fact that some are older. Further research has shown that what really counts is for a child to have the opportunity to interact with older, more experienced caretakers—mentors and sponsors who do not even need to be related.[85] It helps of course if these older individuals express an interest in the child's feelings and mental state.[86]

Children growing up in extended families with kin and as-if kin in residence not only benefit in all the material ways detailed in the preceding chapter, they also enjoy new cognitive dimensions to their social lives. Not surprisingly, children accustomed to interacting with others perform better on false-belief tests and in games that require an ability to read and empathize with other people's mental states, including being able to read between the lines of expressed motivations. Children with lots of caregivers exhibit these capacities at an earlier age. Similar processes of "contagion" may explain the case of human-reared chimpanzees who, with their extra exposure to human allomothers, end up performing better at tasks requiring a theory of mind and the interpreta-

Capacities for intersubjective engagement begin to develop right from birth but are refined and expanded with age as maturing infants spend more time in the custody of older children. But fathers, older kinswomen, and especially juvenile allomothers can also be direct competitors for food and other resources. A !Kung toddler's time spent in a mixed age play-group provides novel opportunities to learn about status-seeking, posturing, and deceit, and to expand earlier lessons on how to read emotional commitment and predict generosity versus stinginess. (Peabody Museum/Marshall Expedition image 2001.29.412)

tion of someone else's intentions. Even though humans are generally much better than other apes at recognizing that another individual has a mental state and intentions they can affect, apes too (especially those reared by people) possess quasi-human mind-reading capacities that are activated under particular developmental conditions.[87]

No one doubts that large-brained, anatomically modern humans who start to toddle upright by one year of age and begin to talk by two, and who right from an early age exhibit earnest concern for others and take pleasure in sharing their mental states, are different from orangutans or chimpanzees. It is from interactions with more mature minds both "benign and reflective" that children begin to think of themselves as an organism with a mind. What I am proposing, however, is that some of these emotional qualities that distinguish modern humans from other apes, especially mind reading combined with empathy and developing a sense of self, emerged earlier in our evolutionary history than anatomically modern humans did.[88] The critical factor in this emergence of intersubjective capacities was the novel developmental context in which generation after generation of early humans grew up, different from that of any other ape before.

The ancestors of modern orangutans probably grew up in the company of just their mother or possibly one older sibling. Ancestors of chimpanzees spent at least the first six months of life interacting mostly with their mothers, rarely encountering other members of the community and, importantly, never depending on them.[89] As apes mature, older infants and especially juveniles will eagerly seek out available playmates—any age and indeed almost any species will do. The urge to play and seek out partners to play with does not distinguish humans from other apes. What would have distinguished the ancestors of humans from their shared ancestors with other apes would have been that, right from the first days and months of life, they needed to monitor and engage others. Early humans would have been born into social worlds that were more complex and more challenging from the outset. If empathy is contagious, caught from older associates, creatures living like orangutans or chimpanzees would have started later and never had anything like the opportunity humans had to "catch" and then use the requisite neural equipment from an early age. Whatever mind-reading potentials there might have been among the ancestors of chimpanzees and orangutans were left largely latent. Thus, Mother Nature had neither the opportunity nor the occasion to favor and refine them.

Compared with modern chimpanzees or with 6-million-year-old common ancestors of humans and other apes, people today are born with different social aptitudes, and—I am convinced—so were our ancestors at the beginning of the Pleistocene who would have been emotionally modern long before they were big-brained and anatomically modern. Join me in a thought experiment. Pretend that cognitive psychologists could go back in time and carry out experiments aimed at determining how infants among our early hominin ancestors acquired mental attribution skills. At the end of the first year of life, how would a sample of protohuman ape babies who were cared for exclusively by their mother differ from comparable babies with multiple caretakers? Based on what we know from the studies summarized above, I believe we could predict with some confidence the following outcomes. First, ape babies held by others would pay more attention to their mother, to where she was, to her facial expression, voice, and moods. Second, babies cared for by multiple caretakers would be more aware of distinctions between self and others, better able to read the mental states of conspecifics, and capable of integrating information about their own intentions and those of others—indeed, perhaps several others.

As a four-month-old Trobriand girl sits in her mother's lap, an older sibling crawls up behind her and playfully makes eye contact, then waves her hand in front of the baby. This little girl is probably wondering what her brother is doing, and perhaps what he is intending. No wonder children with older siblings are more likely to develop a theory of mind sooner; they need one. (I. Eibl-Eibesfeldt/Human Ethology Archives)

By the end of the first year of life, then, little apes with multiple caretakers would have been challenged in ways that no young ape had ever been challenged before. These tremendously needy hominin youngsters would have had to attend to and learn to read cues of maternal commitment as well as to decipher moods and intentions of others who might be seduced into caring for them. How best to do so? Through crying or through coyness? With smiles, funny faces, gurgling, or babbling? Or failing that, by forgoing enticing communication and resorting to angry attempts to control them—a topic to which I return in Chapter 9. Early hominins had genotypes almost identical to those of their mother-care-only ape relations, but their early experiences would have turned them into quite different, emotionally more modern organisms.

PSYCHOLOGICAL IMPLICATIONS OF SHARED CARE

Few animals are born needier or remain dependent longer than humans. At some point in our distant past, care and provisioning from alloparents began to permit human mothers to breed at a faster pace than any ape ever before. Some anthropologists date this transformation around 1.8 million years ago, and in Chapter 9 I elaborate on why I agree with them, though I do not claim to know for sure. Nevertheless, once mothers embarked on an evolutionary course of producing unusually large, slow-maturing, needy, and long-dependent offspring, there was no turning back. Without help from others, such children could not survive.

No wonder human mothers and their children are sensitive to how much social support they are likely to receive. Like marmosets and tamarin mothers, who also depend on others to help them care for and provi-

Most visiting anthropologists surveying this spirited four-way interaction would assume that the two adult Trobrianders are fathers and the infants they hold are their offspring. In fact, as Eibl-Eibesfeldt notes, both men are alloparents. As the man on the right initiates a greeting by urging the infants to shake hands, the more extroverted ten-month-old looks eagerly at his fellow, smiles, and opens his mouth wide with excitement. The six-month-old looks first to the initiating alloparent, then at the other infant, then over at his nearby father, shrinks back a bit, shakes hands, but then timidly pulls his hand back and nestles closer to the alloparent, who seems to be enjoying this quintessentially human comedy of manners very much. (I. Eibl-Eibesfeldt/Human Ethology Archives)

sion their young, hominin mothers took their perception of alloparental support into account before emotionally committing. Like callitrichids, but in contrast to other apes, early hominin babies were born into a world where nonmaternal caregivers were vitally important not just for the nourishment and protection of infants but for the emergence of full-fledged maternal solicitude.

And yet these creatures were also apes. Thus the stage was set for clever, socially intelligent youngsters to more fully develop the innate gifts for interacting with and manipulating others that all apes are born with. The result was the emergence of quite novel ape phenotypes, which would be exposed to novel selection pressures. Individuals better at meeting the terms of this challenge and developing new dimensions to mind reading would be those best cared for and best fed, and their own mothers would also be more likely to survive. This novel developmental context provided youngsters immediate opportunities and incentives to develop innate aptitudes for engaging others.

In environments with high child mortality, those with more alloparental assistance would have profited not only by being better comforted or entertained (for babies do enjoy this) but, more importantly, by being better protected and better fed in infancy and through childhood. Once upon a time, "feeling neglected" was more than just "the child's experience."[90] The others' level of commitment had life-or-death consequences. Whenever it was that our ancestors adopted alloparental care, it is clear that this mode of childcare—novel for creatures with the minds of apes—would have had profound implications for developing young. So just who were these alloparents likely to be? And why did they help?

5

WILL THE REAL PLEISTOCENE FAMILY PLEASE STEP FORWARD?

There may be human potentialities which date far back in evolutionary
time for which new artificially created conditions may find a new use.

—Margaret Mead (1966)

Think of the typical textbook image or museum di-
orama of the early human family. Perhaps a beetle-browed caveman will
have his arm draped protectively about his mate. She will be holding
their baby. Or perhaps there will be a clustering of beetle-brows near a
campfire, with men hauling back the carcass of a just killed antelope. If
there is a baby, he is held in the arms of an adult female, likely a woman
with milk-swollen breasts. We are meant to take for granted that she is
the baby's mother, for any mother in a state of nature is assumed to remain in continuous contact with her baby, just as any other ape would.
But there is a disconnect between iconic portraits of stone-age families
and firsthand observations of people who actually live by gathering and

Exclusive maternal care is implied by museum dioramas and popular illustrations of australopithecines in nuclear family arrangements. (© John Gurche)

hunting. The person holding the baby would often have been an aunt, sibling, or grandmother.

When politicians lament the "decline of the family," they have in mind departures from the nuclear family: a man, his wife, and their biological children. However, the template for this kind of family dates back only a century or so, at most to Victorian times, and in American contexts not a lot further than the 1950s, when my generation of baby boomers grew up in mostly single-family homes. According to the cultural stereotype, the mother cared for the children while the father went off to his job. Even though there was only a blip in time when a single wage-earner could reliably and predictably support an average family, this myth of the nuclear family, with a nurturing mother at home and a providing father at work, became an American ideal.[1]

My library is filled with books having titles like *Life without Father: Compelling Evidence That Fatherhood and Marriage Are Indispensable for the Good of Children and for Society*, or *Fatherless in America: Confronting Our Most Urgent Social Problem*, books written by sociologists of the family who, without asking under what historical or economic or social conditions this will be so, take for granted that "children develop best when they are provided with the opportunity to have warm, intimate, continuous and enduring relationships with both their fathers and their mothers."[2] Once it is assumed that paternal investment is "an essential determinant of child and societal well-being," or that the best way to rear children is in a nuclear family, or that only a man whose "paternity confidence . . . is high" will be willing to care for children, such propositions not only shape public policy, they also shape the questions researchers ask.[3]

Routinely, studies are designed to contrast outcomes when children are raised by single mothers versus both parents. Invariably, the results show that children with just one parent, especially children already at risk, do less well, grow up more prone to get into trouble, drop out of school, get pregnant, become unemployed, or go to jail if they are reared by one overburdened person rather than two. Of course, it takes more than one person to rear a child. However, the studies have not been designed to determine whether that second person needs to be male and a genetic parent. What about children raised by a mother plus a grandparent, uncle, or older sibling, compared with those from two-parent families, controlled for socioeconomic status? What about three caretakers, none of whom is the biological parent? Under what circumstances does attention from individuals without a genetic relationship to a child contribute to the child's well-being? Are there multiple caretaker arrangements that are almost as good, just as good, or even better than two parents? We don't know, because we rarely asked.[4]

Even those who claim to have grown up in a "dysfunctional" family subscribe to widespread stereotypes of what a "functional" family should look like. Religious conservatives took their lead from Adam and Eve, while even secularists—including many scientists—tend to view monogamous nuclear families as "biological phenomena . . . rooted in organs and physiological structures" of the "human animal."[5] Once the idea took hold that the nuclear family is "at heart a biological arrangement for raising children that has always involved fathers as well as mothers," even otherwise very thoughtful researchers overlooked the need to continuously challenge their underlying assumptions about what children need in order to prosper.[6] In particular, they forgot to ask questions about what happens to children living in a wide variety of other human social arrangements. Even without the relevant information at their disposal, politicians concerned with the "breakdown of the family" still manage to sound quite confident about what the optimal childrearing arrangement ought to look like.[7]

"Studies have shown," declared the U.S. president in 2003, "that the ideal is where a child is raised in a married family with a man and a woman." Thus, instead of funding childcare programs, $1.6 billion was earmarked to fund pro-marriage programs that would tutor people in how to sustain a long-term monogamous relationship.[8] Similar preconceptions about what sort of families are best for rearing children led to the expulsion of a 14-year-old California girl from her Christian school not because of anything she had done but because her parents were both women.[9] That same year, 2005, the U.S. Supreme Court left standing a Florida law banning adoption of children by two gay men, refusing to hear a challenge to it, apparently because the justices subscribed to the rationale being used to uphold the law by a three-judge panel at the 11th U.S. Circuit Court of Appeals. As the justices put it: "The accumulated wisdom of several millennia of human experience" has demonstrated that the "optimal family structure in which to raise children was one with a mother and father married to each other."[10] Given the role that alloparents have played over the course of human evolution, how did such vital benefactors go unacknowledged for so long?

"SEX CONTRACTS" FOR REARING COSTLY CHILDREN

No creature in the world (unless, just possibly, a bowhead whale) takes longer to mature than a human child does. Nor does any other creature need so much for so long before his acquisition and production of resources matches his consumption.[11] Sensitive to this mismatch, evolutionists correctly concluded that *someone* had to have helped mothers make up the difference between what children need and what a mother by herself could provide. From the outset, they assumed they knew who that someone was. That provider must have been her mate, as Darwin himself opined in *The Descent of Man and Selection in Relation to Sex* (1871). Indeed, it was the hunter's need to finance slow-maturing children, Darwin thought, that provided the main catalyst for the evolution of our big brains. "The most able men succeeded best in defending and providing for themselves and their wives and offspring," he wrote. It was the offspring of hunters with "greater intellectual vigor and power of invention" who were most likely to survive.

According to this logic, males with bigger brains would have been more successful hunters, better providers, and more able to obtain mates and thereby pass their genes to children whose survival was underwritten by a better diet. Meat would subsidize the long childhoods needed to develop larger brains, leading eventually to the expansion of brains from the size of an australopithecine's to the size of Darwin's own. Thus did the "hunting hypothesis" morph into one of the most long-lasting and influential models in anthropology.[12] Subsequent versions wove together increasingly coherent scenarios in which early human evolution was a "direct consequence of brain expansion and material culture" fueled by an increasingly bipedal, increasingly effective hunter. Big brains, and with them superior intelligence, were viewed as "the sine qua non of human origin."[13]

At the heart of the model lay a pact between a hunter who provided for his mate and a mate who repaid him with sexual fidelity so the provider could be certain that children he invested in carried at least half of his genes. This "sex contract" assumed pride of place as the "prodigious adaptation central to the success of early hominids."[14]

Over time, minor alterations have been made to accommodate new findings such as the importance of vegetable foods in the diets of African foragers. As it became apparent that among some foragers (like the !Kung) plant foods accounted for slightly more calories than meat, researchers started paying more attention to female contributions.[15] In the wake of revived theoretical interest in Darwin's ideas about female mate choice, and with the realization of just how much variation there was in the lifetime reproductive success of one mother relative to another, scientists also started paying more attention to the reproductive strategizing of females. Nevertheless, after a century and a half, the central assumptions underlying the hunting hypothesis still persist.

WHEN THE SEX CONTRACT FALLS SHORT

The following extract from a 2004 textbook (the two authors happen to be at Harvard, where the hunting hypothesis has long been a centerpiece of the teaching curriculum) is typical. They take for granted that "monogamous pair-bonding and nuclear families were dominant throughout human history in hunter-gatherer societies" and go on to argue that the "most straightforward explanation of the trend toward monogamy is that smart female hominids went to work on chimpanzee-like hominid-males and—step by step, mate selection by mate selection—shaped them up into loving husbands and fathers with true family values" by choosing the cleverest hunters best able to support their wives and children.[16]

No mention is made of what happens when this "loving father" fails to adequately provide because all the eland have migrated elsewhere, or because he had bad luck or poor aim that day, or because he got himself killed or took up with an additional woman, leaving his mate and her progeny with a smaller share, or left them altogether. There is no mention of help from any other quarter, because it has been so long assumed that we knew who provided what to whom. According to a 2003 article in *Newsweek,* "Since the beginning of time . . . women have been programmed to seek a mate who can provide for a family."[17] This ancient heritage supposedly explains why women today remain perpetually on the prowl for wealthy men.[18]

However, a new breed of paleoanthropologists, trained to decipher fossils and stone tools but also to study the subsistence strategies of living hunter-gatherers, were less convinced. They were aware how extremely egalitarian hunter-gatherers tend to be. It made no sense to project onto such people the within-group wealth differentials typical of more stratified societies.

More to the point, these ecologically-minded fieldworkers asked how a Pliocene-Pleistocene hunter would be able to provision his mate and her offspring, assuming he wanted to. New and better evidence on how African *Homo erectus* actually obtained meat, along with more realistic assessments of how rarely even the best contemporary hunters succeed in killing big game (perhaps once or twice a month), challenged underlying assumptions of the model. Newly available quantitative information on the highly communal way foragers share with the whole group made it clear that the most successful hunter would often get no more for his family than the most hapless did. Criticisms of the hunting hypothesis, simmering for more than a century, came to a head.[19] By the end of the twentieth century, as James O'Connell, one of this new breed of behavioral ecologist/archaeologist, put it, the hunting hypothesis had "effectively collapsed."[20]

> Like all young primates, *H. ergaster* [that is, the African branch of *Homo erectus*] juveniles probably had to eat several times a day, *every* day. Like modern children, they probably relied on others to provide most of their food for years after weaning. The hunting hypothesis holds that early human males were the main source of this support, yet traditional East African hunters living in similar habitats today cannot meet this need, despite their use of sophisticated weapons. Though meat represents a sizable fraction of their families' *annual* caloric intake, it is not acquired reliably enough to satisfy the *daily* nutritional needs of their children.[21]

Hundreds of thousands of years after *Homo erectus*, men hunting in arid African habitats like those occupied by the !Kung—armed with spears, bows, and poisoned arrows—still provide less than half of all calories for their group. Even in game-rich areas like Hadza land in northwest Tanzania, hunters succeed only a fraction of the time, perhaps four of the hundred days they go hunting.[22] When hunters do manage to kill a much-sought-after eland or other large ungulate, protein arrives in the form of occasional bonanzas shared by the whole group rather than as predictable meals for the hunter's wife and children. It is left to women to gather nuts, tubers, and berries or pick up more readily acquired but less prestigious prey like tortoises (arguably mankind's original "slow food") in order to reliably provide the next meal.[23]

Beyond the difficulty a hunter would have had providing for his family, there was the other problem with the sex-contract model: the likelihood that a man would die, defect, or divert food to additional women. In this respect, the situation among our hunter-gatherer ancestors may not have been that different from what goes on in much of the world today. The needs of children outstrip what most fathers are able or willing to provide. Worldwide, the proportion of households headed by women without men ranges between 10 and 25 percent and is rising.[24] In countries such as Botswana, Swaziland, Barbados, Grenada, and elsewhere in the Caribbean, 40 percent of households contain children with no father present. In Zimbabwe, Norway, Germany, and the United States, the proportion is closer to 30 percent. Even where fathers are present, their contributions vary, which is why in countries such as Guatemala, Kenya, and Malawi children in female-headed households may be better nourished than those in families with both genetic parents present.[25]

Accurate statistics for men who sire children without knowing or acknowledging it are elusive. What we do know is how often fathers lose contact with their children. In industrialized nations like the United States, close to half of all children whose parents divorce lose contact with their fathers shortly afterward. Within ten years, the proportion rises to two-thirds. For many reasons, not all of which have to do with male priorities, only 52 percent of divorced mothers receive full child support; for children born out of wedlock, the proportion receiving support falls to 32 percent.[26] Many men pair with a mate and father a child, hoping to earn a living or planning to stick around, but find themselves unable to. Others start new families with a new wife. Some have no realistic prospect of watching their children grow up (consider Saul Bellow, who fathered a child at age 84). Clearly, caring for all—or any—of the children that he sires is not automatically the top priority of these progenitors. This is why development agencies concerned with child well-being recommend channeling aid directly to mothers, bypassing fathers. That way, money is more likely to be spent on food for the family, medicine, and school fees rather than cigarettes, alcohol, or status symbols to impress peers or other women.[27]

Paternal defections are not necessarily recent casualties of capitalist economies, globalization, or postcolonial breakdown in family organization. When Frank Marlowe interviewed Hadza still living by hunting and gathering, he learned that only 36 percent of children had fathers living in their same group.[28] A hemisphere away, among Yanomamo tribespeople in remote regions of Venezuela and Brazil, the chance of a 10-year-old child having both a father and a mother still living in the same group was one in three, while the chance that a Central African Aka youngster between the ages of 11 and 15 was living with both natural parents was closer to 58 percent. Pity the Ongee foragers living on the Andaman Islands: none of the 11- to 15-year-olds in that ethnographic sample still lived with either natural parent.[29]

Does this mean that fathers are not important? No. However, it does mean that a mother giving birth to slow-maturing, costly young does so without being able to count on help from the father. The impact on child well-being of variable paternal commitment depends on local conditions and on who else is around, able, and willing to help. In some environments, presence of the father is absolutely essential to keep an infant safe or provisioned. In other places, especially if alloparents fill in, disappearance of the father has no detectable impact on child survival. When anthropologists reviewed a sample of fifteen traditional societies, in eight of them the presence or absence of the father had no apparent effect on the survival of children to age five, provided other caregivers in addition to the mother were on hand and in a position to help.[30]

WHERE FATHERS MATTER MOST

Through time and across cultures, among individuals living along the banks of rivers and lakes, in dense forests, or in arid savannas, there has always been variation in what fathers could do to help provision their families. In northern climates and in many areas of South America, most calories came from game. The importance of having a father has been especially well documented for some heavily meat-dependent South American forager-horticulturalists. Many such groups are also characterized by high levels of violence, as was true for the Ache when they still lived exclusively as forest nomads (before they settled near mission stations) and for many twentieth-century groups living in the center of the Yanomamo tribe's range during much of the twentieth century. When such peoples become "crowded in their landscapes compared to true family-level societies . . . [and] can no longer avoid resource competition simply by moving elsewhere," anthropologists Allen Johnson and Timothy Earl remind us, the bravest and most aggressive men begin to be regarded as "valuable allies rather than dangerous outcasts."[31] Not surprisingly, being killed by someone else was a main cause of death for children and adults alike.

Like so many other primates, what mothers and infants most urgently needed a male for was to protect them—not just from predators but from conspecific males.[32] Compared with Ache children whose parents remained married, Ache youngsters whose parents divorced had a nearly double death rate. If the father actually died or disappeared altogether, chances of the child dying before his ninth birthday rose threefold.[33] Risks to infants from stepfathers are well-documented, and in the Ache case, survival chances for the fatherless were so compromised that a pregnant woman who found herself widowed (and especially if she expected to remarry) might bury her fatherless child at birth rather than continue to invest in a doomed enterprise.[34]

Heavy reliance on meat among foragers like the Cuiva, or again the Ache (who derived a whopping 87 percent of their annual calories from game), put fatherless children at a particular disadvantage.[35] As among African foragers, these South Americans have a communal system whereby the best hunter's share is no bigger than that allocated to the worst. Meat is shared according to a strict "from each according to his means" ethic of "cooperate frequently and share fully." A participant's contribution need be no more significant than loaning an arrow or providing information about where game was last seen, but to receive a share a man had to participate. A father who was not around would not be viewed as deserving a share, and neither would his children.[36]

As important as fathers can be, providing for children is not necessarily their top priority. Even though Hadza hunters could acquire protein more reliably by targeting small game, such as hares, they preferred hunting for more prestigious but elusive large game.[37] Maximizing prestige was a higher priority than maximizing yields. Thus the anthropologist Kristen Hawkes proposed what is now known as the "show-off hypothesis," according to which big-game hunting is considered more like an athletic sport than a subsistence mode, with men seeking to burnish their reputations in the eyes of other men, and to impress women.

No one argues that men, or the meat they provide, are unimportant in traditional societies. Indeed, one reason good hunters are so admired is precisely because meat *is* highly valued and much desired, and with good reason. The more food available, the more fertile women are, potentially enhancing the reproductive opportunities of both sexes as well as the survival chances of better-nourished children. Thus, not surprisingly, when Frank Marlowe analyzed the composition of typical diets across foraging societies, he found a significant correlation between female fertility and how much food was provided by men.[38]

The big challenge confronting mothers who give birth to costly young, then, is not that goods and services provided by men are unimportant but rather that women have no reliable way to guarantee paternal support. As one way to hedge their bets and garner alternative sources of support for their children in societies with chronically unpredictable resources or high rates of adult mortality, some mothers manage to line up an "extra" father.

ADDING EXTRA FATHERS OR PARTS OF FATHERS

Contrary to the widely held dogma that only men who are certain of their paternity provide for young, in many widely separated corners of the world there exist customs and beliefs that help mothers elicit tolerance, protection, or assistance from men who are only possibly, rather than certainly, related. Among Eskimos, Montagnais-Naskapi, and some other North American Indian tribes, as well as among Central American people like the Siriono and many tribes in Amazonian South America as well as across the ocean in parts of pre- and postcolonial west, central, and east Africa, women are permitted or even encouraged to have sex with real or fictive brothers of their husbands. A range of innovations permits mothers in traditional societies from southwestern China and central Japan, as well as among people like the Lusi of Papua and New Guinea and in areas of Polynesia, to line up extra "fathers."[39] Even in times and places renowned for patriarchal family structures, such as the Qing dynasty in China or in traditional India, desperately poor parents sometimes made ends meet by incorporating an extra man (preferably some kind of wage earner) into the marital unit.[40]

In an increasingly globalized world where rapidly expanding underclasses are characterized by scarce, unpredictable resources and where men have a hard time earning enough to support a family, and in any event are liable to die young or otherwise disappear, mothers ranging from Africa and the Caribbean to the *banlieues* of Europe and U.S. inner

The Yanomamo forager-horticulturalists of South America have become widely known for their fierceness and belligerence, and—in the twentieth century—for raids to steal women and sometimes even for killing children sired by rivals. Yet on closer examination the temperaments of Yanomamo vary enormously, in part depending on where and among whom they live. Yanomamo living in the lowland forests at the center of this tribal group's range are indeed characterized by high rates of polygyny and conflict between men over women, resulting in many homicides. But members of the same tribe living in less densely populated highland regions on the outskirts of this core area were relatively peaceful, monogamous, and—according to the anthropologist Napoleon Chagnon—inclined to smile more. In both locales, fathers and maternal uncles were extremely affectionate toward their young relations, as illustrated in this counter-iconic image of a Yanomamo dad delightedly juggling his baby daughter. (I. Eibl-Eibesfeldt/Human Ethology Archives)

cities routinely enter into sequential polyandrous (one woman, several men) relationships to make do, hedge bets, or improve their lot.[41] The behavior of these women is more accurately described as "assiduously maternal" than "promiscuous."[42] Across large swaths of tribal Amazonia, among forager-horticulturalists like the Bari of Venezuela, the Ache of Paraguay, Wayano of French Guiana, Matis of Peru, Takana of Bolivia, or the Arawete, Kulina, Kuikuru, Mehinaku, or Canela of Brazil, it is socially acceptable, even expected, for a husband to permit real or fictive ceremonial "brothers" to sleep with his wife.[43] Even among the Yanomamo, a people famous for their many-wived, polygynous headmen, many women spend at least brief phases of their lives in polyandrous marriages.[44] Odds are, a woman's official husband will be the father of any child she bears. But not necessarily.

Given what a powerful emotion sexual jealousy is, polyandrous liaisons are a risky strategy, dangerous for all concerned.[45] But widely held beliefs about "partible paternity" help ease some of this tension. In these cultures, semen from every man a woman has sex with in the months before her infant is born supposedly contributes to the growth of her fetus, resulting in chimeralike composite young sired by multiple men. Each possible father is subsequently expected to offer gifts of food to the pregnant woman and to help provide for the resulting child.

If there are too many possible fathers, or if a mother is deemed too promiscuous, men will be discouraged from helping her, and she will be out of luck. Nevertheless, among the Ache and the Bari (the two tribes for which we have the best data), children with two designated "fathers" were better fed and on average more likely to survive, making two seem like the optimal number of fathers under these social and ecological conditions.[46]

Belief in partible paternity and other customs that facilitate maternal manipulation of information about paternity tend to be more feasible in groups with long-standing matrilineal traditions where sexual attitudes and childcare options are already tilted in favor of maternal interests. Such mindsets are very different from those in Western society, where a long history of patrilineally transmitted resources leaves men preoccupied with genetic paternity and puts children whose paternity is in doubt at a serious disadvantage. But in partible-paternity societies, where relying on a single father is an even bigger than usual gamble, having several possible fathers has the opposite effect.

It is presumably with the ultimate goal of promoting child survival under perilous conditions that customary rituals among South American tribes like the Canela or the Kulina provide publicly sanctioned ways for mothers to pick up an extramarital provisioner.[47] When they find themselves "hungry for meat," Kulina women order men to go hunting. On their return, each woman selects a hunter other than her own husband as a partner. "At the end of the day the men return in a group to the village, where the adult women form a large semicircle and sing erotically provocative songs . . . asking for their 'meat.' The men drop their catch in a large pile in the middle of the semicircle, often hurling it down with dramatic gestures and smug smiles, after which the women scramble to grab a good sized portion. After cooking the meat and eating, each woman retires with the man whom she selected as her partner for the sexual tryst."[48]

Through regularly enacted rituals where sex is used to forge bonds with multiple partners, virtually every Kulina child is guaranteed more than one father. Through ritual sex, a mother lines up extra provisions for both herself and the child while at the same time taking out insurance lest her current husband default or die. "Extra" fathers are socially recognized and expected to observe the same dietary restrictions around the time of the birth as the mother's official husband does. Nevertheless, as a matter of prudence and a courtesy to the husband, extra fathers, who have their own complex web of liaisons, are expected to be discreet.[49]

CULTURALLY PRODUCED CHIMERAS

It is vanishingly rare for any ape to produce litters or twin sets sired by different males the way lions, cheetahs, wild dogs, prairie dogs, and voles do. Over millions of years, these species have had ample opportunities to evolve uterine and ovulatory quirks that spread genetic paternity among several males, but this is not the case for apes. Thus, humans do not ordinarily produce multi-fathered twin sets, much less chimeric young who combine several male gene lines within a single individual, adding bits and pieces of extra fathers in the way cooperatively breeding marmosets do. Human twinning is unusual, and only 8 percent or so of human twins and 21 percent of triplets exhibit even low levels of chimerism; human twins with completely different fathers are exceedingly rare.[50]

As relative newcomers to the cooperative breeding scene, humans have been left to extract help from extra males by other means. Solutions to this persistent posterity problem are culturally rather than biologically transmitted. In parts of the world where one father was unlikely to suffice, lineages that invented and retained beliefs about partible paternity proved best adapted to persist and so pass on these customs to subsequent generations. People have converged upon ideological solutions functionally similar to the physiological solutions that in other cooperatively breeding animals evolved through natural selection. Without actually producing genetic chimeras, women give birth to children that men *believe* to be chimeras.

Chimeric paternity is an alien concept to Westerners. Our ideas about what it means to be a father have been shaped not only by our evolutionary history but by hundreds of years of patrilineal social history, not to mention scientific advances in the understanding of genetics. The recent "gening of America" has brought with it new markets as well as inventions, including new DNA paternity test kits.[51] Whether or not accurate information about paternity is a good idea depends on who is asking. Is it a man who feels duped? A mother who feels entitled to more support? A grown child seeking his or her identity? Or is it a growing child who needs a lot of care, regardless of who provides it?

When I consider how unprecedented actual knowledge about paternity is, and when I start to worry about how it is likely to affect the well-being of children, I am reminded of the long-ago Naskapi tribesman who was taken to task by an early Jesuit missionary in North America. Seeing the priest's dismay at the group's sexual promiscuity and uncertain paternity, the man responded: "Thou hast no sense. You French people love your own children; but we love all the children of our tribe."[52] Spoken like a true cooperative breeder.

THE MIXED MOTIVES OF MEN

All primate males are interested when they perceive that another male is having sex with a female in their group, and they exhibit various degrees of agitation. It is scarcely surprising that most Darwinians, including Darwin himself, took for granted that "our early semi-human ancestors" could not have practiced polyandry because there is no way a male could ever be "so devoid of sexual jealousy" or be willing to invest in children whose paternity he was less than certain of.[53]

There is no denying the potentially disruptive effects of infidelity or the power of nepotistic impulses. Men with the option to choose between putative genetic offspring and stepchildren are likely to spend more time with the former. Among the Hadza, their ethic of communal meat-sharing notwithstanding, Marlowe found that men with biological children in camp seemed more motivated to hunt and also more inclined to channel extra meat to children they believed they had actually sired. The one stepchild in Marlowe's sample who fared unusually well was also a nephew, the child of a deceased brother whose mother the hunter had married.[54] Marlowe's account is especially pertinent because in foraging contexts the majority of children alloparents provision are likely to be cousins, nephews, and nieces rather than unrelated children. It is also consistent with new research showing how adept both nonhuman and human primate males are at gauging possible paternity.

As is the case with many primates, savanna baboon females go out of their way to mate with multiple males. Only males who have never mated with the mother, and thus can be certain at least of their nonpaternity, are potentially infanticidal. Males who have mated with the mother, by contrast, are more likely to single out her subsequently born offspring for special protection.[55] But while male estimations of paternity are fairly good, they are never perfect. Thus, baboon infants often find themselves with more than one male protector even though (baboons not being marmosets) they only have one actual progenitor.

As they mature, young baboons continue to benefit from the support of their mother's former consorts. Among the baboons at Amboseli, Kenya—arguably the best-studied primates on earth—researchers working with Jeanne Altmann are zeroing in on some of the long-term benefits of paternal attention. In the case of daughters, the presence of their genetic father in the same troop is correlated with a faster rate of maturation. This means that a daughter with her dad nearby will begin to reproduce at an earlier age, enhancing her chances of higher overall lifetime reproductive success. Sons with a father present also mature faster, but only if their father was high-ranking at the time of their birth and presumably dominant to other males who might challenge him. The father's rank matters less in a daughter's case because even the lowest-ranking male would be dominant to all females in the troop who might harass or challenge her.[56]

No one knows yet exactly what cues are involved, but men as well as baboons are pretty good at assessing whether or not they actually sired children attributed to them. When the anthropologist Kermyt Anderson set out to analyze rates of misattributed paternity in different groups from around the world, he divided people into two categories. One contained putative fathers who felt sufficiently uncertain about paternity to demand a DNA test on their child. The other group was composed of men with no reason to doubt their paternity but who for some reason got tested. Actual rates of nonpaternity were far higher in the first group (around 30 percent) than in the second (2–3 percent).[57] Presumably, male sensibilities are as good as they are precisely because at some level paternity does matter. But this does not mean that primate males *only* nurture young whom they are sure they have sired. So long as care is neither too exclusive nor too costly, being certain of paternity is just one of several factors that affect whether or not males protect, provision, babysit, or love children.

Later in this chapter, I consider some of the other factors that affect the nurturing tendencies of males. In addition to protective responses toward infants in the group at large or targeted toward those born to recent consorts, or males' concern for "reputation" and their eagerness to display what good fathers they would be, some of the most important factors involve the male's past experience with a particular infant. A fixation with genetic paternity obscures the full range of emotions and motives that influence nurturing tendencies in men, and may also obscure their impacts on child survival. This holds true for other animals as well, as we will see in Chapter 6. Nevertheless, the unreliability and contingent nature of men's nurturing responses raises a perplexing theoretical question: How can something so potentially important vary so much? Let me address that question first, before turning to specific mechanisms involved in nurturing impulses.

THE PARADOX OF FACULTATIVE FATHERING

To put men in perspective, step back for a moment and consider paternal behavior in broad comparative perspective, across all 5,400 or so species of mammals in the world. In the majority of them, fathers do remarkably little beyond stake out territories, compete with other males, and mate with females. With outlandish auditory and visual displays which often entail specially evolved weaponry, bellowing, barking, or roaring, males engage in fierce contests to rout their competitors. Then "Slam, bam, thank you ma'am" and the inseminator is off. Male caretaking is found in only a fraction of mammals. By comparison, males in the order Primates stand out as paragons of nurturing, unusual for how much protection and even direct care of young they provide.

In the vast majority of primates, males remain year-round in the same group as females with whom they have mated. Even in species where males do not directly care for infants, males play a generalized role in the protection of young. They remain in the vicinity of the mothers, jealously protecting access to local resources (including once and future mates), and in the process males keep infants they might have sired from being attacked by rival males. Since lactation lasts a long time in primates, the incentive for would-be progenitors to eliminate infants sired by another male is enormous. By destroying unweaned infants and reducing the amount of time until the no-longer-lactating mother becomes fertile again, a newcomer can improve his chances of breeding during the limited period he is likely to have reproductive access to her. Ironically, the same prolonged dependence that makes extra help so beneficial to mothers renders infants especially vulnerable to this particularly ruthless form of male-male competition.[58]

There is almost no direct male care in apes. Orangutan and chimpanzee fathers spend little, if any, time in the vicinity of their young, while contact between gorilla and bonobo fathers and their babies is limited to just being nearby. After birth, a mother gorilla may seek out her group's protective alpha and attempt to stay close to this silverback. Once her infant is mobile, the youngster may follow his mother's example by staying near his father, as this older infant gorilla is doing, but males do not hold or carry infants, and never provision them or their mothers. (© A. H. Harcourt/AnthroPhoto)

Generalized protection of young is widespread, and in many species male attentions go beyond that to include staying near to and looking out for specific infants, the way some baboon males do, as well as more direct care (carrying, retrieving, huddling with infants to keep them warm) in perhaps as many as 40 percent of all primate species. Extensive male care seems especially likely to have evolved in prosimians and New World monkeys, and males in the genera *Aotus* and *Callicebus* actually provision their young.[59] As primates go, then, the nurturing behaviors exhibited by some men are not particularly unusual. As Great Apes go, however, direct male care is very unusual indeed.

Over the 70 million years that primates have been evolving, what mothers most needed from males was protection of their young from other males. Yet given that primate males remained year-round in the vicinity of mothers and infants anyway, there were myriad opportunities for selection to favor fathers inclined to do a bit more than just protect. This led to the evolution of male behaviors that range from occasional babysitting by baboons (who literally sit near the baby) to the nearly obligate male care (meaning that infants don't survive without it) exhibited in various titi monkeys, night monkeys, and marmosets of South America. In our own species, fathers, although often helpful, are not nearly so predictable.

While some men exhibit a marmosetlike devotion to their young and do so for a far longer time span than any other primates, other men ignore their children's very existence. Pondering this state of affairs, I have sometimes asked myself whether there might be different morphs of men. Regardless of whether or not this is so (and there is no science of the subject, nor any way I know to tell ahead of time, for readers who might be wondering), what we do know is that nurturing responses in human fathers are extremely facultative—that is, situation-dependent and expressed only under certain conditions. This generalization holds true whether we consider provisioning or the observable intimacies between father and child.

Overall, the frequency of father-child interactions is higher in the case of foraging peoples than among agricultural, pastoral, or most postindustrial societies. This tells us something important about both the history of our species and the different component parts involved in the evolution of paternal commitment.[60] Like other mammals with a lot of male care, men are physiologically altered just from spending time in intimate association with pregnant mothers and new babies. To me, this implies that care by males has been an integral part of human adaptations for a long time. Male nurturing potentials are there, encoded in the

DNA of our species. Yet unlike other mammals with extremely costly young and nearly obligate biparental care, human males may nurture young a little, a lot, or not at all. Compared with a titi monkey male, whose top priority in all the world is to remain close to any baby produced by his mate, or to a bare-faced marmoset, who vies with his mate to be the first to grab babies emerging from her birth canal so as to gobble up the hormone-rich placenta, men's priorities are nowhere near so single-minded. Mating with a man hardwired to help rear young, even young almost certainly his, is not a trait human mothers can realistically count on.

Some primates exhibit very high levels of direct male care, others do so only in emergencies, while still others exhibit no care at all. But the extent of this between-species variation pales when compared with the tremendous variation found within the single species *Homo sapiens*. Contributions of material or emotional support range from semen only to the obsessive devotion of a Mrs. Doubtfire, where a father will go to almost any lengths to remain close to his children. Across cultures and between individuals, more variation exists in the form and extent of paternal investment in humans than in all other primates combined.

It is an understatement to say that men's emotions in this respect are complex. Communal ideals and quests for local prestige are important. So is sexual access to women. Then there is the personal affection or the nepotistic urges men may feel, emotions which can trump communal values. But at the end of the day, we are still left with a perplexing paradox: If men's investment in children is so important, why hasn't natural selection produced fathers as single-minded and devoted to childcare as titi monkeys, California mice, or dwarf hamsters? And given that male care is so idiosyncratically and contingently expressed, how could natural selection have favored human mothers who invariably produced offspring beyond their means to rear alone? How can it be that some men tenderly care for children who might not even be theirs, while other fathers certain of their paternity feel no compulsion to care at all?

It's time to consider some specific cases. Even though individuals vary in how affectionate they are, most anthropologists would agree that as groups go, men among people like the Aka are unusually involved in infant care. Let's consider why.

Both Aka parents are more or less equally responsible for provisioning children, and women as well as men participate in communal net-hunting. Aka fathers spend a lot of time in camp, and they remain within eyesight of babies a whopping 88 percent of the time. This is the highest average figure for paternal proximity recorded for any human society.[61] The Aka case supports Barry Hewlett's argument that time spent in proximity is a very important factor. Proximity provides opportunities for the nurturing potentials present in many (all?) men to be activated and tapped. Men who spend a lot of leisure time in camp have more op-portunities for positive or even intimate interactions.[62] But where par-ents live, and who else is around, can also be important. Courtney Mee-han, a Washington State University anthropologist, decided to learn precisely how important.

Whether or not female primates reside among familiar matrilineal kin is an important factor influencing whether they will accept offers of childcare assistance. But among African hunter-gatherers, individuals are unusually flexible and opportunistic, often moving many times over the course of their adult lives, visiting family and gravitating toward lo-cally available resources, including not just material resources but good childcare. At any given point in time, mothers may have more or fewer matrilineal kin at hand. This was the situation among the Aka that Mee-han studied. Mothers rarely remained in the same group their whole lives. This provided Meehan with a natural experiment for comparing how much care children received depending on whether parents lived ei-ther with the mother's kin or with the father's.

An Aka husband customarily resides for a time with his wife and her family. The new husband will hunt on their behalf for a period of years (known as "bride service") until one or more children have been born. Thereafter, the couple may stay, move with their children back to his people, or in some cases join another group altogether. The practice of remaining near the wife's kin until after children are born means that inexperienced young mothers are likely to be among their own kin when they give birth for the first time, an especially vulnerable time for moth-ers and even more vulnerable for firstborns. Across primates, infants born to inexperienced, first-time mothers are at high risk of death from, among other causes, maternal inexperience and incompetence. Like all first-time primate mothers, only more so, young women need extra sup-port and guidance as they learn to mother.[63] As she expected, Meehan found that a mother residing around her own mother and her mother's kin (that is, living "matrilocally") does indeed receive a great deal more assistance.

Even with small sample sizes, differences were large enough for Meehan to identify a clear pattern. Infants whose mothers lived matrilocally received more than twice as much alloparental care as infants born to mothers living near their husband's kin ("patrilocally"). Care from older siblings was a constant for infants living in both locations. The difference was the extra help provided by an infant's maternal aunts and uncles and especially by its maternal grandmother. When interviewed, all but two Aka women specifically mentioned that they preferred living in their natal community because of the availability of kin support.

To Meehan's surprise, the total amount of care an infant received did not differ much in the two settings. This was so even though mothers themselves spent about the same amount of time holding their babies. How could this be? The question brings us back to fathers. In the absence of mother's kin, fathers compensated by caring more. Meehan found that in patrilocal settings, fathers were doing nearly 20 times more caretaking.[64] This flexibility provides the key to the paradox of facultative fathering. Care is a fungible commodity, and humans have always been unusually flexible and opportunistic not just in eliciting care but also in providing it, relocating, adjusting, juggling, and compensating in strategic ways.

Over the long span of human evolution, even if a dad defaulted, alloparents could—at least potentially—fill the yawning chasm between what children needed and what their mothers alone could provide. In some situations, death or defection of the mother's mate would doom their offspring. Undoubtedly, huge numbers succumbed. Yet if humans evolved as cooperative breeders, theirs had to be a dynamic system with built-in flexibility. If, instead of being a devoted dad, a father turned out to be only an indifferent nurturer, or even if he deserted altogether, decamping to seek alternative mates, his offspring still might pull through with help from alloparents, permitting a "cad" to enjoy his cake and reproductive fitness too. Cynical as all this sounds, there is a growing body of empirical evidence about the psychology of fathers and the behavior of alloparents consistent with such a scenario. Flexibility was, and continues to be, the hallmark of the human family.[65]

Even though Hadza fathers are typically indulgent and just as affectionate with their children as Aka fathers are, the only time they hold infants is when they are in camp, and they do so much less of the time, closer to 7 percent than to 22 percent.[66] Yet even among the Hadza, anthropologists Alyssa Crittenden and Frank Marlowe found a similar pattern to the one Meehan described for the Aka: With or without a dad present, a Hadza infant's quota of direct alloparental care remains more or less constant.[67]

Once again the explanation has to do with how flexible, opportunistic, and also mobile the Hadza are, readily moving where they are needed or where they need to be. If a father died or defected, a Hadza infant's grandmother was more likely to come to live nearby and spend more time holding her fatherless grandchildren.[68] When fathers were alive and well and living in the same camp, they accounted for a quarter of all nonmaternal caretaking, holding babies twice as often as the babies' grandmothers did. But when the father was absent, the amount of time maternal grandmothers held grandchildren increased, rising to 70 percent of the time that someone other than the mother held infants. If the mother remarried so that children were living with a stepfather, grandmothers again stepped into the breach, moving nearby. In this situation, the proportion of time infants were held by grandmothers rose to 83 percent of the total time they were held by nonmaternal caregivers.[69]

In other words, the effects of father absence are attenuated through proactive and strategic maneuvering by kin, especially by the mother's mother, as well as through the mother's own maneuvering.[70] We've already seen how mothers may strategize by lining up extra fathers even before a child is born. But mothers have other options as well. For example, when the !Kung woman Nisa lined up one too many extra fathers and her jealous husband opted for a Bushman divorce by simply leaving, Nisa trekked across the desert to join her distant brother. She remained with her child's maternal uncle while she looked for another mate willing to be a stepfather to her children.[71] Of course, having a surviving older brother willing to help her rear his nieces and nephews is not much more certain than having a husband. And as we will see in Chapter 8, the availability of a grandmother is less certain still.

The higher the mortality risks, the less either a mother or her slow-maturing children can afford to depend on any specific family composition and the more critical it becomes for children and their parents to be flexible in eliciting support. If a parent dies, it becomes more crucial than ever for collateral kin or older siblings to compensate, and evidence suggests that they often (alas, not always) do. When Patricia Draper, a child development expert, joined forces with Nancy Howell, a demographer, to study growth rates of Ju/'hoansi children using data collected when the Bushmen still lived as nomadic foragers, they found that children, though hardly well-nourished, grew at fairly constant rates regardless of fluctuations in the precise configurations of kin on hand to provision them. Draper and Howell speculated that this smoothing out of food availability was due to the sharing ethic typical of hunter-gatherers, combined with the residential flexibility of parents and alloparents.[72] By 2005 Lawrence Sugiyama and Richard Chacon documented just such a pattern among Yora forager-horticulturalists of southeastern Peru. On average, weaned juveniles spent about 40 percent of time eating in households other than their own. But in the case of juveniles with only one living parent, they were more likely to be found in households with more alloparents, presumably buffering them against parental loss.[73] In such a system, the children most at risk from paternal defection are going to be those short on alloparents.

Most hunter-gatherers live in close-knit family units. To this extent, conventional views about family life among our ancestors are correct. But the composition of these families fluctuates through time. What we idealize as the nuclear family (father, mother, and their children) was often just a temporary phase, a less-than-optimal phase at that, since by themselves two parents would have been unable to meet the needs of several children. In describing the typical or natural Pleistocene family, the descriptors I prefer are kin-based, child-centered, opportunistic, mobile, and very, very flexible. Childrearing units were inherently elastic, expanding and contracting as individuals gravitated away from adversity and toward not only food and water but locations where either they anticipated social support or had reason to expect that their support was needed by other family members. These alloparental safety nets provided the conditions in which highly variable paternal commitment could evolve.

The seeming paradox posed by Darwinian selection—favoring mothers who produced children beyond their means, paired with fathers whose help is far from guaranteed—actually represents two sides of the same coin. On either side, the paradox is resolved the same way. Mothers can overshoot their capabilities to provide, and fathers can vary, because both sexes evolved in a highly fluid system where alloparents often provided the compensatory assistance.

BIOLOGICAL UNDERPINNINGS OF DADS VS. CADS

In my book *Mother Nature* I analyzed the combination of love and ambivalence in the maternal side of the human parental equation. Here I have focused on the paternal side, on the variable devotion of fathers and on the role that cooperative breeding played in the evolution of such facultative care. It's time to consider biological mechanisms involved in determining whether a man will behave like a dad or a cad.

A January 3, 2007, news story in the *New York Times* described two men in the Bronx who rushed forward to catch a boy falling from a fourth-floor window, saving his life.[74] When the second of the two men, Pedro Nevarez, who had a 19-year-old foster son, was interviewed afterward, he modestly asserted that "I'm not a hero. I did what any other father would do. When you're a father, you would do this whether it's your child or not." Mr. Nevarez was making an important point about the relevance of experience. Thresholds vary, but men who have lived with and come to love small children are more likely to feel a reflexive urge to rescue a child, even one who does not share his genes. At the same time, there are innumerable cases where even a father confident in his paternity behaves as if he is oblivious to the well-being of his own children. The extremely variable nature of men's nurturing impulses makes it essential to consider the experiential as well as the social and ecological conditions under which paternal devotion emerges.

Take two foraging societies, the !Kung San and the Aka. Both are characterized by affectionate fathers with relatively high certainty of paternity.[75] Yet !Kung fathers engage in little direct care of infants (holding them maybe 2 percent of the time), while Aka fathers engage in ten times that much. According to Hewlett, the difference may be explained by opportunities for male-infant proximity. Whereas !Kung men go off with

In contrast to !Kung fathers, who spend relatively little time holding infants, and do so only when in camp, Aka fathers spend more time holding infants both in camp and when both parents go on hunting expeditions in the forest, as shown here. (Barry Hewlett)

other men for long periods while hunting, Aka men use nets to hunt game and go off as a group together with wives, children, and others. Aka (and also Efe) men spend a lot of time around camp and have more leisure time to interact with infants and children. Obviously, feeling more certain about paternity will be a common corollary of a husband accustomed to spending time in close proximity to his wife. But certainty about paternity, which has been such an obsessive focus for evolutionary interpretations of male behavior, is only one factor influencing men's nurturing responses to babies. Time spent in proximity with pregnant women and their infants and the act of caring for babies, in and of themselves, render men—even a man who is not the genetic father—more nurturing. Thus far (in Chapters 3 and 4) I have paid more attention to the effects of cooperative breeding on the well-being of mothers and their infants. Let's briefly consider the experiential, endocrinological, and neurological effects on males—men and boys alike.

Endocrinological transformations during pregnancy, birth, and lactation, as well as neurophysiological responses to the powerful stimuli babies emit, are far more pronounced in mothers than in fathers. But men as well as women can be physiologically altered by exposure to babies. Prolactin, a hormone commonly associated with brooding behavior in female birds and lactation in mammals, provides a case in point.[76] Prolactin levels in men residing in intimate association with pregnant women or new babies are significantly higher than those in other men. Other hormones linked to maternal sensitivity to infants, such as cortisol, also rise in fathers when they are in contact with pregnant mothers and subsequently with their newborns. On the other hand, testosterone levels fall.[77] Not surprisingly, such changes are correlated, since fathers who are more involved during pregnancy also tend to be fathers more involved in caring for the baby during the first year of life.[78] The more prior childcare experience a man has had, the longer he has been exposed to babies, and the more emotionally involved and sensitive to their needs he is, the more pronounced the physiological effects tend to be.

Some wags attribute higher prolactin levels in new fathers to sleep deprivation, a familiar stressor for new parents. Sure, sleeplessness could be a factor, but there has to be more to it. In one preliminary study, Hewlett found that just a mere 15 minutes of holding an infant could produce measurable increases in a man's circulating levels of prolactin.[79] Furthermore, such prolactin effects are more pronounced in experienced fathers holding their second-born infant against their chest than in less-experienced men, possibly because experienced fathers are presensitized. Such men also hold babies more.[80]

These correlations are most pronounced in species with biparental care, extensive shared care, or full-fledged cooperative breeding. They are found both in mammals, where of course only females lactate, and in birds, where neither sex does. Among scrub jays, pigeons, voles, marmosets, hamsters, and humans, higher prolactin levels are associated with nurturing behaviors by males. Calibrations differ by sex, of course, with levels especially high in lactating mothers. Nevertheless, the association between prolactin levels and nurturing holds across birds and mammals, both males and females, parents and nonparents, allomothers as well as mothers.[81]

In the first study of its kind, Canadians Katherine Wynne-Edwards, a zoologist, and Anne Storey, a psychologist, recruited 34 couples by requesting volunteers from prenatal classes at a hospital in Newfoundland. Couples were then visited at home and blood samples taken. Men in the study tended to have higher levels of prolactin and cortisol in the last three weeks prior to birth than was the case earlier in the pregnancy. Furthermore, stimuli from newborns produced further transformations as determined by a clever experimental design involving a second blood sample.

The first blood sample was taken shortly after the researchers arrived; the second was taken after the (probably bemused) subjects had been bombarded with the scent, sounds, and sight of newborn babies. Men were requested to hold either their own newborn or, if prepartum, a soft doll wrapped in a blanket that had recently held (and still smelled like) a newborn baby, while listening to tape recordings of a neonate crying inconsolably. Next, subjects watched a brief video of a newborn struggling to breastfeed for the first time. The men were then asked how they felt about their wife's pregnancy and about the crying baby (for example, they were asked how anxious they were to comfort it).

Strong reactions to an infant in need were disproportionately exhibited by men who experienced couvade symptoms during their partner's pregnancy. This term comes from the French *couver* (to incubate or hatch) and refers to various cultural practices whereby a man whose wife is pregnant or in labor displays physical symptoms similar to hers. Couvade symptoms range from weight gain and fatigue all the way to morning sickness and loss of appetite. Men most affected by their mates' pregnancy, as well as those most responsive to babies, had the highest prolactin levels and the most pronounced declines in testosterone.[82]

Endocrinological researchers are at pains to point out that such hormone changes, by themselves, do not necessarily cause males to behave in nurturing ways.[83] Rather, fluctuations in hormone levels—themselves influenced by particular behaviors and past personal histories—enhance male sensitivity to infant cries and other cues. This is one of the take-home messages from the work of University of Toronto psychologist Alison Fleming, who together with her colleagues has been working for years to tease apart the complex interactions between biological and social factors that influence parental responsiveness.[84]

Fleming's early work focused on mothers, but as she expanded her experimental field of vision to include fathers' responses as well, her team discovered interesting similarities—and differences. Their results show that "not only do the cries produce changes in fathers' hormones, but fathers' endocrine states prior to hearing the cries are related to how they respond to those cries. Fathers with lower baseline testosterone levels are more sympathetic and show a greater need to respond." As in mothers, hormones function in conjunction with past experiences and experiential cues to alter the chances that a male will respond in a nurturing way. When Fleming combined endocrine measures with behavioral observations of men whose past childcare histories were well known, she discovered that the more previous caretaking experience a man has had, the more pronounced the hormonal changes turned out to be.

Again, this is not to say that women and men are equivalent in their responses. Transformations in mothers are far more dramatic. Scientists have to use a completely different calibration to measure the hormonal changes in the two sexes, and rather than responding to internal cues from pregnancy and the birth process, men must depend on as-yet-unidentified sensory cues from the mother or baby. Furthermore, thresholds for responses to a fretting infant are set lower in new mothers than in new fathers.[85] All the same, it is increasingly clear that a biological potential for nurturing behaviors lies latent in some if not all men—even though it takes particular conditions and past experiences to induce the behaviors, and even though the potential is only sometimes expressed.[86]

To date, the most widely replicated hormonal effects have to do with a drop in testosterone levels reported for men living in close association with pregnant women and for men living with infants after they are born.[87] The more responsive to infants men are, the more likely their testosterone will continue to drop with continued childcare. It makes me fantasize about bottling essence of neonate to spray about the rooms of teenage boys.

OF MARMOSETS AND MEN

Earlier in this chapter we saw how Aka and Hadza men adjust levels of paternal investment in line with past experience and with the local availability of alloparents. These hunter-gatherers are anatomically and cognitively modern humans. They are fully endowed with language and have the foresight to consciously calculate the costs and consequences of their actions. By what logic, then, can I argue that smaller brained, prelinguistic hominins, with far more rudimentary technologies at their disposal and living as long as 2 million years ago, experienced similar emotions and were similarly capable of adjusting parental and alloparental effort and cooperating with one another this way? The answer, quite simply, is that all primates are social opportunists. Even those with nowhere near human levels of cognitive processing capacities, foresight, tool kits, or language are nevertheless adept at social compensation.

Consider some particularly well documented monkey examples. If a savanna baboon female loses her mother, she sets out to strengthen her relationships with her sisters; and if her sisters die, she cultivates tighter friendships with more distant kin; failing those, she turns to nonkin.[88] Cooperatively breeding primates (as well as cooperatively breeding birds and mammals outside the Primate order) appear just as flexible, or perhaps even more so, when it comes to adjusting levels of care in line with variable family composition.

As in the case of men, male marmosets paired with pregnant females experience a cascade of hormonal changes that not only induce these callitrichid males to gain weight—the marmoset version of couvade—but also lower their threshold for responding to babies and becoming more nurturing.[89] Just the scent of his infant is enough to produce a drop in the serum levels of circulating testosterone in a male marmoset.[90]

So far, surges in prolactin synonymous with male nurture have been reported only in New World monkeys such as marmosets and in men who hold and carry infants. However, declines in testosterone levels in males just spending time in close association with a pregnant or lactating female have also been reported for wild olive baboons, even though care in this species is largely confined to protectively remaining nearby and vigilant and does not usually include carrying infants.[91] In the few cases where scientists have compared hormonal changes in closely related species with and without male care, the species without male care do not exhibit these pronounced hormonal responses around the time of birth.[92]

Much of what we know about callitrichids comes from captive studies. However, the psychobiologist Karen Bales and her coworkers have also studied sources of variation in parental care among rare and highly endangered golden lion tamarins in the forests of their native Brazil. Just as in the studies of human foragers, the more alloparents in a tamarin group, the less help the father provided. That is, the total amount of care the infant received remained roughly the same, even as the father's contribution declined.[93] But when alternative caretakers were not around, fathers helped more. The nonhuman primate mothers were similarly flexible and opportunistic, responding to the local caretaking situation and also to their own condition, investing more when they were in good physical shape (as measured by body weight) and when they labored under fewer energetic constraints. Bales summed up their findings this way: Mothers invest more than the absolute minimum either when "they have to or when they can."[94]

Similarly opportunistic mothers and high- and low-investing fathers have also been described among the black tufted-ear marmosets at Jeff French's Callitrichid Research Center in Omaha.[95] With just 10 grams of gray matter—a hazelnut-size brain only 1/125th the size of an anatomically modern human one—tamarins and marmosets competently adjust parental and alloparental effort in line with their current physical condition, breeding prospects, and the availability, willingness, and competence of the assistance on hand. Cooperatively breeding nonprimate animals like meerkats are also opportunistic, helping or declining to help depending on a similar set of contingencies.[96]

Even before we begin to factor in the role of culture and conscious foresight in explaining the behaviors of parents and alloparents, we need to consider the wide range of situational, experiential, and endocrinological variables that affect individuals' unconscious as well as conscious responses to infants. The importance of hormones initially came as quite a surprise when over a quarter century ago researchers first noticed that prolactin levels went up among male marmosets carrying babies. Although these research results were initially met with skepticism, they have since been replicated many times.[97] Yet, even as evidence mounted that males experience hormonal changes when their mates give birth, it was not until 2000 that Wynne-Edwards and Storey looked for and found comparable hormonal changes in men.

There is no doubt in my mind that long-standing stereotypes about mothers who nurture and fathers who provide, stereotypes left over from the sex-contract era of anthropology, contributed to this delay. Even now when I mention hormonal changes in fathers, as I did recently to a nephew who was expecting his first child, the idea strikes many as too weird to possibly be true. "I thought prolactin was a woman's hormone!" he exclaimed. But with new evidence and new ways of thinking about human childrearing, as the "real"—and very flexible—Pleistocene family steps forward, new questions along with new answers about what children need and how they got it during humankind's long evolutionary past are emerging.

Only since the beginning of this century have scientists really begun to study the physiological underpinnings of male commitment in humans and to compare these effects with those in other animals. As this work gets under way, it is already clear that some remarkable, heretofore undreamed of similarities exist between marmosets and men. I am convinced that these parallels reveal important convergences in taxonomically quite distant primates, albeit primates who happen to share a deep evolutionary history of cooperative breeding. I also believe that this new physiological evidence underscores a conclusion arrived at some time ago by workers from social service agencies concerned about the global prevalence of deadbeat dads: There is a vast but all too often untapped potential for male nurturing out there.

6

MEET THE ALLOPARENTS

In the ants and other social insects, we are thus privileged to see not only
how complex societies have evolved independently of those of humans . . .
[but also] the forces of natural selection that formed and shaped them.

—E. O. Wilson and Bert Hölldobler (2005)

Self-conscious as we humans are, we cannot help cred-
iting our mind-reading capacities and giving impulses to another distinctively human trait, a big brain and with it greater intelligence. Animals like chimpanzees and corvids show signs of anticipating future
events and planning ahead, but not as routinely, inventively, or rationally
as humans do. None combine "forethought" with our unusually well-
developed impulses to share and cooperate. Nor does any other animal
have anything like our species' infinitely expandable language. It is taken
for granted that big brains and language account for what is most special about humans.[1]

At first glance, the claim that Pleistocene apes in the line leading directly to *Homo sapiens* were also the only apes to share care of young appears to posit a connection between big brains and enlightened child-care. Yet shared care of young along with strategic maneuverings by al-loparents are also found in primates with nothing like big brains. Tiny-brained marmosets and tamarins excel at sharing and coordinating care. Obviously brains are important. Human behavior cannot be understood without taking into account all the vast and intricate coevolutionary processes that contribute to the evolution of sapient intellects. But not every aspect of our humanness is explained by bigger brains.

We have no basis for presuming an essential connection between sa-pient brains and the ability of both kin and nonkin to coordinate need-sensitive care and to provision young. In my view, cooperative breeding came before braininess. It set the stage so that apes with longer child-hoods and greater intersubjectivity could evolve, and these traits in turn paved the way for the evolution of big-brained, anatomically modern people. Brains require care more than caring requires brains.

To underscore this point, in the present chapter I broaden my scope beyond the Primate order (composed of monkeys and apes who do by and large have big brains relative to their body size) and examine allopa-rental caretaking in species that are taxonomically more remote: wolves, wild dogs, meerkats, bee-eaters, scrub jays, cichlid fish, paper wasps, and many others. In doing so, I emphasize how nonessential a sapient or, for that matter, even a primate mentality is for the sort of situation-depen-dent decisions cooperative breeders routinely make. Strategic alloparent-ing was well within the capacities of our prehuman ancestors long before our craniums started to expand. This is my primary reason for casting the net wide enough to include nonprimate cooperative breeders. But there is also another reason.

We have no time machine to return to the Pleistocene and observe hominins with shared care going about their lives. There are no firsthand observations to inform reconstructions of how early hominin mothers became less possessive of their newborns and began to relinquish exclu-sive access, or to explain why others were willing to accept such a charge. Yet, for several decades sociobiologists have been asking questions about a range of cooperatively breeding animals, some of them living under ecological and social conditions reminiscent of the challenges that Pleis-tocene hominins also faced. These studies can help us understand the processes through which cooperative breeding evolves.

From the outset, the study of cooperative breeding, particularly theoretical efforts to explain altruism toward the young of others, was central to the field of sociobiology.[2] There is now a vast body of evidence and theory aimed at elucidating the evolution of alloparental care and provisioning in social insects, birds, and carnivores. We know far more about the behavior, ecology, and genetic relationships of these animals than will ever be the case for extinct hominins. Comparisons across cooperatively breeding animal species provide our best hope for understanding what sort of selection pressures induce individuals to help rear someone else's young rather than attempt to breed themselves. Insights thus gained can also help explain why mothers among highly social apes living in Africa two million years ago might have abandoned their long-standing practice of mother-only care.

BIRDS OF A FEATHER, AND WHY WE NEED TO CONSIDER THEM

No one was giving much thought to the evolution of cooperative breeding (the term did not even exist) back in 1935 when an article "Helpers at the Nest in Birds" first appeared in the journal *Auk*.[3] By the 1960s, primatologists were reporting on "aunting" behavior by females other than the mother in monkeys, and soon after terms like "communal care" were being used to describe co-mothering in rodents and lions.[4] Meanwhile, the evolutionary theorist William D. Hamilton was still pondering a question that had puzzled Darwin a century before: How could such seemingly altruistic behavior evolve?

With the publication in 1975 of Edward O. Wilson's *Sociobiology: The New Synthesis,* "cooperative breeder" became the umbrella term applied to any species with alloparental care and provisioning.[5] By now we know that cooperative breeding occurs in a taxonomically diverse array of arthropod, avian, and mammalian species, including some 9 percent of roughly 10,000 species of birds and at least 3 percent of all mammals.[6]

The demographic consequences come as no surprise. Cooperatively breeding birds like Florida scrub jays manage to successfully rear young in exposed habitats that would be inhospitable to other jays. With alloparents to help guard them, their nests are less vulnerable to predation. Cooperative breeding and the flexibility it permits for rearing young successfully in a wide range of habitats, including otherwise adverse ones,

Right from birth, an elephant calf is protected by his maternal aunts and grand-mother, as well as by his mother. Any of these closely related allomothers may allow the infant to nurse. Siblings and cousins too young to lactate may engage in "comfort suckling." Not surprisingly, calf survival is correlated with how many allomothers are in the family unit. (Oxford Scientific)

allowed wolves, elephants, and lions (all of which were once much more widely spread around the world than they are today), along with various species like corvids, mice, and humans (all species that remain unusually abundant and widespread today), to move out of Africa or, as in the case of many cooperatively breeding birds, Australia, migrating to almost every continent of the world.[7] Alloparental assistance means that mothers conserve energy, stay better nourished, remain safer from predation and other hazards, and survive to lead longer lives. Because mothers with help wean babies sooner, many reproduce at an accelerated pace. This means more young born over the mother's lifetime and, even more importantly, more young likely to survive.[8]

Mothers sufficiently confident of the benevolence of groupmates can entrust helpless and delectably edible offspring to their charge while they devote energy to producing more and bigger babies. With others, often including dads, to help, mothers are able to provision their youngsters, who in turn can afford the luxury of growing up slowly, building stronger bodies, better immune systems, and in some cases bigger brains without succumbing to starvation in the process. Among cooperatively breeding social carnivores—African wild dogs, gray wolves, red foxes, lions, banded mongooses, and meerkats—alloparents offer pups milk, meat, or both as well as protection. As with marmosets, alloparental provisioning—of mothers during pregnancy and of their young after parturition—permits significantly heavier litters. On average, each pup weighs proportionally more and grows faster than do pups in closely related, noncooperatively breeding carnivores.[9] Across avian as well as mammalian taxa, the number of alloparents correlates with pup survival.[10] In meerkats, Australian apostle birds, and white-winged choughs, chicks or pups do not survive without alloparental care.[11] The same "obligate" care may have applied to child survival under the high-mortality conditions that characterized foraging populations among our Pleistocene ancestors.

From Charles Darwin to Edward O. Wilson, great naturalists have been intrigued by societies with divisions of labor and levels of cooperation as extreme as those found in honeybees and humans, and have sought their evolutionary rationales. By behaving like "superorganisms," Wilson proposed, such creatures have been able to occupy their respective "pinnacles of social evolution" through better survival and preemptive exclusion of competing organisms, thereby spreading around the globe with spectacular success.[12] In an influential paper entitled "An Evolutionary Theory of the Family," the ornithologist Steve Emlen detailed finer-grained similarities between human families and cooperatively breeding birds known as African bee-eaters.

It is no accident that the language of ornithology has always been rich in anthropomorphic descriptors for the behavior of avian "husbands" and "wives." Emlen's parallels included "adultery" and "incest avoidance," problems with "stepparents," as well as Freudian-style father-son conflicts over who gets to breed, with dads chasing away their sons' prospective mates to force their sons to work for the family unit instead.[13] Yet until recently, mammal researchers studying cooperative breeding were surprisingly silent about where big-brained, bipedal human mammals fit in. When lists of cooperatively breeding mammals were drawn up, humans were rarely included.[14]

By the close of the twentieth century, however, this situation began to change. My own investigation of cooperative breeding was piqued by an interest in maternal emotions and infant needs. In 1999 I argued that unless early hominin mothers had been able to count on significant alloparental as well as paternal contributions for the care and provisioning of extremely costly, slow-maturing young, the human species simply could not have evolved.[15]

Today, comparisons with humans are increasingly cited as reasons for studying mammals with cooperative breeding. Such justifications can focus either on the highly specialized division of labor and group-level arguments offered by Wilson or on Emlen's arguments about how complex families work.[16] But whether one approaches cooperative breeding from the perspective of the "superorganism," the family's internal workings, the mother's interests, or child well-being, the same evolutionary conundrum pops up: How could natural selection favor alloparental behaviors leading individuals to care for and provision someone else's young?

THE CRITICAL IMPORTANCE OF SHARING FOOD

Part of the explanation for the evolution of alloparental care is that these behaviors are not always as self-sacrificing as they appear. In many instances, babysitting is occasional, engaged in for the most part when an animal has little else to do. Gifts of food may be proffered only when not actually needed by the donor. Over lifetimes, alloparents strategically schedule assistance so as to reduce the cost, volunteering only when helpers have energy to spare or when they are still too young or too disadvantageously situated to be able to reproduce themselves.[17] In animals where practice is critical for learning how to parent, as is the case in many primates, babysitters derive valuable experience from caring for someone else's young.[18] But what about cases where care actually is costly, as when allomothers provide hard-earned food or give up their lives altogether?

The easiest way to get bitten by a dog or other animal is to reach for its food. Yet alloparents routinely volunteer food. In many cooperative breeders, allomothers even provide breast milk, which is, metabolically speaking, the costliest substance a mammal produces. Milk is so precious that in herd-dwelling mammals like sheep or elephant seals, mothers resolutely refuse to share it—viciously butting aside orphaned or separated infants who attempt to pirate their "white gold." How odd then that an animal who had taken risks and gone to so much effort to catch or collect food, especially after converting the food into milk, would then deliver this hard-won prize to someone else's offspring. And yet humans and marmosets are far from the only creatures where allomothers not only routinely guard, defend, keep warm, groom, or carry about infants other than their own but also provision or suckle them.

Among birds, alloparental care almost always entails provisioning. Crested magpie jays who have never reproduced themselves bring back beakful after beakful of food to fledglings who flit to conspicuous perches beside their nest and beg for it. Avian helpers often provide more food than the chicks' own parents do. Some allomaternal feeding involves reciprocal arrangements, especially in mammals with co-suckling. Among cooperatively breeding mice, lions, elephants, or brown hyenas, a co-mother will allow the young of a co-resident mother (who may be her sister or mother) to join her own young at her teats, freeing each female in turn to forage and ensuring shorter gaps between snacks for pups.[19]

In the case of house mice, females able to set up nestkeeping with a sister enjoy significantly higher reproductive success than either those who choose an unrelated female or those who rear their young alone. Cooperative as this arrangement sounds, sometimes pregnant female house mice kill several of their partner's pups, with the effect of increasing the amount of milk on offer when their own young are born. Both females still gain from cooperating, but the killer benefits more, at the expense of her partner.[20] In other cases, helping is more of a one-way street. Subordinate wolf, wild dog, or meerkat females who have never (and may never) conceive sometimes undergo a "pseudopregnancy," with a swollen belly and mammary glands. Then once the alpha female's pups are born, these lactating nulliparas are used as wet nurses, secreting milk for the alpha's pups. One wild dog who had never given birth herself spontaneously began to lactate ten days after the alpha female's pups were born, and this allomother suckled them more than their own mother did.[21] It is not known why this happens, but by becoming a wet nurse the subordinate may increase her chance of being tolerated in the group. And eventually, she may have an opportunity to conceive.

Among cooperatively breeding canids, wolves, coyotes, red foxes, silver-backed jackals, Semyen foxes, Indian dholes, or—my personal fa-

In cooperatively breeding canids like these African wild dogs, adults return from hunting to regurgitate predigested meat into the mouths of eager pups. (Chris Johns/National Geographic Image Collection)

vorites—African wild dogs, allomothers (and also mothers) consume and partially digest prey, then return to the den to regurgitate this special "formula" into the eager mouths of pups. Youngsters who until then were nourished entirely on breast milk rush forward to lick the donor's muzzle. The lactating mother may be fed regurgitated meat as well.[22] Even less appetizing, but every bit as important, are the *caecotrophes* (partially digested fecal pellets) that naked mole rat alloparents excrete for nearly weaned pups. Along with the preprocessed nutrients, pups ingest endosymbiotic gut flora needed to digest cellulose in the mole rat's staple diet of fibrous underground tubers.[23]

The importance to immatures of being provisioned during this highly vulnerable weaning phase is huge, for weanlings are still too small to compete successfully for food with older group members. Across cooperatively breeding species, alloparents continue to subsidize small but rapidly growing young long after they have been fledged or weaned. The ornithologist Tom Langen was the first to systematically quantify prolonged dependence among cooperatively breeding birds. Analyzing data for 261 species of passerine birds, Langen discovered that species did not differ in how long they incubated their eggs or fed nestlings. The duration of postfledging provisioning, however, was twice as long (just over 50 days) in the cooperatively breeding species compared with species without help (20 days). Duration of postfledging dependence for only-occasionally-cooperative bird species fell neatly between these two extremes (30 days).[24]

It is not yet clear whether animals that grow up slowly are more likely to evolve cooperative breeding, or whether cooperative provisioning permits prolonged dependence and with it a longer preadult life phase.[25] Most likely it is a bit of both, since these traits could coevolve. What is apparent is that young who are protected from starvation by cooperatively breeding parents have the luxury of growing slowly and can use the extra time to master complex subsistence skills. Like children learning to make a living, the crested magpie jays that Langen studied have to learn to recognize and catch appropriate insect prey, and to identify and gather palatable berries. In other words, these beguiling jays must learn how to become hunters and gatherers in their own right.[26]

The correlation between cooperative breeding and long post-weaning dependence is not as well documented for mammals as it is for birds. Still, we know that alloparental provisioning offers valuable learning opportunities at the same time that it also subsidizes longer learning phases for immatures.[27] Young lions, wild dogs, and other social carnivores rely on game brought back by older group members to keep from starving while they gradually, awkwardly, master such arts as stalking and downing highly mobile, elusive, and often dangerous prey. The only way weaned but still inexperienced immatures survive their early bungling is through the generosity of other group members, who allow youngsters privileged access to carcasses.[28]

Among some cooperative breeders, provisioning by alloparents goes a step further. In addition to providing immatures opportunities to learn subsistence techniques for themselves, alloparents actually act as mentors. The best-documented instances of animal teaching occur among pied babblers, a species of ant, and meerkats—animals with lots of alloparental care but few brains and even less general learning. In the ant case, mentors merely reflexively guide naive nestmates to food. Meerkat alloparents actually help pups learn by preprocessing prey for them to practice with.

In response to begging calls from pups, meerkat helpers bring small prey and then remain nearby to supervise how pups handle the meal. The most striking case of monitoring involves scorpions. Even though scorpions have stingers that can deliver dangerous neurotoxins, they account for some 5 percent of the meerkat's diet. When pups are very young, helpers kill scorpions before delivering them. As pups mature, the helper delivers live scorpions but first disables them by removing their stinger. Gradually, as the pups gain experience, helpers deliver intact scorpions. Should the scorpion scamper off, the helper recaptures it and hands it back to the pup. As Cambridge University researchers Alex Thornton and Katherine McAuliffe point out, teaching in meerkats "can be based on simple mechanisms without the need for intentionality and the attribution of mental states."[29] Nevertheless, there is little question that these alloparents exhibit a powerful urge to respond to the needs of youngsters. In some species, alloparents take dedication even further: They forgo breeding careers altogether in order to help rear the young of others.

SHERMAN'S "EUSOCIAL CONTINUUM"

In eusocial (truly social) animals, alloparents routinely put survival of the group or hive ahead of their individual interests. To qualify as eusocial, organisms must meet three criteria: (1) they must live in groups with overlapping generations; (2) they must provide alloparental care; and (3) they must divide reproductive labor to such a degree that many (or even all) helpers never breed. In the most extreme cases, helpers belong to sterile castes.[30] They not only never breed, they are anatomically unequipped to do so.

In the view of the Cornell University zoologist Paul Sherman, animals with shared care can best be understood by locating them along a continuum. At one end are groups where many or most members eventually breed, and at the other end are groups where successful reproduction is concentrated—or "skewed"—to favor the ovaries of just a few females, perhaps even a single especially fecund female, as in the case of a honeybee queen. At the skewed end of the continuum, nonreproductives completely subordinate their direct reproductive interests to those of the group. Many entomologists regard eusociality as a distinct category, but here I follow Sherman, treating eusocial societies as points along a continuum with varying degrees of reproductive skew.[31]

Social insects such as ants, termites, and the more highly organized species of bees and wasps, along with a rare mammalian case, the naked mole rat, live in large colony societies with the kind of extreme reproductive skew that qualifies them as eusocial. Unlike cooperatively breeding birds, eusocial alloparents do *all* of the provisioning. Worker ants lug prey back to the hive, then gently place helpless larvae atop their food source. Or the larvae rock their heads and beckon with dancing mandibles to induce alloparents to regurgitate nutritious syrup into their waiting maws. Bee larvae are either fed directly this way or else "bottle-fed" from specially constructed overhead wax pouches filled with pollen and honey.[32]

Eusocial species with extremely skewed reproduction are distinguished from other cooperative breeders by their typically larger group sizes and their unusually strict, often lifelong, division of labor. Honeybee colonies provide a good example. The grubs that are fed a special concoction called royal jelly develop into queen bees who devote their long lives to producing most or all of the colony's young, while hard-working nonbreeders tend them. Among some eusocial insects like fire ants, workers are permanently sterile. In others, a few workers, should they live long enough or be so lucky, may get a chance to breed. But the distinguishing feature of eusocial insects is that helpers are not just biding their time or waiting out adverse conditions until they manage to breed themselves. Rather, they spend their entire lives tending and feeding the offspring of one or several superfecund females—often their own mother or sister. Untold numbers actually give their lives for the cause. Per capita death rates for workers defending or provisioning colonies in which they themselves have never bred are staggering.[33]

Such rigid division of labor goes way beyond the allomaternal dedication found in cooperatively breeding birds or mammals, with one exception. The exceptional case is the naked mole rat, the only vertebrate with a breeding caste and morphological differences between castes.[34] Efforts to resolve the puzzle of eusociality in social insects led to the development of the first rigorous theoretical explanation for the evolution of cooperative breeding, known as kin selection.

Looking more like a bad dream than a mammal, naked mole rats (*Heterocephalus glaber*), with their hairless, wrinkled hides and protruding teeth adapted for tunneling through desert hard-pan, come closer than any mammal known to the skewed reproductive success characteristic of eusocial insects. Fewer than 5 percent of mole rats ever have an opportunity to breed. Females who manage to dominate other group members and achieve breeding status undergo massive morphological changes, including lengthening of the lumbar vertebrae, permitting the "queen" (the bulgingly pregnant female above) to produce large litters. Even more remarkably, male and female mole rats who achieve breeding status develop significantly more brain cells than subordinates, especially in the hypothalamus. Differences in brain morphology between breeding and nonbreeding females are more pronounced than any differences between the sexes. (Jennifer Jarvis)

HAMILTON'S RULE EXTENDS BEYOND KIN SELECTION

Owing to peculiar asymmetries in the genetics of haplodiploid insects, full sisters in ants, bees, and wasps share three quarters of their genes by common descent, instead of the one half typical of full siblings. In 1964 this extra dollop of genetic relatedness caught the attention of the evolutionary theorist and wasp specialist William D. Hamilton. Hamilton hypothesized that a higher-than-usual degree of genetic relatedness between the queen and her sisters in species like honeybees made it especially advantageous for workers to opt out of reproducing themselves, since they could increase their genetic representation in succeeding generations indirectly by investing in their superfecund sister's young instead of directly in their own. Rather than breed oneself, why not help the queen? She not only carried the same genes by common descent, but as long as she was protected and provisioned by her kin, she could remain safely inside the hive, using her specialized anatomical equipment to pump out eggs at a rate of 5 or 6 a minute, as many as 2,500 in a day. By contrast, a solitary bee trying to breed on her own would be hard put to reproduce at all, much less produce a vast number of offspring likely to survive.

Put this way, altruistic worker bees participate in a win-win scenario benefiting all hive members. It makes perfect evolutionary sense for individuals to behave cooperatively in ways that enhance the reproductive success of relatives with whom they share such a high proportion of genes by common descent. Hamilton termed the combined effects of an animal's behavior on his or her own direct reproductive success plus the indirect effects on the fitness of close kin "inclusive fitness."

The logic behind such kin selection is summarized in a deceptively simple expression: $C < Br$. According to what has become widely known as Hamilton's rule, altruistic helping should evolve whenever the cost to the helper (designated as C) is less than the fitness benefits (B) obtained from helping another individual who is related by the value of r.

Hamilton's rule is widely accepted today. Almost all evolutionary biologists assume that without sufficiently close genetic relatedness and an appropriate ratio of benefits to costs, caretaking and other cooperative propensities that do not directly increase the helper's own reproductive success would not have evolved. By now, however, especially close degrees of relatedness between the helper and the helped such as are found in the haplodiploid social insects or, for that matter, among chimeric marmosets seem more nearly special circumstances that lower the threshold for the maintenance of high levels of cooperation through evolutionary time rather than an essential condition without which they could not persist.[35] For one thing, many eusocial creatures are neither haplodiploid nor chimeric. Termites are a case in point. They are eusocial even though workers are not necessarily super-related to the queen. Not only is close kinship less essential than was at first assumed, but "helping behaviors" themselves are not always quite as altruistic as they first appear.

Even though kinship is not essential for the persistence of cooperation, clearly it matters. The neural and physiological underpinnings for helpful behaviors first evolved in the context of mother-infant relationships and subsequently became extended to others in groups of closely related animals. Degree of relatedness often makes a difference in whether helpers help at all, as well as in how far individuals will go to help. The more alloparental assistance matters for fitness, the more likely kinship is to make a difference.[36] Studies of the nondescript brown birds called dunnocks provide one of the best-documented examples.

As with many cooperatively breeding birds (and similar to many traditional human societies), dunnocks have very flexible breeding systems. A female may breed either monandrously (with just one mate) or polyandrously (with several males), just as males may breed with either one or several females. Over the course of their lifetimes, the same individuals may mix and match these various permutations, but so far as caretaking goes, relatedness still matters. When females mate with several males, possible fathers calibrate the amount of food they bring back to chicks according to when and how often they copulated, and hence according to that male's probability of paternity.[37] Such male propensities help explain why some cooperatively breeding females who find themselves short on helpers engage in extrapair copulations with other males in their group, trading copulations for help, as has been reported for African superb starlings (and of course some humans).[38]

Whether dunnocks, brown hyenas, or Hadza foragers, it is a reasonable bet that helpers provide more food to the infants they feel more closely related to.[39] But in the early years of the Hamiltonian era, kin revelations seemed so powerful that they overshadowed other considerations. Today, with more information available, it is increasingly apparent that once the neural and physiological underpinnings for helping behavior were in place, helpers did not necessarily have to be close kin. Researchers are paying more attention to other reasons, besides genetic relatedness, that explain why helpers help in any particular situation. Male superb fairy wrens of Australia, who help rear chicks that they are only occasionally related to, provide a spectacular segue into this topic.

Tiny, wag-tailed, insectivorous birds, constantly hopping about on the ground and flitting from spot to spot, superb fairy wrens can be hard to get a good look at. Even so, it is difficult to miss the stunning flashes of blue from male feathers that catch and reflect light like the avian equivalent of iridescent blue Morpho butterflies. Superb (and they really are) fairy wrens are typically found in groups with a single breeding female assisted by one to four males—the territory owner plus younger males, often sons of the breeding female who help defend the territory as well as protect and provision her chicks. Because territories are in such short supply and a fairy wren without a territory has little chance of surviving long, females driven out of their natal groups by their mothers are compelled to take the first opening on offer, rather than holding out for the best and the brightest mate. But no matter. As it turns out, the owner of her territory only fathers a fraction of her offspring anyway.

Once DNA testing became standard issue in ornithological toolkits, researchers were stunned to discover that the vast majority (over 75 percent) of fairy wren chicks were sired by outside males. Female promiscuity notwithstanding, all care was provided by males in the mother's group. When the Australian ornithologists Michael Double and Andrew Cockburn attached tiny radio transmitters to females, they discovered that just before daylight, fertile females were flying off for quick liaisons, then returning just as quickly to the territory where their mate and other helpers remained.[40] In a paper fetchingly titled "Pre-Dawn Infidelity: Females Control Extra-Pair Mating in Superb Fairy Wrens," Double and Cockburn hypothesized that females unable to choose the male that best suited them when selecting a territory subsequently take matters into their own wings. Her partner makes the best of his cuckolded lot by helping rear her chicks anyway. After all, some unknowable fraction of her offspring is still likely to be sired by him.

Whereas males in cooperatively breeding birds like dunnocks and superb starlings discriminate between chicks, providing more food to chicks likely to be their own (based on how frequently the male copulated with the female around the time those eggs were fertilized), superb fairy wren males have not been observed to exhibit this kind of favoritism toward their own offspring.[41] So what motivates them? So far as the young male helpers go, their motives are complex, but fear is certainly one motive. Helpers who slack off will be attacked by the territory owner.[42] Given how few chances a male is likely to have to sire offspring during his lifetime, the dominant male not only helps to rear broods whose paternity he is less than certain of, he pressures subordinates to help out as well. When you think about it, the fairy wren territory holder's options are not really much different from those confronted by Bari and Ache husbands, as described in Chapter 5. Constrained by harsh conditions, unpredictable resources, and high mortality rates, they too tolerate high levels of infidelity by their mates in exchange for the chance of pulling at least a few offspring through.[43]

SITUATIONS WHERE IT IS MORE COSTLY NOT TO CARE

No question about it, kinship is integral to the origin of caregiving. But by itself, degrees of relatedness are insufficient to explain all observed cases of alloparental care. The cost/benefit components in Hamilton's famous expression play a much larger role in explaining cooperative breeding than was initially assumed. These include costs attendant on being attacked or ostracized from a group as well as the benefits of remaining in a group's territory when all other suitable habitats are filled.[44] Consistent with this "ecological-constraints hypothesis," high adult survival rates are often correlated with low rates of adult dispersal. With no new breeding opportunities open to them, nonbreeders remain in their natal group, biding their time, available to help rear a dominant breeder's young.[45]

Yet the cooperation of these cooperative breeders is not always as voluntary as it appears. On closer inspection, it turns out that quite a few seemingly utopian colonies swarming with civic-minded altruists bent on helping their kin more nearly resemble police states where dominant breeders attempt to control groupmates. A second-generation Hamiltonian entomologist, David Queller, recently summed up current thinking as follows: "A little more or less kinship can matter less than larger differences in the costs and benefits of altruism."[46]

Tie a thin filament around the wasp waist of a paper wasp queen to constrain her, as the entomologist Mary Jane West-Eberhard did, and then what happens? Once the breeding female can no longer keep wayward relatives away from empty brood cells, the workers start filling them with their own eggs.[47] Sensitive to any threat of defection, a paper wasp queen normally retaliates against any worker who slacks off grub-tending or gets too close to empty cells. Considering how few neurons they have in their brains, workers are remarkably astute at predicting just when their boss is and is not likely to punish them. When experimenters literally caused the queen to "chill" by lowering her body temperature, the workers (whose body temps were not affected) also slacked off, as if sensing that the queen would not be doing anything about it.[48]

Or consider what goes on in the subterranean tunnels occupied by naked mole rats. Among these endearingly ugly mammals, a single highly fecund breeding female mates with one to three males, who subsequently help their queen and other hivemates defend and maintain the colony. The trouble is, some workers aspire to reproduce themselves. Toward that end, they cut corners so as to conserve vital bodily reserves for the big push. This is why, as the biologist Hudson Reeve put it in the title of an article in *Nature* magazine, there has to be "queen activation of lazy workers in colonies of the eusocial naked mole-rat." Ever on the *qui vive* either for slackers or for a female who might be inclined to operationalize an ovary of her own, the queen attacks them, shoving and hissing. Remove the queen, though, and workers work less—especially the larger workers with the best breeding prospects, or workers who happen to be less closely related to the queen. As Harvard's cynical former president, Larry Summers, once noted, "Conscience is the knowledge that someone [powerful] is watching." Fear has long been an effective way to induce individuals to cooperate.

Animals with brains no bigger than a bird's, with no more neurons than a paper wasp, motivated by no more empathy than a mole rat, respond to the appropriate cues and go through the motions of being cooperative team players, even when their hearts (or stomachs) are not in it. Among Australia's white-winged choughs, helpers fly back to the nest and deliver food into the gaping mouths of begging chicks, only to snatch the food back from the chicks and gulp it down themselves when the parents are not looking.[49] The need for subterfuge underscores one of several other-than-altruistic rationales for helping. These birds are not really behaving altruistically—they just have to pay to stay, and occasionally they only pretend to pay at that. Indeed, even in the most highly "cooperative" breeders, such as eusocial insects with sterile castes, cheating is widespread if unconstrained by the policing of other hive members. Among leaf-cutting ants, for example, a few fathers sire larvae that grow larger and in other ways bias their chances in favor of growing up to be the hive's designated breeder.[50]

Some of the best-documented examples of paying rent and reaping the repercussions of cheating derive from experiments with creatures who are far from warm-hearted. Think scaly, cold-blooded fishes, creatures so insensitive that for centuries anglers (wrongly) convinced themselves that fish feel no pain when hooked in the mouth. Not only do brain scans reveal that fish do indeed register pain, but cooperatively breeding fish behave in ways consistent with the same cost/benefit calculations that can also be documented in marmosets, mole rats, meerkats, and men. As Emlen stressed from the outset, whether in birds, men, or fish, "natural selection can operate on the decision-making process itself."[51]

Allomaternal care (not including provisioning) has been reported in eight species of fish, almost all of them belonging to the Cichlidae, a highly social family characterized by extensive parental care.[52] Even though warm-blooded mammals are arguably cuddlier, more affectionate, and more interested in tactile contact, the Walt Disney story about finding Nemo, the empathetic-seeming fish with the obsessively caring dad, is actually not as far-fetched as all that. To learn why not, travel with me to the clear waters of Lake Tanganyika in east Africa, home to many species of mouth-brooding cichlids.

Neolamprologus pulcher is the species that biologists Ralph Bergmuller and Michael Taborsky selected in order to learn how breeders "decide" which helpers to tolerate and which to exile. Cichlid helpers assiduously tend broods, using their tails to fan eggs and newly hatched larvae in order to keep them parasite-free. Alloparents also housekeep by nibbling up detritus and by preventing sand from collapsing on the eggs. Some alloparents who are not even particularly close relatives of the breeders nevertheless act as guards, keeping predators away. Even when the territory-owning occupants are replaced by newcomers, helpers keep right on helping.

By staying in the group, young fish not only remain safer from predators, they continue to grow and reserve their place in line, should they survive long enough to inherit the territory and its attendant breeding opportunities. But there is a revealing twist to this tale. Once helpers reach a certain size, parents become less tolerant of their tenants, allowing them to remain only during the period in the parents' reproductive cycle when help is actually needed. Furthermore, if workers slack off (as when Bergmuller and Taborsky experimentally interfered with their performance), territory owners cease to tolerate them altogether and drive the slackers off.[53]

Nor should we overlook the misfortunes that await subordinates who do manage to breed. In the most ambitious long-term field study ever undertaken of a cooperatively breeding mammal, Tim Clutton-Brock and his team from Cambridge University have monitored a population of nearly 200 meerkats (Suricata suricatta) living in 13 groups in the Northern Cape of South Africa, including several groups recently elevated to stardom in the Meerkat Manor television series. Even though social mongooses live in groups of 3–50 individuals, a single dominant female usually accounts for about 80 percent of the pups produced. The soap opera could just as well have been called Meerkat Dynasty.

Once promoted to top female, a meerkat undergoes a remarkable estrogen- and progesterone-linked growth spurt. She literally grows into her new role. Like a newly elevated naked mole rat alpha, who undergoes a lengthening of her torso and a marked increase in brain cells, the meerkat alpha gains 6 percent of her body weight and develops a swollen head (expanding by 3 percent).[54] Thus buffed up, she is ready for her new job as breeder in residence. She will produce litters of 3–8 pups as often as four times a year. The bigger she is, the more pups she produces. Should any of the smaller, subordinate females in the group (usually her own daughters) manage to mate and conceive, she will drive out the wayward breeder, especially if she is pregnant herself. Even if the reigning alpha allows a pregnant subordinate to remain (perhaps because help is short at the time), she will likely kill and cannibalize her pups rather than share allomaternal assistance.[55] But there is an intriguing meerkat tit-for-tat. Given the opportunity, pregnant daughters have also been known to kill their mother's pups.

GOOD HELP IS HARD TO FIND

Only a dozen or so meerkat infanticides have actually occurred above ground and been witnessed by researchers. Hence, it is impossible to precisely quantify how many pups are lost in these unseemly family squabbles over who gets to use the babysitters. But it's a lot. If even a single killing is observed above ground, the rest of the litter (left underground) is never seen again. Tim Clutton-Brock along with his coworker Andrew Young now believe that such infanticides are a main cause of litter failure. On 13 of 16 occasions when dominant females lost litters, there was a pregnant subordinate still in the group at the time with both opportunity and motive. It is probably in order to preclude such lethal and literal "aunting to death" that dominant females preemptively expel daughters who become pregnant.[56] Thus does a meerkat *mater familias* enhance the survival chances of her forthcoming litter by condemning her grandoffspring to an untimely death.

Kin they may be, but meerkat alphas are decidedly less than kind. Nor are alpha meerkats the only cooperative breeders prone to kill their subordinates' progeny. Wild dogs, dingos, and brown hyenas, as well as marmosets, exhibit similarly lethal proclivities, especially when the alphas are in the final stages of pregnancy or have new pups themselves.[57] Infant death may be a direct result of wounds inflicted by the dominant female, or it may come about from neglect when a dominant female prevents the subordinate mother from nursing or otherwise caring for her offspring. Among African wild dogs, an infanticidal alpha has even been known to leave one or more of the offender's pups alive so she will continue to produce milk that the alpha female's larger pups can use, exploiting the subordinate female like a wet nurse.[58]

The all-too-real threat of infanticide explains why many subordinates opt to forgo conceiving. From marmosets to mongooses, subordinate females respond to domination by suppressing their own ovulation rather than waste resources on a doomed gamble. Suppressed reproduction was such a striking part of family life among marmosets, meerkats, wolves, and wild dogs that many mammalogists initially considered it an essential attribute of cooperative breeding and made it part of the definition.[59] However, it now seems clear that interference by dominants that leads subordinates to suppress their own reproduction is just one of several possible tactics by which some mothers ensure care for their own offspring. Eliminating the offspring of subordinates, extracting help from kin, tolerating outsiders in the group, punishing slackers, or (as we will see in Chapter 8) evolving females with long postreproductive lifespans so that postmenopausal grandmothers and great-aunts will be on hand are all just different routes to the same end: ensuring advantageous ratios of helpers to infants. When help is really in short supply, some cooperative breeders even set out to recruit or kidnap caretakers from other groups.

A pair of white-winged choughs that attempts to breed without having sufficient help is doomed to fail. This is probably why, when group size falls below the set point for success, group members (sometimes the helpers rather than the breeding pair) may raid a smaller neighboring group and kidnap recently fledged young. Over a period of days, the neighbors will be attacked and harassed, sometimes resulting in destruction of some of their eggs. Then, with the weaker group's adults diverted by defensive skirmishes, some of the attackers herd young choughs back to their own territory. The kidnappers provision the stolen fledglings until they complete maturation, at which point these foster children help rear chicks in their new group (their alternatives at this point being too limited to do otherwise).[60]

BENEFITS OF GROUP MEMBERSHIP

This brief survey of cooperative breeding animals leaves little doubt that alloparental care need not always be directed toward close kin. Even for nonrelatives kidnapped or fostered in from smaller or weaker groups, remaining as a second-class citizen can be preferable to life as a vulnerable vagrant. Plus, there is always the chance that local opportunities will open up. Some helpers take advantage of their situation to advertise their particular merits. In other words, many alloparents are helping because they lack better options or because they seek to avoid punishment or, worse still, they dread ostracism from the group. For social animals, living outside a group, even during temporary migrations, represents an unusually dangerous condition. Alloparents have many excellent reasons for staying put, rather than simply decamping to seek less oppressive company.

There are also good reasons for remaining in a familiar and demonstrably habitable place, where one has an inside track on local resources and escape routes. The benefits of remaining in one's birthplace (philopatry) are augmented still further when local habitats are saturated, and suitable places to live and breed are in short supply, or when access to local resources are worth preserving and being passed down through the generations.⁶¹ Acorn woodpeckers, found throughout the oak woodlands of California, provide the best-studied example, apart from our own species, of how philopatry and family togetherness can be motivated by inheritance prospects from accumulated resources.

As I write, one of these handsome red-crowned woodpeckers is laboriously drilling a hole in an oak tree outside my window. Acorn woodpeckers will drill line after line of these carefully spaced holes, then stuff each hole with a single gathered acorn that is pressed tightly in place to prevent squirrels and other marauders from prying them loose. These stashed meals serve as emergency rations to tide the woodpeckers over when food is scarce. In a big colony, these labor-intensive granaries may contain tens of thousands of acorns that will be passed down from generation to generation as insurance against highly seasonal and unpredictable food supplies.⁶²

Besides having access to physical resources, animals have access to social resources in their natal group, since kin are typically more supportive than strangers. Networks of kin are a big reason why animals who can afford to do so stay home. For a maturing son, philopatry means access to his father and brothers, the males likely to make the most reliable allies. The downside of philopatry is that females eager to avoid breeding with a male familiar from birth will refuse to mate with him, putting a stay-at-home male at a disadvantage. Female preferences for novel or unfamiliar males—a defense against inbreeding—is a big reason why in many species, including the majority of primates, males take the risk of migrating while the females remain behind, joined by males from outside their natal group.

For females, the greatest benefit of philopatry is that matrilineal kin will be on hand. This is especially important for a primate at the time of her first birth, when an inexperienced young female is especially in need of social support and has so much to learn in order to be a competent mother and pull her especially vulnerable firstborn infant through.⁶³ For relatively long-lived mammals like whales or elephants, and also some primates, nearby matrilineal kin pass along knowledge about local resources and childrearing to the next generation.⁶⁴ Yet the long-lived Great Apes are exceptions to the widespread mammalian pattern of female philopatry. As in many bird species, by and large it is males rather than females who remain in their natal place. Typically, Great Ape females push off as they approach breeding age, though important exceptions are known where particularly dominant or well-connected chimpanzee females managed to stay (discussed in Chapter 8).

As we return to primates, two points need to be kept in mind. For almost all members of this order it is extremely important to live in a viable group, and other things being equal it is advantageous for a mother to be in a group that contains close kin. Nowhere has this principle been more clearly demonstrated than among the well-studied savanna baboons at Amboseli. Analysis of the long-term behavioral, demographic, and genetic data from this population reveals that the more socially integrated a female is and the more social contacts she is able to maintain, the more likely her young are to survive. And what better way to be integrated than to grow up among close kin.[65] Never easy to precisely measure, the cost/benefit components in Hamilton's rule are nevertheless omnipresent. Relatedness is not the whole story, but almost invariably kinship plays some role in biasing the ratio toward helpfulness.

Once the practice of helping immatures gets started, the benefits of direct and indirect reproductive fitness can keep cooperative breeding going, especially in situations where costs are imposed on group members for *not* helping.[66] But how does alloparental care get started in the first place? This question requires us to consider both ecological factors, such as those promoting philopatry, low turnover in group membership, and long lifespans, and factors having to do with behavior that shapes the architecture of animal brains through deep evolutionary time. Let's begin with some ecological factors.

ECOLOGICAL FACTORS IN THE EVOLUTION OF COOPERATIVE BREEDING

When ornithologists surveyed the avian lineages where cooperative breeding has independently evolved or re-evolved, three sets of conditions stood out as important. First, birds who took a long time to mature and were likely to live a long time—that is, who had relatively slow life histories—were predisposed to evolve cooperative breeding. Second, cooperative breeding tends to be found in lineages that evolved under ecological conditions favoring year-round occupation of the same area.[67]

This is because in more seasonal climates, youngsters who did not disperse early or migrate someplace else to spend the winter would starve. Year-round occupation in the same locale is important and helps explain why so many of the avian taxa most prone to evolve cooperative breeding originated in Africa, Australia, and other regions in the southern hemisphere.[68] For example, in Afrotropical regions, the proportion of avian species with cooperative breeding rises to 15 percent, higher than the proportion of cooperative breeding (9 percent) for birds worldwide.[69] As it happens, many of the best-studied examples of cooperative breeding belong to the Australian-derived family Corvidae.

Cooperative breeders of Australian origin include scrub jays, magpie jays, and other corvids such as jackdaws, famous for their eagerness to proffer food to individuals other than their own offspring, including nonrelatives. Corvid species not only seem preadapted to evolve cooperative breeding, they are also unusually adept at manipulating their environments in inventive ways.[70] Their unparalleled problem-solving abilities along with their ingenuity in making and using simple tools (the star of this show being the tool-making New Caledonian crow) once led the cognitive psychologist Nathan Emery to ask provocatively if corvids should be considered "feathered apes." It leads me to inquire whether there is some interaction between a deep history of cooperative breeding and offspring that grow up to be especially good at learning from others and manipulating their physical as well as social environments.

The third factor conducive to the evolution of cooperative breeding has to do with special environmental challenges such as unpredictable rainfall or fluctuating food availability, which would make it especially hard to stay fed or keep young provisioned.[71] Even among creatures that remain year-round in the same locale, seasonal shortages and harsh conditions may make some local resources especially worth defending, as is the case with stashes of acorns stored by woodpeckers. When such resources are passed on between generations, it adds extra value to philopatry.

In spite of their nomadic lifestyles, hunter-gatherers often transmit customary rights to certain hunting areas and especially waterholes from generation to generation.[72] Heritable resources, even when routinely shared with others, are still worth defending and add value to philopatry, as well as helping to maintain a viable group size. Other ecological factors conducive to the evolution of cooperative breeding that would also have pertained in the case of Pleistocene hominins include their year-round occupation of foraging areas in tropical Africa during a period when increasingly unpredictable rainfall meant significant fluctuations in food resources. All these factors would have made philopatry, extra providers, and alloparental assistance especially attractive.

But even if early hominins encountered ecological conditions conducive to cooperative breeding, at a behavioral level what happened? What was the probable sequence of events through which apes who had not previously shared care and provisioning of young evolved cooperative breeding? In the case of still-extant cooperative breeders, we not only know a great deal about the phylogeny of different groups, but the consequences of individual behaviors can still be observed and measured, so that once again, birds of a feather provide useful models for comparison.

BEHAVIORAL FACTORS IN THE EVOLUTION OF COOPERATIVE BREEDING

The most persuasive explanation to date for the behavioral origins of cooperative breeding is known as the misplaced-parental-care hypothesis. Two ornithologists, David Ligon and Brent Burt, proposed this two-step process. Start with a species that bears particularly helpless and slow-maturing young, a species with a deep history of parental care requiring parents to be sensitive to cues emanating from these needy immatures. According to Ligon and Burt, a legacy of intense parental care in lineages with helpless young would predispose members of that species who remained in their natal groups to engage in alloparental care—provided that nonbreeders enjoy sufficient proximity to begging young.[73]

Their hypothesis is consistent with the recent finding that cooperative breeding is nearly three times more likely to evolve in taxa that produce altricial (helpless) versus precocial (soon able to survive on their own) chicks.[74] As Ligon and Burt put it, "The genetic basis for helping behavior is much older than previously appreciated . . . Helping behavior had its origins as a simple by-product of misplaced parental care associated with delayed dispersal or colonial living in lineages with altricial young."[75]

The best-studied cases of misplaced parental care involve brood parasitism in birds, a type of nurturing by alloparents that is unlikely to be adaptive for the duped. In most such cases, insufficiently discriminating responses of parents toward eggs (and eventually chicks) deposited in a nest by members of another species divert resources away from the nest-owners' own young to young left by the brood parasite, often with disastrous consequences for the alloparents' own reproductive success. Reed warblers duped by common cuckoos who lay eggs in their nests are essentially making an alloparental mistake. Once the alien hatches, a strapping cuckoo chick uses its body to heave its hosts' own eggs up and out of the nest. With the nest all to himself, the unrelated chick then clamors to be fed with loud calls and a vivid, yawning yellow gape sufficient to mimic a whole clutch of its hosts' own young. Duped parents find the urge to respond to this super-stimulus and satisfy this request irresistible. They respond so diligently, and for so long, that the imposter may grow to eight times the size of his hosts.[76]

Over many generations, species subject to recurrent parasitization eventually adapt. For example, selection may favor more discriminating parents or else parents who abandon their nest as soon as they detect intrusions. But these are only the parasitized species that have survived to the present day. More often than we realize, I suspect that alloparental carelessness led to extinction.

Based only on creatures that persisted long enough to be observed, the ultimate Darwin Award for maladaptive nurture goes to mouth-brooding cichlids. These mothers sequester their eggs inside their own mouths to keep them out of someone else's. They are so eager to get all their eggs safely stashed that in the process they sometimes ingest the eggs of a local parasitic catfish. Catfish scoot in just behind the male cichlid as he fertilizes the female's eggs and deposit their fertilized eggs right beside the cichlid caviar, where they too get gulped into the mom's mouth. Once again, natural selection has set the bar low. Even if protection gets indiscriminately extended to the young of another, this outcome is usually a better option than condemning one's eggs to immediate predation.

Unfortunately, in this instance the much smaller eggs of the parasitic catfish quickly exhaust the nutrients stored in their own yolk sacs. Maturing posthaste, tiny, voracious changelings hatch and then bite into

Birds have a hardwired feeding response. It is not uncommon to see one species feeding another—something that nest parasites like cuckoos have evolved to take advantage of. Begging behavior by altricial chicks can trigger feeding behavior even in species that do not normally exhibit alloparental care, regardless of species—provided that the relevant cues are broadcast, as in this famous image of a cardinal responding to the open mouth of a goldfish from Welty and Baptista's classic text, *The Life of Birds*. (Paul Lemmons)

the yolk sacs of the other eggs in their nursery, digesting them and continuing to grow bigger and bigger until the catfish fry are able to swallow whole their mouth-brooding host's entire wriggling clutch. Having eaten all their mouthmates, the predators signal their foster mother to let them out. Off they go to feed, returning to the cichlid mother's hospitably open mouth when danger threatens—houseguests from hell. Whereas birds in populations chronically subjected to parasitism by cuckoos may eventually be selected to discriminate their own eggs from imposters, poor mother cichlids appear not to do so. How could they? So heavy is the predation pressure in Lake Tanganyika that a moment's hesitation in the mouth-brooder's uptake means her eggs would be eaten anyway.

The misplaced-parental-care hypothesis assumes that ancient potentials for nurturing young were present in both males and females, along with opportunities for selection to favor responses to young that promoted caretaking—even in nonparents. This is one reason philopatry is so important to the evolution of cooperative breeding—because social and ecological conditions promoting repeated exposure to young are needed to activate the relevant behaviors. The reason food sharing is crucial is because it means that infants can remain dependent without imposing an overwhelming burden on their mothers. The precise formula for helping varies from species to species, but over time the availability of alloparental care sets the parameters for what a mother herself needs to provide. Among cooperatively breeding birds like superb fairy wrens, the more help a mother has, the less she has to provide herself. This means the mother can afford to lay smaller eggs with fewer nutrients—the avian equivalent of early weaning.[77] In other situations (as with marmosets), good help means the mother can produce larger, more, or more closely spaced young.

The misplaced-parental-care hypothesis looks promising at a theoretical level and is consistent with much natural history. But at a mechanistic level, in terms of the genes involved, can evolution actually work like that? New evidence from the comparative genomics of eusocial insects is gratifyingly consistent with this hypothesized link between maternal behavior and the evolution of shared care. A team in the Department of Entomology and the Institute for Genomic Biology at the University of Illinois has taken the first steps toward understanding the underlying processes at a molecular level.

The entomologists analyzed the genomes from different individuals belonging to a primitively eusocial paper wasp (*Polistes metricus*). Early in the colony-building process, before the queen has daughters around to help her provision her larvae, she does it all, both producing and provisioning her own broods. Later in the course of colony development, once she has allomaternal assistance, the queen quits provisioning and devotes all her energy to egg production. When the researchers examined the genomes of the lone nest-founding queens as well as the daughter-workers, they found that gene expression in foundresses who still combine brood production and brood-tending is very similar to gene expression in workers. But once foundresses get a working colony established and cease to provision their broods, gene expression in these breeders becomes significantly different from that of the workers.[78] These differences need not involve novel mutations. Rather, selection can operate on the molecular regulators in DNA that determine when, in the course of development, a gene for a particular trait will be expressed, or under what circumstances. In the case of established queens, genetic instructions for the provisioning trait are simply skipped over and are no longer expressed.

That genes for brood production, nurturing, and provisioning behaviors could be expressed either together (as in the case of the solitary foundresses) or separately (as in the case of queens and workers who divide these tasks between them) illustrates the importance of flexibility in gene expression over the course of an organism's development in a particular environment—the importance, in other words, of phenotypic flexibility. Even without novel mutations, genes that are expressed differently over the course of development produce novel phenotypes on which natural selection can act. This is what Mary Jane West-Eberhard terms "the dynamic role of development in the production of selectable variation"—a central concept for the argument developed in this book about the cognitive and emotional implications of cooperative breeding.

Five years before these molecular genetic findings, West-Eberhard's interest in the role of phenotypic flexibility had led her to anticipate the role trait loss was likely to play in the evolution of alloparental care and eusocial breeding systems.[79] As she put it, "Brood care by worker females that have not themselves laid eggs may be stimulated out of sequence when a subordinate female encounters a hungry larva, even though it is not her own offspring, thus causing her to skip ahead in the normal reproductive cycle, deleting the oviposition phase. If such behavior happens to be advantageous (e.g., when the hungry larvae are genetic relatives), selection may favor maintaining such altered behavioral sequences in the new context."[80] Provided that caretaking enhanced the fitness of nonmothers, such a scenario would explain how allomaternal provisioning could get started and continue to be selected.

DO HUMANS HAVE ANY EQUIVALENTS TO STERILE CASTES?

Alpha female meerkats, marmosets, and wild dogs forge vicious contracts with subordinates, sometimes including their own daughters: "Breed now and I will kill your progeny, but if you help rear my young, perhaps even lactating to feed them, I will tolerate you, and you just might get a chance to breed one day yourself." Readers who have come this far may sense a disconnect between hunter-gatherers and other co-operative breeders with their high levels of reproductive skew and the all-out, even murderous, competition between mothers seeking to monopolize resources for their own young. Nothing in the ethnographic literature for hunters and gatherers suggests that a single dominant woman monopolizes breeding opportunities or that reproduction among subordinates is suppressed. Nor among African foragers do we find infanticidal co-mothers. Is this due to some bias in the way anthropologists view their subject? Or is there a real difference between human and the many nonhuman cooperative breeders?

The recognition that humans must have evolved as cooperative breeders is relatively new, and to date most research has focused on the benefits of alloparents. Far less attention has been paid to ways in which allomothers might compete with or interfere with mothers.[81] I suspect there is much more to learn about competition between mothers for resources, as well as between their children, not to mention competition between the alloparents, yet I do not think we should ignore the assessment of generations of ethnographers. Furthermore, even if some lacunae in the ethnographic record on competition between mothers and cheating by alloparents are due to observational bias, we still have to explain why self-serving behaviors are so subtle as to confound trained observers.

Virtually all African peoples who were living by gathering and hunting when first encountered by Europeans stand out for how hard they strive to maintain the egalitarian character of their groups, employing sanctions against bullies, braggarts, or those deemed stingy, consciously keeping social stratification and extreme skews in access to resources or in reproduction to a minimum. Men are socialized to suppress more chimpanzeelike domineering tendencies, and women may be as well. Both in their lifestyle and in their genetic histories, these south African !Kung, east African Hadza, and central African foragers provide the best available windows we are ever likely to have into the social lives of our ancestors.

Among people living in small foraging bands, it is not uncommon for a woman to allow another woman's baby to nurse at her breast. Such suckling appears to be carried out on a voluntary, sometimes reciprocal, basis. Other forms of shared care also appear voluntary, but when the young anthropologist Adam Boyette recently interviewed Aka children, asking them what would happen should they refuse to care for their younger siblings, nieces, nephews, or cousins, 57 percent answered that their mother might refuse them food; 30 percent mentioned "hitting"; 23 percent, insults. In fact, Boyette never actually saw any evidence of mothers punishing children by withholding food or hitting them (which is very rare among hunter-gatherers). The point is, children felt social pressure to help. When asked who taught them this, most replied that it was their mother. Not all children dragooned into helping are close kin. Another young anthropologist, Alyssa Crittenden, described a Hadza mother tying a sling with her infant in it onto a "protesting unrelated girl." Reprimanding the babysitter, the mother then walked away, leaving the girl with little choice but to care for the child or risk further, even more general, disapproval. Oppressive expectations for help may also be placed on an orphan or distant relative fostered in from another group.[82]

When I specifically asked Paula Ivey Henry, who worked among the patrilocal Efe, why there was so little competition among women, she replied that she had wondered the same thing. Do women new to the group compete for scarce and difficult-to-find resources? Jostle for place at fruiting trees or wild tuber patches? What happens when a woman does less work in communal fish-trapping ventures but still claims her share? When women go off to forage, she told me, "there is an interesting hierarchy in the way women position themselves at a food patch . . . The more established women in the group often gain more advantaged access. They were also able to send their children (multiple is better!) up through the limbs of trees to gather more." When resources were scarce, there might be competition, but most plant foods were there for the taking by those willing to gather or extract them, and (for reasons explained in Chapters 8 and 9) there were almost always plenty of babysitters to go around.[83]

To find reports even remotely comparable to the coercion and reproductive exploitation found in cooperatively breeding animals with high levels of reproductive skew, we must leave hunter-gatherers behind and turn to archaeological and especially written records from more settled and more stratified human societies. As far as is known, such social systems emerged relatively late in the history of our remarkably young species, within the past 10,000 years. Only in much larger scale societies, with people living at higher population densities with more pressure on resources, and in particular with opportunities for some individuals to monopolize resources, do we find stratified societies like those of ancient China, Japan, the Near East, early Hawaii, Africa, or medieval and early modern Europe.[84] Such societies provide plenty of meerkat-worthy instances of subordinate allomothers recruited to rear the young of the powerful.

From classical times in ancient Rome and throughout much of medieval Europe, reaching a peak in seventeenth- and eighteenth-century France, Italy, Spain, and Russia, hundreds of thousands of socially more advantaged and more powerful women relied on coerced assistance from enslaved, indentured, or poorly paid wet nurses and nursemaids to maintain their extremely high fertility levels. Having their babies suckled by other women enabled elite women to breed at almost yearly intervals, at least for a time, without jeopardizing the survival chances of their young. By contrast, the wet nurse's own baby, denied her breast milk, suffered a high probability of dying, at the same time that the wet nurse's own subsequent ovulations were suppressed by prolonged lactation. Wet nurses who suckled successive charges year after year might go on producing milk for decades, effectively transforming them into a sterile caste. If the authors of the Code of Hammurabi in 1700 BCE deemed it necessary to outlaw the substitution by a wet nurse of one baby (her own perhaps) for one of her charges, it is probably because cheating by alloparents was a problem.[85]

Despite eerily convergent parallels between coerced human wet-nursing and the coerced wet nurses found in canids, meerkats, and other cooperative breeders, or the sterile castes typical of eusocial breeders, such cases represent derived post-Neolithic cultural (and perhaps also biological) adaptations subsequent to the time when our ancestors lived in small-scale hunting and gathering groups. As far as the origins of emotionally modern humans go, these cases are after the fact. Taking into account the ecological and demographic realities of foragers' lives, it seems unlikely that such heavily skewed reproduction, with dominant females forcing subordinates to spend their lives helping rather than breeding themselves, could have been universal or species-typical when cooperative breeding first got started.

In spite of recent human history that amply testifies to a species capable of ruthless exploitation of others by those powerful enough to get away with it, there is no evidence that humans evolved sterile castes per se. Rather, nursemaids became anovulatory because they were forced to continuously lactate, while eunuchs—ideal tenders for a powerful ruler's harem—were rendered sterile by surgical castration. Neither method is a physiological adaptation comparable to the sterile castes that evolved in social insects. Women who ovulate but fail to conceive do not spontaneously undergo pseudopregnancies and lactate so as to suckle young born to a more dominant female the way canids do. Still, there are respects in which Mother Nature equipped our species with what, in terms of cooperative breeding, is an ergonomically convenient life history, characterized by long prereproductive and postreproductive life phases among women (before menarche and after menopause). These peculiarities of the human species effectively increase the ratio of caretakers to youngsters needing care.

A few evolutionary biologists have speculated that postmenopausal females might be the human equivalent of sterile castes, manifestations of reproductive suppression by other means. Indeed, Kevin Foster and L. W. Ratnieks have gone so far as to propose that, like naked mole rats, humans should be considered *eusocial* mammals because they evolved to rely on alloparental care, live in multigenerational societies, and have a specialized class of sterile helpers in the form of postmenopausal women. Pushing this proposal further, British biologists Michael Cant and Rufus Johnstone have hypothesized that early cessation of reproduction in women may reflect "the ghost of reproductive competition past," and that early cessation of ovulation in women evolved to "reduce the degree of reproductive overlap between generations" and "give younger females a decisive advantage in reproductive conflict with older females."[86]

However, to me, this sequence seems out of order. Females cease to reproduce with age in other primates as well—that is, ovaries that peter out are a preexisting condition. What is different about humans is their longer lifespan afterward. I will come back in Chapter 9 to this idea of derived traits like longer lifespans which represent evolutionary elaborations on preexisting conditions such as cooperative breeding. But first we need to consider the attributes that make primates so susceptible to misdirected maternal care and prone to the evolution of shared care in the first place.

After all, the majority of primates exhibit some form of biparental or alloparental care. No wonder then that some 20 percent of primates have evolved shared provisioning as well as shared care, nearly twice the proportion of cooperative breeders as are found among birds. With their highly social natures and costly young, primates as an order are wide open to the evolution of cooperative breeding. With this in mind, it is time to consider specific traits that made primates so susceptible to shared care, and then consider what had to change in a particular line of apes to make shared care—widely present in primates generally, but virtually nonexistent among apes—such a feasible and attractive option for mothers in the line leading to the genus *Homo*.

7

BABIES AS SENSORY TRAPS

What natural selection cannot do, is to modify the structure of one
species, without giving it any advantage, for the good of another species;
and though statements to this effect may be found in works of natural
history, I cannot find one case which will bear investigation.

—Charles Darwin (1859)

Charles Darwin was convinced that if an animal ever
did something purely for the benefit of another species it would annihi-
late his entire theory. Yet in a seeming contradiction to all that is Darwinian, many birds and mammals are surprisingly susceptible to the
charms not only of babies that are no kin to them but even babies belonging to a different species altogether. Not long ago, in an incident
reminiscent of the legendary lion who befriended Androcles, a real-life
lioness in north central Kenya nicknamed Kamuniak adopted rather
than ate first one, then another, and another—five in all—baby antelopes.
One fawn, alas, the lioness did eventually eat. However, the other four

were tenderly nurtured by the indiscriminately mothering lioness until they died of starvation or else were finally retrieved by desperate oryx mothers. That lioness "must have a mental aberration," opined a perplexed UNESCO official back in Nairobi.[1]

Around that time, another story appeared about a mother leopard who killed a baboon, then discovered a baby clinging to her prey. "The little baboon called out," explained the nature cinematographer who had been filming the scene, "and we thought we were going to hear a major crunch and the leopard smacking her lips, but instead, the baby baboon put its paws out and walked towards the leopard . . . [who] gently picked it up in her mouth, holding it by the scruff of its neck and carrying the infant up a tree." Its foster mother guarded the baby overnight, but by next morning the infant had succumbed, presumably to starvation. Yet, it was still being protected by the leopard. "It's as if nature was turned on its head completely," marveled the filmmaker.[2]

No doubt the filmmaker was aware of instances when a mammal, say a male mouse, encounters an infant and either ignores it or eats it. But in fact, responding to cues from someone else's baby is not all that rare. What was unusual in Kamuniak's case was that the beneficiaries of misplaced maternal largesse would ordinarily have been lunch. Indiscriminate mothering has been reported now for a broad assortment of creatures. Animals such as primates, canids, or felines that have shared care in their lineages appear to be especially susceptible. Even mothers with infants of their own may sometimes take up an additional baby, but usually not for long or at the expense of care to their own young.

Hyper-nurturing barnyard hens may indiscriminately gather nearby chicks beneath the brood-patch on their breast to keep them warm. Beneficiaries of their broodiness include baby geese, ducks, or even kittens if they happen to be nearby. My neighbor's female Jack Russell terrier once underwent a pseudopregnancy, chased away a mother cat, and spontaneously began to produce milk to suckle her foundling kittens, which she reared to maturity. The Associated Press recently ran a story about a mother cat returning this canine favor by adopting a newborn Rottweiler.[3] Far down the Great Chain of Being, about a quarter of the fry in broods of some cichlid fish are fostered in from other broods.[4] As long as they happen to be the right shape and size, "eggs" eliciting protection need not even actually be eggs. Mothers in those earwig species that ex-

Kamuniak, whose name means "blessed one" in the language of the local Samburu pastoralists, is shown here with one of her wobbly-legged adoptees. (Reuters)

hibit maternal care can be tricked into protecting balls of wax provided they are the same size as their eggs.[5] Birds can be just as suggestible. The cardinal shown in Chapter 6 just could not resist the impulse to deposit food in the gaping mouth of that goldfish. Throughout the Animal Kingdom, and most especially in species that produce immobile, utterly helpless babies that need a lot of maternal care (the way baby primates do), infants exude potent signals, captivating the susceptible. Related or not, infants can be powerful sensory traps.

How to reconcile such susceptibilities with Darwinian logic? Rather than disproving the theory, indiscriminate mothering more nearly illustrates the little exceptions that confirm Darwin's big rule. Through evolutionary time, these mistaken recipients of care were likely to be related. Foster mothers had more to lose, genetically speaking, by *not* responding than by over-responding. Thus does the bar for responding get set quite low—so low that parental care is occasionally diverted to someone else's young. But this logic pertains only as long as the risk of misplaced parental care has not been *too* common over the past evolutionary history of that organism. If risks of misplaced care are substantial, as is the case in herd animals with highly mobile young prone to wander over and latch onto some unrelated mother's teat, preventive safeguards evolved. A lamb who strays from his mother and tries to pirate milk from the teats of another nearby ewe will be rudely butted away. A mother will reject all comers except those lambs whose coats wear the scent she specifically imprinted on in the minutes after she gave birth. In many other animals, however, especially those with young unable to move about much on their own (which includes most primates and many nesting birds), maternal affections remain more flexible. Whether the yawning gullet of a fish that happens to resemble the gape of a hungry chick or ultrasonic calls from a chilled pup, these cues induce recipients to respond.

The brains of animals with helpless young are wired to register signals of infants' needs. Their endocrine systems are calibrated to urge a rapid response, and their neuronal reward systems are designed to reinforce these nurturing behaviors. Being near babies, or in the human mother's case holding her baby close, becomes almost addictively pleasurable. Selection favoring caring parents was essential to start the ball rolling; but once under way, kin selection intensified selection pressures favoring more generalized caregiving. In time, selection favoring nurturing responses can take on a life of its own. Once members of a given population have been selected to respond to infant cues by helping, caregivers need not be close relatives in order to respond. The stage is set for cooperative breeding—and for such totally unexpected possibilities as blessed Kamuniak, the oryx-adopting lion.

INNATE RESPONSIVENESS TO INFANTS

Animals with the most at stake have the lowest thresholds for responding to babies. Thresholds are set lower still during particular life phases when individuals are most likely to encounter tiny relatives in need. In female mammals, sensitivity to infant cues is particularly acute in the postpartum period. New mothers are primed by hormonal changes during pregnancy, topped off by a surge of the neuropeptide oxytocin during birth. They are supremely attuned to the shapes, cries, and smells of babies. As the little creature near her begins to suck on and stimulate her nipples, a mother's circulating level of the nurture-promoting hormone prolactin rises.

Describing baby lust as "addictive" is more than poetic license. Experiments with lactating rats show that the same dopamine-based reward systems that make sucking on their nipples pleasurable also renders some animals susceptible to drug addiction. Either way, whether from having their pups close by and sucking on their nipples or from consuming cocaine, the experience leaves females desperately anxious to have that experience repeated. Pups are such a powerfully rewarding stimulus that when experimenters gave mother rats a choice between pushing a lever that would administer cocaine or one that would cause pups to tumble one after another into her cage, the mother filled her cage with pups.[6]

Most research on infant-activated reward systems in the brain is done with laboratory rats, mice, or voles. However, rhesus macaques are known to have similar reward systems. Indeed, when members of Eric Keverne's lab at the University of Cambridge chemically blocked the action of endogenous opioids, maternal responsiveness to infants declined.[7] Infants have similarly rewarding effects on human mothers. It should not be surprising that studies using MRIs show activation of dopamine-associated reward centers in the brains of first-time human mothers when they look at photographs of their smiling infant.[8] Any number of cues would probably have a similar effect—suckling, soft coos, a familiar baby's chuckle, the seductive smells emitted from the glands on her baby's scalp.

A key assumption of the misplaced-parental-care hypothesis is that allomothers respond to infants as well, but most of the neurophysiological research has been done only with mothers. Nevertheless, preliminary evidence suggests that dopamine- and oxytocin-related reward systems are implicated in allomaternal care as well. Mothers are supersensitive to infantile cues, but in mammals characterized by a lot of shared care, juveniles and subadult females who have never been pregnant or given birth also spontaneously respond to infants, huddling over pups to keep them warm. In infant-sharing primates such as langurs, these females exhibit irrepressible urges to sniff, touch, cuddle, and repeatedly take and carry new babies. In marmosets and tamarins, males—especially those with prior caretaking experience—also eagerly respond to infant vocalization and other cues, and they may be even more eager than females are to caretake.[9]

The underlying organization for maternal and alloparental brains is probably about the same, but studies of different primate species with and without alloparental care are beginning to reveal some interesting neuroendocrinological differences. In both marmosets and men, males who engage in a lot of care have higher prolactin levels than males who do not. Other species characterized by nurturing males include California mice, Mongolian gerbils, African meerkats, and Djungerian hamsters.[10] The inclination to care for infants derives from ancient and fairly universal physiological systems that are normally operational only in mothers. In these species, however, nurturing tendencies get switched on in males as well. In addition to (or perhaps instead of?) piggy-backing on highly conserved maternal systems, it is possible that selection may have favored the evolution of separate neuronal systems that are specific to nonmaternal caregivers. Marmosets may provide such an example.

As in many mammals, pregnant monkeys near term are sometimes especially attentive to babies. Very pregnant langurs, for example, are second only to inexperienced young females in how eager they are to take and carry another female's infant and in how much time they are willing to spend holding another female's baby. The most obvious explanation is that these very pregnant females are hormonally primed for motherhood. Yet this pattern is not found in all monkeys, and the responsiveness of a pregnant female to another's infant may unfold very differently in species with pronounced reproductive skew, where there is competition between females to be the breeding female or to gain access to available alloparental care. In contrast to the usual monkey model, common marmosets in the late stages of pregnancy are the antithesis of nurturing. Indeed, late-term marmosets can be absolutely lethal allomothers. Experiencing the other female's infants clinging to her as aversive, she attacks them, sometimes literally biting their heads off—thus eliminating young who might compete with the infants she herself would soon produce.[11]

To date, most neurophysiological research has focused on how infants respond to parents, or, in a few cases, on how fathers respond to babies. Far less attention has been paid to the neurophysiology of how alloparents react to infants. I expect this situation to change in the near future as laboratory scientists increasingly recognize what important roles these caregivers played in human evolution.[12] Already, scientists comparing species of voles with and without alloparental care have discovered that prairie voles, who exhibit shared care, have a higher density of oxytocin receptors in certain regions of their brains (the nucleus accumbens) than do closely related meadow voles who do not jointly care for young. Furthermore, even within the same species there is considerable variation between individuals. For example, the more responsive prairie vole females who spontaneously lick and groom their pups also turn out to be the ones with the highest concentrations of oxytocin receptors.[13]

Right from the outset, then, brains of potential caregivers can be different. Such differences are likely to be further magnified by variation in caretaking opportunities, life experiences, and specific behaviors. A behavior known as placentophagia, placenta-eating, provides a case in point.

CONSUMING QUESTIONS

The placenta is an endocrine organ that synthesizes various hormones, including several steroids. At birth, both the "afterbirth" and the accompanying amniotic fluid are awash in opioid analgesics. Some scientists speculate that mothers giving birth to litters eagerly lick off amniotic fluid from each pup during short breaks in the delivery process and consume the liverlike placenta as a means of self-medicating. This is not just a matter of good house- (or, more precisely, den-) keeping. The mother's anesthetizing cocktail eases the pain of birth and keeps her calm and on task. For even though birth in other mammals is not as tight a squeeze as it is in humans, it still hurts. A dog, for example, may give a little "yelp" as each pup emerges. The same regions of the brain that influence maternal behaviors also influence whether a mother consumes the afterbirth.

The act of eating the placenta can in turn accelerate the onset of maternal behaviors.[14] This is why it is worth noting just which individuals are interested in eating the placenta. In species with a lot of nonmaternal caregiving, such as marmosets and some hamsters, males as well as females, and in some cases prereproductives of both sexes, are as eager to eat placentas as mothers are, yet these juveniles and males have no need to dull birth pangs. I still recall how stunned I was when the primatologist Jeff French showed a video clip of birth among Brazilian bare-eared marmosets (*Callithrix argentata*). At first I had trouble comprehending the actions of the struggling bodies on the screen. As the first of two babies emerged from his mother's birth canal, a fierce tug-of-war was going on between the mother and an adult male who was trying to wrest control of the emerging baby. Then, after the second baby, as the placenta emerged, the male was vying with the mother for that as well, eager to have the first bite.[15]

Placentophagia has been particularly well studied among the Djungarian hamsters (*Phodopus cambelli*) that the Canadian biologist Katherine Wynne-Edwards brought back from Mongolia so she could study them in her lab. The male in these hamsters, and sometimes prereproductive juveniles as well, serve as midwives, mechanically assisting the female as she gives birth. When on hand, these midwives may also greedily eat the placenta. By contrast, sheep, which lack allomaternal care by fathers or by anyone else, are repulsed by the smell of amniotic fluid and will not go near a placenta unless they have just given birth. In that case, rather magically, and for a brief period only, the newly delivered mother will find the smell and taste of the placenta and the amniotic fluid still coating it absolutely irresistible.

In other words, it is not just babies that can be sensory traps. The chemical paraphernalia that accompany them into the world can be cues every bit as potent, providing their consumers with extra doses of nurture-promoting molecules.[16] Placentophagia on the part of new mothers occurs nearly universally across carnivorous and herbivorous mammals with only a few exceptions, such as camilids and marine mammals. Across primates, however, the distribution of placenta-eating mothers is more sporadic, especially in the Great Apes. A new mother chimpanzee or gorilla will sometimes consume the placenta right after birth, even before she picks up the newborn lying beside her. At other times the mother will ignore the afterbirth, perhaps leaving it behind in the makeshift nest where she delivered her baby or, seemingly oblivious to it, dragging the placenta along behind her, still attached to her infant by the umbilical cord.

Nonhuman ape mothers lack the fixed action patterns around the time of birth that are seen in other mammals like mice or dogs. Responses are even less automatic among humans. There are virtually no traditional societies in which mothers routinely eat the placenta. Even among people starved for protein, where meat of any kind is a highly desired commodity (as is the case among the Eipo of highland New Guinea and among Australian Aborigines) placentas are not eaten. Typically, the afterbirth is buried or otherwise discarded, sometimes with a special ceremony or other ritual treatment. Ironically, most reports of placentophagia in humans come from New Age parents, who mistakenly imagine they are reverting to a more traditional or "natural" mode of childbirth.[17] Clearly, though, the custom is only natural if people are emulating prehuman rather than human ancestors.

COMMODITIES IN THEIR OWN RIGHT

Whether or not they eat the placenta, many primates are sensitive to infant cues and alert to their well-being. Even the most aloof male will rush to protect a threatened infant. Yet group members are not equally likely to seek to get their hands on or actually hold babies. In the next chapter, we will see how among langur monkeys it is the mother's older female kin who are the most intrepid and determined in defending babies. Yet these same old females exhibit little interest in holding the babies they protect. Rather, it is the prereproductive juvenile and subadult females, those most in need of babies to practice with in advance of becoming mothers, who are most eager to touch, take, and carry infants. Young females go to the most trouble to keep babies content and quiet. More experienced adult females will occasionally take a baby and hold it for a few minutes, but they seem relatively blasé about the baby's complaints. Younger, prereproductive females are more attentive and seem more concerned lest their charge's cries attract a competing allomother. These immatures strive harder to keep their charges all to themselves and hold them the most number of minutes.[18] That said, virtually all primate females find babies at least initially attractive and are eager for a closer look.

This is certainly the case among savanna baboons. These mothers are exclusive caretakers of their infants during the first weeks of life, carrying them 100 percent of the time. Nevertheless, newborns attract intense interest from other females. Juveniles, subadults, and adults seek to sniff, inspect, and, if they possibly can, get their hands on the new baby. They persist in spite of the baboon mother's possessive oversight, the tone of which can be summed up as "Touch maybe, if you must, but unless you happen to be much, much more dominant than me, don't you dare take." The only exceptions to this rule are low-ranking mothers who simply are not always able to assert their "parental rights," as the Amboseli baboon researcher Jeanne Altmann puts it. In these circumstances, a dominant animal may forcibly kidnap a baby, which she then may or may not return.[19] In species of cercopithecine monkeys with rigid dominance hierarchies, such kidnappings can have disastrous results if a nonlactating female refuses to give the baby back; in a few cases, infants have starved to death. The threat of kidnap is one reason mothers in species with rigid female dominance hierarchies (like baboons or rhesus macaques) are so unwilling to give up their infants. In species with more relaxed hierarchies, such as langurs, there is no such thing as a within-group kidnapping. Mothers can always get their babies back.[20]

From the savannas of Africa to the forests of southern Mexico, baby monkeys are so attractive that little baboons and spider monkeys become commodities in a bustling simian marketplace. According to primatologists Peter Henzi and Louise Barrett, females essentially bargain for the right to touch babies. Adult female baboons who do not currently have an infant of their own provide many minutes of nonreciprocated grooming in exchange for being able to briefly touch another female's three-month-old or younger infant. The younger the infant and the fewer other infants there are in the group at the time, the more attractive a specific infant tends to be. In line with conventional marketplace rules of supply-and-demand, the rarer the baby, the more minutes of grooming—or in the case of the New World spider monkeys, who rarely groom but hug instead, the more social massaging—is required for access. As Henzi and Barrett put it: "Grooming bout duration (the baboon price 'paid' for handling) was inversely related to the number of infants present in the group."[21]

Why strive so hard for access? Part of the answer is the need for experience. Far from automatic, competent caretaking requires practice. Lack of experience is a big factor in the extremely high mortality rates for firstborn infants recorded in every primate species for which we have data.[22] This penalty for being born to a first-time (primiparous) mother may be especially high in species with a touch-but-don't-take policy. We know from long-term records for the savanna baboons at Amboseli that infants of experienced mothers are twice as likely to survive as are those of primiparas (63 percent survival rate vs. 29 percent).[23]

In infant-sharing species such as langurs, mothers may be reluctant to give up infants to very young females (under 13 months of age themselves), but as they age, and especially as they become more competent caretakers, prereproductive females get more access. Developmental age is clearly a factor in competence, but practice matters as well, including among females who have given birth before. Even experienced mothers benefit from brief refresher courses with borrowed babies, especially if they are pregnant and need a bit of priming to ensure that they respond appropriately as soon as their new baby emerges.[24]

Among infant-sharing species, access to babies and opportunities to practice holding babies are a routine part of a maturing female's life, with the result that by the time she first gives birth she is well versed in how to hold a baby and keep it comfortable and content.[25] Practice is so important that, in situations where no new babies are present in a female's own troop, an inexperienced young female may feel compelled by baby-lust to make a risky foray into a neighboring troop to try to steal one. In most cases the darting interloper is chased away, but very, very occasionally a langur succeeds in taking a new baby from a female in another troop.

The magnetic attraction of neonates incites spirited competition between inexperienced young langur allomothers to get hold of the newest arrival, especially when babies are scarce. An allomother will run off three-legged, holding her prize with one arm against her body, stopping every so often to pat and cajole it so as to cut down on the baby's whining. It's as if the nursemaid recognizes that the cries might attract a competing caregiver. They remind me of Gollum in *The Lord of the Rings*, obsessively eager to hold tight to his "precious."

NATAL ATTRACTIONS

Once natural selection starts to favor parents and alloparents who are responsive to babies, this changes the playing field for the infants themselves. Wherever babies who attract the most care are most likely to survive, natural selection is going to favor those who broadcast even more appealing cues or whose attractive signals are broadcast further. After all, other immatures may be competing for allomaternal attention as well. Thus maternal or allomaternal biases in favor of the youngest and most vulnerable immatures produces selection for traits that accentuate "babiness," rendering immatures cuter and cuddlier still, more delectable to protect or hold.

A self-reinforcing evolutionary process produces parents and alloparents who are more sensitive to infantile signals and babies who are better at emitting them. Such processes have certainly been at work in humans, as evidenced by recent neurophysiological research at Oxford University. Twelve adults, three of them parents, nine of them childless, were shown portraits of unfamiliar infants. Within a seventh of a second, brain scans detected specific neural signatures in the medial orbitofrontal cortex, a region of the brain implicated in monitoring, learning, and remembering rewarding experiences.[26] The response was quite different from the signature produced when the same people looked at the faces of other adults, and occurred far too fast to be conscious.

The media went wild. One headline read: "Neural Basis for Parental Instinct Found." Yet only three of the study subjects had actually been parents. Magnetoencephalographic scans of the remaining nine nonparents revealed the same highly specific brain activity. Hence, this near-immediate response to a baby's face was a generalized reaction found in parents and nonparents alike. I predict that similar neural signatures will also be found in other primates exposed to infantile traits. By then I hope the headlines read: "Neural Basis for Alloparental Responses Confirmed."

Most primates are born looking very different from adults. Even in rhesus macaques or savanna baboons, among whom mothers do not allow other group members to take their newborns, babies wear black natal coats accessorized by bright pink skin around their ears, feet, and rump, as if to reinforce the brand "Really New Baby." (I have even wondered if perhaps the recently reported preference for the color pink found in women but not in men might not be a leftover maternal response to infant coloration in primates.)[27] In infant-sharing species where several new babies are simultaneously available, as when births are clustered in

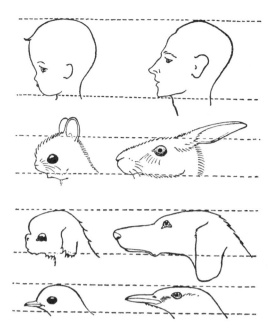

Like other primates, humans find babies irresistible. The discovery of this innate human attraction to infantile traits was one of the early triumphs of ethology, and this attraction continues to provide an important source of revenue for Walt Disney and Madison Avenue. As early as the 1950s, Konrad Lorenz identified a suite of traits contributing to the perception of infants as adorable, what he called *kinden-schema* (infant schema). These include a relatively large head; large, low-lying eyes; and pudgy cheeks. Together with short, thick extremities and clumsy, gamboling movements, such infantile features render baby animals luscious and irresistibly appealing. Infantilized dog breeds (like pug-nosed Pekinese) and manufactured baby dolls exploit these innate responses. Even though humans are universally responsive to infant cues, the thresholds for responding vary with the receiver's age, sex, and experience (both past and recent) with babies. Thirty years after Lorenz published this diagram, the ethologist Thomas Alley asked 120 childless undergraduates to examine drawings of children that differed in size and in how immature the proportions seemed. For both sexes the "mean cuddliness rating" decreased with perceived age, but subjects with younger siblings proved most responsive. Even though women were on average significantly more protective than men were, both sexes became responsive to infants after prolonged exposure. Given such propensities, it is perhaps not surprising that so many members of our species become attached to puppies and other pets with babylike attributes. U.S. pet owners spend some $41 billion a year on the purchase, grooming, boarding, feeding, and veterinary care of their dogs, cats, and other miscellaneous pets. Based on a 2004 survey by the American Pet Products Manufacturers Association, one third of such small animal owners specifically say that they consider their pets as immature family members. (Lorenz 1950, rpt. 1971:155)

one season, there is going to be intense competition between babies to attract the attention of caretakers. The outcome can be spectacular.[28]

Among some of the infant-sharing primates where allomaternal care of infants is beneficial to their mothers and where infants are in competition with other infants born around the same time to attract this care, neonatal coats have evolved to be more than just distinctive; they are positively flamboyant, visible to would-be caregivers from far away. But since birds of prey, often the biggest predators upon arboreal monkeys, have excellent color vision, flamboyant natal coats are visible to them as well. From high above the forest, these raptors can also pick up the message "New baby on board," suggesting that the advantages to infants from being desirable commodities must have been great enough to outweigh this extra risk.

Within the far-flung subfamily Colobinae, infant-sharing species across Africa, Asia, Southeast Asia, Borneo, and Sumatra have evolved a diverse wardrobe of natal coats. Ebony langurs from Java, dusky leaf monkeys from Malaya, and silver leaf monkeys from Borneo are all born bright orange, reflecting the sunlight like spun gold. Sumatran mitered leaf monkeys are born white with a dark stripe down the back crisscrossed by another stripe across the shoulders, while Bornean proboscis monkeys are born with robin's-egg-blue faces and distinctive, upturned blue noses. African black-and-white colobus babies are born covered in snowy white fur. Are these monkeys really so different from the dowdy jeans-wearing parents in Harvard Square who squire about children wearing brightly colored designer outfits?

Locale to locale, Mother Nature had to make do with the genetic materials she had at hand, but wherever benefits outweighed the costs, natural selection favored the production of infants that advertised their status as really new babies, helping to ensure their care. Over the hundreds of thousands of years it took to evolve flamboyant natal coats, attracting allomothers must have been sufficiently important to parental reproductive success to make this a good bet despite the increased predation risks.

But wait, some primate-savvy reader might say. Given how especially important alloparents are to callitrichids, why is it that marmoset and tamarin infants arrive in the world dressed so much like their grown-up parents? Baby golden lion tamarins, for example, are born the same

In some infant-sharing monkeys there has been selection on infants to attract allo-maternal attentions by evolving distinctive natal coats visible at a distance. These black-and-white colobus monkey babies arrive in the world snow-white, then gradually over the first months of life morph into the black-and-white dress of adults. As far as allomothers are concerned, the younger the baby, the more powerful the stimulus. Gradual loss of the natal coat coincides with declining alloma-ternal interest. (Noel Rowe/All The World's Primates)

color as their parents, distinguished only by a contrasting black stripe down the middle of their forehead. Such drabness seems to challenge the hypothesis that reliance on shared care favors the evolution of fancy natal coats. Rather than brightly broadcasting their neonativity, babies whose survival will depend absolutely on allomaternal attention wear uniforms that blend discreetly into the fur of the adult to whose back they cling. One possible explanation is that marmoset babies do not have to compete for alloparental attentions as much, since ordinarily only one mother is producing at a time. Alternatively, such seeming anomalies may be reminders of the constraints past evolutionary history places on natural selection. Rather than devising the perfect solution in the most efficient possible way, Old Mother Nature had to make do with what she had on hand, the ingredients in her cupboard left over from previous creations, a matter of phylogeny.

As it happens, callitrichids do not register color quite the same way colobine monkeys do. Whereas the retinas of apes and Old World monkeys are characterized by three types of cone photoreceptors (trichromacy), marmosets and tamarins, like many New World primates, typically lack trichromacy.[29] Thus, while a marmoset baby's main predators, raptorial birds, would still be able to pick out a flamboyantly colored baby, the signal would be lost on potentially helpful conspecifics—all the costs and none of the benefits. Furthermore, since hawks, eagles, and falcons all originally evolved in South America between 50 and 80 million years ago, New World monkeys have been under pressure from above for a very long time. Under the circumstances, it is perhaps no wonder Mother Nature opted for camo.

Fancy natal dress is not always advantageous, nor is it always feasible to evolve. The object after all is natal, not fatal, attraction. But in species with color vision, where alloparental attentions do indeed enhance the survival of immatures even by a small degree, over generations the evolutionary advantage of eye-catching natal dress is potentially enormous. There is every reason to assume that distinctive natal coats are biological traits that evolved through natural selection because they increased the reproductive success of the parents who carried genes for them. In humans, however—who recently shared a common primate ancestor with non-infant-sharing apes—the raw material for colorful babies may not have been there, or perhaps time was just too short, or maybe human babies appeal through other means, by being expressive and unusually plump. Humans are born far fatter than other apes are, advertising in this way that they are full-term babies worth keeping.[30]

Even though physical traits like coat color typically take many generations to evolve, new behaviors can emerge more swiftly. In the human case, magnifiers of nurturing responses may be culturally introduced by what mothers do to their babies. Perhaps they noticed that babies who were "dressed up" survived better. Hence it is time to examine how the cooperative breeding model alters the way anthropologists interpret some of the curious things that people do to, and with, their babies.

Unlike infant-sharing monkeys, human babies are not born wearing fancy natal dress. Their appeal is broadcast by big heads, plump bodies, and, in time, smiles and chortles. Their infantile appeal is in the eye of their beholders, their message designed primarily for very local consumption, their immediate priority being to appeal to their unusually discerning human mothers.[31] But other than being a lot less scrawny than other apes are, human babies are not born looking any fancier at birth than an orangutan or chimpanzee baby does. Presumably, the common ancestor of humans and other apes were fairly drab as well. Yet through their actions human mothers have managed to converge on the same sorts of solution to their childcare and posterity problem that infant-sharing monkeys arrived at through the evolution of physical traits. Mothers themselves decorate, arrange, and train their babies in ways that make them more flamboyantly attractive to other caregivers.

In her richly textured account of "the culture of infancy" in a West African Beng village, the cultural anthropologist Alma Gottlieb describes infant care practices that initially seem puzzling. To Gottlieb, the way the Beng treat their babies seemed so nonsensical that she became convinced that their mode of childcare could be understood only within their peculiar symbolic system. Like many cultural anthropologists, she saw little point in considering evolutionary contexts or adaptive functions.

At first glance, her prejudice against adaptive explanations in this instance seems well-founded. For Beng mothers engage in some remarkably counterintuitive, maladaptive-seeming behaviors. They force babies to drink water before allowing them access to the breast. They also administer herbal enemas several times a day, and decorate their babies' faces and bodies with protective painted symbols thought to promote health and growth, as well as to advertise tribal status or identity. Such practices, Gottlieb argues, flow from belief systems specific to the Beng, having to do with the sacredness of water and the origin of babies who enter the world reincarnated from ancestors, and can only be understood within the context of a specifically Beng worldview.

At first glance, such practices seem to defy common sense and functional explanation. How could enemas and body paint have anything to do with keeping babies healthier or enhancing their survival? If any customs fly in the face of theories about adaptive behavior, surely these do. Symbolic decorations are not going to encourage babies to grow faster or make them healthier, and parasite- and bacteria-laden water forced down a baby's throat is likely to do the reverse, causing diarrhea. And what use are excretion-promoting enemas when the big problem in this society is malnutrition? Combined with all the other economic and environmental challenges Beng children face—protein shortage, disease, the backbreaking work their mothers must combine with childcare—it is no wonder that nearly all are malnourished and more than 20 percent die before age five.[32]

And yet stand back and consider Beng maternal practice in terms of the universal dilemma confronting primate mothers who find themselves torn between heavy subsistence loads and the need to care for infants in the face of high rates of mortality. These are mothers who cannot possibly rear their infants without assistance from others. Next, consider the Beng in the context of a species that must have evolved as a cooperative breeder. Again and again, Gottlieb mentions the "enormous labor demands" on Beng mothers who farm full-time, chop and haul firewood, provide water, do the laundry, and prepare food using labor-intensive methods.[33] A woman, especially an undernourished woman with several children, could not possibly manage these tasks without enlisting kin and other villagers to help her care for her infant. As it turns out, each of the seemingly useless cultural practices mentioned above also just happens to make babies more attractive to allomothers.

"Every Beng mother," Gottlieb writes, "makes great efforts to toilet-train her baby from birth so as to attract a possible [caretaker] who can be recruited to the job without fear of being soiled. The goal is for the infant to defecate only once or twice a day, during bath time, so as never to dirty anyone between baths, especially while being carried."[34] It is to make a baby more easily comforted by a nonlactating allomother that they are taught early—and forcibly—to be satisfied by a drink of water if no one is available to breastfeed. It is specifically to make her infant more attractive to caretakers that a mother beautifies her baby with painted symbols, for "if a baby is irresistibly beautiful, someone will be eager to carry the little one for a few hours, and the mother can get her work done."[35] Cultural practices may be infinitely variable, and many customs do definitely take on lives of their own, spinning off idiosyncratic elaborations. But mothers in the genus *Homo* still need a lot of help with their children. Even though villages idiosyncratically vary, it is still going to take one.

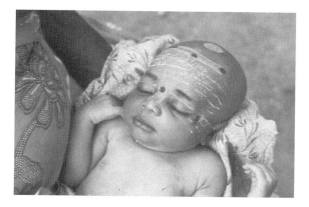

One of the reasons that Beng mothers decorate their babies with eyebrow pencil, bright orange cola nut paste, and green-tinted growth lines is to make them more attractive to allomothers, a sort of culturally applied flamboyant natal coat. (Alma Gottlieb)

PROMISING CANDIDATES FOR SHARED CARE

Primate babies are all born altricial, meaning that they need a lot of care in order to survive, and they are magnetically attractive to at least some other group members. To top it off, some primate mothers can be extraordinarily nonchalant about whether the babies they care for are their own. Their lack of discernment has led some fieldworkers to question whether primates are even capable of distinguishing their own new infants from those of others—although in humans, at least, there is evidence that they can. Still, consider the remarkably undiscriminating mothers described in a recent issue of the journal *Primates*.

Researchers studying northern muriqui monkeys in the forests of Minas Gerais in Brazil watched as two multiparous, experienced mothers descended from the trees to drink. Each held a new infant, one a male born eight days before, the other a four-day-old female. Somehow, in the course of their terrestrial excursion, the mother of the younger baby ended up carrying—and suckling—both babies, one on each teat. Not until some 36 hours later did the mother of the older infant manage to retrieve a baby, but she retrieved the wrong one—the younger female rather than her own son. The swapped infants were subsequently raised to independence by their respective foster mothers. Had the infants in question not been different sexes, known to the researchers from birth, it is possible they would never have detected the mismatch. Apparently neither mother did.[36]

Although the circumstances were unusually well observed, the muriqui mismatch was by no means an isolated incident. On rare occasions when wild cebus monkeys have happened upon orphaned infants, females have picked them up. A wild spider monkey once picked up a howler monkey infant abandoned in the forest for unknown reasons.[37] Monkey mothers who have lost their own infants sometimes steal and then adopt the infant of another female. Even the most seemingly aloof chimpanzee male will adopt and successfully rear an orphaned sibling (provided the infant is close enough to weaning age). They remind me of the seemingly misanthropic old hermit Silas Marner, who finds himself mesmerized by the abandoned toddler Eppie's golden hair. Thus does the appeal of babies override ordinary powers of discrimination.

Unquestionably, the raw material for misdirected parental care, and with it the potential for the evolution of shared care and even cooperative breeding, is present among monkeys and apes. Like the warblers and other birds whose nests are routinely parasitized by cuckoos, primates find all infants attractive, including infants not their own. Aware of how easily monkeys and apes accept new babies, professionals managing primates in captivity frequently recommend cross-fostering (removing a mother's baby and substituting another) as a discord-free technique for introducing new "blood" into a breeding colony to keep it from becoming too inbred. Were the keeper to release a strange adult into the troop, he or she might be attacked and yet would be unable to flee or to skulk on the outskirts, until becoming accepted by others in the group, as occurs in the wild. By introducing strangers as infants, keepers ensure that the new group member will be immediately accepted, picked up, carried, and introduced around by a local female, and therefore accepted by the adult male as well, avoiding much potential mayhem.

Having learned about this unabashed readiness of mothers to accept substitute babies from the colony managers, researchers now use cross-fostering as a tool in behavioral experiments, placing an infant from one species with a mother of another and observing outcomes. This has become a research method of choice to tease apart "nature" and "nurture" and to study the interaction between genetic instructions and rearing environments.

Innate primate responsiveness to infants plays out similarly among humans. People readily accept and bond with adopted babies, especially infants shortly after birth.[38] Roughly 120,000 legal adoptions take place every year in the United States. Foster-care situations total four to five times that number.[39] Per capita, adoptions are probably even more common in traditional societies, although in those cases adopted children are often relatives, and nepotism looms large.[40] Adoptees may be orphans, overstock, or children fostered in from families willing to loan or let them go altogether, in the hopes that their children will encounter better prospects or because they are too great a burden at home.

As in other cooperative breeders, many of these fostered young help out, "paying to stay." They are not necessarily well-treated. There is no longer any doubt that—primatewide—infants are at risk of being killed by unrelated members of their same species, and that in humans foster children and stepchildren run a significantly higher risk of discrimination, exploitation, and abuse.[41] Years ago, I had trouble convincing colleagues that this was so. Today the pendulum has swung the other way, so that genetic relatedness is too simplistically and dogmatically invoked, leading evolutionists to overlook powerful human urges to look out for children. As in other animals, genetic relatedness and self-interest are not the *only* explanations for "the kindness of strangers." A lot depends on circumstances, on the individuals involved, on their past histories, and on where and how babies are encountered, as we saw in Chapter 5.

An innate attraction to babies is a highly conserved primate trait present in most monkeys and apes. The neural mechanisms for neonatal attraction were almost certainly present in the common ancestors of Great Apes and humans, especially in females. Timing and the particular circumstances under which adopters and stepparents are exposed to infant cues will have important effects on how they subsequently treat unrelated infants. Like all primates, humans can be magnetically attracted to infants, and some people adopt babies simply because, to use a phrase adoptive parents frequently use, they "fall in love" with them.

The general responsiveness to infant signals so typical of primates highlights what promising candidates for the evolution of shared care apes would be. Not only can we take for granted that the neural mechanisms and underlying endocrinology for responding to needy immatures were already in place, but other circumstances as well would have favored shared care. Like many other primates, the African Great Apes are highly social and are also characterized by relatively slow life histories. Paleontological evidence as well as comparative behavior from extant ape species indicate that our ancestors lived year-round in highly gregarious, mixed-age communities with slow-maturing young. Babies would have been born excruciatingly helpless, taking years to grow up. Membership in a group would have been essential for mothers to rear young, and groupmates would have been chronically exposed to cues emanating from babies.

We also know that all African apes passed through the late Pliocene–Pleistocene crucible of unpredictable climate change with recurring periods of food shortage, the sort of conditions that might force mothers to seek provisioning help from others. These are precisely the sort of conditions that in other animals promoted shared care, if not the evolution of full-fledged cooperative breeding. Yet even though shared care—and, in the case of callitrichids, cooperative breeding—did evolve in many other species of nonhuman primates, none of the Great Apes living under natural conditions in the wild exhibits shared care. Why not?

And so, once again, we come back to the same question. In Chapter 1 I pointed out that mind reading and the quest for intersubjective engagement were far more developed in humans than in other apes. In Chapter 2 I asked why our ancestors evolved in this direction, while other apes never did, even though they would have presumably benefited as much or more from enhanced social learning or in-group cooperation. In Chapters 3 and 5 I showed that allomaternal care in the form of provisioning would have been essential to infant and child survival among ancestral humans, and I explained how such shared care produced developmental contexts where infants who paid more attention to both mothers and others would benefit from correctly gauging their intentions and engaging their solicitude. The children good at doing so were both more likely to survive and also cognitively and emotionally transformed.

In Chapter 4 I explained how shared care and provisioning was conducive to the development of infants' capacities for monitoring both mothers and others. Such increased attention to their feelings and intentions was accompanied by Darwinian selection favoring survival of youngsters who excelled at mind reading, so that, through time, intersubjective engagement became increasingly important in the genus *Homo*. In Chapter 6 I took readers on a comparative excursion of cooperative breeding outside the order Primates and summarized the most important explanatory theories for why alloparents would ever be willing to care for the young of others. I discussed how cooperative breeding evolves in the first place and how it is maintained. Finally, in this chapter, I returned specifically to the primate case, stressing how responsive primates are to infants and how preadapted they are for the evolution of shared care.

If shared care really was a crucial precondition for the evolution of intersubjectivity, and if all primates are to some extent preadapted to evolve it, the absence of shared care in other apes brings us back to the initial question: Why us and not them? We may have explained why our ancestors embarked on an evolutionary path that left them more sensitive to the mental states, feelings, and intentions of others (because they started out as cooperative breeders), but we have not explained why only this line of apes adopted this mode of infant care and childrearing in the first place. After all, other apes are also extremely clever social strategists. The more we learn about chimpanzees, for example, especially "enculturated" chimpanzees with exposure to human alloparents, the clearer it becomes that they have at least rough ideas about what others know and intend. Furthermore, given how competitive life is at least in groups of common chimpanzees, presumably their ancestors as well would have benefited from traits that enhanced in-group cooperation.

All this only increases the mystery: What are the missing ingredients that encouraged or permitted one line of apes to evolve this profound reliance on allomaternal caregivers while other apes stuck with exclusively maternal care? In the next chapter I propose a twofold answer having to do with just who was available to help, and the sort of help that was on offer under conditions where allomothers were needed not just to care for but also to help provision children.

8

GRANDMOTHERS AMONG OTHERS

What everyone needs in the [new] millennium is
access to the Internet and a grandmother.

—Anonymous (cited in Farmer 2000)

If allomaternal assistance is so beneficial for maternal
fitness, why don't all mother apes solicit help? It can't be lack of interest
by prospective allomothers—most primates are fascinated by babies. As
we just saw, the neural underpinnings for *kindenschema* are in place, and
apes are no exception. Rather, the main obstacle to shared care is the
mother's lack of trust in her surroundings and reluctance to allow anyone else to hold her infant. Mother apes in the wild are obsessively anxious about their babies. Frankly, if I were a mother chimpanzee, I would
be too.

Primatewide, mothers have to worry about strange males, and in
both chimpanzees and gorillas, infanticide by males is a major source of
infant mortality. But because females typically leave their natal kin to

Great Ape mothers are notoriously possessive. When Flo, one of Jane Goodall's Gombe chimpanzees, gave birth to the infant Flint, his older sister Fifi (on the left) was not allowed to take him, although she was obviously interested and eager to do so. In this photograph, Fifi appears to be eying her brother with what looks to me like resigned yearning. (Hugo van Lawick/Jane Goodall Institute)

breed in other communities, they have to worry about unrelated and potentially infanticidal females as well. This is especially true of highly omnivorous common chimpanzees, who eat baby gazelles and colobus monkeys when they can get them. Baby chimpanzees are a no less delectable source of proteins and lipids. Furthermore, because chimpanzees' primary diet is ripe fruit, elimination of a rival mother's infant means greater access to a finite local resource for the killer's own line.[1]

Provided they can be dispatched with impunity, baby chimpanzees are fair game. Fortunately for mothers, rival females are rarely any bigger than they are, and few are willing to take the risks males do. The stakes don't warrant it. Elimination of a nursing infant provides a male one of his few chances to inseminate a fertile female, but infanticidal females merely gain a meal or eliminate a tiny rival who might never grow up anyway—scarcely worth the risk of being wounded by his protective mother. Not surprisingly, the first observations of infanticide by chimpanzee females targeted babies of mothers with some disability that hampered retaliation—illness, a paralyzed wrist, extreme subordination.[2] Infants of strange females attempting to immigrate into the community are especially vulnerable because community females may gang up on her.

One February day in 2006 a team of primatologists studying chimpanzees in the Budongo forest of Uganda noticed an unfamiliar female moving in from another community. Young adult females usually migrate earlier in their reproductive careers, but this new arrival was already a mother, carrying a week-old infant. The pair was attacked by six resident females. Five had infants of their own, clinging tight to their mothers as they charged. Screaming and bleeding, the strange female was no match for this xenophobic consortium. As her attackers caught hold and pounded on her back, she crouched low to the ground, shielding her baby. Three community males approached, also screaming, noisily ricocheting off tree trunks, but none attacked. One old male actually looked as though he was trying to pry a resident female off, but to no avail. The alpha female wrested the baby away, only to lose it to another female who snatched it from her and delivered a lethal, neck-spanning bite.[3]

Given the company chimpanzees keep, it is understandable that a mother would be reluctant to allow even a well-intentioned older sibling to hold her baby. Caring and attentive as a sister would be, she might not be sufficiently experienced or imposing to ward off a more dominant adult. If ape mothers insist on carrying babies everywhere, it is not because they instinctively seek continuous tactile contact with babies; it is because the available alternatives are not safe enough.

I vividly recall the incident that first brought home this realization. I was watching a group of bonobos at a zoo in the Netherlands. The apes were in their winter quarters—several indoor cages connected by open doors. The only other person around was my host, a young scientist who had just provided sugar cane, a favorite food. The dominant female and the rest of the group were in a connecting cage, some distance away from a mother and baby. Apparently feeling quite safe, the mother actually set her baby down so she could use both hands to eat.

Something similar was observed among common chimpanzees in a zoo in Singapore. The mother even allowed cagemates to carry her 3-month-old infant.[4] But I know of only one published account, described by its author as "an unusual incident," in which a wild ape mother voluntarily permitted another female to not only hold but actually adopt her newborn infant. This involved a 13-year-old Gombe chimpanzee named Gaia who happened to be living in the same community as her own mother when she gave birth for the first time. As females from a more dominant matriline approached and tried to inspect the baby, the grandmother (Gremlin) took the baby from her inexperienced daughter and "turned her back toward them" in a protective mode. Thereafter, the grandmother retained the baby, nursing him along with her own two-year-old son right up until Gaia's baby died at age five months.[5]

There are more than a dozen cases of wild chimpanzee orphans being adopted by another group member (usually a close relative). What was so unprecedented about this case was that the mother was still alive. All other reported lapses in maternal possessiveness involve new mothers under more protected conditions. Particularly telling is the case of the chimpanzee Ai who allowed Tetsuro Matsuzawa, her unusually reliable friend, access to her new baby, access such as no scientist had ever before been voluntarily permitted. In another instance, an inexperienced mother gorilla at the San Diego Zoo allowed her own mother to carry her baby.

Ordinarily, a wild gorilla would have left her natal group long before she gave birth for the first time, and as in the Gombe case, it was unusual for this 11-year-old female to be living with her mother. Having lost her first infant, this new mother was still inexperienced and, like many first-time primate mothers, seemed unsure what to do. She left the neonate on the floor. As Masayuki Nakamichi, a Japanese primatologist then working in San Diego, apprehensively watched, the grandmother came over, picked up the baby, and held it out near her daughter's face, as if demonstrating what needed doing. The grandmother then handed the baby to its mother, who eventually learned to care for it.[6]

In this rare photo, the grandmother held the newborn under the face of her daughter for 15 seconds (shown here) before gently pushing the baby gorilla toward its young and inexperienced mother, who finally took it. (Masayuki Nakamichi from Nakamichi et al. 2004:76)

With the exception of the Gombe case, which was more nearly a concerned grandmother taking protective custody of a baby from an inexperienced and inept daughter, all the other exceptions to exclusive maternal care of newborns in Great Apes occurred in captivity without predators or potentially infanticidal conspecifics lurking nearby. Even more importantly, I suspect, in all cases the mothers were in unusual company, alone with a familiar, competent, trusted adult. Such admittedly rare incidents nevertheless reveal something important. Sufficiently confident of their physical and social surroundings, even gorilla, chimpanzee, or bonobo mothers will share care.

So why do hunter-gatherers differ from other apes in this respect, by *routinely* sharing care? Might there be neurochemical differences that encourage postpartum women to be more trusting than other apes? Different monkey species in the genus *Macaca* range from the highly aggressive and rigidly hierarchical rhesus and pigtail macaques, among whom mothers never voluntarily allow access to their infants for fear that the dominant female would kidnap the infant and not give it back, to the unusually tolerant and far less competitive Barbary and Tonkean macaques, who freely share care. These species-specific behavioral differences are correlated with neurophysiological differences. Highly possessive rhesus and pigtailed macaque mothers are reported to have reduced serotonin activity compared with the more tolerant, infant-sharing Barbary and Tonkean macaques.[7]

Since both birth and lactation coincide with higher-than-usual levels of the tolerance-and-trust-promoting neurotransmitter oxytocin, it would be particularly interesting to know if there are physiological differences between human mothers and other apes in how they respond to neuropeptides like oxytocin in the postpartum period. Might such differences affect receptors to such "affiliative" and trust-promoting hormones?[8] Complete sequences of all ape genomes may one day make possible the kind of comparisons already being done with closely related species of social insects. At present so little is known about the comparative neurobiology of maternal behavior in apes that we can neither confirm nor rule out physiological differences postpartum. No one knows, for example, why nonhuman ape mothers often feel compelled to eat the placenta right after birth, while women (even more omnivorous than other apes) eschew this potent dose of extra hormones. Might women already be more responsive to oxytocin, less anxious about social contacts postpartum, and therefore less in need of a nurture-promoting cocktail?

Research from other mammals reveals that adults dosed with oxytocin do indeed become more trusting and affiliative.[9] Voles exposed to higher levels of oxytocin in early infancy exhibit greater propensity to bond with others and behave in more nurturing ways later in life.[10] Furthermore, a species such as prairie voles in which parents rely on others to help care for their young has more oxytocin receptors in certain brain regions than does a closely related species that does not form pair bonds or tolerate alloparental care. Whereas prairie vole mothers readily accept help, other vole mothers attack anyone who approaches their young.[11]

It is entirely possible that neurological differences between humans and other apes affect how these mothers behave after giving birth. But I know of no studies showing this. Furthermore, even if differences could be documented, we would still need to explain how infant sharing became common enough for natural selection to act on and favor a subset of mother apes whose underlying physiologies inclined them to be more tolerant of others postpartum. Rather than dwell on what we do not yet know about the comparative physiology of apes and humans, let's turn to what the ethological evidence tells us to expect from mothers under various circumstances.

In order for a hyperprotective Pleistocene hominin to voluntarily allow access to her infant, she would have to be in the company of others who were competent and trusted, perhaps her own mother—a full-grown and experienced caregiver familiar from birth. Until recently, most evolutionists took for granted that hominin females had no such candidate around. Now new evidence forces us to reassess this assumption and to consider whether it was not only possible but likely that early hominin mothers gave birth in the vicinity of matrilineal kin. This new way of thinking about the company kept by Pleistocene mothers completely alters the theoretical feasibility of shared care in an ape.

In this chapter, I describe new findings about both Great Ape and hunter-gatherer residence patterns, showing that these creatures were more flexible than previously assumed and that it was not impossible for ancestral apes to give birth near matrilineal kin. In the case of Pleistocene foragers, there is reason to believe that they were not only living under circumstances where alloparental care was feasible but also where food sharing was increasingly important for survival and successful childrearing. I conclude by discussing the different qualifications and variable availability of different kinds of caretakers—older siblings, cousins, co-mothers, fathers, possible fathers, and especially grandmothers, whose impact on child survival has only recently begun to be studied but is already yielding some surprising twists.

ON THE IMPORTANCE OF GIVING BIRTH NEAR KIN

Primate social organization is famously variable. But across species, two generalizations hold up remarkably well. First, females who live among kin are better able to defend their interests than those who leave their natal groups to forage and breed among nonkin. Second, mothers are most prone to share infants when they feel confident that they can readily get them back unharmed.

Until recently, however, it was taken for granted that, like other apes, hominin females left their natal groups to give birth for the first time in another community, to rear young among unrelated, possibly rival, females who were unlikely to be supportive. Just suggesting that early humans lived in matrilocal settings was viewed by evolutionists as some heretical throwback to outmoded views about matriarchal stages in human evolution, bringing to mind advocates for Mother Right or Goddess Cults.[12] There were two reasons for discounting such views. The first had to do with entrenched assumptions about the patrilocal tendencies of all hominid apes—Great Apes, australopithecines, and humans alike. The second reason was a tendency to project onto early Paleolithic ancestors patriarchal attributes from later time periods.

By "patriarchal" I mean a society with patrilocal residence patterns, patrilineal inheritance, and social institutions biased toward patrilineal interests. By this definition, few tropical gathering-and-hunting societies that have not yet adopted horticulture are patriarchal. Yet somehow, patrilocal living arrangements, and even patriarchal elaborations correlated with patrilocality, are routinely assumed to be human universals and are projected back in time onto our early Pleistocene ancestors.[13] The supposed antiquity of patrilocality was further bolstered by comparisons with the African Great Apes, since both gorillas and chimpanzees exhibit marked patrilocal tendencies, with females migrating out to breed among nonkin. Given such entrenched assumptions, it was difficult to imagine hominins ever being sufficiently matrilocal to evolve shared care.

The preeminence of the man-the-hunter/sex-contract paradigm, with its accompanying stereotypes about nuclear families and maternal caregiving, was another obvious obstacle. So too was the habit among mammal researchers of assuming that cooperative breeding meant that a single dominant female would monopolize the group's reproduction. Since marmosetlike reproductive suppression has never been reported for hunter-gatherers, this criterion if applied excluded early humans.[14] But the most persistent barrier to thinking humans might have evolved with shared care had to do with residence patterns.

Three widely accepted lines of evidence pointed to male philopatry as a hominid universal. First, behavioral evidence from the African Great Apes initially suggested that females always left their natal group to breed. Second, apart from the special sex-induced alliances in bonobos, none of the Great Apes exhibited the strong female-female social bonds typical of matrilocal species.[15] Third, and most impressive, George Peter Murdock's classic cross-cultural compilations seemed to document a prevalence of patrilocality in humans as well. Murdock's analyses of ethnographic information on 862 representative cultures from around the world, expressly coded for use in the Human Relations Area Files and in his *Ethnographic Atlas,* indicated that the vast majority of human cultures were patrilocal. This included hunter-gatherer societies, 62 percent of which, according to Murdock's information, were patrilocal.[16] Therefore, it seemed both logical and parsimonious to assume that the common ancestors of apes and humans also lived in male kin groups.[17]

Evolutionists had little incentive to challenge this received wisdom. Assumptions about the universality of patrilocal residence patterns were consistent with other widely accepted assumptions about naturally dominant males and "men in groups" who forged alliances with fathers and brothers to hunt and to protect their mates and natal territories. Furthermore, having men stay put while exchanging their daughters and sisters with other groups seemed like an adaptive way for fathers and brothers to avoid excessive inbreeding while simultaneously forging alliances with other groups—critical building blocks for early human social organization. At the time, sisters and daughters were viewed as essentially passive pawns in largely male-orchestrated transactions.[18]

Patrilocal residence became an integral feature of hominin family life as reconstructed by physical anthropologists in the twentieth century. The resulting assumptions were subsequently incorporated wholesale into early sociobiology and evolutionary psychology. By the early 1980s a few anthropologists were pointing out that female interests and strategies were being overlooked.[19] By the late 1980s, human behavioral ecologists studying foraging peoples were specifically asking why postreproductive women worked so hard. And by the 1990s, Kristen Hawkes and colleagues were arguing that assistance from maternal grandmothers had played a critical role in early hominin evolution—a hypothesis initially met with considerable skepticism.[20] The main objection was that even if their older matrilineal kin survived long enough to be helpful (which many doubted), older women would not have lived near daughters (and new mothers) who needed their help.

A Hadza boy is shown sitting with his great-grandmother and her sister (on the right). Classically "hard-working" Hadza grandmothers energetically sharpen their digging sticks in preparation for a gathering expedition. When a mother has a new baby, as this boy's mother did, Hawkes and company found that their older children's nutritional status was correlated with how much time older kinswomen spent foraging. (James O'Connell)

Biologists and anthropologists alike—who in the early years were mostly male—had long taken for granted that the function of women was to bear and rear a man's children. From this perspective, women past childbearing age were deemed irrelevant and of no theoretical interest. This prejudice surfaced occasionally in ethnographic descriptions of old women as "physically quite revolting" or "nuisances." They were depicted as objects of ridicule—"old hags" whose behavior was obviously not worth studying.[21] Such accounts took for granted that in our evolutionary past, postmenopausal females would have been too decrepit or short-lived to be of use. Demographic and archaeological evidence suggesting otherwise was discounted.[22]

Yet careful demographic analysis revealed that a forager who sur-

Hunter-gatherer women who survive to middle age have a reasonable chance of surviving past reproductive age. Like this !Kung grandmother, they continue to interact lovingly with children and grandchildren. (Peabody Museum/Marshall Expedition image 2001.29.414)

vived to age 15 had about a 60 percent chance of living to 45. And those who made it to 45 had a good chance of surviving into old age.[23] Consider the !Kung during the period when they still lived as hunter-gatherers. The average life expectancy was only 30. But for those who survived childhood, the odds improved. Of the girls who survived to age 15, the majority (62.5 percent) survived to age 45. About 8 percent of the population lived on to 60 or older.[24] Today, there is a remarkable convergence among demographic anthropologists, evolutionary-minded historians, and human biologists who study life history patterns across primates that the bodies of *Homo sapiens* are "designed" to last about 72 years.[25]

Once behavioral ecologists recognized that substantial numbers of women were living long lives, efficiently gathering and processing food for decades after menopause, it became important to explain why creatures who could no longer directly contribute to the gene pool of the next generation would do so. In early versions of "the grandmother hypothesis," evolutionary biologists George Williams and William Hamilton proposed that postreproductive lifespans are favored when the mother's continued survival enhances the survival of her last-born offspring.[26] A "prudent" mother could not afford to die before her last child was independent. Struck by how especially hardworking old females were, Hawkes proposed an alternative version of the grandmother hypothesis, arguing that the reason women lived longer than other apes after they ceased to ovulate had to do with their impact on *grandchildren*. But even with compelling evidence for the longevity and industry of grandmothers, a seemingly insurmountable obstacle remained: Even if she were still alive, a hunter-gatherer woman's mother was unlikely to live in the same group as her daughter—or so it was thought.[27]

THE ALVAREZ CORRECTIVE

Not until near the end of the twentieth century did accumulating information from long-term studies of Great Apes in the wild prompt primatologists to reassess their assumptions about residence patterns. These field observations revealed that the breeding systems of chimpanzees and gorillas were more flexible, and the apes themselves more opportunistic, than previously supposed.

If they could do so and still be safe and find enough fruit to eat, some females (like Gremlin's daughter Gaia) *did* remain in their natal place. Fifi, daughter of Jane Goodall's famous chimpanzee matriarch Old Flo, provides a case in point. Born to a locally dominant mother, Fifi remained in Flo's relatively secure and food-rich home range, within her mother and brothers' sphere of influence. Advantaged by this legacy, Fifi went on to produce nine offspring, the all-time record for a wild chimpanzee, and almost all of them survived. In 2004 when Fifi together with her last infant daughter disappeared and were presumed dead, a few of her older daughters and all of her sons still resided at Gombe in the same community as their mother and grandmother.[28] Several of Flo's daughters and some of her granddaughters continue to live in their natal place, enjoying what sociobiologists refer to as "the benefits of philopatry."

In addition to these field studies, new DNA evidence revealed that co-resident males who jointly defended their community against neighboring males were not necessarily close kin. Thus, even though females were more likely than males to migrate, community males—even males who were close allies—were on average no more closely related to one another than females were.[29] Gorillas too were turning out to be more flexible, with both sexes routinely transferring between groups, often more than once.[30] Then came a reanalysis of the ethnographic evidence for hunter-gatherers which suggested that they too were more flexible in their residence patterns than previously assumed.

Undeniably, Murdock's early efforts to make cross-cultural comparisons more evidence-based and amenable to statistical analysis represented a tremendous advance. From the 1960s onward, he and his followers strove to lay empirical foundations for "the science of human behavior." But the devil was in the details, in translating complex, often very incomplete published records into simple codes that accurately reflected the complex realities of people's residence decisions. When the University of Utah anthropologist Helen Alvarez went back to the original ethnographies for a painstaking reexamination of how Murdock had determined hunter-gatherer residence patterns, her reassessment came as a shock.

Murdock had set up strict criteria for assigning each culture to a particular residence category. For example, a specified proportion of couples had to conform to particular residence rules in order to be assigned as either *patrilocal, bilocal* (or what Murdock called "ambilocal"), with residence established optionally near parents of either husband or wife and perhaps alternating over time, or *matrilocal* ("uxorilocal" in Murdock's terminology). Yet as Alvarez reread the ethnographies, she realized that the numerical census data needed to meet Murdock's criteria were rarely there. His exacting, explicit specifications not withstanding, residence patterns were often assigned on the basis of hunches. When Alvarez recoded the ethnographies, this time using only the 48 hunter-gatherer societies for which empirical evidence on residence patterns was actually available, she found that only 6 of the 48 (12.5 percent) were patrilocal. The majority, 26 of 48 (54 percent), were bilocal.[31]

Notwithstanding dogmatic pronouncements about how humans "tend to be patrilocal" because "in traditional societies sons stay near their families and daughters move away," this underlying assumption about human nature is not supported by evidence from people actually living as hunter-gatherers.[32] Rather than being naturally patrilocal, most hunter-gatherer societies have remarkably flexible and opportunistic residence patterns as couples move between the woman's natal group and the man's.[33] Furthermore, various customs increase the likelihood women will have matrilineal kin nearby when they first give birth. The same pattern we saw among the !Kung can also be found a continent away, among such bilocal foragers as the Pomo Indians of northern California: "The married couple kept moving from one family to the other . . . [but] when a child was expected they always went to live with the wife's family."[34]

Even among unequivocally patrilocal peoples such as the Maidu foragers of northern California, the ethnographer specifically noted that "before residing permanently in the husband's village, the married couple lived for a time with the wife's family, and the new husband rendered service to them by providing food."[35] Murdock along with early ethnographers even had a name for it: "matri-patrilocal."

IF DAUGHTERS HAD MOTHERS NEARBY AFTER ALL . . .

In less than a decade, the starting assumptions of evolutionary-minded anthropologists studying societies who still subsist (at least partly) by gathering and hunting have changed. Fieldworkers take seriously the proposal that humans evolved as cooperative breeders and so include information on available alloparents in their censuses and record the effects of their presence on child survival. Thus, when Brooke Scelza and Rebecca Bliege Bird recently went back to study the Mardu, a traditionally patrilineal and patrilocal people who still actively hunt and gather wild foods in the Western Desert of Australia—albeit these days with trucks and government food subsidies—the researchers specifically asked women how much they were able to rely on matrilineal kin to help rear their children. Following the lead of researchers working in Africa among Aka and Hadza, they also wanted to know how grandmothers and sisters strategized so as to be nearby when help was needed.

Even though the Mardu are, like many Australian Aborigines, traditionally patrilocal, women still manage to line up matrilineal assistance. In particular, women will urge their husbands to take a kinswoman as their second or third wife. As in earlier times, sororal polygyny (when the man marries his wife's sister) was a preferred form of marriage. Marriage to the wife's cousin was also common. Fifty-one percent of women were in polygynous unions with co-wives who were close relatives. Usually, polygynous marriage with more than one wife favors the husband's reproductive interests. Several wives bear him children, but competition between wives for limited family resources can undermine child well-being. Rivalry is less pronounced when wives are related. In line with this logic, elsewhere in Australia, among the Aborigines of Arnhem Land, child survival to age five was significantly higher for polygynous families where co-wives were close relatives. In search of social support and help, Aboriginal wives actively lobby husbands to marry their sisters, and in the interests of harmony (and perhaps child well-being) men oblige.[36]

Among the Mardu, 68 percent of polygynously married women were in sororal unions. Mardu mothers also obtained help from their own mothers, who often relocated to be near daughters of childbearing age, especially if the daughter was monogamously married and lacked an older co-wife to advise and help her. Mothers were especially eager to join a daughter if she was married to the same man as her sister. Traditionally patrilocal or not, half of married Mardu women ages 14 to 40 have a mother in the same group. Between footloose mothers-in-law and related co-wives, average degree of relatedness between females in a Mardu band is high, with women related to each other on average as closely as cousins and having an 11 percent chance of sharing genes by common descent. This average degree of relatedness turns out to be virtually the same as that found among infant-sharing matrilocal monkeys like langurs.[37]

Did ancestral hunter-gatherers likewise have matrilineal kin nearby? We cannot know for sure, but post-Alvarez, long-standing barriers against thinking this was possible have disappeared. Instead of some highly conserved tendency, the cross-cultural prevalence of patrilocal residence patterns looks less like an evolved human universal than a more recent adaptation to post-Pleistocene conditions, as hunters moved into northern climes where women could no longer gather wild plants year-round or as groups settled into circumscribed areas. In the Middle East, people began to herd livestock and became increasingly dependent on growing crops, storing the surplus, and accumulating property. As group sizes along with population densities increased, people adjusted their behavior to these new demographic, dietary, epidemiological, and social realities.

For settled people, shorter birth intervals and faster population growth, along with the accumulation of resources and the emergence of social stratification, brought with them the need to protect livestock and cultivable land as well as wives and children. Protecting such valuable resources became a higher priority than maintaining cordial and reciprocal exchange with neighbors. As outside invasions became more routine, men needed allies they could count on. Who better to rely on than close male kin? Increasingly, men sought to remain near fathers and brothers, obtaining wives from other groups. Only in the past 10,000 or so years has interclan warfare become an integral part of human lives, necessitating patrilocal residence patterns and in the process changing the way that children are reared.

As in all primates, mothers without support from matrilineal kin lost some of their autonomy. The reproductive interests of patrilines increasingly took priority. With both patrilocal living arrangements and shorter birth intervals, the alloparents at hand were more likely to be older siblings of the current infant than maternal grandmothers or great aunts, with mixed results for children, not always good.

GENETIC EVIDENCE ABOUT RESIDENCE IN THE RECENT PAST

Based on genetic evidence from the past few thousand years, after the introduction of herding, horticulture, and social stratification, we know that women in many parts of the world were marrying out and moving between groups. But so far, genes cannot tell us much about residence patterns during the Paleolithic when our ancestors still lived exclusively by gathering and hunting. Let me explain.

Analyses of non-recombining portions of the Y chromosome, which is passed only from fathers to sons, as well as comparative frequencies of mitochondrial DNA, which is passed exclusively from mothers to both daughters and sons, reveal that in the past five thousand years or so women were more likely to move between populations than men were. If residence was patrilocal, we would also expect reproductive behavior to have been more tightly regulated, since men living in patrilocal clans tend to guard their mates from outsiders. Such reproductive control could explain why gene flow between patrilocal populations was largely confined to women.[38]

Consider an admittedly extreme but very telling case involving the recent migration of people between Africa and the Middle East. While there was little male-mediated gene flow from sub-Saharan Africa into the area around Yemen about 2,500 years ago, as evidenced by Y-chromosome data, mitochondrial DNA indicates a tremendous influx of fertile women of African origin around this time. This genetic information, combined with historical accounts, means that captured or enslaved African women bore children to Middle Eastern Arab men. African men either were not taken to the new location or, if taken, left no surviving offspring.[39] Conquests yielding access to women are starkly inscribed in genetic records from other parts of the world as well. The most famous case involves genetic evidence from a particular haplotype on the Y chromosome that points to a rapid spread of genes from one particular male lineage linked to Genghis Khan. It is consistent with the dates of his army's conquests across Asia from the Pacific to the Caspian Sea.[40]

Such reproductively skewed patterns contrast with those from matrilocal societies, which tend to be more relaxed about who breeds with whom. Routinely, both sexes move around, although men usually move somewhat more. Over the past 10,000 years or so, matrilocal and matrilineal societies have increasingly given way to pressures from expansionist, patrilineal neighbors and invaders so that patterns of conquest are widely documented across Europe, Africa, Asia, and South America.[41]

Genes tell us a surprising amount about patterns of conquest. They even tell us when people started to live in cities, rely on milk products, or suffer from various diseases. They can shed light on when dogs and cats began to be domesticated. Comparing the genetic histories of lice that live in body hair with lice that cling to garments even allows us to make an educated guess at when humans started wearing clothes.[42] But genetic evidence tells us almost nothing about the *residence patterns* of men and women prior to a few thousand years ago, with one possible exception.

In 2000 scientists working on the Human Genome Project reported that genes involved in sperm production turn out to have evolved at an unusually fast rate compared with other genes. This curious finding suggests that there may have been selection pressure on our hominin ancestors to produce quantities of competitive sperm, a trait critical for the reproductive success of males in primates where females mate with more than one male.[43] Polyandrous matings would not be at all consistent with females being captured or exchanged between patrilineal clans, where reproductive access to women is closely guarded. However, occasional polyandrous matings are perfectly consistent with the more flexible breeding combinations (alternately monogamous, polyandrous, and polygynous) found in cooperative breeders.

Even if this admittedly speculative interpretation concerning sperm-related genes holds up, genetic evidence still does not tell us whether or not matrilineal kin were on hand to help mothers rear their children among African *Homo erectus* 1.8 million years ago. What it does do, though, is remind us how much evolution has gone on since humans last shared a common ancestor with gorillas (whose females mate with a single alpha male and where sperm competition is virtually nonexistent) and with chimpanzees and bonobos (whose females mate with many males and where sperm competition plays an important role in reproductive fitness). Each species of ape differs from every other, and none of them breed like women do today.

Chimpanzee females advertise ovulation with large red swellings around the time of ovulation, and they only copulate around midcycle. Bonobos, by contrast, exhibit swellings that last for weeks and copulate with multiple partners throughout most of their cycle. Gorillas, orangutans, and women do not advertise ovulation with conspicuous swellings at all.[44] In other words, reproductive traits like the sexual swellings of chimpanzees can evolve quite fast, and 5–10 million years have elapsed since humans last shared a common ancestor with primarily patrilocal African Great Apes. This is the main reason I agree with Alvarez that as far as residence patterns are concerned, the best we can do is extrapolate from people who still lived as nomadic foragers when first described.

Granted, the residence patterns of modern hunter-gatherers may or may not resemble those of the first anatomically modern humans. As humans became behaviorally modern—armed with higher-caliber tools and weapons, with fire to cook food, and with language to communicate—their subsistence strategies would likely have diverged from those of the earliest Pleistocene hunter-gatherers. Their lifeways would have been altered further still by contacts with post-Neolithic herders and neighboring farmers, not to mention anthropologists. Yet ethnographic evidence about these people reveals the sorts of behaviors, customs, and strategic maneuvering by parents and alloparents that make it feasible for highly mobile foraging peoples to survive and rear unusually costly and slow-maturing children. This is the basis for arguing that in order to successfully reproduce, foragers needed to be, and were, opportunistic and flexible in their mating and residence patterns.

If correct, Helen Alvarez's revised interpretation of hunter-gatherer residence patterns removes the last barrier for taking seriously the hypothesis that maternal grandmothers and other matrilineal kin helped early hominin mothers rear their young. But even if a mother had older matrilineal kin nearby to help, would they want to?

ON THE ALTRUISM OF AGING FEMALES

As they age, female primates behave differently from younger females. If they are still breeding, mothers spend more time in direct contact with infants and wean them later than younger mothers do. In general, older mothers are more committed to these last installments on their lifetime reproductive success. In addition to their aging ovaries, such heavier investment may be one reason why older mothers experience longer intervals between births.[45] For female primates at or near the end of their reproductive careers, this tendency to "give of themselves" may also lead them to audaciously defend offspring born to female kin.

As with most Old World monkeys, the maximum lifespan for a langur is around 30 years. As they approach this age, females become less active in troop affairs, avoid competition with other animals, and—even in those matrilocal species with routine infant-sharing—rarely take infants just to carry them around. In an emergency, however, these same socially marginalized old matrons become the most active in defending the group's feeding grounds from neighboring groups. They are also the most daring in defending infants attacked by infanticidal males. Among langurs, sooty mangabeys, and savanna baboons, it is these 20- to 30-year-olds who take bigger risks to defend an endangered infant than the victim's own mother does.[46]

Such episodes are uncommon, but the heroics are unforgettable. Some time ago, scientists observing baboons at Moremi, Botswana, watched as a new male arrived in the troop. Shortly after, he attacked an infant sired by his predecessor. The newcomer chased the seven-month-old female, knocked her down, and dragged her along the ground, then threw her six feet into the air. Nearby group members vocalized and rushed forward but were rebuffed by the male, who resumed his attack on the stunned infant, "biting her in the head, the groin and below the navel." At this point, several females rushed to intervene. The defenders included both the infant's mother and *her* mother, who in spite of being older, smaller, and weighing much less than the muscular young male, was the most audacious. "The grandmother attacked . . . with particular persistence," prompting retaliation from the male, who inflicted a deep cut on the crown of the old female's head. Despite her wound, the grandmother continued to harass the male, managing to temporarily hold him off before he renewed his attack, once again dragging the infant and biting her in the stomach and ribs. Twenty-two minutes later, the baby was dead.[47]

Another instance of matronly heroics involved the langur monkeys I studied at Mount Abu in Rajasthan. A usurping male had been stalking a young mother and her infant for several days. After each abortive attempt, the male would give up for a time, then resume. To evade him, the mother retreated onto the flimsy outer branches of a jacaranda tree when suddenly the infant (but not his mother) fell. The male, who had been riveted to the pair, immediately bounded to the ground and was the first to reach the fallen infant. He was pursued seconds later by the two oldest females in the group. After a fierce struggle, they managed to retrieve the superficially injured infant and return him to his mother. Then the oldest of the two, a solitary female I called Sol because she spent so much time on the margins of the group, continued to harass the male.

This female had ceased to menstruate and no longer bore offspring. She spent her days foraging on the outskirts of the troop and never attempted to take and hold babies. Her main contact with other females was to give way when they displaced her from a feeding position. To all appearances Sol was just biding her time until she died. Yet the striking thing was how abruptly Sol could transform herself into a super-hero. I was a young woman myself, 26 years old and still childless when I watched, astounded, as again and again this worn-toothed old female fought with a male twice her weight and armed with dagger-sharp canine teeth.

In general, monkeys are cautious about escalating aggression, warily

(Top) After retrieving the slightly wounded infant from the male, a grimacing Sol continued to punish the male, slapping at his face and pulling the hairs on his face with one hand while fending off his bites with the other. To me this postmenopausal old female was signaling: "Attack this baby one more time, and it is going to cost you." (Bottom) Nevertheless, four days later, the male was able to grab the infant again (his body can be seen swinging from the male's muzzle like a rag), and Sol together with another old female charged to the rescue. Although they succeeded in getting the baby back, he was horribly wounded, with cuts in his head and deep wounds in his groin. (S. B. Hrdy/AnthroPhoto)

sizing up the opposition in advance so as to avoid being wounded. I marveled at Sol's audacity. Based on what is known about the breeding structure of langur groups, she was almost certainly either a grandmother or great-aunt to the infant she defended.[48] It was her extraordinary selflessness that first inspired my interest in the evolutionary importance of old females.

Since then, systematic observations across species have shown that the presence of a mother makes her daughter more secure. Across the very hierarchical cercopithecine Old World monkeys, among vervets, baboons, and macaques where a female's rank is inherited from her mother, having a grandmother nearby has a significant impact on the childrearing success of younger kin. This is so even if the grandmother is still fertile and preoccupied by her own infants. Just her quotidian presence results in modest improvements to her daughter's or her grandchild's security. In the case of vervet monkeys, a young mother foraging with her own mother nearby will allow an older infant to wander about more freely than at other times. The independence permitted a two-month-old vervet with his or her maternal grandmother present was comparable to that of a three-month-old who did not have a grandmother's support.[49]

Modest differences add up, especially in the case of young and inexperienced mothers. When vervet matriarchs were experimentally removed, their absence was correlated with a marked decline in survival and fertility of daughters between the ages of four and six years. Vervet females were less likely to be threatened or attacked by competing females and were more effective at keeping their babies alive if their own mother was in the same group. Similarly, Japanese macaque females who have a postreproductive mother nearby give birth for the first time at earlier ages, and give birth again after a shorter interval than do females without a mother present.[50] Since females of higher rank give birth at a younger age and produce more offspring who reach adulthood, over many generations the cumulative effects of mother-supported rank are potentially enormous.

When an older female has more than one daughter in the troop, she spends more time near the youngest or least experienced daughter, the one who most benefits from her support.[51] In the langur case, aging females with little potential for directly contributing to the next generation's gene pool (that is, females whose reproductive value was low) were much more willing to defend the offspring of their kin, with whom they shared some genes.[52] The objection might be raised that valiant old females like Sol or the Moremi baboon grandmother were just defending a group member the way *any* adult female would.[53] But no other adult females present, not even the infants' own mothers, took anything like the risks their elders did.

The strongest evidence for the generalization that primate mothers breed more successfully with social support comes from Amboseli baboons. In five different groups, the mothers with the highest rates of infant survival were the most socially integrated. The most successful females all had a half-dozen or so close female associates.[54] Taking into account the fact that "giving impulses" go up with age, it is easy to see why young females would benefit from remaining in their natal groups to take advantage of such selfless allies.[55]

Yet only a minority of mother apes have matrilineal kin nearby. Most social mammals, and the majority of monkeys, are matrilocal, but not Great Apes—even though their residence patterns are somewhat more flexible than previously assumed. However, if we accept Alvarez's corrective, hunter-gatherer mothers (who among other things have different dietary needs than other apes) depart from the Great Ape pattern, and in this respect more nearly resemble Old World monkeys.

So what changed in the line leading to *Homo sapiens* to make it more advantageous and more possible for daughters to be near their mothers when they breed? What tipped the cost/benefit balance among early hominins in favor of young females remaining near kin? Or, alternatively, what made it possible for old females to relocate to be near female relatives who needed them? And what so increased the benefits of having aging kin nearby that natural selection began to favor longer postmenopausal lifespans? For these things to happen, three conditions had to be met.

First, great-aunts and grandmothers needed sufficient freedom of movement so they could live near kin or move to be where they were needed—that is, they had to have the *opportunity* to help. Second, old primate females needed some *motive* for their increasing helpfulness or altruism on behalf of kin. Finally, these old matriarchs had to find some *means* to help—something useful they could do to enhance the reproductive success of younger kin, something so chronically useful that it outweighed the extra pressure that females past breeding age put on local resources.

IT'S TIME TO TALK ABOUT FOOD

What little we know about australopithecines suggests that although they walked on two legs, these tiny-brained 80-pound apes were built a lot like chimpanzees. By 2.5 million years ago, *Homo habilis* was starting to look more human, walking upright and using tools. No one knows for sure what led some of these creatures to evolve into heavier, larger-bodied, longer-legged, longer-faced, and larger-brained *Homo erectus*.[56] Various factors were involved, as we will see in the next chapter, but one thing seems clear. Whatever else was going on, *Homo erectus* had found new ways to find, process, and digest the food needed to support both their larger bodies and, especially, their energetically more expensive larger brains.[57] To date, the most plausible scenario is one set forth by anthropologists James O'Connell, Kristen Hawkes, and Nicholas Blurton Jones. According to their version of the grandmother hypothesis, new opportunities to help kin generated selection pressures favoring longer lifespans among postmenopausal women. But what were the new opportunities?

O'Connell and colleagues propose that long-term trends toward a cooler, drier climate at the end of the Pliocene pressured the precursors of *Homo erectus* to seek new ways to supplement their primary diet of fruit. By around two million years ago, game was increasingly important, but its availability was unpredictable. A division of labor between men who hunted and women who gathered also became more critical. O'Connell and others suggest that when neither meat nor more nutritious plant foods like nuts were available, our ancestors fell back on large underground tubers that plants in dry areas use to stockpile carbohydrates.

These storage organs occur throughout the savanna but are protected by a deep layer of sun-baked earth and are hard to extract. Savanna-dwelling baboons access shallower rhizomes and corms, and chimpanzees in the only population ever to be studied in a savanna habitat use pieces of wood to dig out shallower tubers, suggesting that australopithecines may have done so as well.[58] But it takes special equipment to dig out the larger, deeply buried tubers. This is why, except for a few burrowing mammals like mole rats equipped with shovel-shaped incisors, humans are the only primates who exploit this widely available but difficult-to-access food source.[59]

Tubers are not only hard to extract, they can be fibrous and difficult to digest, hardly ideal food for children. Like nuts, they need to be premasticated or processed in some other way. To eat them, weaned youngsters would have to depend on older providers. Nevertheless, evidence is increasing that starchy tubers were an important fallback food among our ancestors. A 2007 report in *Nature Genetics* revealed that people like the Hadza who rely on roots and tubers have accumulated extra copies of a gene positively correlated with salivary amylase enzymes useful for the digestion of starch. Such copies are absent in Siberian Yakut herders and others with little starch in their diets. Tellingly, three times more copies of these genes are found in foragers who rely on starchy tubers than among chimpanzees, who, except for rare savanna populations, do not eat them.[60]

Not only do savanna-dwelling foragers have salivary juices specifically adapted for digesting starch, but African *Homo erectus* possessed the right teeth for the job. Isotopic analysis of their flat, thickly enameled molars yields results consistent with a diet containing underground roots.[61] Once *Homo erectus* developed the use of fire, perhaps as early as 800,000 years ago, roasting tough, fibrous tubers would have rendered them more digestible and more useful still.[62]

Even before cooking, the addition of tubers to the other plant foods gathered by women would have provided new incentives for food sharing between hunters and gatherers, as well as new opportunities for postreproductive women willing to enhance the survival of kin. For women who knew where to look and who were willing to walk long distances, dig into hard earth, and carry their bounty back to camp, tubers provided a widely available if not particularly palatable source of calories when other foods were in short supply.[63]

The experience and diligence of old women would have been useful in other contexts as well. In many parts of Africa today, tree nuts provide a protein-rich staple for chimpanzees and humans alike. But perfecting the art of cracking their hard outer shells can take years.[64] Furthermore, if every gatherer is a botanist—expert at identifying which plants are edible versus poisonous and predicting their availability—older women are the PhDs. Paula Ivey Henry describes one old Efe woman's uncanny ability to locate medicinal plants and vegetable foods rarely used except during famines. Her own children had all died, yet this wizened old woman spent hours in the forest collecting fish, shellfish, nuts, fruits, and roots too scarce or hard to locate at that time of year for other women to bother with or even remember.[65]

The significance of ethnobotanical knowledge for the well-being of children in parts of the world where most people are perpetually undernourished is only beginning to be studied. In 2007 a team of American and Spanish anthropologists working among Tsimane forager-horticulturalists in Amazonian Bolivia reported a significant correlation between how much mothers knew about the diversity and uses of local plants and the nutritional status and health of their children. The effects were independent of other measures like household income or years of schooling.[66] Although the researchers did not report *how* mothers acquired their special knowledge, most likely it was transmitted woman-to-woman.

Other forms of traditional knowledge—about environmental hazards, diseases, or people in distant communities—are less likely to be gender-specific. Across primates, aged females and, when they are still around, aged males provide vital reservoirs for intergenerationally transmitted knowledge. Whether Hamadryas baboons or foragers, it is the oldest group members who remember where to find water in drought years when all the usual sources have dried up. But with the exception of humans, information and skills are primarily transmitted through demonstration rather than through teaching or the intentional sharing of knowledge. When suffering from diarrhea, for example, chimpanzees seek out a particular plant that hinders intestinal parasites. But as far as I know, chimpanzees only medicate themselves. It was the skilled utilization of new food sources and technologies in the genus *Homo,* combined with the increased importance of sharing and teaching, that opened up new possibilities for kin-directed assistance between generations and for altering the cost/benefit ratio of keeping older group members around.[67]

THE MORPHING OF GRANDMOTHERS

We have come a long way since the days when evolutionists and anthropologists alike ignored females past reproductive age. Today, the presence or absence of postmenopausal women, their longevity, their efficiency, along with their dedication to kin have become legitimate research topics. The new significance accorded postreproductive females was very much in evidence in 2002, when I attended the first-of-its-kind international symposium on "the psychological, social, and reproductive significance of the second half of life" at the Hanse Institute for Advanced Study in Delmenhorst, Germany.

Throughout the last quarter of the twentieth century, sociobiologists, many of us women, had worked hard to expand evolutionary theory to include selection pressures on both sexes. Along with other fieldworkers, I had also been studying the contributions to infants' well-being of both mothers and allomothers, old females included.[68] But this meeting was the first time that researchers from around the world convened specifically to discuss the impact of grandmothers.[69] Well past menopause myself, yearning for grandchildren, I was anything but a disinterested participant.

Kristen Hawkes was there, along with Ruth Mace, who two years previously had reported that the presence of a maternal grandmother halved child mortality among the Mandinka. The German primatologist Andreas Paul summarized accumulating evidence that menopause can no longer be considered uniquely human and that other primates, if they live long enough, may also cease to menstruate before they die, and also exhibit strong impulses to help younger kin. What is unusual about humans, Paul stressed, is not that follicles in a woman's ovaries peter out around age 40 but how long women go on living afterward.[70] Just why this might be useful was explained by the anthropologist Donna Leonetti as she described what she and colleagues were learning about Khasi tribal peoples from Meghalaya in northeast India.

The Khasi are among the few matrilineal peoples to retain their traditional way of life. Daughters, especially the youngest daughter, continue living with their mothers after they begin to bear children, and this residence pattern pays off in higher child survival. Twelve percent of Khasi mothers had lost one or more children before the age of ten, but the chances of a child dying were 74 percent greater if no grandmother lived with them.[71]

A young woman who does not happen to reside matrilocally may nevertheless return to her mother around the time of first birth. The Bavarian medical anthropologist Wulf Schiefenhövel stressed the value of such customs. Not only is support at hand during childbirth, but if the mother dies before her children are independent, or chooses not to rear her children, matrilineal kin are available to help. Among the Trobriand Islanders Schiefenhövel studied, 27 percent of children, especially firstborns, end up being fostered out shortly after weaning and are reared by allomothers. In about a third of these cases, the adopter was their grandmother.[72]

For society after society, grandmothers have been shown to influence the reproductive success of kin. For European and North American farming communities where written records were available, the increased lifetime reproductive success of mothers with a grandmother to help could be traced over several generations.[73] Birth and death records for 500 Finnish women and 2,400 Canadian women leading hardscrabble peasant lives and destined to lose 40 percent of all infants born to them revealed that if these mothers had their own mother still living in the same community they lost significantly fewer children. In both samples, numbers of surviving grandchildren depended on how much longer the woman herself survived after the birth of her last child. Postreproductive women gained roughly two extra grandchildren for every ten years they survived past completion of their childbearing.[74] But these effects were significant only in the case of the first three grandchildren. This suggested that either mothers were gaining valuable experience or else help from older children compensated for the increasing frailty or absence of a grandmother.

News about hardworking postmenopausal women among the Hadza and the stunning impact of grandmothers on child survival among Mandinka horticulturalists (discussed in Chapter 3) spread fast among anthropologists. Researchers working in highland Peru, Senegal, rural Ethiopia, northeasternmost India, and the deserts of Western Australia began to ask new questions. Others scoured archives in Europe, North America, and Japan. All confirmed the importance of postmenopausal altruists.[75] Wherever populations were characterized by high average rates of child mortality, grandmothers—if available—made a difference to child survival.

Galvanized by the new findings, Rebecca Sear and Ruth Mace set out to review evidence for 28 traditional societies where we already had fairly good demographic information. In all of them, death of the mother in the first two years proved catastrophic, presumably because substitutes for mother's milk and maternal care were so inadequate. But the lethal impact of losing one's mother decreased with the child's age, and in five societies a motherless child who survived to age two had as good a chance of reaching adulthood as a child whose mother had not died. Since two-year-olds were still far from independent, other caregivers had to be stepping in. And no single class of caregivers made a bigger difference than grandmothers. Their presence was correlated with higher child survival in every one of the twelve societies for which relevant data had been recorded.[76]

WHEN AND EXACTLY HOW DO GRANDMOTHERS HELP?

Overall, grandmothers were turning out to be the most reliably beneficial of all alloparents. Under some ecological conditions, for example in foraging societies when game is short, their presence had an even bigger impact on child survival than the father's did. At other times grandmothers proved most useful when mothers were young, inexperienced, or lacked older children to help out.[77] Children's age was also a factor since, statistically, children benefited most from having a grandmother present around the age of weaning.[78] Whereas some youngsters are nonchalant about the end of nursing and may even wean themselves, more often little monkeys and apes (including human ones) find rejection from the mother's breast quite stressful. Not only do youngsters lose access to the emotional comfort of sucking there, but they have to compete for available food with larger group members, and may suffer pangs of jealousy if they see a younger sibling nestling where they want to be. It is no wonder that weaning sometimes feels like a death sentence. To some already malnourished and immunologically challenged toddlers, it may actually be one.[79]

Recollecting her earliest years, the !Kung woman Nisa recalled how jealous she felt when her newborn brother displaced her at her mother's breast. Tension between Nisa and her mother erupted whenever he nursed, so what did she do? "I went to the village where mother's mother lived and told myself I would eat with her. When I arrived at her hut, grandma roasted [food], and I ate and ate and ate. I slept beside her and lived there for a while." Later, her grandmother returned Nisa to her parents, making a point of scolding her adult daughter in front of Nisa for punishing instead of being nice to her. Nisa was comforted by knowing that she had such an influential ally.[80]

Kindly old grannies are a long-standing cultural stereotype. Yet researchers have only begun to zero in on the stress-reducing component of their benevolence. In 2006, seventeen years after he had first gone to Trinidad to find out whether alloparents affected maternal reproductive success, Mark Flinn was still doing research there and published a paper describing the physiological benefits of having supportive alloparents. As predicted, a traumatic social event—such as being threatened or witnessing a fight between parents—led to increases in salivary cortisol levels by anywhere from 100 percent to 2000 percent. But the negative effects of early social trauma (as measured by cortisol levels) was moderated for children with alloparental support, including children with a grandmother on hand.[81]

Such demographic circumstances are crucial. The more inexperienced the mother or the fewer older children around to help (her own or perhaps their cousins), the more a grandmother or great-aunt matters.[82] Fortuitously, the same high child mortality rates that make grandmaternal contributions so critical also make it likely that postmenopausal women will have few direct descendants vying for their help. Grandmothers can also distribute themselves and channel contributions according to those who need their help the most.[83] But demographics aside, it also matters *whose* mother a grandmother was.

MOTHER'S MOTHER VS. MOTHER-IN-LAW

Clearly grandmothers have a range of beneficial effects, even in some cases dramatically reducing child mortality. However, the type of effect she has may vary depending on whether the nearby grandmother happens to be the mother's mother or the father's. Across traditional societies, the presence of a maternal grandmother is more likely to be correlated with the enhanced well-being of grandchildren, whereas the presence of the father's mother is more likely to be correlated with increased maternal fecundity, earlier reproduction, and shorter intervals between birth.[84] Such increased maternal fecundity may be a boon for her mate's reproductive success, but it will not necessarily enhance the well-being of children born in rapid succession and forced to compete for family resources with more siblings. Furthermore, the benevolence of *every* grandmother is far from guaranteed. Under some circumstances her ministrations prove downright detrimental.

We need only turn to case studies from some of humanity's more stratified and highly patriarchal societies to find grandmaternal interventions reminiscent of murderous marmoset and meerkat "grandmothers from hell." For example, long-standing preferences for particular family configurations in some parts of the world, especially a preference for sons, may result in a paternal grandmother taking the initiative to dispatch an unwanted granddaughter. I am still haunted by a photograph sent to me once by a colleague depicting a pair of brother-sister twins born to a Pakistani mother. The much-desired son, who had remained with his mother to breastfeed, was healthy and robust, while the daughter, who had been taken at birth by the paternal grandmother and bottlefed with a lethal mixture of powdered milk and unboiled water, was limp and emaciated. Shortly after the photograph was taken, the little girl died from chronic diarrhea and malnutrition.[85]

Another case of what is better termed a mother-in-law than a grandmother effect can be found in Eckart Voland and Jan Beise's reconstruction of eighteenth- and nineteenth-century families from Germany's Krummhörn region. As expected, child survival rates were higher if the postreproductive caregiver was the wife's mother.[86] If the husband's mother lived in the house, the most salient effect was her daughter-in-law's shorter intervals between births and higher overall fertility. Although one might expect this higher fertility to result in higher overall reproductive success, it did not. Having a live-in mother-in-law turned out to be correlated with a significantly higher rate of stillbirths and neonatal mortality.[87] According to Voland and Beise, these poor outcomes may have been artifacts of pregnant wives living in a dour Calvinist community, separated from their own families and under the oppressive and presumably highly stressful surveillance of their husband's mother.

Clearly the impact of paternal grandmothers on the survival of grandchildren is not as uniformly beneficial as is that of the maternal grandmother. Several authors attribute reported differences in solicitude to the level of uncertainty that surrounds paternity. If "it is a wise child who knows his own father," it will take an even wiser, unusually well-informed grandmother to distinguish her son's child. A paternal grandmother may feel less emotionally committed to grandchildren to whom she might or might not be related.[88] It is also possible, of course, that the two women simply do not like each other.

Whatever the reasons, opposing effects from paternal versus maternal grandmothers similar to those reported for German peasants have also been documented for patrilineal societies in mid-twentieth-century West Africa and eighteenth- to nineteenth-century Quebec.[89] Rice-growing peasants from seventeenth- to nineteenth-century Tokugawa, Japan, also conform to this pattern, albeit with extra twists. It was very unusual in this patrilocal, patrilineal, extremely patriarchal society for a mother to be living with her daughter, but a few did, and the maternal grandmother's presence was correlated with increased survival rates for both her grandsons and granddaughters. More commonly, it was the father's mother in the household, and although her presence had no effect on granddaughters, it was detrimental to the survival of grandsons.[90] One possibility is that in this rigidly patrilineal system, paternal grandmothers had a stake in reducing the number of heirs competing to inherit the land.[91]

Different roles played by grandmothers depend on a range of factors—residence patterns for sure, but also local subsistence conditions, the family's socioeconomic status, family composition, and inheritance patterns—which will obviously be more important for settled people than among hunter-gatherers who have few possessions.[92] Leonetti and her coworkers have undertaken the first study aimed at teasing apart such factors. They are comparing childcare patterns among the mother-centered Khasi community in the northeastern Indian state of Megahalaya with those in a patrilineal and patrilocal Bengali community in the neighboring state of Assam. Among these patriarchal Bengalis, men monitor and seek to control women's movements, and mothers and their children alike suffer from a lack of direct access to resources.

Owing to the importance of patrilineally inherited farmland, female chastity is a matter of tremendous concern to Bengalis. Wives are under chronic surveillance, with the father's mother in her stereotypical role as watchdog, and (as in the case of the eighteenth-century German peasants) her presence is correlated with shorter intervals between births and an overall increase in the number of children born (some women have as many as eleven children). Nevertheless (and this diverges from the German case), the paternal grandmother's presence is more helpful than harmful in keeping infants alive, even though the fast reproductive pace probably takes a toll on their mothers.[93]

In contrast to Bengali mothers, Khasi mothers own property, have considerably more freedom of movement, and benefit from having matrilineal kin nearby. Maternal grandmothers in particular attach high priority to keeping the mother and her children as well-nourished and healthy as possible. Not surprisingly, the grandmother's labor is positively correlated with how much children weigh, which is on average significantly more than Bengali children of the same ages. Even though the socioeconomic status of the two groups is roughly similar (with no one being that well off), on average Khasi mothers are taller, better nourished, and weigh more than their Bengali counterparts, who by and large are fed less well in childhood and all through adulthood.[94] Among 2,666 Khasi infants in this study, those with maternal grandmothers present as opposed to absent were more likely to survive to age ten.[95]

Are maternal kin invariably good news then? Not necessarily. Even within matrilocal societies, growing population density can increase competition between kin for matrilineally inherited resources. This appears to be the case in parts of contemporary Malawi, where having the mother's mother or sisters around actually proves detrimental to child survival. In the case of Malawi, I suspect that this situation is due to the decreasing availability of farmland women need to support their families. In the terminology of Sherman's eusocial continuum, such competition increases the degree of reproductive skew, since mothers with access to more land can rear more young. This speculation is consistent with the fact that the correlation between nearby matrilineal kin and child mortality was confined to girls and most pronounced in families that had heritable land.[96] This 2008 study from Malawi is important, reminding us how much we still have to learn about humans as cooperative breeders.

PATRIARCHAL COMPLICATIONS SINCE THE PLEISTOCENE

Patrilineal concerns are one reason why the impact of the husband's mother on the well-being of grandchildren can be so variable. Universally, people in traditional societies want children, but residence patterns, family compositions, values, and priorities regarding children differ. Whereas people with matrilineal/matrilocal histories award high priority to maternal interests, those in patrilineal, and especially full-fledged patriarchal, societies where property is passed from fathers to sons are more concerned with ensuring the husband's paternity and preserving patrilineal access to resources, even when this entails practices detrimental to the well-being of mothers (and children too), such as sequestering women or sewing up their vaginas (infibulation).

Through time, a fixation with chastity can take on a symbolic and institutional life of its own, so that tremendous mental energy and effort gets channeled into policing and controlling female sexuality and convincing women that it is essential for their own and their children's sake to be "good" (that is, chaste, dutiful, submissive, and self-sacrificing) mothers.[97] It's not that men and their mothers in these societies don't care about children. They do, often desiring lots of them, especially several sons (an heir plus a spare). But preservation of the patriline and patrilineal institutions still takes priority, even to the point of depriving children of grandmothers. Consider the once widely practiced South Asian custom of *suttee*. When a man died, it was his widow's "sacred duty" to burn herself alive. Her suicide forestalled diversion of resources for her continued support as well as eliminating risks that she might dishonor the patriline by taking up with another man. However, *suttee* was not just hard on virtuous widows. It deprived dependent children of grandmothers and great-aunts, as well as mothers.[98]

WHAT ABOUT GRAMPS?

Even among foragers like the Efe, where lots of hands-on male care can be found, grandfathers spend surprisingly little time holding babies. Fathers, cousins, and older brothers spend more than twice as long babysitting as grandfathers do (also more than five times more than uncles). Among the Hadza, grandfathers are far less likely than grandmothers to even be in the same camps as their grandchildren. In Sear and Mace's 2008 overview, the proximity of grandfathers had little detectable impact on the survival of their grandchildren.[99] Does this mean grandfathers don't matter?

Certainly as they age, most men continue to be interested in what happens to their descendants. In patrilineal societies, older men take a special (if not particularly hands-on) interest in sons and grandsons, while in matrilineal societies uncles (mother's brothers) are especially important mentors. In societies like our own, where intergenerational transmission of property is both very important and unusually well-documented, men go to more trouble than women do to channel wealth down the generations to blood descendants, to keep property "in the family."[100] In hunter-gatherer societies, property does not have anything like the same importance, but social relationships are no less complex—or prone to generate discord. Respected middle-aged and older men, aging fathers, grandfathers, and uncles help relatives broker disputes between rivals or co-wives, increase the likelihood that groups retain the use of waterholes, and perhaps most importantly help arrange suitable matches and influence group recruitment and retention.

As Polly Wiessner has shown for the !Kung, the combined hunting, healing, and political skills of "elder statesmen" diffuse tensions, promote solidarity, attract useful group members, and otherwise promote the group's solidarity and continued access to resources. The impact of a respected man can persist long after he passes his prime. In a follow-up study tracing the fates of different Bushmen families, Wiessner found that a man skilled in setting up long-term *hxaro* relationships and in other ways could keep his group together in the same area almost twice as long as less-gifted elders could. As she put it, "Thirty-four years later, the wives of men who excelled in these activities had an 84% chance of living with their mature, married children as opposed to the 34% chance of women married to less skilled men."[101] Whether or not old men continue to reproduce themselves, or even whether or not they are actually the progenitors of children born to younger wives, such elder statesmen have kin in the groups whose long-term interests they promote.[102] Such men are not so much uninterested in children as they are uninvolved in childcare.

There are few primate analogues for the stabilizing influence of postprime men. With physical decline, nonhuman primate males tend to become marginalized or are driven out of the group altogether. The closest parallel might be a silverback male gorilla accompanied by a younger black-backed male apprentice in his same group. Even after the older male has passed his prime, the silverback continues to play a protective role, and the presence of multiple males in the group increases infant survival.[103]

In gerontocratic human breeding systems, where old men not only control the marriage options of younger men but monopolize younger women themselves (think Aboriginal Australia), old "silverbacks" continue to exercise influence. This led Frank Marlowe to hypothesize that selection favoring longevity might have operated even more strongly on these old patriarchs than on grandmothers (the "patriarchs hypothesis").[104] Bear in mind, however, that uniquely human ideologies promoting respect for elders long after they have lost their physical edge probably required language. If lifespans were already longer by the time humans acquired language (a proposition I will examine in the next chapter), this brings us back to grandmothers.

THE LUCK OF THE DEMOGRAPHIC DRAW

Apart from human females, no other primates, and very few other mammals, take decades to mature before they begin to breed and then live for decades after their ovaries peter out. Among the rare exceptions, short-finned pilot whales and orcas quit breeding around age 40 but live decades longer.[105] Nonhuman female primates who survive long enough to cease menstruating go on to live only a few years afterward, or a decade at most in the case of chimpanzees, who reproduce for the last time around age 42. Even the most long-lived of these females spend only 16–25 percent of their lives as postreproductives, not nearly as long as women, who cease to cycle some time after age 40 and then potentially live on for twice that long.[106] The proposal mentioned in Chapter 6 that menopause might have evolved to produce in humans a sort of "sterile caste" to forestall competition between older and younger breeding females overlooks the fact that what is different about human apes is not cessation of reproduction around age 40—that is, menopause itself—but how long women go on living afterward.[107]

Experienced in childcare, sensitive to infant cues, adept at local subsistence tasks, undistracted by babies of their own or even the possibility of having them, and (like old men as well) repositories of useful knowledge, postmenopausal females are also unusually altruistic. Given the flexibility of forager lifestyles, these ideal allomothers can readily relocate near needy kin—though it is well to keep in mind that the meat a new husband provides members of his wife's group may also be part of the attraction. Across the societies in the Sear and Mace overview, grandmothers were second only to mothers, and rivaled only by older siblings, in their beneficial impact on child survival. But postmenopausal allomothers also have a drawback: the probability they will eventually grow frail.

Nothing guarantees that a postreproductive woman will survive long enough to be of use. In an unusually well-researched thought experiment, anthropologists Jeffrey Kurland and Corey Sparks used archaeological records from late Paleolithic gravesites to compile demographic parameters and then used these to estimate probable lifespans for foragers under a range of ecological conditions. Under good conditions with low mortality, they estimated that a 20-year-old mother would have a roughly 50 percent chance of having a 40-year-old grandmother alive to help her raise her children. As mortality went up, this chance drops to around 25 percent. Using census data from ethnographies, Kristen Hawkes and Nick Blurton Jones came up with lifespan estimates that fell between those two extremes. Their low estimate was consistent with that for a sample of 20 Efe infants—four had surviving grandmothers. At the high end, 7 of 15 Aka infants had either maternal or paternal grandmothers present.[108]

Fewer than half of Pleistocene mothers would be likely to have had a mother alive or living in the same group when they first gave birth. The chances of a mother having an older sibling still alive were several times higher than that. The chance of her infant having older siblings or cousins, or having either a father, possible fathers, or a would-be father, or some combination thereof would have been higher still. Depending on the circumstances, some combinations would be more beneficial than others, even though—all other things being equal—those with a helpful grandmother would be better off than those without. In the terminology of five card stud poker, where only the very lucky are likely to be dealt a full house or even a matching pair, having a grandmother nearby was like having an ace in the hole. Given equivalently mediocre hands, a grandmother was often the winning card in the Darwinian game of life—but only for those lucky enough to have been dealt one.

The probability of different types of help varied with circumstances. So did the kind of help different alloparents provided and how such help

Cousins and older sibs can be good for a snack, but children's most common allo-maternal contributions are as role models and child-minders (usually with adult supervision not far off). (Peabody Museum/Marshall Expedition image 2001.29.416)

was weighted. Children make adept berry-pickers and lizard-catchers but lack the upper body strength and long arms to dig out deep tubers.[109] Nor do they come close to being as practiced and single-minded at tasks like gathering or nut-cracking as old women are. But prereproductive babysitters have the merit of availability. Supervision by a nearby adult would have made older children more usable still, freeing mothers to forage more efficiently. And of course after the Neolithic, with all the chores typical of farming societies, children became productive assets in their own right.[110]

Helpful as grannies are, a grim final question remains: What happens when they cease to be useful? Medicare, Social Security, and other features of the modern safety net make Westerners some of the only people (and the only primates) where resources routinely flow from the young to the very old. More often in primates, resources flow from grandparents and parents down to breeding adults and their offspring.[111] Inevitably among our ancestors there came a time when even the most helpful old female became too decrepit to provision herself, much less share with others.

In some species, grandmothers voluntarily opt out of competition for food with younger kin, falling in rank, giving way to younger relatives, marginalizing themselves and being marginalized by others. Across human societies, treatment of old people varies from reverence to astonishing callousness.[112] Just as in modern America, where children telephone grandparents more times each month if they possess significant heritable resources, old women in foraging societies are more valued when the food they gather is an important component of the diet. Along with women generally, they are less valued in societies subsisting primarily on game brought in by men.

Customs for coping with decrepitude range from reverse solicitude (the young caring for the old) to voluntary euthanasia (as in traditional Japan), from reverence to marginalization, abandonment, or outright execution. As Kim Hill listened, an old Ache man recalled when as a young man he used to sneak up with his axe behind old women who had become a burden on the group. "I would step on them, then they all died, there by the big river . . . I didn't used to wait until they were completely dead to bury them. When they were still moving I would [break their backs and necks]."[113] In other words, it may not be purely altruism that motivates an Ache woman my age to work so hard.

THE ART OF MANUFACTURING ALLOMOTHERS

Given the neediness of human children and the vagaries of a hunter-gatherer existence, humans were fortunate to be so flexible, mobile, and well-equipped to consciously strategize. For unlike marmosets, human children are not chimerically related to several fathers who are also brothers. Nor can they rely on allomothers who are genetically more closely related to them than the helpers are to their own young, the way honeybee grubs can. This is why the special talent human parents have for cultivating future caretaking prospects, even to the point of manufacturing fictive kinship, is so important. The sort of sexual liaisons described in Chapter 5 provide a taste of myriad possible ploys. Once acquired, language and kinship customs equip women with an even wider range of options for manufacturing kin. Humans are expert at forging alliances on their children's behalf.

Beginning in girlhood, and as they mature, women become increasingly adept at making friends. The roots of such predispositions do not grow out of men's quest for hunting partners or brothers-in-arms. Whether consciously or not, women seek "sisters" with whom to share care of our children. Even the obsession with being popular and "belonging" so poignantly evident in teenage girls, rendering them both acutely sensitive to what others think and also causing them to be competitive and ruthlessly mean in excluding others, may possibly have much to do with forging bonds which in ancestral environments would have been critical for successful childrearing. From adolescence onward, many girls are more concerned with popularity and belonging than with achievements per se, so much so that their "sense of self becomes . . . organized around being able to make, and then to maintain, affiliations and relationships," and they dread the rupture of friendships and other social ties.[114]

Some evolutionary psychologists attribute such tendencies to the innate powerlessness of women in ancestral worlds, where they were carried off from their natal communities to breed among less-than-supportive members of another patriline.[115] Others see in the human female's urge to "tend and befriend" a way to obtain support in times of stress (such as during attack by a saber-tooth tiger).[116] But neither of these hypotheses explains why women became so much more affiliative than say chimpanzees, who also usually left home to breed and also had to worry about big cats. These psychologists overlook a key difference between women and other apes. Girls as they matured to breeding age and throughout life needed to line up help from more individuals than just their mates. The bonds themselves became the resource to be protected.

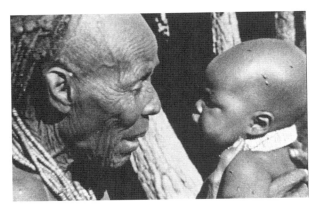

Grandmothers are not the only aged females who forge loving relationships with children. Her dimming eyesight notwithstanding, this 85-year-old Himba woman peers expectantly into the face of her grandson's four- to five-month-old daughter as she makes a soft grrrr-sound and gently shakes the baby. The girl looks back tentatively, the more intently as the old woman's forehead touches hers and she begins to rhythmically sing while patting the baby on the back. Meanwhile, the baby looks away from the old woman, to her mother, and back again to her *great*-grandmother. (I. Eibl-Eibesfeldt/Human Ethology Archives)

Over generations, devices for manufacturing kin have been culturally elaborated and maintained. "It is intriguing to speculate," Wiessner writes, "that the roots of human kinship systems might lie in cooperative breeding communities where maternal-like care comes from a number of individuals other than the mother, thereby extending concepts of who constitutes family."[117] Stratagems include honorary naming devices, systems of classificatory kin, as well as customs such as designating "extra fathers." Females in many species use polyandrous matings to line up possible fathers, while bonobos use sexual gratification as well as grooming and occasional gifts to strengthen social bonds with members of both sexes.[118] No species, however, proves as clever or opportunistic and—once language became part of the species repertoire—so endlessly inventive as humans are in the manufacture of partners to share with and alloparents to rely on. If long-lived grandmothers were humankind's ace in the hole, all these classificatory kin—distant relatives, godparents, possible fathers, namesakes, trading partners, and other manufactured alloparents—became their wild cards.

9

CHILDHOOD AND THE DESCENT OF MAN

All of us long to be at home in the world, to find our singular passions
reflected in a larger pond than the selves we swim in.

—Daphne Merkin (2002)

No mammal in the world has produced young that take longer to mature or depend on so many others for so long as did humans in the Pleistocene. Cared for by alloparents as well as parents, these incredibly costly, large-brained offspring grew up slowly and survived in sufficient numbers to produce a founding population that could move into new habitats, rear children there, spread out, and eventually people the globe.

Provisioned not just by their mothers but by other members of the group, even offspring weaned long before they were able to fend for themselves could nevertheless mature slowly without starving. The African hunter-gatherers studied by anthropologists in the twentieth century were already very different creatures from the hominins of the Pleis-

Over thousands of generations, uncounted numbers of prereproductives of both sexes played with, reacted to, distracted, soothed, carried, teased, occasionally fed, sometimes competed with, and (more or less) kept safe and happy the almost incessantly needy babies and toddlers left partially or entirely in their charge. It will be some years—not until she is nineteen or so—before the !Kung girl on the left gives birth herself. This means she will have abundant opportunities to practice caretaking prior to becoming a parent. (Peabody Museum/Marshall Expedition image 2001.29.413)

tocene, but the challenges they faced staying alive, staying fed, and rearing their children provide the most realistic models we have for reconstructing the challenges faced by our ancestors. Among the !Kung, girls rarely reached menarche before age 16 or so and usually did not give birth for the first time before age 19 or older. Even more time elapsed before these young women produced as much as they consumed. Yet once we step back to view maturing humans in broad comparative perspective, we see that such prolonged periods of postweaning (or in the case of birds, postfledging) dependence are not, in and of themselves, out of the ordinary for cooperative breeders, even though the sheer extent of dependence is on the long side in the case of modern humans. The really distinctive feature of the human story is not longer childhoods per se but a larger mosaic of life-history traits that derived from cooperative breeding: bigger brains that are metabolically more costly than those of other apes; extended lifespans for females after they pass menopause; and peculiarly prosocial tendencies, especially where food sharing is involved, that distinguish humans from chimpanzees, bonobos, orangutans, and gorillas.

In this chapter, I briefly consider long childhoods and other life-history traits with origins in cooperative breeding, and then consider how pinpointing their appearance in the fossil record could help resolve the vexed question of just when in the history of the genus *Homo* such an unapelike mode of childrearing got started, and with it the greater capacities for intersubjective engagement that coevolved with cooperative breeding. Finally, I consider some of the unusual liabilities that these peculiar emotional aptitudes impose upon immatures as socially intelligent and sensitive to separation as all apes are, and speculate about our future evolution.

EXTENDED LIVES, LONGER CHILDHOODS, BIGGER BRAINS

Although shared care is not found in other Great Apes, it is found in nearly half of all primates. Alloparental care is accompanied by provisioning in approximately one fifth of primate species, even though with the exception of humans and some Callitrichidae (the galago or ruffed lemur nestmates who allow one another's young to suckle, for example) such provisioning is fairly minimal. Outside of primates, alloparental care and provisioning have also evolved multiple times in a broad array of insects, birds, and other mammals. The remarkable thing about humans, then, is not so much cooperative breeding as it is *cooperative breeding in an ape*—and the highly unusual traits that emerged as a consequence of this unprecedented combination.

Consider the case of long postmenopausal lifespans. Provided they survive long enough, many female primates cease to menstruate before they die. Yet apart from women and some whales, no other mammals in the world go on living for decades after they are no longer able to reproduce. So what processes led to the extension of postmenopausal lifespans in humans? Well, if mothers with help are better nourished and safer from hazards, their chances of surviving long enough for genes favoring slightly longer lifespans to be expressed go up. And if help from surviving older females increases the survival of their kin, as Kristen Hawkes proposed was the case among *Homo erectus,* then genes conducive to even greater longevity would have been favored over evolutionary time.[1] So cooperative breeding (which, based on its frequency in nature, evolves more readily than long postmenopausal lifespans do) would have set the stage for this highly unusual and derived life-history trait to evolve in humans.

As a general biological rule, the costs imposed by reproduction mean that individuals who breed tend to die sooner than those who have not bred. However, this rule is often reversed for females among cooperative breeders. In such extreme cases as the eusocial naked mole rat, ants, bees, or termites, breeding females are coddled and kept safe deep within tunnels or hives, thereby surviving longer than their nonbreeding helpers do. The lifespan of a honeybee queen is measured in years, while that of a worker is counted in weeks. The queen's long lifespan is a derived life-history trait that could evolve only because other hive members expended the effort and took the risks to rear her young.[2]

Similarly to extended lifespans, the prolonged childhoods and bigger brains of humans also appear to be derived traits that evolved in the context of cooperative breeding. Whenever natural selection favors longer lifespans (which in the case of the genus *Homo* might be because of the help postmenopausal women provided to their relatives, or because of some other reason), longer childhoods follow as a matter of course.[3] Once the likelihood of dying young is reduced, a later age of maturity becomes an evolutionary advantage. By waiting longer before diverting bodily resources to reproduction, animals can grow bigger bodies and possibly also develop more target-specific immune systems—an important investment for the long haul. Slower maturation also provides immatures the option to "pay as they grow," opportunistically shifting to a slower pace of growth during times of food shortages and then catching up in times of plenty.[4]

A prolonged childhood, in turn, may have relaxed the selection pressures opposing the evolution of bigger brains. Brains are enormously expensive organs, second only to hearts in how much energy they require. Only well-fed youngsters—such as those with fairly reliable allomaternal provisioning—could afford to grow and maintain such expensive tissue.[5] Because evolutionary increases in brain size tend to be incremental, being modestly more cerebral than a competitor would scarcely be a sufficient advantage to compensate for the big handicap of taking nearly two decades to mature. A faster-maturing albeit dumber competitor could still outbreed her. But if apes in the hominin line were already living longer, and—because they were provisioned by others—already enjoying the luxury of growing up slowly, then incremental increases in brain size could evolve at a discount.[6] Even without off-setting the full costs of waiting so late to breed, brains could gradually get bigger until they reached a size that actually enhanced the relative fitness of possessors— by allowing them to learn more, know more, become more efficient at food procurement, out-compete others for mates, and so forth.

Without a doubt, highly complex *coevolutionary* processes were involved in the evolution of extended lifespans, prolonged childhoods, and bigger brains.[7] What I want to stress here, however, is that cooperative breeding was the *pre-existing condition* that permitted the evolution of these traits in the hominin line. Creatures may not need big brains to evolve cooperative breeding, but hominins needed shared care and provisioning to evolve big brains. Cooperative breeding had to come first.

But when? One place we might turn to answer this question is the fossil record. If fossil evidence allows us to attach a date to the emergence of longer childhoods or bigger brains or extended lifespans, we would be in a position to estimate the point by which cooperative breeding had already become established in the hominin line, and with it (I believe) the emergence of emotionally modern humans. So is there any fossil evidence to support my contention that modern emotional sensibilities emerged in the hominin line long before our late Pleistocene sprint into behavioral modernity?

WHEN DID COOPERATIVE BREEDING FIRST BEGIN?

We now know that by the beginning of the Pleistocene—a million and a half years before humans with fully sapient-sized brains were on the scene—the average African *Homo erectus* was twice as big as *Australopithecus afarensis* (believed to be a predecessor of the genus *Homo*). Males weighed around 130 pounds, with some individuals nearly six feet tall. Their 800–1,100 cc brains were nearly twice as large as those of australopithecines or chimpanzees—smaller than the brains of *Homo sapiens* but moving into their range (1,100–1,700 cc).[8]

Animals this big almost certainly took longer to grow, suggesting that African *Homo erectus* matured later than did either australopithecines or modern chimpanzees, although probably not nearly as late as modern humans. In all likelihood, these early Pleistocene hominins were already enjoying the prolonged postweaning dependence we would expect to find in a cooperative breeder. Evidence from *Homo erectus* leg bones and molar development (suggesting slightly later molar eruption) may also be consistent with slower development.[9] While much controversy surrounds the interpretation of all the fossil evidence, one thing we can be certain of is that by 1.8 million years ago African *Homo erectus* were growing bigger brains than any of their known predecessors.

Another thing we know from the fossil record is that, while both sexes were taller and weighed more, this increase in body size was more pronounced in females than in males. Instead of being nearly twice as big as females, as is the case of australopithecines, *Homo erectus* males were only 18 percent larger than females.[10] This degree of sexual dimorphism is only slightly more pronounced than that of modern humans. Why is increased growth among these females important? To grow bodies and especially brains this big, both sexes—but especially *Homo erectus* mothers and their children—needed high-quality diets. Yet as the behavioral ecologist and paleontologist James O'Connell and his colleagues emphasize, climatic conditions at the beginning of the Pleistocene would have decreased the availability of the palatable shoots and soft fruit that ape immatures in Africa fed on.[11] Among bipedal apes in an arid habitat of mixed savanna and woodland, weanlings would have had to rely on foods obtained, processed, or premasticated by others before being shared. Their survival would have depended on food sharing by adults in their group.

In addition to eating starchy tubers when meat was in short supply, these hominins probably also obtained protein and lipids by efficient harvesting and processing of nuts, insect grubs, and perhaps shellfish.

The omega-3 fatty acids in these foods would have been especially critical for pregnant women and nursing mothers, to fuel the fast-growing brains of late-stage fetuses and nursing young.[12] Such a diet accentuates the interdependence between male hunters, who were eager for both meat and prestige, and female gatherers, who were likewise keen on meat but put an even higher priority on reliable meals. Such conditions would have greatly increased the survival value of food sharing and division of labor, as well as the flexible residence patterns that allowed pregnant females to remain or move near relatives—including their own mothers—who could be counted on to help with provisioning.

Rare as it is in other apes for new mothers to have their own mother in the same group, many other primates, including most of the cercopithecine Old World monkeys, opt for matrilocal residence, and with good reason.[13] Social support from matrilineal kin means that a female can forage, breed, and rear young more nearly on her own terms. By contrast, patrilocal residence puts females at a disadvantage with respect to how much freedom of movement or control over their reproductive lives they have.[14] Whether daughters stayed near their mothers or returned to be with them at childbirth, or whether mothers themselves moved, the added support from having matrilineal kin nearby would have made new mothers feel more secure and would have promoted the kind of inter-individual trust essential for hominin mothers to be willing to share care of their young.

For my money, such a living arrangement where mothers had nearby kin and came to depend upon assistance from others in rearing their young provides the most promising answer to the question "Why us and not them?" Other apes in the early Pleistocene would have benefited every bit as much as humans from being better able to read the intentions of competitors or from evolving an even more Machiavellian intelligence than they did. One need only recall the fierce and highly strategic intra- and intergroup competition that researchers like Goodall, de Waal, Mitani, Nishida, and Wrangham all document for common chimpanzees to wonder why enhanced capacities for mind reading and cooperation did not evolve in them as well. The most compelling solution to the puzzle, in my view, has to do with the cognitive and emotional implications of cooperative breeding.

I don't think humans ended up with greater inter-individual tolerance, aptitudes for mind reading and learning, and with them greater capacities for cooperation than other apes because they already possessed sapient-sized brains, symbolic thinking, and sophisticated language. Rather, I am convinced that our line of hominins ended up with these attributes because of an unprecedented convergence—the evolution of cooperative breeding in a primate already possessing the cognitive capacities, Machiavellian intelligences, and incipient "theory of mind" typical of all Great Apes. The ancestors of humans started from a different place than chimpanzees did.

From the outset, I have stressed that no one knows for sure when hominins began to share care. Nor do we know when hominins began to undergo the cognitive and emotional transformations that laid the groundwork for higher levels of cooperation—transformations that would eventually became hallmarks of the human species. Perhaps one day new methods for analyzing fossil bones and teeth will yield new insights into when hominin mothers started to wean babies earlier than other apes did, or began surviving longer. Perhaps comparisons between different ape genomes (including ancient DNA from fossil hominins) will shed light on when postpartum mothers became more tolerant of others. So far, however, the fossil record has not yielded a definitive answer.

WHEN DID HUMANS BECOME EMOTIONALLY MODERN?

Almost all of those who study child development now accept the primate origins of human infants' need to feel secure (the basis of attachment theory). But few speculate on the evolutionary origins of humankind's unusual capacities for intuiting intentions, learning from others, sharing resources, and communicating ideas. Of the select few who have published on this topic, most assume that the quest for intersubjective engagement with others emerged later in the Pleistocene than suggested above, within the last 200,000 years, more or less concurrently with anatomically and behaviorally modern humans—big-brained animals complete with language and symbolic culture.

"After they understand others as intentional agents like themselves," writes Michael Tomasello, "a whole new world of intersubjectively shared reality begins to open up. It is a world populated by material and symbolic artifacts that members of their culture, both past and present, have created for the use of others."[15] Karlen Lyons-Ruth of Harvard Medical School, another developmental psychologist whose ideas about the origins of intersubjective engagement have profoundly influenced me, likewise tilts toward a late Pleistocene origin. As she puts it, humans used their new awareness about mental states "to learn from and transmit knowledge to others and [this] capacity for conceiving of other minds accounts for the explosive rate of cultural evolution over the last 200,000 years."[16]

None of these researchers claims to know for sure when humans became emotionally modern. But there has been this tendency to assume that new aptitudes for mind reading coevolved with language, symbolic thinking, new modes of cultural transmission, and art—in other words, to assume that emotional modernity emerged among humans who already possessed sapient-sized brains as well as language and symbol manipulation and who combined quests for intersubjective engagement with modern capacities for learning and cultural evolution. That is, in the late Paleolithic. Although there are hints that hominins might have been molding clay into anthropomorphic forms as far back as 250,000 years ago, the first unambiguous evidence that people were looking about their world and selecting materials in order to "make them special" come from the Middle Paleolithic, some 150,000 years later. This evidence includes barbed points made of bone (for a spear, perhaps, or a harpoon?) and perforated shell beads (for jewelry?). From about 30,000 years onward, cave paintings and carvings testify unequivocally to humankind's signature creativity.[17]

Without question, the creators of the carefully observed and beautifully rendered lions, bison, and rhinoceroses on the rock walls of places like Chauvet Cave in France held complicated belief systems and were interested in sharing their personalized symbolic worlds with others. These artists were capable of new modes of learning and cultural transmission, and they built on one another's inspiration and techniques. Indeed, at least some of the paintings were probably joint products created by many hands over time. It is not much of a stretch to assume that individuals who punctuated their paintings of animals with shamanlike half-men/half-animal bipeds would judge others according to whether they conformed to the same belief system. This represents an enormous divide between humans and other animals.[18]

Other primates possess social conventions as well, and individuals that fail to conform may be at a disadvantage. For example, sick animals who behave strangely may be shunned or ostracized, while those who ignore dominance protocols may be attacked. But we have no evidence that other animals monitor anything other than overt phenotypic signals such as physical appearance, smells, or behavior.[19] In the case of behaviorally modern humans, however, socially transmitted knowledge is cumulative, resulting in increasingly elaborate conventions to which group members may be expected to conform, often in very detailed and seemingly arbitrary ways, as in ritual or public ceremonies. As the ethnographer and evolutionary ecologist Kim Hill points out, people everywhere become inordinately concerned not only with how others perform but with how they feel, think, and believe, and they monitor such conformity both in ceremonial contexts and in everyday life. Failures to conform may generate deep feelings of guilt or cause others to be angry. Given the universality of such emotions, they presumably predated the time within the past 200,000 years when the common ancestors of all modern humans migrated out of Africa—but by how much?[20]

To answer this question, it is important, first, to distinguish between tangible manifestations of behavioral modernity expressed in art and language, and intangible manifestations of emotional modernity expressed in the attention individuals pay to what others are thinking and feeling. Although the linguistic and symbolic gifts of behaviorally modern humans allow them to take intersubjectivity to new heights, in and of itself intersubjective engagement does not require language or symbol manipulation. Indeed, the former almost certainly evolved before the latter. The ability to intuit the needs and desires of others and respond appropriately doesn't even require much of a brain—recall the tiny-brained meerkat allomothers who take developmental stage into account when teaching youngsters how to eat dangerous scorpions. There is no reason why emotional modernity could not have evolved long before humans became behaviorally or even physically modern.

Infants whose brains are immature and who cannot yet talk or draw pictures are nevertheless attuned to the expectations and emotional reactions of caregivers. As the psychologist Vasudevi Reddy and others have shown, children less than a year old exhibit embarrassment and what looks very much like shame, as if they are acutely aware of how they might have failed to meet the expectations of someone else. These infants are not just afraid of punishment (other animals—dogs, for example—when caught doing something they were trained not to do, can act "embarrassed"). Rather, at a much earlier age than previously realized or even considered possible, and long before they acquire language, human children appear to monitor what others think of them and care deeply about what others feel and intend. By age four, around the time a child in a foraging society would be weaned, modern children begin to use their intersubjective gifts and growing language skills in quite sophisticated ways, not only to intuit what others want but also to intuit what they want to hear. Four-year-olds are already able to use such knowledge to flatter others and to ingratiate themselves with the sort of people upon whom children's survival once depended.[21]

At some point in the course of hominin evolution, then, our ancestors adopted modes of food sharing and childcare that were very different from those observed in other apes, with profound implications for the nature of maternal commitment, the intention-reading aptitudes of their young, and the prosocial impulses of other group members. That is why in a book about the origins of emotionally modern humans I focused on the early hominin prequel rather than on the main human feature film, the great cultural leaps forward that cooperative tendencies and language eventually made possible. For in such modest beginnings— perhaps as long as two million years ago—I believe we can identify the groundwork for spectacular later developments.

If communal childcare goes back in the human lineage as far as I believe it does, then quests for intersubjective engagement emerged among creatures who looked quite different from us, who could not talk nor transmit knowledge the same way we do, but who were already attributing mental states to others and empathizing with them more than living Great Apes do. But regardless of whether emotional modernity originated among *Homo sapiens* or *Homo erectus*—that is, among people who either did or did not look like us and behave like us, and who did or did not use language the way we do—at some point human mothers began to bear offspring too costly to rear by themselves. This made a mother's commitment to any given child contingent on her perception of social support. Indeed, I have wondered whether this might not be one reason for the correlation researchers still find between a new mother's perception of low social support and postpartum depression.[22] My focus

This reconstruction is based on fossils from Dmanisi, the Republic of Georgia (sometimes designated *Homo georgicus*), and shows how *Homo erectus* might have looked 1.8 million years ago. Quite possibly these distant ancestors were already beginning to reflect on the subjective mental states and intentions of others, long before anatomically modern, large-brained *Homo sapiens* emerged. (Sawyer and Deak 2007:155, Nèvraumont Publishing)

here, however, is not on the psychological risks to mothers but on the psychological risks that prolonged dependency and highly contingent commitment set up in *infants*, who, unlike other apes, lack the same guarantee of maternal succor.

NEW DIMENSIONS TO THE TIES THAT BIND

As novel contexts for development produced novel phenotypes and generated new selection pressures to act on those phenotypes, the outcome was little apes who were every bit as manipulative and socially astute as other apes but were in addition emotionally more sensitized to cues of commitment than any ape had ever needed to be before. The rest of course was history—literally. But there was a downside to such sensibilities.

All babies have different needs and priorities than their mothers do, and very different notions about when their mothers should carry them versus delegating their care to someone else or providing no immediate attention at all.[23] Like all primates, human infants need to feel connected. Just as Bowlby pointed out more than half a century ago, dread of separation is the most powerful motivating force in the lives of infant primates. But intersubjectively gifted human infants seek more than the security that comes from tactile contact (though they certainly seek that as well). These special-needs primates want (in the words of poet Daphne Merkin) to see their "singular passions" reflected in some "larger pond" of emotional attachment. They feel a chronic need to factor perceived intentions into their quest for reassurance.

To my knowledge, Karlen Lyons-Ruth is the first child psychologist engaged in clinical practice to attempt to integrate Bowlbian attachment theory with new findings about humankind's legacy of cooperative breeding. It is part of her search to understand the peculiar need for infant–caretaker attunement that she and her colleagues have been documenting in our species. "As the explicit sharing of intentional states became a more powerful force in human evolution," she wrote in 2005 together with her colleague Katherine Hennighausen, "this shift also affected the infant–parent attachment system, moving the center of the attachment relationship to primarily intersubjective processes." All infant primates are soothed by close bodily contact, but in humans the sharing of emotional cues became a more important part of the quest for continuing commitment.[24]

Post-Bowlby, generations of developmental psychologists, infant psychiatrists, and psychoanalysts have worked to demonstrate the importance of early attachments for security and self-confidence as infants gradually learn how to regulate their emotions. We already know that early in development these little connoisseurs of commitment become attuned to facial expressions, rhythms, and tones of voice—the entire spectrum of cues with which caretakers (most of this research was done with mothers, of course) signal how sensitive they are to the infant's mental state and needs.[25] Now for the first time, a growing awareness of this unusual dimension to the needs of human infants, different from the emotional needs of other apes, is being combined with an evolutionary explanation for *why* this should be so.

When a (usually older) child complains that "no one understands me," and we ask ourselves why a child would care, a big part of the answer has to be that we descended from creatures whose minds were preadapted to evaluate the understanding and commitment of others. No other social creature is capable of feeling quite so "lonely" even when surrounded by familiar conspecifics. Beginning with Emile Durkheim on *anomie* and continuing with Robert Putnam in *Bowling Alone*, Shelley Taylor in *The Tending Instinct*, or John Cacioppo and William Patrick in *Loneliness*, a number of distinguished writers have commented on how the centrifugal pressures of modern life are diminishing our sense of community. The modern emphasis on individualism and personal independence along with consumption-oriented economies, compartmentalized living arrangements in highrise apartments or suburban homes, and neolocal residence patterns combine to undermine social connectedness.

But from my perspective as an evolutionist interested in the role that childrearing played in the evolution of prosocial impulses, the trouble started earlier. All through the Pleistocene, infant survival depended on the ability of infants to maintain contact and solicit nurture from both mothers and others. If, in African foraging societies like those of the Efe or the Aka, children grew up feeling surrounded by responsive caretakers, it was because as a matter of fact they were. Those who were not were unlikely to survive. No wonder these children learned to perceive their world as a "giving place." Within the first two years of life, infants fortunate enough to be reared in responsive caretaking relationships develop innate potentials for empathy, mind reading, and collaboration, and often do so with astonishing speed. Such behavior is the outcome of complex interactions between genes and nurture, and this drama is played out on the stage of the developing brains. Thus, the development of innate potentials is far from guaranteed.

The end of the Pleistocene marked a consequential divide in the way children were raised, as people began to settle in one place, build walled houses, grow and store food. While predation rates declined, malnutrition remained a problem, and deaths from diseases like malaria and cholera actually increased. Nevertheless, child survival became increasingly decoupled from the need to be in constant physical contact with another person, or surrounded by responsive, protective caretakers, in order to pull through. Many other things began to change as well. For one thing, girls growing up in sedentary agricultural societies reached puberty sooner and became capable of giving birth at younger ages. Among foragers, any girl sufficiently well-fed to ovulate in her early teens was, almost by definition, a girl surrounded by supportive kin, people who after she gave birth were likely to be willing to help her rear her young. After the Pleistocene, and increasingly over the ensuing centuries, even young women still psychologically immature and woefully lacking in sympathy or social support could nevertheless be well-fed enough to ovulate and conceive while still in their early teens.

Cultivated fields, livestock, and food stores were accompanied by population growth and social stratification, and with them the need to defend property and, even more than before, to defend women as well. Property, higher population densities, and larger group sizes all put new pressures on men to remain near fathers and brothers, their most reliable allies. "In-group amity" as a way to survive in the face of "out-group enmity" took on greater importance. With men remaining near their own kin, it was women who moved—either exchanged between groups or perhaps captured. With a diminished role for the mother's kin in rearing young, old compunctions against raiding with the purpose of taking women by force began to fade.

As property accumulated and residence patterns also became more patrilocal, inheritance patterns became patrilineal. Male heirs were better positioned to hold on to intergenerationally transmitted resources. Such developments led to an increased emphasis on being certain about paternity. As cultures emphasizing female chastity flourished, women's freedom of movement was severely curtailed. No longer could women use sexuality to line up extra "fathers"; no longer could daughters move to be near kin at birth, or mothers move to be near daughters who needed their help. Increasingly, young women found themselves giving birth for the first time far from their own mothers and sisters, more likely to be in competition with, rather than bonded to, the women they saw around them.

More important, patriarchal ideologies that focused on both the chastity of women and the perpetuation and augmentation of male lineages undercut the long-standing priority of putting children's well-being first. Customs such as sequestration of women, chaperoning, veiling, and *suttee* took a huge toll on women, but they also took a toll on children. With settled lifestyles, intervals between births were already growing shorter. At the same time, the need for competing clans to out-man rivals put even greater emphasis on large numbers of heirs, particularly males. The fecundity of women took priority over the health or quality of life of any individual child. Conventions that kept men separated from women and children discouraged the development of the nurturing potentials of fathers, depriving children of yet another source of allomaternal care.

Fast forward now to the modern postindustrial era, as patriarchal institutions have begun to lapse and women in many parts of the developed world have begun to regain considerable freedom of movement and control over reproduction and mating choices. As always, though, mothers still need a tremendous amount of help to successfully rear their young, and yet they often reside far from supportive kin. Among many immigrants from the Old World to the New, or more recently from Latin America to the United States, extended kin were left far behind, and mothers in these truncated families were forced to abandon older traditions of childrearing and invent new ones.

As mothers began to work outside their homes, in locations incompatible with childcare, many became accustomed to using paid allomothers, often creching infants together in one supervised place. The highest quality daycare centers do an excellent job of simulating the nurture on offer from extended families, with high ratios of adults to infants and stable cadres of responsive caretakers. But daycare of this caliber is not necessarily available, or if available, rarely affordable. Many women, who for the first time in the history of our species have a choice, are opting to delay childbirth or forgo it altogether. Yet those children who do come into the world are now surviving at higher rates than ever before.

Child mortality in developed countries has plummeted. More than 99 percent of those born survive to age 5, and those who do not are more likely to die from accidents (automobiles being the biggest killers) than from malnutrition or disease. Meanwhile, in the developing world, child mortality from disease and malnutrition remains high, and in war-torn or AIDs-stricken regions with burgeoning populations of under-nurtured orphans, their chance of surviving is little better than in the Pleistocene. But as everywhere in the post-Neolithic era, survival of even the neediest youngsters has become largely decoupled from the responsiveness of caretakers. And perhaps for the first time in human history, exceedingly high rates of child survival coincide with sobering statistics about the emotional well-being of children.

In a finding that is not so surprising, developmental psychologists report that as many as 80 percent of children from populations at high risk for abuse or neglect grow up confused by or even fearful of their main caretakers, suffering from a condition known as "disorganized attachment." Far more unsettling is the finding that 15 percent of children in what are described as "normal, middle-class families," children not ostensibly at special risk, are also unable to derive comfort from or to constructively organize their emotions around a caretaker they trust; these children too exhibit symptoms of disorganized attachment.[26]

From the outset there was always a number of children who could not be categorized using attachment theory's classic designations of "secure" versus "insecure" attachment.[27] In 1990, the psychologist Mary Main at the University of California–Berkeley recognized that many of these difficult-to-classify children seemed dazed or disoriented. Some appeared dissociated from where they were, or would suddenly freeze for no apparent reason, as if alarmed by the proximity of their caretaker and paralyzed by their own contradictory emotions of fear and need. As Main put it, the attachment figure is normally "the primate infant's haven of safety in times of alarm," but not for these children. She hypothesized that infants repeatedly exposed to frightening behavior by their caretakers, or whose caretakers seem to be frightened themselves—rendering them insensitive or unresponsive to infants' needs—encountered an irreconcilable dilemma that left them unable to mount any coherent strategy to elicit the attention and nurturing they required. She called this disorganized attachment.[28]

So far, follow-up studies of these children extend only as far as the late teens, but already we know that by the time they reach school age, children classified with disorganized attachment as infants have difficulty interpreting the feelings of others, are significantly more aggressive toward their peers, and are prone to behavior disorders.[29] Patterns of attachment between infants and their caretakers have not been studied long enough for psychologists to be able to say whether they might be changing over time, or whether they are predictive of adult behavior and emotional health. But what we can confidently surmise is that prior to about 15,000 years ago, the conditions leading to a serious attachment disorder in a child would not have been compatible with that child's survival.

Perverse as it sounds, when viewed this way, it appears that children today have begun to survive *too well*. Pleistocene parents and other kin were selected to respond to grave threats to their children's survival—predation and starvation—by providing constant physical protection. As they held infants and passed them around to provisioning group members, who in the course of these intimate interactions became emotionally primed to nurture their charges, parents and alloparents communicated their commitment to the children in their group. Back in the Pleistocene, any child who was fortunate enough to grow up acquired a sense of emotional security by default. Those without committed mothers and also lacking allomothers responsive to their needs would rarely have survived long enough for the emotional sequelae of neglect to matter. Today, this is no longer true, and the unintended consequences are unfolding in ways that we are only beginning to appreciate.

ARE WE LOSING THE ART OF NURTURE?

As in all higher primates, only more so in the human case, prior experience and learning loom large in the way mothers and allomothers nurture infants in their charge. Compared with other mammals, like dogs or cats, human mothers have a near absence of what ethologists call "fixed action patterns." Nurture, in our species, is more nearly an art form passed down from mothers or others to subsequent generations. Contrary to the notion of a "maternal instinct," a person's responsiveness to the needs of infants is to a large degree acquired through experience—through both the experience of nurturing and the experience of being nurtured. As we have seen throughout this book, both males and females start out with an innate capacity for empathy with others and for nurture, but past experiences along with proximate cues are critically important for the development and expression of nurturing responses. A study of foster mothers and the way they responded to their charges, undertaken by the University of Delaware psychologist Mary Dozier and her colleagues, illustrates my point here.

Fifty infants between birth and 20 months of age were placed with women who had no biological relationship to them. Prior to placement, each of these foster mothers was asked to describe her own attachment experiences as a child, during an in-depth "Adult Attachment Interview." The interviews were recorded, transcribed, coded, and classified by four independent specially trained raters. Some of the foster mothers clearly remembered and valued their own early attachment relationships. Others were more dismissive about them. In their analysis, the researchers took into account race, socioeconomic status, number of prior placements, and especially age of the infant at the time he or she was placed with a particular foster parent. Age at placement mattered, as we might expect. But the single best predictor of how securely attached an infant would become to a given caregiver turned out to be the way the foster mother recalled her own childhood experiences. Her state of mind about her past relationships dwarfed other effects.[30]

It is well known that genetics plays a role in personality development, and of course these babies did not arrive in foster care as "blank slates." Just as in other primates, some individuals are innately calm while others are more reactive. Some children are extroverted, others shy; and such traits are clearly heritable. However, attachment styles are known *not* to be heritable in the same way, and certainly in this instance the degree of concordance between the attachment styles of caregivers and their charges was clearly not due to shared genes.[31] Rather, the quality of the attachment relationship that babies forged reflected the emotional state of the allomothers currently providing their care.

Human infants are born monitoring the intentions of others, and by the second year of life their increasingly sophisticated sense of self, along with their awareness of the connections between self and others, helps them to understand the various goals that someone else might have in mind, as well as to communicate their own. These capacities provide the underpinnings for inter-individual communication and cooperation.[32] Children cared for by responsive others exhibit a high potential for collaboration, and this may help explain why infants who are classified as securely attached become better at making friends in preschool.[33] But "equally impressive," Lyons-Ruth reminds us, "is the potential for derailment."[34]

We are learning that a subset of children today grow up and survive to adulthood without ever forging trusting relationships with caring adults, and their childhood experiences are likely to be predictive of how they in turn will take care of others. For hundreds of thousands of years, an interest in mind reading and in sharing mental and emotional states has provided the raw material for the evolution of our unusually prosocial natures. But if the empathic capacities of infants find expression only under certain rearing conditions, and if natural selection can only act on genetic traits that are actually expressed in the phenotype, perhaps we need to be asking how even the most useful innate predispositions can persist if their development is not encouraged?

After all, "the" human species is no more static than other species are. If our environment changes (or, more pertinent in the human case, as we transform our environment), we change with it. So why wouldn't novel modes of childrearing continue to shape not just child development but human nature? To anyone who wonders if processes postulated in this book could ever be reversible, I would say that there is no reason why not. Just because humans have become "advanced" enough to vaccinate their young, write histories, and speculate about our origins, this does not mean that evolutionary processes have ceased to operate.

Far from it. Indeed, some anthropologists such as Henry Harpending at the University of Utah and John Hawks of the University of Michigan are convinced that over the last 40,000 years or so—since the Upper Paleolithic and especially since the Neolithic—selection on our species has actually *accelerated* as human activities and population pressure transformed local environments and as an exponentially expanding population generated many more mutations for selection to act on. The best-documented cases of post-Pleistocene selection involve adaptations for resisting new diseases like cholera, smallpox, yellow fever, typhus, malaria, and, more recently, AIDS, as well as digestive mechanisms for coping with novel diets.[35] But there is no reason why cognitive and behavioral traits would be any less susceptible to ongoing selection than digestive enzymes.

Indeed, Hawks argues that some of the fastest-evolving genes in the human genome are those associated with the development of the central nervous system. His views are consistent with the discovery of new genetic variants responsible for increased brain size that are probably no more than 6,000 years old. Under strong positive selection, these variants have spread rapidly.[36] As one evolutionist has quipped: "The ten or so [hominin] species that preceded modern humans came and went at a rate of about 200,000 years per species. Ours began some 130,000 years ago, so we could be just about due for a change."[37] It will not matter how spectacularly well prosocial tendencies served humans in the past if the underpinnings for such traits remain unexpressed and thus can no longer be favored by selection. Over evolutionary time, traits no longer used eventually disappear.

No one doubts that organisms like fish benefit from being able to see. That is why they have eyes. When reared in total darkness, however, fish like the small cave-dwelling characin fish of Mexico cease to develop their capacity for vision. Even when reintroduced to sunlight and reared outside, populations of characin fry long isolated in the dark fail to regain sight. As a simple matter of somatic economy, unused traits no longer favored by natural selection are lost, while somatic or neurological resources are diverted for uses elsewhere.

Viewed from the perspective of some evolutionary theorist surveying humans 20,000 years hence, our powerful impulses to empathize with others, to give, share, and seek reciprocation, might seem like nothing more than transient phases in the ongoing evolution of the species. Although there is a widely held assumption (known as Dollo's Law) that evolutionary processes are irreversible, don't count on it. Dollo's Law is more nearly a description of the deep history of some organisms than a universally applicable natural law like gravity.[38] A far more basic and universal tenet of evolutionary biology states that "the removal of an agent of selection can sometimes bring about rapid evolutionary consequences."[39]

To all the reasons people might have to worry about the future of our species—including the usual depressing litany of nuclear proliferation, global warming, emerging infectious diseases, or crashing meteorites—add one more having to do with just what sort of species our descendants millennia hence might belong to. If empathy and understanding develop only under particular rearing conditions, and if an ever-increasing proportion of the species fails to encounter those conditions but nevertheless survives to reproduce, it won't matter how valuable the underpinnings for collaboration were in the past. Compassion and the quest for emotional connection will fade away as surely as sight in cave-dwelling fish.

I have no doubt that our descendants thousands of years from now (whether on this planet or some other) will be bipedal, symbol-generating apes. They will probably be technologically proficient in realms we do not even dream of yet, as well as every bit as competitive and Machiavellian as chimpanzees are now, and probably even more intelligent than people today. What is not certain is whether they will still be human in ways we now think of as distinguishing our species—that is, empathic and curious about the emotions of others, shaped by our ancient heritage of communal care.

NOTES

1. APES ON A PLANE

1. The study of theory of mind dates from Premack and Woodruff 1978. For an update on the literature, begin with Penn and Povinelli 2007 and references therein.

2. Psychiatrists Daniel Stern (2002) and Peter Hobson (2004) and developmental psychologists Karlen Lyons-Ruth (Hennighausen and Lyons-Ruth 2005) and Colwyn Trevarthen (2005; Trevarthen and Aitken 2001) prefer to talk about "intersubjectivity" or "affective sharing," terms which encompass both the sharing of attitudes about the world and the affective components of the relationship between the individuals involved. Eager questing for such emotional sharing is thought to emerge very early in human infant development (Reddy 2003, 2007) and to precede and guide later theories of mind and inferences about what others know or believe.

3. This account appeared in 1884 in the *Proceedings of the Asiatic Society of Bengal* and is cited in full in Hrdy 1977a:5-6.

4. Neuroimaging studies by Jean Decety, Perrine Ruby, and others are reviewed in Decety and Jackson 2004, see esp. pp. 86-87.

5. Rilling et al. 2004a:1695; Fehr and Fischbacher 2003.

6. Cosmides and Tooby 1994; Ostrom 1998; Trivers 1971.

7. Wiessner 1977, 1982; Thomas 2006.

8. Trivers 1971; Burnham and Johnson 2005; Nesse 2007.

9. Trivers 2006; Warneken and Tomasello 2006; Hamlin et al. 2007.

10. Rilling, Gutman, Zeh, et al. 2002.

11. For quotation about "wired to cooperate" see Damasio 2003:172–173. For an economist's perspective, see Ostrom 1998:7. For experimental evidence that our brains work differently when we are making decisions based on

what other people, as opposed to computers, are doing, see Rilling et al. 2002; Rilling, Sanfey, et al. 2004a.

12. Trevarthen and Logotheti 1989:43. Although controversial when first proposed, Trevarthen's views have since gained considerable support (Draghi-Lorenz et al. 2001).

13. Marci et al. 2007.

14. We are "hardwired, it appears, to feel each other's happiness and pain—more deeply than we ever knew," cautions psychotherapist Babette Rothschild in her warning to fellow therapists (2004).

15. Sober and Wilson 1998; Tomasello 1999; Hammerstein, ed. 2003; Fehr and Fischbacher 2003; Boyd 2006. I know of no better introduction to the evolution of cooperation and altruism than Matt Ridley's beautiful 1996 book on *The Origins of Virtue*.

16. Bowles and Gintis 2003:433.

17. For excellent overviews see McGrew 1992; Whiten et al. 1999; van Schaik et al. 2003. As early as 1874, Darwin was describing observations of chimpanzees cracking nuts with stones (1974:78–79).

18. For chimpanzees see McGrew 1992; Boesch and Boesch-Achermann 2000; Pruetz and Bertolani 2007; Matsuzawa 1996. For captive bonobos see Savage-Rumbaugh and McDonald 1988; Parish and de Waal 1992. For captive gorillas see Gomez 2004. For wild orangutans see van Schaik et al. 2000.

19. Mercader et al. 2007.

20. Mulcahy and Call 2006; Raby et al. 2007.

21. Inoue and Matsuzawa 2007.

22. Matsuzawa 2001; Herrmann, Call, et al. 2007.

23. For an overview of the role of bipedalism in human evolution, see Stanford 2003.

24. Herrmann, Call, et al. 2007.

25. Tomasello et al. 2005:675

26. Tomasello et al. 2005:676.

27. Tomasello et al. 2005.

28. Tomasello 1999:59; Boyd and Richerson 1996.

29. Tomasello et al. (2005) review arguments for considering humans as "hypersocial," in line with Tomasello's 1999 proposal. They also update earlier comparisons between humans and other chimpanzees to take into account more recent findings in what is a rapidly developing field of inquiry.

30. According to the taxonomy now preferred by many geneticists, the superfamily Hominoidae is composed of the so-called Lesser Apes (gibbons and siamangs) plus what are commonly known as the Great Apes (orangutans, gorillas, chimpanzees, and bonobos) plus humans. But unlike the old days when the term "hominid" was used to distinguish humans and their various bipedal ape ancestors (such as *Australopithecus*) from the "Great Apes,"

current phylogenies include the Great Apes as well as humans among the creatures called hominids. Thus, many specialists now divide hominoid apes into two families, the Hylobatidae (gibbons and apes) and the Hominidae, with these hominid apes in turn divided into two subfamilies, Ponginae for the orangutan and its fossil relatives and Homininae for African apes and humans. All members of our lineage subsequent to their divergence from chimpanzees are placed in the tribe Hominini. Hominins include *Australopithecus, Homo habilis, Homo erectus, Homo heidelbergensis,* and *Homo sapiens.*

31. Darwin 1890:240.
32. Rilling, Gutman, et al. 2002; Rilling, Sanfey, et al. 2004a.
33. Ingman et al. 2000; Wade 2006:52–60; Behar et al. 2008.
34. Kaplan et al. 1990; see also Cashdan 1990; Hawkes 2001, esp. Table 4; Smith 2003.
35. See esp. Kelly 2005.
36. Wiessner 1977, 1996, 2002b.
37. Wiessner, personal communication, March 5, 2007, elaborating on her written account; see also Marshall 1976: 310–311.
38. Rodseth and Wrangham 2004:393ff and references therein.
39. Dunn et al. 2008.
40. Wiessner 2002b:421.
41. Forty-six percent of the partnerships in her sample were with partners related as closely as first cousins. Yet in spite of the tendency to favor kin, many partnerships were with fairly distant relatives; Wiessner 2002a:31.
42. Wiessner 2002a.
43. Richard Lee, who originally explained this system, learned that the elder in any "namesake" dyad gets to determine which kinship term is to be used, adding to its flexibility over a person's lifetime (2003:64–76).
44. Wiessner 2002b.
45. See Marlowe 2004 for a comparison using 36 foraging societies.
46. Sealy 2006; Johnson and Earle 2000:54ff.
47. McHenry 2009, with thanks to John Fleagle.
48. Cohen 1995:29; Stiner et al. 1999; Johnson and Earle 2000, esp. ch. 1; Behar et al. 2008.
49. Choi and Bowles 2007; cited and discussed in Jones 2008:514 and references therein.
50. Kelly 2005 and esp. Wiessner 2006. For the logic of "behavioral scaling" that explains the link between population density and human aggression, see Wilson 1971b or 1975:20ff.
51. Washburn and Lancaster 1968; Wrangham and Peterson 1996:199; Wrangham 1999:1; Jones 2008 and references therein.
52. See Kelly 2005 for "Paleolithic warlessness" and esp. Fry 2007 for recent overview and Johnson and Earle 2000 for general introduction. Even ar-

chaeologists who stress the prevalence of "prehistoric war" acknowledge that there is no evidence for warfare from the Pleistocene (e.g., Keeley 1996).

53. Marshall 1976; Lee 1979, esp. pp. 24, 244–248, 343–346, 390–400, 458; Johnson and Earle 2000; Hewlett 2001:52; Kelly 2005; Wiessner 2006, discussed at length in Boehm 1999. See esp. Boehm's discussion of how fiercely egalitarian hunter-gatherers can be.

54. See esp. Lee 1979:390–400. Even though this monograph on the !Kung San is often cited to support the claim that Paleolithic people were more violent than modern people, with homicide rates comparable to those of America's most violent cities (see Jones 2008 and references therein), Lee is explicit that the !Kung San do not engage in warfare, and if American deaths due to warfare are included, !Kung homicide rates would be far lower than those in America (1979:398).

55. Take a look at the index to one of the best and most widely adopted textbooks on *Evolution and Human Behavior* by John Cartwright (2000). Terms like "sharing" and "childrearing" do not appear. There are no references to "maternal," "paternal," or "allomaternal care," but there are two to "maternal-fetal conflict" and ten to "paternity confidence"; no mention of "infants" or "infant care" but two to "infanticide." This same criticism could be applied to many of my own earlier publications.

56. This bias can be found in some of the best books in the field, e.g., Wade 2006:148–150, n. 189. A 2000 essay by Parish and de Waal discusses the bias and suggests some antidotes.

57. See, for example, experiments demonstrating the role of interindividual tolerance in cooperation among chimpanzees (Melis et al. 2006a) along with research documenting the more relaxed temperaments of bonobos relative to chimpanzees (Hare et al. 2007).

58. Parish and de Waal 2000; Höhmann 2001. It is not known whether this is a species-typical difference between bonobos and chimpanzees, an artifact of bonobos having been studied less, or a consequence of habitat differences. What we do know from studying other primates, such as langur monkeys, is that behaviors such as territorial encounters, male-male aggression, and infanticide by adult males are highly variable, reported in some populations but not others. More often than not, population density is the key variable (Hrdy 1979).

59. De Waal 1997. On the significance of semicontinuous receptivity and "concealed" (or, more precisely, inconspicuously advertised) ovulation see Hrdy 1981a, ch. 7; 1997.

60. Silk 1978; Parish 1998; White 1994; de Waal 1997; Kano 1992:74, 166–170. A chimpanzee or orangutan baby may beg for food but would be likely to get anything only if the possessor was its mother, and even then delivery would be grudging.

61. Melis et al. 2006a; de Waal 1996, 1997.
62. Pollick and de Waal 2007.
63. See Wiessner 2005 for ways in which talking can substitute for, as well as fan, aggression.
64. Bird-David 1990; Hewlett, Lamb, et al. 2000. The developmental implications of growing up in what these researchers call a "giving" environment are discussed below in Chapter 4.
65. Shostak 1976:256.
66. Blurton Jones 1984; Moore 1984.
67. Parish 1998; Parish and de Waal 2000; Kano 1992:74, 166–170.
68. Höhmann and Fruth 1996:53. Most other cases of "tolerated taking" in primates are likely to involve infants getting a brief pick-me-up from the breast milk of an allomother—for example, O'Brien 1998 for capuchin monkeys; Smith et al. 2001 for tamarins; Pereira and Izard 1989 for lemurs.
69. Burkart et al. 2007. See also de Kort, Emery, and Clayton 2006 for jackdaws.
70. Cosmides 1989; Ridley 1996.
71. Rilling et al. 2002, 2004b.
72. Ambrose 1998. This point continues to be debated, but archaeologists Marwick (2003) and McBrearty and Brooks (2000) make a convincing case.
73. For discussion of how humans get psychologically prepared to commit genocide through propaganda and other means, see Roscoe 2007. For case study see Browning 1998. On role of competition for resources see Diamond 2005, esp. pp. 323ff. For more on situation-based compunctions against murder see Hauser 2006.
74. See Zinn 2003:1–3; Earle 1997:37.
75. Discussed in van der Dennen 1995.
76. For an authoritative overview, see Johnson and Earle 2000 and references therein. For spread of conquerors' genes in the case of Genghis Khan, see Zerjal et al. 2003.
77. Dawkins 1976:75ff for elaboration of underlying logic.
78. I am indebted to the novelist Edmund White (2001:14) for his articulation of what being "compassionate" means.
79. Harpending et al. 1996; Wade 2006 and references therein.
80. I have in mind figures on the order of one person per square mile, as is typical of some twentieth-century Kalahari desert foragers (Thomas 2006). Several people per square mile, as reported for Andaman Islanders, would probably be on the high end (Kelly 2005).
81. Smith 2007 and references therein, quotations from pp. 141–142. See also Bowles 2006, following Darwin 1874, for similar conclusions.
82. Hare and Tomasello 2004.

83. Polly Wiessner, personal communication, 2005.

84. Lancaster and Lancaster 1987; Kaplan 1994.

2. WHY US AND NOT THEM?

1. Examples selected from the chapter titles of Darwin's *The Expression of the Emotions in Man and Animals*, first published in 1872.

2. Hobson 2004:270.

3. Melis et al. 2006a, 2006b.

4. Long considered uniquely human, socially contagious yawning also occurs in chimpanzees (Anderson and Matsuzawa 2006). For helping see Warneken and Tomasello 2006 and Boesch and Boesch-Achermann 2000:246–248. For adoptions of orphaned kin see Goodall 1986.

5. For a published version of this story, see de Waal 1997:156. For more on his views of our "common ground" with other primates see de Waal 2006.

6. Warneken et al. 2006; Warneken and Hare 2007.

7. These experiments were designed by an imaginative young postdoc on Tomasello's team named Brian Hare, now at Duke University. For more on the greater skill displayed by chimps in competitive compared with cooperative tasks, see Hare and Tomasello 2004.

8. Herrmann et al. 2007.

9. Melis et al. 2006a.

10. Jensen et al. 2006. These results are not consistent with claims widely made in the media about how nonhuman primates have an innate sense of fairness that leads them to reject a reward if another monkey gets a better reward for the same effort. These claims derived from an interesting series of experiments in Brosnan and de Waal 2003. See Brosnan, Schiff, and de Waal 2005 for extensions of this work with chimpanzees. See Jensen et al. 2007 for discussion of the differences.

11. Contrast interpretations of de Waal 2006 or de Waal as cited in Zimmer 2006 with those of Silk et al. 2005; also Vonk et al. 2008. In particular, Preston and de Waal (2002) stress the importance of interpreting experiments such as those by Silk et al. within the context of other long-standing experiments in this area. They cite Stanley Milgram's famous experiments years ago in which human subjects were willing to inflict painful electric shocks on others when authority figures instructed them to. They are struck by the contrast between Milgram's Yale undergraduates and those of rhesus macaque monkeys, who opted to starve for days rather than pull a chain that delivered food but in doing so imposed an electric shock on another monkey. Monkeys who had experienced such shocks themselves, as well as monkeys with previous familiarity with their victims, were the least willing to impose a shock and starved longest before pulling the

chain. To de Waal, such findings (e.g., Masserman et al. 1964) imply that monkeys are more caring than people are, rather than the other way around. Monkeys, on the other hand, do not respond to authority figures and experimental stress tests the same way human subjects do. This is an ongoing debate.

12. For example, in a lecture at a conference on attachment held at UCLA in 2002, the psychiatrist Daniel Stern specifically referred to the role of inter-subjectivity in enhancing shared vigilance and thus helping otherwise defenseless early hominins survive on the African savanna.

13. Jane Goodall in an interview with Virginia Morell (2007:52).

14. Hauser 1996.

15. Hobson 2004:2; cf. Premack 2004:320; Tomasello et al. 2005. For insightful discussion of social challenges and primate preadaptations contributing to the cognitive capacities needed for syntax, see Cheney and Seyfarth 2007, ch. 10.

16. Langford et al. 2006 and references therein.

17. Greene et al. 2002.

18. For more on the evolution of maternal emotions, see Leckman et al. 2005.

19. See Keverne et al. 1996; Panksepp 2000; Zahn-Waxler 2000; MacLean 1985.

20. Allman 2000:98–102.

21. Carter 1998.

22. Allman 2000:111–112.

23. Carter, Ahnert, et al. 2005.

24. Silk 1999; Maestripieri 2001.

25. Hrdy 1977a, ch. 7.

26. Hrdy 1999:207–217 and references therein.

27. Silk, Alberts, and Altmann 2003.

28. Ahnert, Pinquart, and Lamb 2006:665; this report is consistent with earlier observations by Gunnar and Donahue (1980).

29. Gunnar and Donahue 1980. For an even stronger statement of this position see Simon Baron-Cohen (2003), who argues that "the female brain is predominantly hard-wired for empathy" (p. 1). For a general review and critical evaluation of the evidence, see Brody 1999, ch. 7.

30. Radke-Yarrow et al. 1994.

31. Stallings et al. 2001.

32. The idea can be traced back to Darwin but has been richly developed by Eibl-Eibesfeldt in his 1989 classic *Human Ethology* as well as by Babchuk et al. 1985; Taylor 2002. For updates and further empirical demonstrations see Baron-Cohen 2003 and esp. Hampson et al. 2006, who demonstrate that young women are quicker and more accurate at reading facial expressions than young men, controlling for their subjects' prior theatrical and childcare experience.

33. For the clearest statement of the mind-reading mums hypothesis see Brockway 2003:95ff.; see also Chisholm 2003; Allman 2000; Panksepp 2000; Preston and de Waal 2002 (esp. their reply to commentaries).

34. Caro and Hauser 1992; Thornton and McAuliffe 2006.

35. Boesch and Boesch-Achermann 2000:202. On maternal modeling of nut-cracking, see also Gagneux 1993 and Matsuzawa 2001.

36. Byrne and Whiten's edited volume on *Machiavellian Intelligence* (1988) includes reprints of the classic early papers on this subject by Alison Jolly, Nicholas Humphrey, and David Premack. For some of the most interesting recent nonhuman primate research see Hauser et al. 2003 on identification of reciprocators. See Silk 2003 or Cheney and Seyfarth 2007 on identification and choice of allies.

37. See esp. Harcourt 1988 on the role of alliance formation in the evolution of social intelligence; quotation appears on p. 144.

38. De Waal 2006 and references therein.

39. For a sensible, highly readable overview, see Dunbar 2003.

40. Byrne and Whiten 1988; Boesch and Boesch-Achermann 1990.

41. According to one of several alternate explanations for apparent coordination, higher success rates during group hunting might just be an artifact of something else, such as the fact that the chances of capturing prey go up as more males participate in the hunt. See Gilby et al. 2006 for overview; also Mitani et al. 2000.

42. See Flinn et al. 2005 for an overview of how human "ecological dominance and social competition" shaped the evolution of the human neocortex. To avoid confusion, however, note that in order for humans to achieve ecological domination over other species (a prerequisite of the version of the Machiavellian intelligence hypothesis that Flinn et al. advocate) I assume that early hominins must already have been cooperating at a higher level than is typical of other apes. Thus, Flinn et al.'s ideas about ecological dominance combined with social competition cannot solve the specific problem we are addressing here.

43. Once again, I am indebted to the observations of the developmental psychologist Andrew Meltzoff (2002). See also Trevarthen 2005 and references to the earlier literature therein. For general introduction to social intelligence, see Goleman (2006).

44. This includes infanticide by males and by female competitors of the mother as well as intergroup raids. See Goodall 1986; Nishida et al. 1985; Wrangham and Peterson 1996; Watts and Mitani 2000; Pusey, Williams, and Goodall 1997; Townsend et al. 2007.

45. Papousek et al. 1991.

46. For the discovery of "mirror neurons," see Rizzolatti et al. 1996.

47. Rizzolatti et al. 2006; see also Gallese et al. 2002; Preston and de Waal 2002; Gomez 2004, ch. 9.

48. Meltzoff and Moore replicated their famous 1977 experiment with much younger babies in 1989. These experiments are reviewed in Meltzoff 2002; quotation appears on p. 11.
49. Tsao, Freiwald, et al. 2006.
50. Meltzoff 2002:24; see also Quinn et al. 2002.
51. Meltzoff 2002:10.
52. Meltzoff 2002:24; see also Preston and de Waal 2002.
53. Meltzoff 2002:24.
54. Holden 2006:25.
55. Eibl-Eibesfeldt 1989; Emery 2000. I am indebted to Karen Bales (personal communication, January 2008) for pointing out that marmosets and tamarins do not find stares to be aversive.
56. I have never seen a chimpanzee, gorilla, or bonobo with white sclera in the visible part of the eyes, though the white on the sides is sometimes visible when an ape "rolls" its eyes wide, as I once observed in an orangutan at a zoo in Perth, Australia. However, primatologist Kim Bard informs me that very rarely one encounters a chimpanzee with white sclera (personal communication 2005).
57. On human responsiveness to fearful eye whites, see Whalen, Kagan, et al. 2004.
58. This logic, sometimes referred to as the cooperative-eye hypothesis, is beautifully laid out by Tomasello (2007).
59. See Leavens 2004 and literature cited therein.
60. Darwin 1874.
61. For overview of primate parenting, see Bard 2002.
62. Papousek et al. 1991; Konner 1991.
63. Quotation from Farroni et al. 2002:9602.
64. Estimates and quotation from Bard 2002:104.
65. Bard 2002, esp. page 107; Hobson 2004:268. Bard's ideas are echoed by cultural anthropologists like Alma Gottlieb (2004:315, n. 31) who stress cross-cultural differences in how long mothers spend looking into their infants' faces or talking to them.
66. Bard 2002 and esp. Leavens, Hopkins, and Bard 2008.
67. Bard et al. 2005.
68. Matsuzawa 2003, and references therein; also Inoue and Matsuzawa 2007.
69. Matsuzawa 2006.
70. Hobson 1989:200.
71. Farroni et al. 2002.
72. Hobson (2004:195), for example, reports that the proportion of empathy-deficient children is 400 times higher among children blind from birth than among sighted children.
73. Whiten and Byrne 1997, and for further discussion Boesch and Boesch-

Achermann 1990, 2000; and brief review in Matsuzawa 2003. For a readable introduction to the topic see de Waal 2001.

74. Tomasello 1999; Gomez 2004:252ff.

75. Myowa 1996; Myowa-Yamakoshi et al. 2004. Myowa's results have subsequently been replicated by Bard, who further found that previous experience with human faces was not necessary for facial imitation by chimpanzee neonates (2007).

76. Tetsuro Matsuzawa, personal communication, 2006; Bard 2007.

77. Ferrari et al. 2006.

78. See pioneering work along these lines by Wood, Glynn, Phillips, and Hauser 2007.

79. Want and Harris 2002.

80. Jones 2007, quotation on p. 598; Want and Harris 2002.

81. Hare et al. 2002.

82. See Dennis 1943, esp. Table 1, for the developmental chronology of Del and Rey, twins reared in social deprivation.

83. See Cole and Cole's text on *The Development of Children* (1993:171) for smiling in a 2.5-month-old blind baby.

84. Dennis 1943.

85. From Stern 2002.

3. WHY IT TAKES A VILLAGE

1. For an excellent overview of the relevant anatomical research and how recent discoveries of the FOXP2 gene help date the origins of language, see Lieberman 2007. For the (still controversial) argument about click languages, see Knight et al. 2003.

2. See Leavens 2006, and literature cited therein; refer back to Chapter 2.

3. See Eibl-Eibesfeldt 1971 for classic ethological account of maternal bonds as roots of "love."

4. On this occasion the old female Flo allowed her daughter Fifi to take baby Flint (Goodall 1969:388).

5. Van Noordwijk and van Schaik 2005. According to Fossey (1979), gorillas fall in the same range, though there are a few reports of transfers after just a few months.

6. Primate taxonomies are in constant flux. Since I was a graduate student, the commonly accepted number of living primates has risen from 175 species to 276, the number I use in this book. This does not mean that many new species were actually discovered. The principal reason for the increase is that existing classifications are continuously being rearranged and split apart in an effort to better characterize the genetic, morphological, and ecological diversity within the order Primates and to more accurately re-

flect their phylogenetic relationships. Species names are constantly changing as well as being added. To keep abreast of such changes, I relied on the
1996 edition of Noel Rowe's *The Pictorial Guide to the Living Primates,* a favorite among primate behaviorists and conservationists. Rowe includes cap-
sule summaries of the distribution and natural history of each species
next to vivid color photos, and it makes a handy reading companion. The
forthcoming edition of Rowe's book will list closer to 400 species. An up-
to-date taxonomy will eventually be available at a website located at www
.alltheworldsprimates.com.

7. For anxiety in pregnant mice approaching term, see D'Amato, Rizzi, and
   Moles 2006. For birth in wild orangutans, see Galdikas 1982.
8. Van Schaik 2004:102.
9. Quotation from Schaller 1972:54; Hrdy 1999:177ff.
10. See Turner et al. 2005 and references therein.
11. Sarah Turner writing from the Awajishima Monkey Center, personal com-
    munication 2007.
12. For up-to-date authoritative overview by one of the pioneers in the field,
    see Fleming and Gonzalez 2009; Gray and Ellison 2009 and references
    therein.
13. Elsewhere (Hrdy 1999, chs. 12 and 14) I examine in some depth the his-
    torical and cross-cultural evidence for infant abandonment as well as cri-
    teria (sex, viability, local conditions) that enter into such painful deci-
    sions.
14. Varki and Altheide 2005.
15. Reed et al. 2007.
16. For example, Bugos and McCarthy 1984.
17. Howell 1979; Schiefenhövel 1989; reviewed in Hrdy 1992, Table 1ff.
18. The foundations for this argument are laid out in Hrdy 1999, esp. chs.
    9–14.
19. See Leckman et al. 1999, 2005 for studies with primarily Western moth-
    ers.
20. See Hill and Hurtado 1989 for intergroup variation in hunter-gatherer
    lifestyles. See Small 1998 or Konner 2005 for more on indulgence toward
    infants.
21. Konner 1972; 1976:306; Lee 1979:310.
22. See Hewlett, Lamb, et al. 1998 for comparisons across foragers, farm-
    ers, and Western postindustrial societies. See esp. Konner 2005 for a de-
    tailed reexamination of the literature on hunter-gatherer infant care
    highlighting how much shared care was actually going on among the
    !Kung.
23. Hill and Hurtado 1989; Hewlett and Lamb 2005.
24. Lancaster 1978; Wall-Scheffler et al. 2007.

25. Konner 1972:292.

26. Blurton Jones 1993:316. See esp. overview of this literature in Konner 2005.

27. Based on observations by Blurton Jones's coworker Frank Marlowe (2005b:182).

28. For the Mbuti see Turnbull 1965; quotation from Turnbull 1978:172, cited in Hewlett 1991b:13.

29. Tronick et al. 1987, writing about the Efe.

30. Hewlett 1989a, 1989b; Rosenberg and Trevathan 1996. For more on placentas, see Chapter 7.

31. Morelli and Tronick 1991; Hewlett, Lamb et al. 2000. In the majority of human societies mothers wait for several days before initiating breastfeeding (Hewlett 1989a).

32. Morelli and Tronick 1991:47.

33. Hewlett 1989a.

34. For Agta case, see Peterson 1978:16, cited by Hewlett 1991a:13.

35. Crittenden and Marlowe 2008.

36. Konner 2005; Hewlett 2001.

37. See Rosenberg and Trevathan 1996.

38. For overview and recent summary of the !Kung data, see Konner 2005. For Efe fieldwork, see Ivey 2000 and Morelli and Tronick 1991. For Aka, Hewlett 2001. I have focused here on foraging societies, but cross-cultural surveys suggest that across many types of human societies it is usual for allomothers to be the first to touch and hold the baby. According to Hewlett 1989a, this applies in some 92 percent of the world's cultures.

39. Ivey 2000, Figs. 3, 4, and 5, Tables 4 and 5.

40. Eibl-Eibesfeldt 1989:138–145; personal communication from Alyssa Crittenden, 2006.

41. Hewlett, Lamb, et al. 2000, Table 1. This allomaternal provisioning included breastfeeding as well as kiss-feeding. The amount of allomaternal provisioning among these foragers was much higher than among neighboring agriculturalists, the Ngandu.

42. Goodall 1969:398.

43. Stern 2002.

44. Watson 1928.

45. Bowlby 1971:319.

46. For infantile preferences for attractive faces see Langlois et al. 1987. For experiments on gaze-following see Farroni et al. 2004. For smells see Porter 1999.

47. See overview in van IJzendoorn and Sagi 1999 and references therein.

48. Bowlby 1971:228–229 and elsewhere. Subsequently Konner incorporated

Bowlby's continuous-care-and-contact model as a key component of "the Catarrhine Mother-Infant Complex" (see, e.g., Konner 2005:39–41).

49. Both vervet and patas monkeys spend about as much time on the African savannas as baboons do, yet in both species mothers allow other females (often nulliparous females gaining practice for motherhood) to take their babies (Lancaster 1971; Hrdy 1976; Nicolson 1987) as early as the first or second day after birth (2007 personal communications from Janice Chism for patas and Lynne Isbell for vervets). Similarly, there is a lot of infant-sharing among some of the more tolerant, albeit less-well-studied semiterrestrial macaque species, including *Macaca sylvanus* (mostly involving male caretakers) and *Macaca tonkeana,* where other females, esp. juveniles or subadults, take and carry infants as young as a few days old (Thierry 2007 and personal communication, 2008).

50. By the time volume 1 of Bowlby's trilogy on *Attachment and Loss* was published (1969), we had early field reports of infant-sharing among langurs and titi monkeys (Jay 1963; Mason 1966).

51. See Pereira et al. 1987 for *Varecia variegata.* For *V. rubra* see Pereira and Izard 1989; Vasey 2008. Pereira and Izard (1989) report a rare case in which an unrelated ring-tailed lemur female spontaneously lactated and nursed twins born to a groupmate. In the vast majority of primates, mothers fiercely resist attempts to suckle by infants not their own.

52. Eberle 2008 for *Microcebus murinus;* Kessler and Nash 2008 for *Galago senegalensis.*

53. Radhakrishna and Singh 2004.

54. Assunção et al. 2007.

55. For detailed early observations of biparental care among wild titi monkeys (*Callicebus molloch*) and grey-necked owl (also called "night") monkeys (*Aotus trivirgatus*), see Wright 1984. For wild *Aotus azarai,* see Wolovich et al. 2007. For gibbons see Nettelbeck 1998.

56. Fernandez-Duque 2007; Wolovich et al. 2007. For titi infants more upset by separation from fathers than mothers, see Hoffman, Mendoza, et al. 1995.

57. Small 1990 (and personal communication 2006) regarding infant transfers on their first day postpartum.

58. Taub 1984.

59. Reviewed in Paul et al. 2000. Although this assertion was highly controversial when first proposed (Hrdy 1977b, 1979), it is now increasingly clear that infanticide by males occurs in prosimians, Old and New World monkeys, and apes, and can be a major source of infant mortality (see for example van Schaik and Janson 2000). In some of the best-documented cases, infanticide accounts for 30 to 50 percent or more of all deaths in in-

fancy (for example, Sommer 1994; Palombit 1999, 2001; Cheney and Seyfarth 2007), swamping other sources of variance in maternal reproductive
success (Fedigan et al. 2007).

60. For calculations explaining why I am convinced that female langurs have a
roughly 0.16 chance of sharing a gene by common descent, see Seger 1977.
Recent genetic findings are consistent with Seger's initial calculation
based on behavioral evidence (Little, Sommer, and Bruford 2002).

61. Hrdy 1976, 1977a. Even in continuous-care-and-contact species like chimpanzees, nulliparous females are the most interested in babies, though
they do not gain much access to them before babies are older than six
months (Nishida 1983).

62. Struhsaker 1975:65–66.

63. Pusey and Packer 1987.

64. This 20 percent estimate derives from Wright 2008 and from an ongoing
classification of infant care among primates by Stacey Tecot, Patricia
Wright, Noel Rowe, and myself.

65. Primates with shared suckling can be found in a number of genera, including *Galago, Lemur, Microcebus, Propithecus, Varecia,* and *Cebus.*

66. For shared care and suckling in the genus *Cebus* see Perry 1996; Manson
1999; Baldovino and Bitetti 2008. For hunting and sharing of even high-
value food items, see Carnegie et al. 2008 and esp. Rose 1997, Table 6.

67. My use of the term cooperative breeding in this way dates from Hrdy 1999,
2005a, although I have since learned that alloparental provisioning is
more widespread in primates than I then realized. For more on the history
of the term and definitional confusion surrounding the way cooperative
breeding is applied, see Chapter 6.

68. Garber 1997.

69. Ross et al. 2007.

70. French 2007.

71. According to calculations by Ross et al. 2007 ("Supporting Information"
available online), the degree of relatedness between marmoset brothers
may be on the order of 57 percent.

72. See calculations by Haig (1999), a Harvard evolutionary geneticist who anticipated the discovery of chimeric germ lines in marmosets.

73. Primate breast milk tends to be quite dilute compared with the very rich
milk of other mammals whose babies spend more time away from their
mothers, as among tree shrews or rabbits, where "absentee" mothers leave
their young behind in dens for long periods. Regardless of whether they
are continuous-care-and-contact or infant-sharing mothers (Hrdy
1999:127–129ff., and references therein), primate mothers tend to produce milk that is low in fat and low in carbohydrates. In the case of infant-
sharing species, babies can make up at night for time away from the lactat-

ing mother during the day. Marmoset milk is an exception, far richer than that of other infant-sharing monkeys with on the order of four times more protein. One possible explanation is that the richness of marmoset milk has more to do with rapid early growth than with time off the mother. (Mother seals, for example, produce very rich milk, not because of shared care but because their babies need to grow fast.) At present, we do not have sufficiently detailed comparative data on mother's milk in primates to assess the various possibilities.

74. See Haig (1999) for a thoughtful reconstruction of this "deep history."

75. Most of the births were triplets, but rarely did more than two survive (McGrew and Barnett 2008).

76. Data for this correlation derive from three of the best-studied species of Callitrichidae, the moustached tamarin (*Saquinus mystax*), common marmosets (*Callithrix jacchus*), and golden lion tamarins (*Leontopithecus rosalia*). Snowdon 1996; Bales et al. 2002; and Karen Bales, personal communication, January 2008. For detailed field observations on alloparental care and provisioning, see Bales et al. 2000; Baker et al. 2002.

77. Killing of infants by females other than the mother has now been so frequently observed, both in captivity and the wild (e.g., Digby 2000; Saltzman and Abbott 2005; Saltzman et al. 2008; Bezerra et al. 2007) that Saltzman et al. 2008:282 propose that pregnant female marmosets *"routinely"* eliminate competitors to their own young.

78. Digby 2000.

79. Garber 1997; Porter and Garber (2008) also reported allomaternal food-sharing for *Callimico goeldii*.

80. Garber 1997.

81. Rapaport and Brown 2008; see also Cronin et al. 2005.

82. Hauser et al. 2003; Cronin et al. 2005; Snowdon and Cronin 2007.

83. Burkart et al. 2007; see also Burkart and van Schaik 2009 and ongoing research by these authors.

84. Hauser et al. 2003.

85. Ziegler et al. 2004, 2006.

86. Schradin and Anzenberger 1999; Schradin et al. 2003.

87. Johnson et al. 1991; Bardi et al. 2001. Except for information from macaque monkeys and ape mothers reared in captivity under conditions of social deprivation, there are almost no other observations of infant abuse or abandonment of full-term young among nonhuman primates.

88. For more detailed examination of this topic, esp. the human evidence, see Hrdy 1999.

89. Varki and Altheide 2005.

90. See classic early paper by Lancaster and Lancaster 1987; see Kramer 2005b for a twenty-first-century update.

91. Kaplan 1994; Kramer 2005a and personal communication, 2005.

92. Van Schaik 2004; Knott 2001; Robson, van Schaik, and Hawkes 2006.

93. For nonhuman primates, see Mitani and Watts 1997, Fig. 3; also Ross and MacLarnon 2000. For association between alloparental care and earlier weaning in humans, see Quinlan and Quinlan 2008, Fig. 2.

94. See Whitten 1983 for the first empirical demonstration of greater feeding efficiency in mothers with help.

95. See Partridge et al. 2005 on costs of reproduction. See Penn and Smith 2007 specifically for the human case. See Hawkes and Paine 2006 for general discussion.

96. Coontz 1992. See also Stone 1977 for families in the English-speaking world. See Stack 1974 for mid-twentieth-century black communities in the United States. See Al Awad and Sonuga-Barke 1992 for contemporary Sudan. For traditional societies in South America and Africa see Weisner and Gallimore 1977; Hames 1988; LeVine et al. 1996. For children "at risk" see esp. Crnic et al. 1986; Durrett et al. 1984; Lyons-Ruth et al. 1990; Pope et al. 1993; Werner and Smith 1992; Spieker and Bensley 1994.

97. Kertzer 1993; Hrdy 1999:371–372.

98. Crittenden 2001:108–109; Pearse 2005; Rosenbloom 2006; Walker 2006.

99. Spieker and Bensley 1994.

100. Furstenberg 1976.

101. Pope et al. 1993.

102. Olds et al. 1986, 2002. See overview of many such interventions by Olds et al. 2007.

103. Coutinho et al. 2005.

104. Turke 1988; see also Hames 1988, another pioneer in this area.

105. Flinn (1989) reported that nine Trinidadian mothers living in households with nonreproductive helpers (typically daughters) on hand had significantly higher reproductive success than 29 mothers without such help. See also Hames 1988 for an early study of "helpers at the nest" in tribal South America.

106. Hawkes, O'Connell, and Blurton Jones 1989.

107. Hawkes, O'Connell, and Blurton Jones 1997.

108. Hawkes, O'Connell, et al. 1998.

109. Hrdy 1999, 2002.

110. Adovasio et al. 2007.

111. Ivey 2000; see also Ivey Henry et al. 2005.

112. Sear et al. 2000, 2002, reanalyzing data first collected in the mid-twentieth century by Dr. Ian McGregor and his collaborators.

113. Sear et al. 2000:1646.

114. Sear et al. 2002.

115. Sear and Mace 2008. How father-absence affected the Mandinka child's

psychological or emotional development is unknown. But for one of the few studies ever to address this issue (and conclude for Western children that the main effect would be closer attachment to the mother), see Golombok et al. 1997.

116. Across wild populations of prosimians, New and Old World monkeys, and Great Apes, roughly half of all infants born die before adulthood. For example, 50 percent death rates in the first year of life are reported for wild slender loris (Radhakrishna and Singh 2004) and several species of wild tamarins (Wright 1984:71). Similarly high death rates over the first several years are reported for baboons (Altmann 1980:41; Altmann and Alberts 2003) and Great Apes (van Noordwijk and van Schaik 2005; Harcourt and Stewart 2007). Mean death rates in the first year are comparable for other apes and humans, around 22 percent. But mortality at older ages varies tremendously between forager groups. Only after the first year, as humans infants approach weaning and during their juvenile years, do we begin to see a lot of variation. The variation reveals interesting contrasts between humans and other apes, probably having to do with how variable post-weaning maternal and allomaternal provisioning can be in humans (Hill et al. 2001). Consider three samples from Central African foragers. At the low end, 14 percent of Efe infants died in the first year, 22 percent at older ages. By contrast 33 percent of Mbuti infants died in the first year, plus another 56 percent by age 15. Among the Aka, 20 percent of infants born during Hewlett's fieldwork died in the first 12 months, 43 percent by age fifteen (Hewlett 1991b, 2001, and supplementary data in Marlowe 2001, Table A). See also Gurven and Kaplan 2007.

117. Strassmann and Gillespie 2007.

4. NOVEL DEVELOPMENTS

1. Murray and Trevarthen 1986; Trevarthen 2005.
2. Henning et al. 2005 and references therein.
3. Personal communication, 2007. Those interested in this topic should look for forthcoming papers by the Japanese anthropologist Akira Takada at Kyoto University.
4. Bakeman et al. 1990, Table 2, using data from Mel Konner's pioneering fieldwork between 1969 and 1970, and during a six-month period in 1975.
5. Bakeman et al. 1990, Fig. 3.
6. For correlation with nutritional status, see esp. Valenzuela (1990), who used the Strange Separation test to measure attachment security in a population of low-income Chilean infants. See also Kermoian and Leiderman 1986 for Gusii horticulturalists in Kenya, and van IJzendoorn and Sagi 1999 for an overview.

7. For example, Kermoian and Leiderman (1986:457) described high levels of childcare among the Gusii as "unusual," and Ivey (2000:856) referred to the Efe as exemplifying a "unique" childcare system.

8. Tronick et al. 1992; van IJzendoorn et al. 1992; Hrdy 1999, 2005a; Hewlett and Lamb, eds. 2005; Voland et al., eds. 2005.

9. See Chisholm (2003) on the connection between theory of mind and the need for infants to cope with contingencies. See also Hrdy 2005a.

10. I specify *monkeys* because there are no studies using apes reared with inanimate sources of security comparable to Harry Harlow's mother-deprived rhesus macaques. And frankly, because of the cruelty such experiments entail, I cannot help but hope comparable studies are never done.

11. Ainsworth 1978:436.

12. See Rajecki, Lamb, and Obsmascher 1978, and esp. Ainsworth's commentary there; Hennighausen and Lyons-Ruth 2005; Trevarthen 2005.

13. Tronick et al. 1978. For an updated review of the vast literature regarding the infant's quest for social responses see Thompson 2006.

14. This phrase from Trevarthen, cited in Bakeman et al. 1990, an analysis of !Kung infancy. See Trevarthen 2005 for Western children.

15. Hamlin et al. 2007. The Yale experimenters were primarily interested in the implications of their findings for the development of morality, a topic far beyond the scope of this book. For an elegant and up-to-date discussion, see Hauser 2006.

16. Tomasello 1999, esp. pp. 61–68; quotation from p. 61.

17. Harlow's discovery that "motherless" rhesus monkeys preferred soft, terry-cloth-covered surrogates to wire ones with a milk bottle attached only served to confirm Bowlby's convictions on this score (Bowlby 1971).

18. See Rilling 2006 for up-to-date overview.

19. Regarding sensitivity, see Murray and Trevarthen 1986; regarding contingent commitment, see Hrdy 1999, chs. 16, 17, 19 and 20; Hennighausen and Lyons-Ruth 2005, and esp. the writings of Jim Chisholm (1999, 2003).

20. Draghi-Lorenz et al. 2001; Reddy 2003, 2007. For more on the importance of emotions like pride and shame for the developing sense of self, see Fonagy et al. 2002:25ff.

21. The only exceptions include some prosimians, such as galagos and ruffed lemurs, who leave their babies in a nest (e.g., Pereira, Klepper, and Symons 1987).

22. Bowlby 1971; Harlow et al. 1966. For the first experiments designed to test Bowlby's theories about attachment using rhesus macaques, see Spencer-Booth and Hinde 1971a; 1971b. The first stages of infant distress will be all too familiar for researchers who use Mary Ainsworth's Strange Situation test, described further in Chapter 9, n. 27.

23. Robert Hinde, personal communication 1996.

24. Bowlby 1971. For infant-initiated adoption of new caretakers in a nonhuman primate model, langur moneys, see Dohlinow and Taff 1993.

25. See Dolhinow 1980 for langur monkey infants separated from mothers. For indiscriminate attachment in emotionally deprived or orphaned human children, see Hennighausen and Lyons-Ruth 2005; O'Connor et al. 2000; and esp. Albus and Dozier 1999.

26. Thompson et al. 2005; Leckman et al. 2005 and references therein.

27. Ainsworth 1978:436.

28. See Fleming and Gonzalez 2009 and references therein for up-to-date review.

29. Trevarthen and Aitken 2001.

30. Hrdy 1999, chs. 19 and 20.

31. Bowlby 1969 (1971 edition).

32. Bard, Myowa-Yamakoshi, et al. 2005; Keller et al. 1988; Keller 2004.

33. Lavelli and Fogel 2002:30. See also Papousek and Papousek 1977, who considered this possibility.

34. Bard, Myowa-Yamakoshi, et al. 2005.

35. Kaye and Fogel 1980; Locke 1993. See Kojima 2001 for humans. See Hrdy 1977a for monkeys.

36. Kojima 2001:193.

37. Kojima 2001.

38. For the best available descriptions of babbling in pygmy marmosets see Elowson, Snowdon, and Lazaro-Perea 1998a; 1998b. For descriptions of infant vocalizations among wild Goeldi's monkey (*Callimico goeldi*) see Masataka 1982.

39. June 3, 2003, SBH interview with Jeff French.

40. Elowson et al. 1998b.

41. For example, Bard 2004, in her discussion of the rarity of "colicky" crying in chimps. Kojima 2001:195, and esp. Nishimura 2006.

42. Falk 2004a. For background on motherese see Fernald et al. 1989.

43. Falk 2004b:530, in response to critics pointing out that foraging mothers rarely set babies on the ground.

44. According to ethnographer Barry Hewlett, when Aka parents take infants with them on hunting expeditions, either parent may briefly put the baby down while actually jumping on netted prey (personal communication 2008).

45. Strier 1992:84.

46. Falk 2004a. See related explanation for language origin in Locke and Bogin 2006. The best starting point for readers interested in the primate origins and subsequent evolution of language is Hauser et al. 2002. See also Hauser 1996 for general introduction.

47. Although outside the scope of this book, there exists an extraordinarily

rich—and contentious—literature on when, how, and why language took on its distinctively human properties. Falk (2004a) and I (Hrdy 2005a) rely on a fairly conventional chronology which places the emergence of human language between 50,000 (Klein and Edgar 2002) and 150,000 or so years ago (McBrearty and Brooks 2000). See also Bickerton 2004; Lieberman 2007. Other anthropologists and linguists place the emergence of language earlier and view it as more tightly correlated with babbling.

48. Scientific accounts of biparental care in titi monkeys and shared care in langurs began to be presented at meetings and to appear in the literature by the 1960s (e.g., Jay 1963; Mason 1966).

49. Tronick et al. 1992:568; van IJzendoorn, Sagi, and Lambermon 1992. Outside of developmental psychology, attachment theory also had its share of criticism from feminists and others concerned with its implications for mothers, but that is another story, told elsewhere (Hrdy 1999, ch. 22).

50. Bowlby 1988:2; see esp. also Rutter 1974.

51. Lamb, Thompson, et al. (1985) following Hinde (1982) were among the first to critique our failure to study the effects of multiple caretakers per se. See also van IJzendoorn, Sagi, and Lambermon 1992 and Ahnert et al. 2006, and references therein.

52. NICHD Early Child Care Research Network 1997; McCartney 2004. See also ongoing analyses available online (www.nichd.nih.gov, www. excellence-earlychildhood.ca).

53. See Hewlett 1991a:172 for one of the first discussions of this topic in the context of paternal care among foragers.

54. See Lamb 1977a for father-infant interactions in the first year of life; 1977b for the second year.

55. These figures derive from comparison of U.S. "time diaries" kept by four samples of men from 1965, 1975, 1985, and 1998. The average time fathers spent with infants in 1998 was more than twice that of the preceding decades, from 17 minutes a day in 1960s and 26 minutes in the 1980s (Sayer et al. 2004; see also Lamb 1981; Lamb et al. 1987).

56. Even among other forest-dwelling hunter-gatherers like the Efe, the proportion of time fathers hold infants is around 2.6 percent. The figure for the veldt-dwelling !Kung is 1.9 percent of daytime. See West and Konner 1976 for the !Kung; Winn et al. 1989 for Efe; see also Hewlett 1988, esp. Tables 16.4 and 16.6; Hewlett 1991b, Table 5; Hewlett 2001; also Katz and Konner 1981.

57. Werner 1984 and esp. Rutter and O'Connor 1999 for discussion of some of the early practical implementations of this dawning awareness that it was neither unusual nor harmful for children to form several attachments; van IJzendoorn et al. 1992; Sagi et al. 1995.

58. Van IJzendoorn et al. 1992:5.

59. Van IJzendoorn et al. 1992. Similar flexibility allowing children to be securely attached to a mother and insecurely attached to an allomother, and vice versa, has since been reported by Lieselotte Ahnert and her coworkers among children in German daycare (Ahnert 2007 and personal communication, 2007, regarding a manuscript in preparation). Assessments of secure vs. insecure attachments rely on Mary Ainsworth's Strange Situation test, described in Chapter 9, n. 27.

60. Van IJzendoorn et al. 1992; Sagi et al. 1995.

61. Specifically, the researchers found less concordance in the child's relationships across caretakers. This finding from kibbutzim is consistent with U.S. and German studies suggesting that a secure attachment to the mother provides a critical foundation for forging other relationships (Grossmann and Grossmann 2005; Ahnert 2007).

62. Barry Hewlett, personal communication 2007; Hewlett 2007. See also McKenna et al. 1993; Small 1998.

63. Fite, French, et al. 2003.

64. Oppenheim et al. 1990; van IJzendoorn et al. 1992.

65. For example, Gusii infants securely attached to child caretakers scored significantly higher on the Bayley Mental Development Index than anxiously attached ones (Kermoian and Leiderman 1986:467–468 and Table 3).

66. Van IJzendoorn and Sagi 1999:723.

67. For example, the kind of integration Sagi and van IJzendoorn reported was less evident to Ahnert and colleagues (2006) in their study of children in German daycare centers.

68. Hewlett and Lamb 2005; Barry Hewlett, personal communication 2008.

69. Emde et al. 1992; Davis et al. 1994.

70. Zahn-Waxler, Radke-Yarrow, et al. 1992; Zahn-Waxler, Robinson, and Emde 1992; Warneken and Tomasello 2006.

71. Draghi-Lorenz et al. 2001; Reddy 2003.

72. Although "nonbasic emotions" such as pride, shame, or guilt are not thought to emerge until the second year of life, Reddy (2003) and others (Draghi-Lorenz et al. 2001) have argued that they emerge much earlier.

73. See Nesse 2001, 2007.

74. Bowlby 1971. See Fonagy et al. 2002 for update on how attachment theorists today view the development of the sense of self.

75. On forager views of their environment as a "giving place" see Bird-David 1990.

76. Quotations from Bird-David 1990:190, who reviews this literature based on her own work and that of other ethnographers.

77. Darnton 1984.

78. Hewlett, Lamb, et al. 2000, quotation from p. 288.

79. Hewlett, Lamb, et al. 2000, esp. Tables 1–3.

80. Clarke-Stewart 1978; Gottlieb 2004:148–164.

81. See Kramer 2005a for the most detailed empirical study available, based on timed observations in addition to interviews, of how farming shapes patterns of childcare.

82. Perner, Ruffman, and Leekam 1994.

83. Harris 2000:54–55ff.

84. From a study of Han children in a large eastern Chinese city, Fu and Lee 2007, discussed by Burkart 2009.

85. Perner et al. 1994; Lewis et al. 1996; Ruffman et al. 1998.

86. Meins et al. 2002.

87. For the best available introduction to this topic, see Tomasello 1999, esp. pp. 21ff.

88. Fonagy et al. 2002, quotation from p. 4.

89. Beuerlein and McGrew 2007.

90. As in, for example, "the child's *experience* of the environment is what counts" (Fonagy et al. 2002:114).

5. WILL THE REAL PLEISTOCENE FAMILY PLEASE STEP FORWARD?

1. For an evocative account of the era, see Hewlett and West 1998; quotation about "lost golden age" appears on p. 103. For historical overview, see Coontz 1992, 2005.

2. Popenoe 1996:191; see also Blankenthorn 1995:220.

3. Hewlett and West 1998:159–160. Popenoe 1996:175; Sylvia Hewlett and Cornel West 1998:159 echo the same point when they write: "Paternal certainty . . . is the most important precondition for paternal investment"; cf. Symons 1979; Gaulin and Schlegel 1980.

4. For important exceptions see Werner 1984; Werner and Smith 1992; Rutter 1974; Rutter and O'Connor 1999; Ahnert 2005.

5. Quotations from La Barre's *The Human Animal* (1967:104). See also the prominently published overview on the "origin of man" published in *Science* (Lovejoy 1981).

6. Popenoe 1996; Blankenthorn 1995. See also Commission on Children at Risk 2003.

7. On the family, see Moynihan 1986; Graglia 1998; Westman 2001.

8. For quotation, see Carey 2005. For more about "Marriage Protection Week" and former President Bush's proclamation in support of the family see www.whitehouse.gov/news/release/2003/10/20031003-12.html. These views continue to be widely expressed, as by the founder of Focus on the Family, James Dobson, who told an audience that years of social research "indicates that children do best co-raised by their married mother and father" (quoted in Seelye 2007).

9. "California girl with lesbian parents expelled," *New York Times*, Sept. 24, 2005.

10. The case was *Lofton v. Secretary of Florida Department of Children and Families*, No. 04-478 (Greenhouse 2005).

11. Lancaster and Lancaster 1987; Lee and Kramer 2002 and references therein.

12. For history and critical overview of the hunting hypothesis see O'Connell et al. 2002; Hawkes 2004b.

13. Quotation from Lovejoy 1981:341. Lovejoy was in turn building on classic papers by Washburn and Hamburg 1968. For critical overview see Hawkes 2004b.

14. Quotation from Lovejoy 1981:341. Updated versions of this hypothesis can still be found in the best textbooks evolutionary anthropology has to offer, for example, Boyd and Silk 1997:435.

15. Lee 1979; Hewlett 1991b.

16. Lawrence and Nohria 2002; see p. 182 for quotation about "true family values."

17. Tyre and McGinn 2003.

18. Buss 1994a; Pinker 1997. My own opinion is that the pursuit of wealthy men has more to do with more recent history—post-Pleistocene social and economic transformations that gave men in patriarchal societies control over the resources women need to reproduce (Hrdy 1999, 2000).

19. See letters in response to Lovejoy 1981 published in subsequent issues by Cann and Wilson 1982, and others; Hrdy and Bennett 1979; Hawkes, O'Connell, and Blurton Jones 2001; Hawkes 2004b.

20. O'Connell et al. 2002:862 and throughout.

21. O'Connell et al. 2002:838.

22. Regarding the 96 percent failure rate, see Hawkes, O'Connell, and Blurton Jones 2001.

23. See Bliege Bird's (2007) lovely case study on women's preferences for "reliable fish" over "big fish" among the Meriam of Australia's Torres Straits.

24. Bruce and Lloyd 1997. For more on the political and ecological pressures contributing to increasing numbers of single-parent households, see Lancaster 1989.

25. Engle and Breaux 1998.

26. Data from 2001, in Dominus 2005. See also Engle and Breaux 1998 for South America; Associated Press 1994.

27. For a rich and impressive literature on this subject, begin with Bruce, Lloyd, et al. 1995; Engle 1995; Engle and Breaux 1998; Ramalingaswami, Jonsson, and Rodhe 1996.

28. Marlowe 2005b.

29. Chagnon 1992:177 for the Yanomamo; Hewlett 1991a for the Aka, 1991b for preindustrial societies.

30. In their 2008 overview of 45 mostly natural fertility, natural mortality populations, Sear and Mace calculate that the presence of fathers had no impact on the survival of young children (usually under age five) in 53 percent of them. This estimate rose to 68 percent when they included data from supplementary societies for which information was less complete. Given how variable paternal impact is, and how much depends on who else is around and willing to help, these percentages should be cited with caution and caveats. See Chapter 8 for further discussion.

31. Johnson and Earle 2000:170.

32. Hill and Hurtado 1996; Marlowe 2001, 2005b; Wood 2006.

33. Hill and Kaplan 1988; Hill and Hurtado 1996:375ff. The minimal role alloparents play in infant care among the Ache may be a factor.

34. See Daly and Wilson 1984, 1999 for overviews; Hill and Hurtado 1996:375ff for Ache case.

35. The 87 percent figure derives from the period when the Ache still lived full-time as forest nomads (Hill and Kaplan 1988, Part I; Hill and Hurtado 1996:424 and Table 13.1).

36. Hill 2002:112.

37. Hawkes's ideas were developed in the course of fieldwork with the Ache as well as the Hadza (Hawkes 1991).

38. Marlowe 2001.

39. See Otterbein 1968 for the Marquesan Islanders in the Pacific; Hakansson 1988 for densely populated areas of Kenya; Sangree 1980 and Guyer 1994, esp. pp. 231–232, for other African cases; Leacock 1980 for Montagnais-Naskapi; Kjellström 1973 for Eskimos; Goodale 1971 for Tiwi of Australia; Sommer 2005 for Qing China; Prince 1963 and Hua 2001 for people of Tibetan origin; and many others reviewed in Hrdy 2000 and in Beckerman and Valentine 2002, esp. the volume's introduction.

40. Briefly summarized in Hrdy 2000. In addition to references there, see Sommer 2005 for very poor in Qing Dynasty China; Freeman 1979:99–100, 131–132 for Indian "untouchables."

41. For case studies see McAdoo 1986 for the United States; Brown 1973 for the Dominican Republic; Stack 1974 for the American South; Bolles 1986 for urban Jamaica; and esp. Borgerhoff Mulder 2009 for the contemporary Tanzanian Pimbe.

42. Lancaster 1989; Hrdy 1999, ch. 10.

43. Carneiro n.d.; Crocker and Crocker 1994; anthology compiled by Beckerman and Valentine (2002). For descriptions of the less bellicose, "gentler," and less polygynous Yanomamo living in highland areas on the periphery

of the Yanomamo heartland, see Chagnon 1992:101–111, writing about fieldwork he did late in his career, after 1991.

44. For early report on Yanomamo polyandry see Peters and Hunt 1975; Peters 1982.

45. In the human case, romantic feelings as well as sexual jealousy may also be involved, e.g., Shostak 1976; Jankowiak 1995; Leckman et al. 2005.

46. Beckerman et al. 1998; Hill and Hurtado 1996.

47. For the Canela see Crocker and Crocker 1994. For the Kulina, Pollock 2002. For matrilineal vs. patrilineal interests, see Hrdy 1999, ch. 10.

48. Pollock 2002:53. For more on "the optimal number of fathers" see Hrdy 2000.

49. Pollock 2002:54.

50. Haig 1999. According to Ely et al. 2006, a few chimpanzee twin sets are born with different fathers. Twinning in humans, and presumably chimerism as well, may increase under certain ecological conditions (e.g., Hrdy 1999:202–203), but nothing like the frequency of chimeras found in marmosets ever occurs in humans.

51. "Who's your daddy?" *Med Headlines,* March 8, 2008 (www.medheadlines .com).

52. Leacock 1980:31.

53. The full quotation reads, "Our early semi-human ancestors would not have practiced infanticide or polyandry. For the instincts of the lower animals are never so perverted as to lead them to regularly destroy their own offspring or to be quite devoid of jealousy" (Darwin 1974:45); this view that polyandrous mating by women could not be other than exceedingly rare because otherwise men would never invest was an early tenet of evolutionary psychology (e.g., Symons 1982) and persists today (e.g., Pinker 1997).

54. Regarding motivation and hunting as "parental effort," see Marlowe 1999b. For meat allocations, see Marlowe 2005b. Data were for children eight years old or younger.

55. Smuts 1985; Palombit 1999, 2001; Palombit et al. 2001; and esp. Alberts 1999.

56. See Charpentier et al. 2008 for this first-ever demonstration of other-than-genetically transmitted "paternal effects" in a nonhuman primate.

57. Anderson 2006.

58. Hrdy 1979; van Schaik and Dunbar 1990. The relationship between infanticide and male care has been well worked out and tested with comparative evidence from primates (Paul et al. 2000). For an up-to-date review of the now vast literature on primate infanticide, see van Schaik and Janson 2000.

59. Kleiman and Malcolm 1981; Taub 1984; Wright 1984; Paul et al. 2000.

60. For overview, see Marlowe 2001 and references therein.

61. Hewlett 1988, see esp. Tables 16.4 and 16.6. See also Konner 2005 for overview.

62. Hewlett 1992.

63. Reviewed in Hrdy 1999, chs. 7 and 8.

64. Meehan 2005, and personal communication 2007.

65. In addition to the Hadza and Aka case studies discussed here, Meehan has recently extended her fieldwork to include Ngandu horticulturalists living near the Aka (Meehan 2008). Winking and Gurven (2007) also report comparable patterns among Tsimane forager-horticulturalists in Bolivia.

66. Literature reviewed in Konner 2005; Crittenden and Marlowe 2008, Table 1.

67. Crittenden and Marlowe 2008.

68. Marlowe 2005b, Fig. 8.3.

69. Marlowe 2005b:184–185, esp. Fig. 8.2. See also Blurton Jones, Hawkes, and O'Connell 2005a.

70. For a particularly careful recent study of such maneuvering, see Sugiyama and Chacon 2005.

71. Shostak 1976. For more on help from older brothers, see Hagen and Barrett 2007.

72. Draper and Howell 2005.

73. Sugiyama and Chacon 2005.

74. Barron and Lee 2007.

75. Hewlett 1991a:137.

76. Carlson, Russell, et al. 2006; Mota and Sousa 2000; Schradin and Anzenberger 1999; Schradin et al. 2003. For more on endocrine monitoring see French, Bales, et al. 2003.

77. For changes in prolactin and cortisol levels linked to changes in the mother, see Storey et al. 2000. For cortisol's role in mother-infant attachment, see Fleming and Corter 1988; Fleming et al. 1997.

78. Bronte-Tinkew et al. 2007.

79. Reported from a preliminary study by Hewlett and Alster (n.d., cited in Hewlett 2001).

80. Delahunty et al. 2007; see also Fleming, Corter, Stallings, and Steiner 2002.

81. For increased secretion of prolactin in birds of both sexes engaged in care of nestlings, see Schoesch 1998 and Schoesch et al. 2004. For mammals and general discussion of prolactin "as the hormone of paternity" see Schradin and Anzenberger 1999. For overview see Ziegler 2000; Wynne-Edwards 2001; Gray et al. 2002; Storey, Delahunty, et al. 2006.

82. Storey et al. 2000; Wynne-Edwards and Reburn 2000.

83. See Wynne-Edwards and Timonin 2007 and Almond, Brown, and Keverne

2006 for experiments with various animal models that fail to show any direct causal relationship between prolactin and caring in males.

84. Two decades of this research are summarized in Fleming and Gonzalez 2009.

85. Stallings et al. 2001.

86. Fleming, Corter, et al. 2002; Fleming 2005. My guess is that nurturing potentials will be found among boys as well as men, but boys have not been studied yet.

87. Gray, Kahlenberg, et al. 2002, and references therein.

88. Silk et al. 2005; Silk 2007; Cheney and Seyfarth 2007.

89. Ziegler 2000.

90. Prudom et al. 2008.

91. When Shur et al. 2008 analyzed fecal samples from wild olive baboon males spending time in close association with former consorts, they found that testosterone levels declined during periods when the female was near term or lactating.

92. I rely heavily here on an excellent overview by Wynne-Edwards (2001). Jones and Wynne-Edwards (2001) undertook the key experiments demonstrating the role of prolactin in promoting male responsiveness to displaced pups among highly paternal Djungarian hamsters but not among relatively nonpaternal Siberian hamsters. Unfortunately we do not yet know much about hormonal changes in other apes in response to cues from pregnant females or infants. However, I would expect hormone levels in chimps to be affected, albeit not nearly so much as in men.

93. Bales, Dietz, et al. 2000.

94. Bales, French, and Dietz 2002.

95. Fite et al. 2005.

96. Russell et al. 2004; social opportunism is also typical of other highly social primates, even those who don't exhibit the same high levels of alloparental care that marmosets do.

97. Dixson and George 1982.

6. MEET THE ALLOPARENTS

1. For example, a sign at the Human Evolution exhibit at the American Museum of Natural History reads: "We owe our creative success to the human brain . . . symbolic consciousness gives us a capacity for spirituality and a shared sense of empathy and morality" (May 15, 2007).

2. Wilson 1975. It's worth noting that the first meeting of sociobiologists, organized by Richard Alexander and held in Ann Arbor, Michigan, in 1976, was largely devoted to the topic of alloparental care in animals. That organization subsequently morphed into the Human Behavior and Evolution Society (www.HBES.com).

3. Skutch 1935.
4. Reviewed in Hrdy 1976; Packer et al. 1992.
5. Wilson 1975; Ligon and Burt 2004.
6. This estimate for birds is based on 852 species out of 5,143 for which patterns of parental care are actually known (Cockburn 2006: Table 1). This new estimate, based on better field data, is three times higher than the old 3 percent figure cited for so long in the literature (Ligon and Burt 2004; Arnold and Owens 1998). The 3 percent estimate for mammals (see Russell 2004 for a recent review) includes a number of mammals like pine voles and prairie voles that have shared care but do not engage in shared provisioning of young. At the same time, the estimate leaves out many primates with shared care but no provisioning. This is a problem because, on the one hand, ornithologists and entomologists consider shared provisioning an integral part of the definition of "alloparental care," so voles, etc., should not be included. This makes the 3 percent figure too high. However, if the definition (just shared care) used by those who study voles is used, the current figure, leaving out all the primates that share care, is way too low. Obviously, there is a desperate need for an updated review and standardized terminology. In the interim, "full-fledged cooperative breeding" is used here to describe mammal species with both shared care and extensive provisioning.
7. Hrdy 2005b:69. See esp. König 1994 for more on the facultative reproductive strategies of mice.
8. For correlations of good help with more mouthfuls of food per minute, see Whitten 1983 for primates. For more increased survival of breeding adults see DuPlessis 2004. For correlations of help with reproductive success for breeders, see reviews in Chapters 3 and 5 for primates, and extensive literature for other animals reviewed in Clutton-Brock, Russell, et al. 2001 as well as in the volume edited by Koenig and Dickinson 2004, esp. the chapter by Russell. For adults with help who live longer, see Arnold and Owens 1998; Rowley and Russell 1990. For correlations between calf survival and number of allomothers in the family unit see Lee 1987; Payne 2003.
9. Gittleman 1986.
10. See Jennions and Macdonald 1994, Table 1, and Russell 2004 for reviews of mammalian cases; Koenig and Dickinson 2004 for birds.
11. Reviewed in Pruett-Jones 2004; Clutton-Brock et al. 2003; Heinsohn 1991.
12. Wilson 1975; see also Wilson and Hölldobler 2005:13371.
13. Emlen (1995, 1997) follows in a venerable ornithological tradition of borrowing terminology from human families to describe their flighty study subjects. For an early critique and further discussion of Emlen's foray into the human family, see Davis and Daly 1997. As yet there has been little response from behavioral scientists who actually study family relations.

14. For example, Solomon and French's ground-breaking compilation (*Cooperative Breeding in Mammals,* 1997) does not include humans. Nor do humans appear on the list of cooperatively breeding mammals in Russell's 2004 overview. For interesting exceptions see Schaller's comparisons between early hominins and savanna-dwelling social carnivores like lions and wild dogs (1972:263), or McGrew 1987 for comparisons between the family lives of humans and marmosets, and of course the work of early human sociobiologists like Turke, Flinn, and Hames described in Chapter 3.

15. Hrdy 1999.

16. Clutton-Brock 2002. Today such comparisons are increasingly mentioned at the end of grant proposals for work on the Callitrichidae.

17. African meerkats provide some of the best-documented cases of alloparents that only volunteer when they can afford to (e.g., Russell, Sharpe, et al. 2003).

18. Hrdy 1977a, ch. 7.

19. König 1994; Drea and Frank 2003. On co-suckling specifically involving grandmothers, see Lee 1987 as well as Gadgil and Vijayakumaran Nair 1984 for elephants; Mills 1990 for brown hyenas. Sperm whales may also have communal suckling (Whitehead and Mann 2000:239).

20. König 1994.

21. Creel and Creel 2002.

22. Macdonald 1980; Malcolm and Marten 1982; Moehlman 1983; Asa 1997; Lacey and Sherman 1997. Pregnant females may also be provisioned.

23. Lacey and Sherman (1997) provide an excellent introduction to the extensive literature on naked mole rats.

24. Of the 261 passerine birds, 217 did not ever breed cooperatively, 10 occasionally did so, while 34 species were frequently cooperative. Duration of postfledging nutritional dependence was more than twice as long for those that bred cooperatively than for noncooperators, while the occasional cooperators fell between the two extremes (Langen 2000, Fig. 1).

25. Contrast Langen (2000), who argues the former, with E. Russell (2000), who suspects the latter. Keep in mind however that the two views are not necessarily mutually exclusive.

26. Langen 1996; Rowley 1978.

27. Boran and Heimlich 1999; Rapaport 2006; Rapaport and Brown 2008; Burkart and van Schaik 2009.

28. Malcolm and Marten 1982; Creel and Creel 2002, esp. p. 165; cf. Bogin 1997:72.

29. Thornton and McAuliffe 2006; quotation appears on page 228. See Rapaport 2006 for pied babbler case.

30. Wilson 1971b; Hölldobler and Wilson 1990.

31. For example, see Sherman et al. 1995; Lacey and Sherman 1997. Even though the idea of a "eusociality continuum" remains controversial

among some entomologists, I use it here because as Lacey and Sherman (2005) point out, the concept is helpful for facilitating potentially revealing cross-taxonomic comparisons. Such comparisons are a main objective of this chapter.

32. Wilson 1975; Hölldobler and Wilson 1990:164.
33. Hölldobler and Wilson 1990.
34. See O'Riain, Jarvis, et al. 2000 for first demonstration of increased body size in breeding mole rats. See Holmes et al. 2007 for differences in brain cells.
35. Wilson and Hölldobler 2005.
36. See esp. Griffin and West 2003 for a meta-analysis of the relation between kin discrimination and the benefits from helpers among vertebrates.
37. Davies 1992.
38. Rubenstein 2007.
39. See Jennions and Macdonald 1994 for an overview and for hyenas; Marlowe 1999b for Hadza.
40. Double and Cockburn 2000; see also Cockburn, Osmond, et al. 2003.
41. Dunn et al. 1995.
42. Mulder and Langmore 1993.
43. Mulder et al. 1994.
44. Emlen (1982, 1991) is the principal architect of this ecological-constraints hypothesis. See also edited volume by Koenig and Dickinson (2004).
45. Arnold and Owens 1998.
46. Queller 2006:42; West-Eberhard 1975.
47. West-Eberhard 1986.
48. Reeve and Gamboa 1987; see also Wenseleers and Ratnieks 2006.
49. Cockburn 1998:161; Boland et al. 1997.
50. Hughes and Boomsma 2008.
51. Emlen et al. 1995:157.
52. Dierkes et al. 1999; Barlow 2000. In addition to having been observed in these fish, alloparental care was also recently reported in reptiles, in skinks belonging to the family Scincidae (O'Connor and Shine 2002).
53. Helpers "pay to stay" by preemptive appeasement (Bergmuller and Taborsky 2005); see also Kokko et al. 2002.
54. Holmes et al. 2007; Russell, Carlson, McIlrath, et al. 2004.
55. Clutton-Brock et al. 1998; Clutton-Brock 2002.
56. Young and Clutton-Brock 2006.
57. See Digby 2000 for the best available review.
58. Suppressed ovulation is not known to occur in humans; however, enforced wet-nursing has been widespread at different times and places, suggesting that some humans may once again have converged through cultural means on behaviors similar to evolved adaptations in other cooperatively breeding mammals (e.g., Hrdy 1999, ch. 14).

59. For example, see Solomon and French 1997.

60. Heinsohn 1991.

61. See Emlen 1991 for classic formulation of relationship between cooperative breeding and saturated habitats.

62. See Koenig and Stacey 1990 for food storage.

63. See Hrdy 1999:155–156, 191–193 and references therein.

64. For example, Whitehead and Mann 2000; Boran and Heimlich (1999)
speculate that some cetacean traditions are deliberately taught.

65. To date, the strongest evidence for the correlation between social integration and maternal reproductive success comes from long-term study of
savanna baboons at Amboseli (Silk et al. 2003; see also Silk 2007).

66. For formal theory behind this idea, actually worked out long ago by
hunter-gatherers themselves, see Fehr and Fischbacher 2003; Bowles and
Gintis 2003.

67. Known as the life-history hypothesis (Arnold and Owens 1998).

68. Cockburn 1996; Russell 2000; Ekman and Ericson 2006.

69. Cockburn 2006.

70. Cockburn 2006.

71. For example, in a controlled study of 45 species of African starlings,
Rubenstein and Lovette (2007) found that cooperative breeding was more
likely to evolve in those living in semi-arid savanna habitats with unpredictable rainfall than in either deserts or forest habitats.

72. Marshall 1976; Lee 1979.

73. Ligon and Burt 2004:6; see also Jamieson 1991; West-Eberhard 1988b.

74. Whereas cooperative breeding is found only 4 percent of avian clades with
precocial young, it is found in 11 percent of those with altricial young
(Cockburn 2006).

75. Ligon and Burt 2004:21.

76. See Kilner and Johnstone 1997; Kilner et al. 1999.

77. Russell, Langmore, et al. 2007.

78. Toth et al. (2007) used the sequenced genome of the eusocial honeybee
(among whom workers but not queens provision) as their baseline for
identifying genes in the genome of *Polistes* workers, foundresses, and
queens, all of which are involved in foraging and reproduction. Genomes
of the late-stage *Polistes* queens more nearly resembled those of honeybee
queens.

79. West-Eberhard 2003. Chapter 11 of her book is specifically devoted to
such "trait loss." The quotation comes from p. 10. As she points out, dele-
tions and other sorts of evolutionary change in developmental sequences
can all be called "heterochrony" (the term preferred by Toth et al.) because
all involve changes in the timing of expression (upward and downward
regulation of gene activity).

80. West-Eberhard 2003, quotation from p. 223; see also 1988b.

81. For non-hunter-gatherer examples see Cashdan 1990; Hrdy 1981a, ch. 7; Strassmann 1997; Strassmann and Hunley 1996; and hopefully more to come.

82. Boyette 2008 and personal communication; Crittenden and Marlowe 2008; on children fostered in, see Hrdy 1999, ch. 11.

83. Paula Ivey Henry, personal communication, May 10, 2008.

84. Betzig 1986; Betzig is preparing a synopsis of the human potential for creating societies with extreme reproductive skews (personal communication 2008).

85. For overviews of extensive literatures on wet-nursing through history see Hrdy 1997, 1999, chs. 12 and 13 and references therein. For an early treatment of this puzzling disconnect between extensive empirical documentation of female-female competition in other primates contrasted with a dearth of such evidence in the human literature, see Hrdy 1981a:129–130.

86. Foster and Ratnieks 2005; Cant and Johnstone 2008.

7. BABIES AS SENSORY TRAPS

1. Lacey 2002.
2. Brennan 2006.
3. Singer 2007.
4. Wisenden and Keenleyside 1992.
5. Costa 2006.
6. See Fleming et al. 1994 for the original experiments. See Ferris et al. 2005 for replication and overview of relevant experiments.
7. Martel et al. 1993; Keverne 2005.
8. Strathearn, Li, et al. 2007.
9. Zahed et al. 2007.
10. Wynne-Edwards and Timonin 2007 and references therein.
11. Whereas pregnant langur monkeys (*Semnopithecus entellus*) are highly motivated to take and hold infants (Hrdy 1977a, Tables 7.4 and 7.8), common marmoset (*Callithrix jacchus*) allomothers in the later stages of pregnancy are surprisingly infanticidal (Bezerra et al. 2007; Saltzman et al. 2008, esp. Fig. 2B).
12. See Roberts et al. 1998 for one of the few early papers to specifically advocate looking at alloparents; also Carter et al. 2005; Bridges 2008.
13. Olazábal and Young 2006.
14. These include the medial preoptic area, medial forebrain bundle, and trigeminal area. See Gregg and Wynne-Edwards 2005 for pioneering overview of this literature.
15. Plenary address, Human Behavior and Evolution Society 2003 meeting, Lincoln, Nebraska; the video was made by Marc van Roosmalen.

16. On placentophagia see Gregg and Wynne-Edwards 2005; Wynne-Edwards and Timonin 2007:6. For more on oxytocin and bonding, see Carter 1998.
17. Menges and Schiefenhövel 2007; I am also indebted to ethnographers W. Schiefenhövel, James Chisholm, and Victoria Burbank for information about the absence of placentophagia among the Eipo and Australian Aborigines.
18. Hrdy 1977a, Tables 7.5 and 7.9.
19. Personal communication, Jeanne Altmann, December 6, 2007.
20. Hrdy 1976; Silk 1999. When the term "kidnapped" is used for infant-sharing monkeys like langurs, the term refers to a female forcibly taking a new infant from a female belonging to a different troop during intertroop encounters (Hrdy 1977a, ch. 7).
21. Henzi and Barrett 2002; see p. 915 for quotation. For more on the spider monkey case see Slater et al. 2007.
22. Seay 1966; Lancaster 1971; Hrdy 1976; Silk 1999.
23. Altmann, Hausfater, and Altmann 1988:412.
24. Hrdy 1977a, ch. 7; Numan 1988.
25. It would be useful to know if, all other things being equal, primiparas suffer on average less infant mortality in infant-sharing species, but to my knowledge data to test this proposition are not currently available.
26. See Kringelbach et al. 2008 for further details which involved a technique called magnetoencephalography.
27. Hurlburt and Ling 2007.
28. At present, we know more about competition for parental and alloparental attentions in nonhuman than human cooperative breeders (e.g., Hodges et al. 2007 and references therein). Part of the reason is that it is easier to quantify competition in litter-bearing species with same-age littermates. In humans, competition is often between offspring of very different ages and capacities. Sibling competition in particular can involve older versus younger sibs, or even sibs yet to be born (Trivers 1974; Hrdy 1999:460–461ff).
29. Sumner and Mellon 2003; Isbell 2006. New World howler monkeys appear to be an exception to this rule since they do have color vision. It may be worth noting in this context that at least one species of howler monkeys exhibits moderate amounts of infant sharing and also bears young with distinctive natal coats (Hrdy 1976). This is a topic that cries out for further study.
30. Discussed in Hrdy 1999, in a chapter entitled "A Matter of Fat."
31. See Hrdy 1999, chs. 19–21, for more on the topic of discriminating human mothers and "runaway selection" for plumpness and other traits likely to appeal to mothers.
32. Gottlieb 2004:329.
33. Gottlieb 2004:163, 188, and throughout.

34. Gottlieb 2004:134.

35. Gottlieb 2004: 95ff., esp. pp. 132, 187–188.

36. Martins et al. 2007.

37. For example, Estrada 1982; briefly reviewed in Hrdy 1999:156–161.

38. For additional information on the practice of "fostering out" see Hrdy 1999:370–376.

39. Statistics from Child Welfare Information Gateway (www.childwelfare .gov) and from U.S. Department of Health and Human Services (www.hhs .gov).

40. Silk 1990.

41. For recent overview of primate infanticide see van Schaik and Janson 2000. In both traditional and industrial human societies, discriminatory treatment of orphans and stepchildren can range from nil or mild (Bledsoe and Brandon 1987; Case and Paxson 2001; Case et al. 2004) to extreme (Chagnon 1990; Daly and Wilson 1999).

8. GRANDMOTHERS AMONG OTHERS

1. Fossey 1984; Goodall 1986; Hamai, Nishida, et al. 1992; Harcourt and Stewart 2007; Pusey, Williams, and Goodall 1997; Townsend et al. 2007.

2. When attacks by a female called Passion on three infants in her community were first observed at Gombe, Goodall (1977) interpreted these "crimes of passion" as pathological behavior. However, sociobiologists immediately recognized the parallels with other species where infanticidal females increase their own, or their offspring's, access to resources by eliminating other females' offspring. When cannibalism is involved, the infant itself becomes a resource (Hrdy 1979, 1981a:108–109; Digby 2000 for recent overview). Today, on the order of 5–20 percent of mortality in the first months of life of infants born at Gombe is attributed to infanticide by females (Pusey et al. 2008).

3. Townsend et al. 2007.

4. Masayuki Nakamichi, personal communication, April 14, 2008.

5. Wroblewski 2008.

6. Nakamichi et al. 2004.

7. See Thierry 2007 for an up-to-date and comprehensive overview.

8. Carter 1998; Carter et al. 2001; Bosch et al. 2005; specifically in regard to oxytocin and trust in humans see Kosfeld et al. 2005.

9. Carter 1998.

10. Bales et al. 2007; also Bales, Pfeiffer, and Carter 2004; Bales, Kim, et al. 2004. It is impossible also not to acknowledge the psychobiologist Sue Carter, who decades ago urged researchers to pay more attention to oxytocin.

11. Olazábal and Young 2006, and references therein.

12. See Knight and Power 2005 for a well-researched overview.

13. For example, Thiessen and Umezawa 1998; Pinker 1997; Buss 1994a.

14. For example, Solomon and French 1997; refer back to Chapter 6. I still recall the first lecture I ever gave on humans as cooperative breeders in 1999, when a prominent zoologist in the audience asked, if so, "Why don't we find reproductive suppression in hunter-gatherers?" His question prompted me to tackle the problem (Hrdy 2002, Part II).

15. For example, in a recent phylogenetic-cum-behavioral analysis, Rendall and Di Fiore (2007, Fig. 2) highlight the lack of tolerance between Great Ape females.

16. Ember 1975; Murdock 1967, reviewed in Alvarez 2004.

17. Ghiglieri 1987; Wrangham 1987; Rodseth et al. 1991.

18. See such early classics as Darwin 1874; Lévi-Strauss 1949; Tiger 1970.

19. I am scarcely an unbiased commentator. I vividly recall these times, and some of the early criticisms were my own (e.g., Hrdy 1981a; Hrdy and Williams 1983).

20. Knight and Power 2005 provide an in-depth historical review of early reactions to the grandmother hypothesis and their background. As a historical note, I was among those convinced early on that apes tended toward patrilocality. I only changed my mind in the course of writing *Mother Nature* (1999). By 1997 I was sufficiently impressed by the flexibility of hunter-gatherer residence patterns that I sponsored Hawkes et al.'s then still controversial, but by now classic, 1998 paper on the grandmother hypothesis for publication in *PNAS*.

21. See Hart and Pilling 1979:124ff for a particularly vivid, if extreme, example; discussed further in Hrdy 2005c.

22. See Hawkes and Blurton Jones's (2005) review of this literature, summarizing reasons why they are now convinced that significant numbers of women in the Pleistocene survived into their sixth and even seventh decades.

23. Gurven and Kaplan 2007:326.

24. Based on demographic analyses by Nancy Howell in 1976, cited in Hawkes and Blurton Jones 2005; Biesele and Howell 1981.

25. Judge and Carey 2000; Lahdenperä et al. 2004; Gurven and Kaplan 2007:349.

26. Williams 1957; quotation from Hamilton 1966. Their ideas were subsequently applied to primates by Hrdy and Hrdy (1976).

27. I review different versions of the grandmother hypothesis as well as the competing prudent-mother hypothesis elsewhere: Hrdy 1999, ch. 11; see also Voland et al. 2005; Paul 2005.

28. Information on this last daughter, Furaha, provided by the Jane Goodall Institute, 2007. For background see Pusey et al. 1997.

29. On the basis of behavioral data alone, prior to the availability of genetic

data, a few authors had suggested that Great Ape breeding systems would turn out to be fairly flexible (e.g., Harcourt et al. 1981). However, this hypothesis was not confirmed until collection of hair and discarded wads of chewed leaves made microsatellite genotyping of wild chimpanzees possible (Vigilant et al. 2001; see also Langergraber, Mitani, and Vigilant 2007).

30. Harcourt and Stewart 2007.
31. Alvarez 2004; Marlowe 2004, whose analysis builds on and supports that of Alvarez.
32. Quotations from Pinker 1997:477 and Pinker 2002:323.
33. Alvarez 2004; Marlowe 2004; Blurton Jones, Hawkes, and O'Connell 2005a, 2005b provide a specific case study; see also Ember 1975, 1978; Ember and Ember 2000; Marlowe 2004.
34. Loeb 1926, cited in Alvarez 2004, Table 18.1.
35. From Riddell 1978, cited in Alvarez 2004, Table 18.1.
36. Wives lobby for sisters as co-wives in many polygynous societies (Irons 1988). See Chisholm and Burbank (1991) for a prescient discussion of the difference between "sororal polygyny," which is often beneficial to wives' interests, and other forms of polygyny that favor the husband's interests. See also Hamilton 1974 on the importance of a mutually supportive social group composed of matrilineally related females—mothers, when a woman is younger; daughters, when older.
37. For estimates of degrees of relatedness among Mardu women, see Scelza and Bliege Bird 2008, Table 3. The average degree of relatedness among langurs was first estimated to be about 0.16 on the basis of behavioral observations (Seger 1977) and later confirmed when genetic evidence became available (Little et al. 2002).
38. See Hamilton, Stoneking, and Excoffier 2005 for a particularly well documented example of more tightly regulated migration in patrilocal societies; see also Seilstad et al. 1998.
39. Richards et al. 2003.
40. Zerjal et al. 2003.
41. See Hrdy 1999:249–265 and references reviewed therein; Knight and Power 2005.
42. Reed et al. 2007. See Wade 2006 for an accessible and comprehensive overview.
43. Wyckoff et al. 2000.
44. Hrdy 1999:214–226. For fuller discussion, see Hrdy 1997, but that article was written before Alvarez and Hawkes convinced me to change my mind about hominin patrilocality.
45. Paul et al. 1993 for Barbary macaques; Nicolson 1987 for olive baboons; Borries 1988 for langurs. Survey data for women who give birth after age 35 similarly suggest increased psychological commitment with age in a sample of contemporary American mothers (Gregory 2007).

46. See Collins et al. 1984 for savanna baboons; Hrdy and Hrdy 1976 and Hrdy 1977a for langurs; Paul 2005 for captive sooty mangabeys and general overview.
47. Collins et al. 1984:208 and Table 4.
48. Seger 1977; Little et al. 2002.
49. Fairbanks 1988.
50. Pavelka, Fedigan, and Zohar 2002; Fairbanks and McGuire 1986; Fairbanks 2000; Hasegawa and Hiraiwa 1980; reviewed in Paul 2005. See Hrdy 1981a:110–111 for discussion of monkey mothers biasing support toward reproductively most "vulnerable" daughters. For parallels among human foragers, see Blurton Jones et al. 2005b; Kramer 2008.
51. Fairbanks 1988, 1993; Paul 2005.
52. Williams 1957; Hamilton 1966; first applied to primates by Hrdy and Hrdy 1976.
53. For example, Pavelka 1990, cited in Paul 2005:22; see also Pavelka and Fedigan 1991.
54. Silk et al. 2003.
55. Paul 2005. For example, Fairbanks and McGuire 1986 for vervets; Pavelka et al. 2002 for Japanese macaques. Although I focus here on primate examples, the presence of the mother's mother means larger litters, fewer losses, and so forth, in some other social mammals as well. Bushy-tailed wood rats (*Neotoma cinerea*) and wood mice (*Apodemus sylvatica*) provide particularly well documented examples (Moses and Millar 1994; Gerlach and Bartmann 2002).
56. McHenry 1992, 1996; Anton 2003.
57. Aiello and Wheeler 1995.
58. Hernandez-Aguilar et al. 2007; McGrew 2007b.
59. O'Connell et al. 1999; Wrangham et al. 1999; Laden and Wrangham 2005.
60. Perry, Dominy, et al. 2007. See Hernandez-Aguilar et al. 2007 for the lone exception of a savanna-dwelling chimpanzee population using shallow corms.
61. Yeakel et al. 2007.
62. See Alperson-Afil et al. 2007 for early use of fire. O'Connell et al. 1999; Wrangham et al. 1999.
63. Hawkes et al. 1998. For early insights into the importance of carrying and sharing, see Lancaster 1978.
64. Bock 2002.
65. Ivey 1993.
66. McDade et al. 2007.
67. Kaplan, Hill, et al. 2000.
68. Hrdy 1981a; Gowaty 1997; reviewed in Liesen 2007.
69. See published proceedings in Voland et al. 2005.
70. Whether or not other primates experience menopause remains a conten-

tious topic (Pavelka and Fedigan 1991), but in his recent overview and evaluation of the literature, Paul (2005) concludes that they do; see also Hrdy 1981b. In the only Great Ape study of its kind, Jones et al. 2007 conclude that ovarian depletion with age occurs in chimpanzees at the same rate as it does in humans.

71. Leonetti et al. 2005:204.
72. Schiefenhövel and Grabolle 2005.
73. Voland and Beise 2002, 2005; Lahdenperä et al. 2004.
74. Lahdenperä et al. 2004; mortality rate calculated from Table 1. The effects were unlikely to be due to fertility differences between lineages since there was no relationship between post-reproductive longevity and the total number of offspring a woman herself bore during her life.
75. In addition to two anthologies edited by Voland et al. (2005) and Bentley and Mace (2009), see Aubel et al. 2004; Crognier et al. 2002; Gibson and Mace 2005; Jamison et al. 2002; Lahdenperä et al. 2004; Scelza and Bliege Bird 2008; Skinner 2004; Valeggia 2009.
76. Sear and Mace 2008. These societies were selected because the relevant information on both group composition and child survival was available rather than because they were a representative human sample across all ecological conditions. For the time being, it's the best we can do.
77. Hawkes et al. 1998 and references therein; Lahdenperä et al. 2004 provide clear evidence that grandmothers have the biggest impact on their daughters' early-born compared to later-born children.
78. Sear, Steele, et al. 2002; Beise 2005.
79. See Schiefenhövel and Grabolle 2005 for Trobrianders. For entry into what is now an enormous literature on the correlation between lack of social support, increased stress, and susceptibility to disease see Taylor 2002 and Flinn et al. 2005 for humans, and Sachser et al. 1998 and Kaiser et al. 2003 for social mammals generally.
80. Shostak 1976:256.
81. Flinn and Leone 2006; Quinlan and Flinn 2005.
82. See Lahdenperä et al. 2004 for an unusually well documented example of greater grandmaternal impact for early-birth-order children.
83. For example, Blurton Jones et al. 2005b.
84. Back in 1999, O'Connell et al. had predicted that "grandmothers could certainly have improved their fitness by aiding sons, but the benefits associated with helping daughters are likely to have been much greater" (p. 477). This is what Sear and Mace found in their 2008 overview using data sets from 28 traditional societies (Tables 2a and 2b). These findings were consistent with the pattern found in their detailed Gambia case study (discussed in Chapter 3) where presence of the mother's mother was correlated with increased child survival, while presence of the father's

mother was correlated with increased fecundity. Sear et al. 2000, 2002; Mace and Sear 2005.

85. See Hrdy 1999, ch. 13, for review of a vast literature on parental preferences for particular offspring sets. See pp. 323–325 and Fig. 13.2 for the case of the ill-fated twin.

86. For why we would expect this, see Smith 1991 and Euler and Weitzel 1996 for early studies of differential solicitude from maternal and paternal grandparents. Similar patterns have since been replicated for a wide range of contemporary and traditional societies (Pashos 2000; Nosaka and Chasiotis 2005; Schölmerich et al. 2005, and references cited below). See esp. recent comparative analysis across 42 societies (Sear and Mace 2008).

87. Voland and Beise 2005; Beise and Voland 2002.

88. Euler and Weitzel 1996; Gaulin et al. 1997; McBurney et al. 2001; Voland and Beise 2005.

89. See Beise 2005 for Canadian case study; Sear and Mace 2008 for West Africa.

90. Jamison et al. 2002. Because of the small sample size, the maternal grandmother's effect was not statistically significant, although with larger numbers the authors expect it probably would be.

91. This hypothesis predicts that such pernicious effects will be most pronounced where there are multiple sons.

92. See Borgerhoff Mulder 2007 for an exemplary case study among the Kipsigis of Kenya.

93. Leonetti et al. 2005:212.

94. Leonetti et al. 2005:209–210.

95. This increased survival was only statistically significant for mothers married for a second time. See Leonetti et al. 2007 for further explanation.

96. Sear 2008.

97. Regarding conflicting maternal and paternal interests see Strassmann 1993; Hrdy 1997, 1999:257–263.

98. On the custom of suttee, see Weinberger-Thomas 1999 and references therein.

99. Ivey 2000 for Efe; Blurton Jones, Hawkes, and O'Connell 2005b for Hadza. Sear and Mace (2008) found that paternal grandfathers had a positive effect on child survival in only 3 of 12 societies, maternal grandfathers in 2 of 12. Even when grandfathers had an effect, it tended to be of borderline statistical significance, or it only applied to granddaughters.

100. Judge and Hrdy 1992.

101. Polly Wiessner, personal communication, March 2008.

102. Wiessner 2002b, esp. pp. 424–425, Table 3, and references therein.

103. Harcourt and Stewart 2007, ch. 11. In the gorilla case, increased infant survival is mostly due to reduced probability of infanticide by outside males.

104. Marlowe (1999a) presents this patriarch hypothesis as an alternative to the grandmother hypothesis.

105. For whales see McAuliffe and Whitehead 2005 and references therein. Elephants are also said to experience menopause, but at least some females are still giving birth in their sixties.

106. Robson et al. 2006, Table 2.1. We do not know yet whether menopause in other apes is a universal trait. See Paul 2005.

107. The proposal by Cant and Johnstone (2008) is also based on the presumption that all apes, including humans, are patrilocal, a view at odds with much work summarized here.

108. Kurland and Sparks 2003; Hawkes and Blurton Jones 2005; Ivey 1993; Meehan 2005.

109. See Hurtado et al. 1992; Hawkes et al. 1995; Bird and Bliege Bird 2005; and Tucker and Young 2005 for empirical evidence from field studies.

110. See Hames and Draper 2004 for an overview of the effects of the transition from hunting and gathering to settled living, and Kramer 2005a for how children help in a farming society. The introduction of wage labor brings further transformation since sons typically earn more and contribute more than daughters to the household economy (e.g., Hagen and Barrett 2007).

111. See Kaplan 1994 for classic paper using data from traditional societies in Africa and elsewhere to demonstrate the direction of resource flow from old to young.

112. See for example the contemporary case of old men in modern Japan denied welfare benefits and permitted to starve to death (Onishi 2007).

113. For attitudes towards and treatment of old women see Biesele and Howell 1981; Hrdy 1999:282 and references therein. For quotation and more on Ache case, see Hill and Hurtado 1996:235–237.

114. Eder 1985. Quotation from Miller 1976, cited in Gilligan 1982:169; see also Taylor 2002 and extensive literature therein.

115. Campbell 2002.

116. Taylor 2002.

117. Wiessner 2002b:411.

118. Hrdy 1999, ch. 10, 2000. Parish 1994.

9. CHILDHOOD AND THE DESCENT OF MAN

1. Hawkes et al. 1998.

2. On the high cost of motherhood and increased mortality risks for mothers in a nonhuman primate, see Altmann 1980:36. For humans, see Penn and Smith 2007. For general case of greater longevity in individuals who fail to breed, see Partridge et al. 2005. For decreased adult mortality in cooperatively breeding birds see Russell 2000. See Keller and Genoud 1997 for eusocial insects and naked mole rats. A honeybee queen can live up to 47 times longer than workers (Page and Peng 2001).

3. I am glossing over important current debates in evolutionary anthropology. For readers seeking a comprehensive overview I highly recommend *The Evolution of Human Life History,* edited by Hawkes and Paine (2006). The conventional anthropological explanation for long childhoods is that an extended period of maturation was essential for the development of big brains. "The adaptive function of prolonged biological youth," it was assumed is "to give the animal time to learn" (Washburn and Hamburg 1965, cited in Hawkes 2006:97). Current versions of this embodied-capital hypothesis emphasize how many years it takes to acquire skills needed to track, hunt, and efficiently process big game; to expertly flake stone tools and craft spears; and to develop language and more fully take advantage of what culture has to offer (Kaplan et al. 2000; see also Kaplan et al. 2001; Bock and Sellen 2002; and Gurven and Kaplan 2007 for more on the importance of learning and benefits of growing slowly). The main alternative explanation for long childhoods relies on models that use "invariant" life history relationships to explain why mammals with larger body sizes have longer lifespans, mature at later ages, and produce babies at a slower pace (Charnov 1993; Robson et al. 2006). There is much to recommend these two hypotheses, which in any event are not mutually exclusive, and depend on complex feedback loops.

4. Hawkes et al. 1998; Robson et al. 2006. Regarding the correlation between large brain size and long juvenile and adolescent life phases see Smith and Tompkins 1995:259ff; Barrickman et al. 2008; Kelly 2004; Dunbar and Shultz 2007. Regarding the significance of larger brain size, see Deaner et al. 2007; Ricklefs 1984. See Janson and van Schaik 1993 on why immatures should grow slowly.

5. On the expensive-tissue hypothesis, see Aiello and Wheeler 1995. For background and overview, see Bogin 1997. On the relation between cooperative breeding and big brains see Isler and van Schaik 2008.

6. Hrdy 1999:287; Kelly 2004.

7. See esp. Robson et al. 2006; Deaner et al. 2007.

8. Walker and Shipman 1996; Anton 2003.

9. Tardieu 1998:173–174; Smith and Tompkins 1995, Table 1; O'Connell et al. 1999:469; Robson et al. 2006; Hawkes 2006, but see Zihlman et al. 2004.

10. Anton 2003; McHenry 1992, 1996.

11. O'Connell et al. 1999, 2002.

12. Presumably, the need of mothers to avoid nutritional depletion from pregnancy and lactation is why among tribal peoples in highland New Guinea, women and children have preferential access to all edible insects that men harvest (Schiefenhövel and Blum n.d.). See Stoll 2001:91–102 for the importance of omega-3s during pregnancy and fetal brain development. Hominins in the early Paleolithic probably did not often, if ever, have access to fish, but we know that wherever and whenever they are available,

tree nuts—often an even denser source of omega-3 fatty acids than fish—
are a staple food among African apes as well as hunter-gatherers (e.g.,
Boesch and Boesch-Achermann 2000:201–204; Lee 1979, ch. 7).

13. Although females are bonded to matrilineal kin in most Old World monkeys, lack of "tolerance" between unrelated females is thought to characterize apes in the line leading to *Pongo, Gorilla,* and *Pan* (e.g., Rendall and Di Fiore 2007, Fig. 2).

14. This was perhaps the most important lesson I learned while researching an earlier book, *The Woman That Never Evolved* (1981a), and references therein.

15. Quotations from Tomasello 1999:60 and 1999:9, and see references therein.

16. Personal communication (2006) from Karlen Lyons-Ruth, who specifically acknowledges her debt to Tomasello (1999); quotation from Hennighausen and Lyons-Ruth 2005.

17. D'Errico et al. 2005; McBrearty and Brooks 2000. For quotation, and much more on origin of art, see Dissanayake 2000.

18. For an excellent discussion, see Hill 2009.

19. One could mention here Old World monkeys who attack an individual who fails to defer to immature offspring of a dominant lineage (Cheney and Seyfarth 2007) or who attack an individual and take away a preferred food item he had found because the finder failed to signal that he was prepared to defend it (as in Hauser 1992). But the closest nonhuman primates come to intention-reading derive from experiments like those done by Marc Hauser and others with cooperatively breeding tamarins and marmosets, described in Chapter 3. It is worth noting that Hauser himself, one of the pioneers in this area, is now reluctant to talk about group sanctioned "punishment" in nonhuman animals (personal communication, August 2008).

20. Hill 2009.

21. Fu and Lee 2007. I am indebted to Judith-Maria Burkart (2009) for this observation.

22. Wile et al. 1999; Miller 2002; Hagen and Barrett 2007.

23. See Trivers 1974, whose theories on parent-offspring conflict are now widely accepted in biology and psychology.

24. Hennighausen and Lyons-Ruth 2005:275.

25. Stern et al. 1983; Stern 2002; Cassidy and Shaver 1999; and esp. Rutter and O'Connor 1999 and Main 1999; O'Connor and Rutter 2000; Fonagy et al. 2002; Belsky 2005.

26. Lyons-Ruth et al. 1999; van IJzendoorn, Schuengel, and Bakermans-Kranenburg 1999.

27. To assess how secure a child feels about his relationship to a main care-

taker, who in most of the research done to date means the mother, psychologists employ Ainsworth's Strange Situation test. In this 20-minute protocol, the mother leaves her toddler together with a kindly "stranger" who is in fact a trained experimenter. The mother then returns, goes away again, and comes back. Most two-year-olds become distressed as soon as they note her absence, but the "securely attached" child will rush to her as soon as she returns and soon be comforted. However, some children fail to find her return reassuring. These "insecurely attached" toddlers can be further subdivided into those who seem "insecure/ambivalent" about just how much comfort they can derive from being near their mother and those who actually "avoid" their mothers, the "insecure/avoidant." For more on this topic, start with Cassidy and Shaver 1999.

28. Main and Hesse 1990; Lyons-Ruth et al. 1999; van IJzendoorn, Schuengel, and Bakermans-Kranenburg 1999; Solomon and George 1999.

29. Lyons-Ruth 1996. See Rutter and O'Connor 1999 for related disorders.

30. Dozier, Stovall, et al. 2001; see also Bates and Dozier 2002. On Adult Attachment Interviews, see Main and Hesse 1990. For a meta-analysis showing the predictive validity of AAI based on 80 studies encompassing some 6,000 children see van IJzendoorn, Schuengel, and Bakermans-Kranenburg 1999.

31. On heritability of personality traits like shyness or sociability, see Kagan and Snidman 2004. On lack of a relationship between attachment styles and the "Big Five" personality traits, see Shaver and Brennan 1992. For temperamental variation in monkey infants see Thierry 2007 and references therein.

32. Hennighausen and Lyons-Ruth 2005:385–386; Lyons-Ruth and Zeanah 1993; Rutter and O'Connor 1999.

33. Berlin and Cassidy 1999. See Vaughn, Azria, et al. 2000 on correlation with friendship and "social competence."

34. Lyons-Ruth 1996, and personal communication in 2008 interview.

35. Hawks, Wang, et al. 2007; see also Harpending and Cochran 2002; Balter 2005. Lactase persistence is perhaps the best-known example of recent selection. Milk, the staff of life for infants, can be difficult stuff for adults to digest unless they produce lactase, the enzyme that breaks down its main sugar, lactose. At some point between 5,000 and 10,000 years ago, as some cultures adopted herding, a gene conferring lactase persistence past infancy began to spread along with cattle-herding immigrants from the Near East to areas of Europe that increasingly relied on milk products. Today, the gene for lactase persistence is found in 80 percent of Europeans and of Americans whose ancestors evolved in Europe. It is also common among Tutsi and other African tribes with histories of herding. However, it is almost entirely absent from groups whose ancestors did not milk

cows, including South African Bantus and many populations in China (Bersaglieri et al. 2004; Burger et al. 2007).

36. J. Hawks, personal communication, December 31, 2007. Regarding rapid spread of new gene variants for increased brain size, see Mekel-Bobrov, Gilbert, et al. 2005.

37. Spier 2002.

38. For general theory see West-Eberhard 2003. On the evolutionary loss of prosocial behaviors, see Wcislo and Danforth 1997. For a case study in rapid evolution, see Lahti 2005. Lahti describes how warbler parents transplanted to locations lacking brood parasitical cuckoos gradually lost the ability to distinguish their own eggs.

39. Lahti 2005.

REFERENCES

Adovasio, J. M., Olga Soffer, and Jake Page. 2007. *The invisible sex: Uncovering the true role of women in prehistory.* Washington, DC: Smithsonian Books.

Ahnert, Lieselotte. 2005. Parenting and alloparenting: The impact on attachment in humans. In *Attachment and bonding: A new synthesis,* ed. C. S. Carter et al., 229–244. Dahlem Workshop Reports. Cambridge: MIT Press.

——. 2007. Mother-child relations with extended social networks in early childhood. Lecture delivered at the University of California–Davis, March 15, 2007.

Ahnert, Lieselotte, Martin Pinquart, and Michael Lamb. 2006. Security of children's relationships with nonparental care providers: A meta-analysis. *Child Development* 74:664–679.

Aiello, Leslie, and P. Wheeler. 1995. The expensive tissue hypothesis: The brain and the digestive system in human and primate evolution. *Current Evolution* 36:199–221.

Ainsworth, Mary D. Salter. 1966. The effects of maternal deprivation: A review of findings and controversy in the context of research strategy. In *Deprivation of maternal care: A reassessment of its effects,* ed. Mary D. S. Ainsworth, 287–357. New York: Schocken Books.

——. 1978. The Bowlby-Ainsworth attachment theory (commentary). *Behavioral and Brain Sciences* 3:436–437.

Al Awad, A. M. E. H., and E. J. S. Sonuga-Barke. 1992. Childhood problems in a Sudanese city: A comparison of extended and nuclear families. *Child Development* 63:906–914.

Alberts, Susan. 1999. Paternal kin discrimination in wild baboons. *Proceedings of the Royal Society of London B* 266:1501–6.

Albus, Kathleen E., and Mary Dozier. 1999. Indiscriminate friendliness and terror of strangers in infancy: Contributions from the study of infants in foster care. *Infant Mental Health Journal* 20 (1):30–41.

Alley, Thomas. 1983. Growth-produced changes in body shape and size as determinants of perceived age and adult caregiving. *Child Development* 54:241–248.

Allman, John. 2000. *Evolving brains*. New York: Scientific American Library.

Almond, Rosamunde E. A., Gillian R. Brown, and Eric B. Keverne. 2006. Suppression of prolactin does not reduce infant care by parentally experienced male common marmosets (*Callithrix jacchus*). *Hormones and Behavior* 49:673–680.

Alperson-Afil, N., D. Richter, and N. Goren-Inbar. 2007. Phantom hearths and the use of fire at Gesher Benot Ya'aqov, Israel. *PaleoAnthropology* 1:1–15.

Altmann, Jeanne. 1980. *Baboon mothers and infants*. Cambridge: Harvard University Press.

Altmann, Jeanne, and Susan C. Alberts. 2003. Intraspecific variability in fertility and offspring survival in a nonhuman primate: Behavioral control of ecological and social sources. In *Offspring: Human Fertility Behavior in Biodemographic Perspective*, edited by Kenneth W. Wachter and Rodolfo A. Bulatao, pp. 140–169. Washington, DC: National Academies Press.

Altmann, Jeanne, Glenn Hausfater, and Stuart A. Altmann. 1988. Determinants of reproductive success in savannah baboons, *Papio cynocephalus*. In *Reproductive success: Studies of individual variation in contrasting breeding systems*, ed. T. H. Clutton-Brock, 403–418. Chicago: University of Chicago Press.

Alvarez, Helen Perich. 2004. Residence groups among hunter-gatherers: A view of the claims and evidence for patrilocal bonds. In *Kinship and behavior in primates*, ed. Bernard Chapais and Carol M. Berman, 420–442. Oxford: Oxford University Press.

Ambrose, S. 1998. Chronology of the later Stone Age and food production in East Africa. *Journal of Archaeological Science* 25:377–392.

Anderson, James, and Tetsuro Matsuzawa. 2006. Yawning: An opening into empathy? In *Cognitive development in chimpanzees*, ed. Tetsuro Matsuzawa, Masaki Tomonaga, and Masayuki Tanaka, 233–245. Tokyo: Springer.

Anderson, Kermyt G. 2006. How well does paternity confidence match with actual paternity? Evidence from worldwide nonpaternity rates. *Current Anthropology* 47:513–520.

Anton, Susan. 2003. Natural history of *Homo erectus*. *Yearbook of Physical Anthropology* 46:126–170.

Arnold, K. E., and I. P. F. Owens. 1998. Cooperative breeding in birds: A comparative test of the life history hypothesis. *Proceedings of the Royal Society of London B* 265:739–745.

Asa, Cheryl S. 1997. Hormonal and experiential factors in the expression of social and parental behavior in canids. In *Cooperative breeding in mammals*, ed. Nancy Solomon and Jeffrey French, 129–149. Cambridge: Cambridge University Press.

Associated Press. 1994. Parents better at car payments than child support, group says. *Sacramento Bee,* June 18, 1994, A8.

Assunção, Maíra de Lorenço, S. L. Mendes, and K. B. Strier. 2007. Grandmaternal infant carrying in wild northern muriquis (*Brachyteles hypoxanthus*). *Neotropical Primate* 14(3):120–122.

Aubel, J., I. Toure, and M. Diagne. 2004. Senegalese grandmothers promote improved maternal and child nutrition practices: The guardians of tradition are not averse to change. *Social Science and Medicine* 59:945–959.

Babchuk, W. B., R. Hames, and R. Thompson. 1985. Sex differences in the recognition of infant facial expressions of emotion: The primary caretaker hypothesis. *Ethology and Sociobiology* 6:89–101.

Bakeman, Roger, Lauren B. Adamson, Melvin Konner, and Ronald G. Barr. 1990. !Kung infancy: The social context of object exploration. *Child Development* 61:794–809.

Baker, A. J., K. Bales, and J. Dietz. 2002. Mating systems and group dynamics in lion tamarins. In *Lion tamarins: Biology and conservation,* ed. D. G. Kleiman and A. B. Rylands, 188–212. Washington, DC: Smithsonian Institution.

Baldovino, M. Celia, and Mario S. Di Bitetti. 2008. Allonursing in tufted capuchin monkeys (*Cebus nigritus*): Milk or pacifier? *Folia Primatologica* 79:79–92.

Bales, Karen, James Dietz, Andrew Baker, Kimran Miller, and Suzette Tardif. 2000. Effects of allocare-givers on fitness of infants and parents in Callitrichid primates. *Folia Primatologica* 71:27–38.

Bales, Karen, Jeffrey A. French, and James M. Dietz. 2002. Explaining variation in maternal care in cooperatively breeding mammals. *Animal Behaviour* 63:453–461.

Bales, Karen, A. J. Kim, A. D. Lewis-Reese, and C. S. Carter. 2004. Both oxytocin and vasopressin may influence alloparental behavior in male prairie voles. *Hormones and Behavior* 45:354–361.

Bales, Karen, L. A. Pfeiffer, and C. Sue Carter. 2004. Sex differences and effects of manipulations of oxytocin on alloparenting and anxiety in prairie voles. *Developmental Psychobiology* 44:123–131.

Bales, Karen, J. A. van Westerhuyzen, A. D. Lewis-Reese, N. Grotte, J. A. Lanter, and C. Sue Carter. 2007. Oxytocin has dose-dependent developmental effects on pair-bonding and alloparental care in female prairie voles. *Hormones and Behavior* 52:274–279.

Balter, Michael. 2005. Are humans still evolving? *Science* 309:234–237.

Bard, Kim. 2002. Primate parenting. In *Handbook of parenting,* 2nd ed., vol. 2, ed. M. Bornstein, 99–140. Mahwah, NJ: L. Erlbaum.

———. 2004. What is the evolutionary basis for colic? (commentary). *Behavioral and Brain Sciences* 27:459.

————. 2007. Neonatal imitation in chimpanzees (*Pan troglodytes*) tested with two paradigms. *Animal Cognition* 10:233–242.

Bard, Kim, Masako Myowa-Yamakoshi, Masaki Tomonaga, Masayuki Tanaka, Alan Costall, and Tetsuro Matsuzawa. 2005. Group differences in the mutual gaze of chimpanzees (*Pan troglodytes*). *Developmental Psychology* 41:616–624.

Bardi, M., A. Petto, and D. Lee-Parritz. 2001. Parental failure in captive cotton-top tamarins (*Saguinus oedipus*). *American Journal of Primatology* 54:150–169.

Barlow, George. 2000. *The cichlid fishes: Nature's grand experiment in evolution.* Cambridge: Perseus.

Baron-Cohen, Simon. 2003. *The essential difference: The truth about the male and female brain.* New York: Basic Books.

Barrickman, Nancy, Meredith L. Bastian, Karin Isler, and Carel van Schaik. 2008. Life history costs and benefits of encephalization: A comparative test using data from long-term studies of primates in the wild. *Journal of Human Evolution* 54:568–590.

Barron, James, and Treymaine Lee. 2007. 2 more city heroes, and one saved child. *New York Times,* January 5, 2007.

Bates, Brady C., and Mary Dozier. 2002. The importance of maternal states of mind regarding attachment and infant age at placement to foster mothers' representations of their foster infants. *Infant Mental Health Journal* 23:417–431.

Beckerman, S., R. Lizarralde, C. Ballew, S. Schroeder, C. Fingelton, A. Garrison, and H. Smith. 1998. The Bari partible paternity project: Preliminary results. *Current Anthropology* 39:164–167.

Beckerman, S., and P. Valentine, eds. 2002. *Cultures of multiple fathers: The theory and practice of partible paternity in lowland South America.* Gainesville: University Press of Florida.

Behar, Doron M., R. Villems, H. Soodyall, J. Blue-Smith, L. Pereira, E. Metspalu, R. Scozzari, H. Makkan, S. Tzur, D. Comas, J. Bertranpetit, L. Quintana-Murci, C. Tyler-Smith, R. Spencer Wells, S. Rosset, and the Genographic Consortium. 2008. The dawn of human matrilineal diversity. *American Journal of Human Genetics* 82:1–11.

Beise, Jan. 2005. The helping and the helpful grandmother: The role of maternal and paternal grandmothers in child mortality in the seventeenth and eighteenth-century population of French settlers in Quebec, Canada. In *Grandmotherhood: The evolutionary significance of the second half of female life,* ed. E. Voland, A. Chasiotis, and W. Schiefenhövel, 215–238. New Brunswick, NJ: Rutgers University Press.

Beise, Jan, and E. Voland. 2002. A multilevel event history analysis of the effects of grandmothers on child mortality in a historical German population (Krummhörn, Ostfriesland, 1720–1874). *Demographic Research* 7:469–497.

Belsky, J. 2005. The developmental and evolutionary psychology of intergenerational transmission of attachment. In *Attachment and bonding: A new synthesis,* ed. C. S. Carter et al., 169–198. Dahlem Workshop Reports. Cambridge: MIT Press.

Bentley, G., and Ruth Mace, eds. 2009. *Substitute parents: Alloparenting in human societies.* New York: Berghahn Books.

Bergmuller, Ralph, and Michael Taborsky. 2005. Experimental manipulation of helping in a cooperative breeder: Helpers "pay to stay" by preemptive appeasement. *Animal Behaviour* 69:19–28.

Berlin, Lisa J., and Jude Cassidy. 1999. Relations among relationships: Contributions from attachment theory and research. In *Handbook of attachment,* ed. J. Cassidy and P. Shaver, 688–712. New York: Guilford.

Bersaglieri, T., P. C. Sabeti, N. Patterson, T. Vanderploeg, S. F. Schaffner, J. A. Drake, M. Rhodes, D. E. Reich, and J. N. Hirschhorn. 2004. Genetic signatures of strong recent positive selection at the lactase gene. *American Journal of Human Genetics* 74:1111–20.

Betzig, Laura. 1986. *Despotism and differential reproduction.* Hawthorne, NY: Aldine de Gruyter.

Beuerlein, M. M., and W. C. McGrew. 2007. It takes a community to raise a child, or does it? Paper presented at the 76th annual meeting of the American Association of Physical Anthropologists, Philadelphia.

Bezerra, Bruna Martins, Antonio da Silva Souto, and Nicola Schiel. 2007. Infanticide and cannibalism in a free-ranging plurally breeding group of common marmosets (*Callithrix jacchus*). *American Journal of Primatology* 69:945–952.

Bickerton, Derek. 2004. Commentary: Mothering plus vocalization doesn't equal language. *Behavioral and Brain Sciences* 27:504–505.

——. 2007. Language evolution: A brief guide for linguists. *Lingua* 117:510–526.

Biesele, Megan, and Nancy Howell. 1981. "The old people give you life": Aging among !Kung hunter-gatherers. In *Other ways of growing old,* ed. Pamela T. Amoss and Stevan Harrell, 77–98. Stanford: Stanford University Press.

Bird, Douglas, and Rebecca Bliege Bird. 2005. Martu children's hunting strategies in the Western Desert, Australia. In *Hunter-gatherer childhoods,* ed. B. Hewlett and M. Lamb, 129–146. Piscataway, NJ: Aldine/Transaction.

Bird-David, Nurit. 1990. The giving environment: Another perspective on the economic system of hunter-gatherers. *Current Anthropology* 31:189–196.

Blankenhorn, David. 1995. *Fatherless in America: Confronting our most urgent social problem.* New York: Harper Perennial.

Bledsoe, Caroline, and A. Brandon. 1987. Child fostering and child mortality in sub-Saharan Africa: Some preliminary questions and answers. In *Mortality and society in sub-Saharan Africa,* ed. E. van der Walle, 287–302. New York: Oxford University Press.

Bliege Bird, Rebecca. 2007. Fishing and the sexual division of labor among the Meriam. *American Anthropologist* 109:442–451.

Blurton Jones, N. G. 1984. A selfish origin for human food-sharing: Tolerated theft. *Ethology and Sociobiology* 5:1–3.

———. 1993. The lives of hunter-gatherer children. In *Juvenile primates: Life history, development and behavior,* ed. Michael Pereira and Lynn Fairbanks, 309–326. Chicago: University of Chicago Press.

———. 2006. Contemporary hunter-gatherers and human life history evolution. In *The evolution of human life history,* ed. Kristen Hawkes and Richard B. Paine, 231–266. Santa Fe: SAR Press.

Blurton Jones, Nick, K. Hawkes, and J. F. O'Connell. 2005a. Older Hadza men and women as helpers: Residence data. In *Hunter-gatherer childhoods,* ed. B. Hewlett and M. Lamb, 214–236. Piscataway, NJ: Aldine/Transaction.

———. 2005b. Hadza grandmothers as helpers: Residence data. In *Grandmother-hood: The evolutionary significance of the second half of female life,* ed. E. Voland, A. Chasiotis, and W. Schiefenhövel, 160–176. New Brunswick, NJ: Rutgers University Press.

Bock, John. 2002. Learning, life history and productivity: Children's lives in the Okavango Delta, Botswana. *Human Nature* 13:161–197.

Bock, J., and D. Sellen, eds. 2002. Special Issue on Childhood and the Evolution of the Human Life Course. *Human Nature* 13(2).

Boehm, Christopher. 1999. *Hierarchy in the forest: The evolution of egalitarian behavior.* Cambridge: Harvard University Press.

Boesch, Christophe, and Hedwige Boesch-Achermann. 1990. Tool use and tool making in wild chimpanzees. *Folia Primatologica* 54:86–99.

———. 2000. *The chimpanzees of the Tai Forest: Behavioural ecology and evolution.* Oxford: Oxford University Press.

Bogin, Barry. 1997. Evolutionary hypotheses for human childhoods. *Yearbook of Physical Anthropology* 40:63–89.

Boland, C. R. J., R. Heinsohn, and A. Cockburn. 1997. Deception by helpers in cooperatively breeding white-winged choughs and its experimental manipulation. *Behavioral Ecology and Sociobiology* 41:251–256.

Bolles, A. L. 1986. Economic crises and female-headed households in urban Jamaica. In *Women and change in Latin America,* ed. J. Nash and H. Safa, 65–82. Hadley: Bergin and Garvey.

Boran, J. R., and S. L. Heimlich. 1999. Social learning in cetaceans. In *Mammalian social learning: Comparative and ecological perspectives,* ed. H. O. Box and K. R. Gibson, 282–307. Cambridge: Cambridge University Press.

Borgerhoff Mulder, Monique. 2007. Hamilton's rule and kin competition: The Kipsigis case. *Evolution and Human Behavior* 28:299–312.

———. 2009. Social monogamy or polygyny or polyandry? Marriage in the Tanzania Pimbwe. *Human Nature* 20.

Borries, Carolla. 1988. Patterns of grandmaternal behavior in free-ranging Hanuman langurs (*Presbytis entellus*). *Human Evolution* 3:239–260.

Bosch, Oliver J., Simone L. Meddle, Daniel I. Beiderbeck, Alison J. Douglas, and Inga Neumann. 2005. Brain oxytocin correlates with maternal aggression: Link to anxiety. *Journal of Neuroscience* 25:6807–15.

Bowlby, John. 1966. *Maternal care and mental health.* New York: Schocken Books. (Orig. pub. 1951.)

——. 1971. *Attachment and loss,* vol. 1: *Attachment.* Harmondsworth, UK: Penguin Books. (Orig. pub. 1969.)

——. 1988. *A secure base: Parent-child attachment and healthy human development.* New York: Basic Books.

Bowles, Samuel. 2006. Group competition, reproductive leveling, and the evolution of human altruism. *Science* 314:1569–72.

Bowles, Samuel, and Herbert Gintis. 2003. Origins of human cooperation. In *Genetic and cultural evolution of cooperation,* ed. Peter Hammerstein, 429–443. Dahlem Workshop Reports. Cambridge: MIT Press.

Boyd, Robert. 2006. The puzzle of human sociality. *Science* 314:1555–56.

Boyd, Robert, and Peter Richerson. 1996. Why culture is common but cultural evolution is rare. *Proceedings of the British Academy* 88:77–93.

Boyd, Robert, and Joan B. Silk. 1997. *How humans evolved.* New York: W. W. Norton.

Boyette, Adam H. 2008. Scaffolding for cooperative breeding among Aka foragers. Paper presented at the annual meeting of the American Anthropological Association, November 21, San Francisco, CA.

Brady, Diane, and Christopher Palmeri. 2007. The pet economy. *BusinessWeek,* August 6, 2007, 45–47.

Brennan, Zoe. 2006. How one leopard changed its spots . . . and saved a baby baboon. *Daily Mail,* December 14, 2006.

Bridges, Robert. 2008. *Neurobiology of the parental mind.* New York: Academic Press.

Brockway, Raewyn. 2003. Evolving to be mentalists: The "mind-reading mums" hypothesis. In *From mating to mentality: Evaluating evolutionary psychology,* ed. Kim Sterelny and Julie Fitness, 95–123. New York: Psychology Press.

Brody, Leslie. 1999. *Gender, emotion, and the family.* Cambridge: Harvard University Press.

Bronte-Tinkew, Jacinta, A. Horowitz, E. Kennedy, and Kate Perper. 2007. Men's pregnancy intentions and prenatal behaviors: What they mean for fathers' involvement with their children. Publication #2007–18. Washington, DC: Child Trends.

Brosnan, Sarah F., and F. B. M. de Waal. 2003. Monkeys reject equal pay. *Nature* 425:297–299.

Brosnan, Sarah F., Hillary C. Schiff, and Frans B. M. de Waal. 2005. Tolerance for inequity may increase with social closeness in chimpanzees. *Proceedings of the Royal Society of London, Series B* 1560:253–258.

Brown, Susan E. 1973. Coping with poverty in the Dominican Republic: Women and their mates. *Current Anthropology* 14:555.

Browning, Christopher. 1998. *Ordinary men: Reserve Police Battalion 101 and the final solution in Poland.* New York: Harper Collins.

Bruce, Judith, and Cynthia B. Lloyd. 1997. Finding the ties that bind: Beyond headship and household. In *Intrahousehold resource allocation in developing countries: Models, methods, and policy,* ed. Lawrence Haddad, John Hoddinott, and Harold Alderman, 213–228. Baltimore: Johns Hopkins University Press.

Bruce, Judith, Cynthia B. Lloyd, and Ann Leonard, with Patrice L. Engle and Niev Duffy. 1995. *Families in focus: New perspectives on mothers, fathers, and children.* New York: Population Council.

Bugos, Paul E., and Lorraine M. McCarthy. 1984. Ayoreo infanticide: A case study. In *Comparative and evolutionary perspectives on infanticide,* ed. G. Hausfater and S. Blaffer Hrdy, 503–520. Hawthorne, NY: Aldine.

Burger, J., M. Kirchner, B. Bramanti, W. Haak, and M. G. Thomas. 2007. Absence of the lactase-persistence-associated allele in early Neolithic Europeans. *Proceedings of the National Academy of Sciences* 104:3736–41.

Burkart, J. M. 2009. Socio-cognitive abilities in cooperative breeding. In *Learning from animals? Examining the nature of human uniqueness,* ed. L. S. Roska-Hardy and E. M. Neumann, 123–141. New York: Psychology Press.

Burkart, Judith-Maria, Ernst Fehr, Charles Efferson, and Carel van Schaik. 2007. Other-regarding preferences in a nonhuman primate: Common marmosets provision food altruistically. *Proceedings of the National Academy of Sciences (USA)* 104:19762–66.

Burkart, Judith-Maria, and Carel van Schaik. 2009. Cognitive consequences of cooperative breeding in primates: A review. *Animal Cognition.*

Burnham, T. C., and D. D. P. Johnson. 2005. The biological and evolutionary logic of human cooperation. *Analyse and Kritik* 27 (2):113–135.

Buss, David M. 1994a. The strategies of human mating. *American Scientist* 82:238–249.

———. 1994b. *The evolution of desire: Strategies of human mating.* New York: Basic Books.

Byrne, Richard W., and Andrew Whiten, eds. 1988. *Machiavellian intelligence: Social expertise and the evolution of intellect in monkeys, apes, and humans.* Oxford: Oxford University Press.

Cacioppo, John T., and William Patrick. 2008. *Loneliness: Human nature and the need for social connection.* New York: W. W. Norton.

Campbell, Anne. 2002. *A mind of her own: The evolutionary psychology of women.* New York: Oxford University Press.

Cann, R. L., and A. C. Wilson. 1982. Models of human evolution. *Science* 217:303–304.

Cant, Michael A., and Rufus A. Johnstone. 2008. Reproductive conflict and the separation of reproductive generations in humans. *Proceedings of the National Academy of Sciences* 105:5332–36.

Carey, Benedict. 2005. Experts dispute Bush on gay-adoption issue. *New York Times,* January 29, 2005, A12.

Carlson, A. A., A. F. Russell, A. J. Young, N. R. Jordan, A. S. McNeilly, A. F. Parlow, and T. Clutton-Brock. 2006. Elevated prolactin levels immediately precede decisions to babysit by male meerkat helpers. *Hormones and Behavior* 50:94–100.

Carnegie, S. K., L. M. Fedigan, and T. E. Ziegler. 2008. Predictors of allomaternal care in *Cebus capucinus.* Abstract. XXII Congress of the International Primatological Society, August 3–8, Edinburgh, UK.

Carneiro, Robert. n.d. The concept of multiple paternity among the Kuikuru: A step toward the new study of ethnoembryology. Ms. in the author's possession.

Caro, T. M., and M. D. Hauser. 1992. Is there teaching in nonhuman animals? *Quarterly Review of Biology* 67:151–174.

Carter, C. Sue. 1998. Neuroendocrine perspectives on social attachment and love. *Psychoneuroendocrinology* 23:779–818.

——. 2005. Biological perspectives on social attachment and bonding. In *Attachment and bonding: A new synthesis,* ed. C. S. Carter et al., 85–100. Dahlem Workshop Reports. Cambridge: MIT Press.

Carter, C. Sue, Lieselotte Ahnert, K. E. Grossmann, S. B. Hrdy, M. E. Lamb, S. W. Porges, and N. Sachser, eds. 2005. *Attachment and bonding: A new synthesis.* Dahlem Workshop Reports. Cambridge: MIT Press.

Carter, C. S., M. Altemus, and G. P. Chrousos. 2001. Neuroendocrine and emotional changes in the post-partum period. *Progress in Brain Research* 133:241–249.

Cartwright, John. 2000. *Evolution and human behavior: Darwinian perspectives on human nature.* Cambridge: MIT Press.

Case, Anne, and C. Paxson. 2001. Mothers and others: Who invests in children's health? *Journal of Health Economics* 20:301–328.

Case, Anne, Christina Paxson, and Joseph Ableidinger. 2004. Orphans in Africa: Parental death, poverty and school enrollment. *Demography* 41:483–508.

Cashdan, Elizabeth, ed. 1990. *Risk and uncertainty in tribal and peasant economies.* Boulder: Westview.

Cassidy, Jude, and Phillip R. Shaver, eds. 1999. *Handbook of attachment: Theory, research and clinical applications.* New York: Guilford.

Chagnon, Napoleon. 1990. Mortality patterns, family structure, orphanage and child care in a tribal population: The Yanomamö of the Amazon Basin. Paper presented at the Symposium on Protection and Abuse of Young in Animals and Man, Ettore Majorana Center for Scientific Culture, June 13–19, Erice, Sicily.

———. 1992. *Yanomamo: The last days of Eden.* New York: Harcourt Brace and Jovanovich.

Charnov, Eric. 1993. *Life history invariants: Some explorations of symmetry in evolutionary ecology.* Oxford: Oxford University Press.

Charpentier, M. J. E., R. C. van Horn, J. Altmann, and S. C. Alberts. 2008. Paternal effects on offspring fitness in a multimale primate society. *Proceedings of the National Academy of Sciences* 105:1988–92.

Cheney, Dorothy L., and Robert M. Seyfarth. 2007. *Baboon metaphysics.* Chicago: University of Chicago Press.

Chisholm, James S. 1999. *Death, hope, and sex: Steps to an evolutionary ecology of mind and morality.* Cambridge: Cambridge University Press.

———. 2003. Uncertainty, contingency and attachment: A life history theory of the mind. In *From mating to mentality: Evaluating evolutionary psychology,* ed. Kim Sterelny and Julie Fitness, 125–153. New York: Psychology Press.

Chisholm, James, and Victoria Burbank. 1991. Monogamy and polygyny in southeast Arnhem Land: Male coercion and female choice. *Ethology and Sociobiology* 12:291–313.

Choi, J. K., and S. Bowles. 2007. The coevolution of parochial altruism and war. *Science* 318:636–640.

Clarke-Stewart, K. Alison. 1978. Recasting the "lone stranger." In *The development of social understanding,* ed. Joseph Glick and K. Alison Clarke-Stewart, 109–176. New York: Gardner.

Clutton-Brock, T. H. 2002. Breeding together: Kin selection and mutualism in cooperative vertebrates. *Science* 296:69–72.

Clutton-Brock, T. H., P. N. M. Brotherton, R. Smith, G. M. McIlrath, R. Kansky, D. Gaynor, M. J. O'Riain, and J. D. Skinner. 1998. Infanticide and expulsion of females in a cooperative mammal. *Proceedings of the Royal Society of London B* 265:2291–95.

Clutton-Brock, T. H., A. F. Russell, and L. L. Sharpe. 2003. Meerkat helpers do not specialize in particular activities. *Animal Behaviour* 66:531–540.

Clutton-Brock, T. H., A. F. Russell, L. L. Sharpe, P. N. M. Brotherton, G. M. McIlrath, S. White, and E. Z. Cameron. 2001. Effects of helpers on juvenile development and survival in meerkats. *Science* 293:2446–50.

Cockburn, Alexander. 1996. Why do so many Australian birds cooperate: Social evolution in the Corvida? In *Frontiers of population ecology,* ed. R. B. Floyd, A. W. Sheppard, and P. J. De Barro, 451–472. Collingwood, Victoria, Australia: CSIRO Publishing.

———. 1998. Evolution of helping behavior in cooperatively breeding birds. *Annual Review of Ecology and Systematics* 29:141–177.

———. 2006. Prevalence of different modes of parental care in birds. *Proceedings of the Royal Society of London B* 273:1375–83, Appendix A.

Cockburn, A., H. L. Osmond, R. A. Mulder, D. J. Green, and M. C. Double. 2003. Divorce, dispersal, density-dependence and incest avoidance in the cooperatively breeding superb fairy-wren *Malarus cyaneus. Journal of Animal Ecology* 72:189–202.

Cohen, Joel. 1995. *How many people can the earth support?* New York: Norton.

Cole, Michael, and Sheila R. Cole. 1993. *The development of children,* 2nd ed. New York: Scientific American Books/W. H. Freeman.

Collins, D. A., C. D. Busse, and Jane Goodall. 1984. Infanticide in two populations of savanna baboons. In *Infanticide: Comparative and evolutionary perspectives,* ed. G. Hausfater and S. B. Hrdy, 193–215. Hawthorne, NY: Aldine.

Commission on Children at Risk. 2003. *Hardwired to connect: The new scientific case for authoritative communities.* New York: Institute for American Values.

Coontz, Stephanie. 1992. *The way we never were: American families and the nostalgia trap.* New York: Basic Books.

———. 2005. *Marriage, a history: From obedience to intimacy, or how love conquered marriage.* New York: Viking.

Cosmides, L. 1989. The logic of social exchange: Has natural selection shaped how humans reason? Studies with the Wason selection task. *Cognition* 31:187–276.

Cosmides, L., and J. Tooby. 1994. Better than rational: Evolutionary psychology and the invisible hand. *American Economic Review* 84 (May):327–332.

Costa, James T. 2006. *The Other Insect Societies.* Cambridge: Harvard University Press.

Coutinho, Sonia Bechara, Pedro Israel Cabral de Lira, Marilia de Carvalho Lima, and Ann Ashworth. 2005. Comparison of the effect of two systems for the promotion of exclusive breastfeeding. *Lancet* 366:1094–1100.

Creel, Scott, and N. Creel. 2002. *The African wild dog: Behavior, ecology and conservation.* Princeton: Princeton University Press.

Crittenden, Ann. 2001. *The price of motherhood: Why the most important job in the world is still the least valued.* New York: Metropolitan Books.

Crittenden, Alyssa N., and Frank Marlowe. 2008. Allomaternal care among the Hadza of Tanzania. *Human Nature* 19:249–262.

Crnic, K., M. T. Greenberg, and N. Slough. 1986. Early stress and social support influences on mothers' and high-risk infants' functioning in late infancy. *Infant Mental Health Journal* 7:9–13.

Crocker, William, and Jean Crocker. 1994. *The Canela: Bonding through kinship, ritual and sex.* Fort Worth: Harcourt Brace.

Crognier, Emile, M. Villena, and E. Vargas. 2002. Helping patterns and reproductive success in Aymara communities. *American Journal of Human Biology* 14:372–379.

Cronin, K. A., A. V. Kurian, and C. T. Snowdon. 2005. Cooperative problem solving in a cooperatively breeding primate (*Saguinus oedipus*). *Animal Behaviour* 69:133–142.

Daly, Martin, and Margo Wilson. 1984. A sociobiological analysis of human infanticide. In *Infanticide: Comparative and evolutionary perspectives,* ed. G. Hausfater and S. B. Hrdy, 487–502. New York: Aldine.

——. 1999. *The truth about Cinderella.* New Haven: Yale University Press.

Damasio, Antonio. 2003. *Looking for Spinoza: Joy, sorrow, and the feeling brain.* New York: Harcourt.

D'Amato, F. R., R. Rizzi, and A. Moles. 2006. Aggression and anxiety in pregnant mice are modulated by offspring characteristics. *Animal Behaviour* 72:773–778.

Darnton, Robert. 1984. The meaning of Mother Goose. *New York Review of Books,* February 2, 1984, 41–47.

Darwin, Charles. 1890. *Journal of researches into the natural history and geology of the countries visited during the voyage round the world of H.M.S. 'Beagle' under the command of Captain Fitz Roy, R.N.* London: John Murray.

——. 1874. *The descent of man and selection in relation to sex.* Reprint of 1874 2nd ed., Chicago: Rand, McNally, 1974.

——. 1872. *The expression of the emotions in man and animals.* Reprint of 1872 ed., with commentaries by Paul Ekman, Oxford: Oxford University Press, 1998.

Davies, N. 1992. *Dunnock behaviour and social evolution.* Oxford: Oxford University Press.

Davis, Jennifer N., and Martin Daly. 1997. Evolutionary theory and the human family. *Quarterly Review of Biology* 72:407–435.

Davis, Mark H., C. Luce, and S. J. Kraus. 1994. The heritability of characteristics associated with dispositional empathy. *Journal of Personality* 62:369–371.

Dawkins, Richard. 1976. *The selfish gene.* Oxford: Oxford University Press.

Deaner, R. O., K. Isler, J. Burkart, and C. van Schaik. 2007. Overall brain size, and not encephalization quotient, best predicts cognitive ability across non-human primates. *Brain, Behavior and Evolution* 70:115–124.

Decety, John, and Philip L. Jackson. 2004. The functional architecture of human empathy. *Behavioral and Cognitive Neuroscience Reviews* 3 (2):71–100.

De Kort, Selvino R., Nathan J. Emery, and Nicola S. Clayton. 2006. Food sharing in jackdaws, *Corvus monedula:* What, why and with whom? *Animal Behaviour* 72:297–304.

Delahunty, Krista M., D. W. McKay, D. E. Noseworthy, and Anne E. Storey. 2007. Prolactin responses to infant cues in men and women: Effects of parental experience and recent infant contact. *Hormones and Behavior* 51:213–220.

Dennis, Wayne. 1943. Development under conditions of restricted practice. *Genetic Psychology Monographs* 23:143–189.

D'Errico, F., Ch. Henshilwood, M. Vanhaeren, and K. van Niekerk. 2005. *Nassarius kraussianus* shell beads from Blombos Cave: Evidence for symbolic behaviour in the Middle Stone Age. *Journal of Human Evolution* 48:3–24.

De Waal, Frans. 1996. *Good natured: The origins of right and wrong in humans and other animals.* Cambridge: Harvard University Press.

——. 1997. *Bonobo: The forgotten ape.* Berkeley: University of California Press.

——. 2001. *The ape and the sushi master: Cultural reflections of a primatologist.* New York: Basic Books.

——. 2006. *Primates and philosophers: How morality evolved.* Princeton: Princeton University Press.

Diamond, Jared. 2005. *Collapse: How societies choose to fail or succeed.* New York: Viking.

Dierkes, P., M. Taborsky, and U. Kohler. 1999. Reproductive parasitism of brood-care helpers in cooperatively breeding fish. *Behavioral Ecology and Sociobiology* 10:510–555.

Digby, L. 2000. Infanticide by female mammals: Implications for the evolution of social systems. In *Infanticide by males and its implications,* ed. C. P. van Schaik and C. H. Janson, 423–465. Cambridge: Cambridge University Press.

Dissanayake, Ellen. 2000. *Art and intimacy: How the arts began.* Seattle: University of Washington Press.

Dixson, A. F., and L. George. 1982. Prolactin and parental behavior in a male New World primate. *Nature* 299:551–553.

Dohlinow, Phyllis Jay. 1980. An experimental study of mother loss in the Indian langur monkey (*Presbytis entellus*). *Folia Primatologica* 33:77–128.

Dohlinow, Phyllis Jay, and Mark A. Taff. 1993. Immature and adult langur monkey (*Presbytis entellus*) males: Infant-initiated adoption in a colony group. *International Journal of Primatology* 14:919–926.

Dominus, Susan. 2005. The fathers' crusade. *New York Times Magazine* (May 8).

Double, M. C., and Alexander Cockburn. 2000. Pre-dawn infidelity: Females control extra-pair mating in superb fairy wrens. *Proceedings of the Royal Society of London B* 267:465–470.

Dozier, Mary K., Chase Stovall, Kathleen E. Albus, and Brady Bates. 2001. Attachment for infants in foster care: The role of caregiver state of mind. *Child Development* 72:1467–77.

Draghi-Lorenz, Riccardo, Vasudevi Reddy, and Alan Costall. 2001. Rethinking the development of "nonbasic" emotions: A critical review of existing theories. *Developmental Review* 21:263–304.

Draper, Patricia, and Nancy Howell. 2005. The growth and kinship resources of Ju/'hoansi children. In *Hunter-gatherer childhoods,* ed. B. Hewlett and Michael Lamb, 262–282. Piscataway, NJ: Aldine/Transaction.

Drea, Christine, and Laurence Frank. 2003. The social complexity of spotted hyenas. In *Animal social complexity,* ed. Frans de Waal and Peter Tyack, 121–148. Cambridge: Harvard University Press.

Dunbar, R. I. M. 2003. The social brain: Mind, language and society in evolutionary perspective. *Annual Review of Anthropology* 3:163–181.

Dunbar, R. I. M., and Susanne Shultz. 2007. Evolution in the social brain. *Science* 317:1344–47.

Dunn, Elizabeth W., L. B. Aknin, and M. I. Norton. 2008. Spending money on others promotes happiness. *Science* 319:1687–88.

Dunn, Peter O., Andrew Cockburn, and Raoul Mulder. 1995. Fairy-wren helpers often care for young to which they are unrelated. *Proceedings of the Royal Society of London B* 259:339–343.

DuPlessis, Morne A. 2004. Physiological ecology. In *Ecology and evolution of cooperative breeding in birds,* ed. Walter Koenig and Janis Dickinson, 117–127. Cambridge: Cambridge University Press.

Durkheim, E. 1893/1933. *The division of labor in society.* Trans. G. Simpson. Glencoe, IL: Free Press.

Durrett, Mary Ellen, Midori Otaki, and Phyllis Richards. 1984. Attachment and the mother's perception of support from the father. *International Journal of Behavioral Development* 7:167–176.

Earle, Timothy. 1997. *How chiefs came to power: The political economy in prehistory.* Stanford: Stanford University Press.

Eberle, Manfred. 2008. Why grouping, why help? Cooperative breeding in a solitary forager (*Microcebus murinus*). Paper presented at the XXII Congress of the International Primatological Society, August 3–8, Edinburgh, UK.

Eder, Donna. 1985. The cycle of popularity: Interpersonal relations among female adolescents. *Sociology of Education* 58:154–165.

Eibl-Eibesfeldt, Irenäus. 1971. *Love and hate: The natural history of behavior patterns.* Trans. Geoffrey Strachan. New York: Holt, Rinehart and Winston.

———. 1989. *Human Ethology.* Trans. Pauline Wiessner and Annette Heunemann. New York: Aldine de Gruyter.

Ekman, Jan, and Per G. P. Ericson. 2006. Out of Gondwanaland: The evolutionary history of cooperative breeding and social behaviour among crows, magpies, jays and allies. *Proceedings of the Royal Society of London B* 273:1117–25.

Elowson, A. Margaret, Charles T. Snowdon, and Christina Lazaro-Perea. 1998a. Infant "babbling" in a nonhuman primate: Complex vocal sequences with repeated call types. *Behaviour* 135:643–664.

———. 1998b. "Babbling" and social context in infant monkeys: Parallels to human infants. *Trends in Cognitive Science* 2:31–37.

Ely, John J., W. I. Frels, S. Howell, M. Kay Izard, M. Keeling, and D. R. Lee. 2006. Twinning and heteroparity in chimpanzees (*Pan troglodytes*). *American Journal of Physical Anthropology* 130:96–102.

Ember, Carol. 1975. Residential variation among hunter-gatherers. *Behavioral Science Research* 3:199–227.

———. 1978. Myths about hunter-gatherers. *Ethnology* 17:439–448.

Ember, Melvin, and Carol Ember. 2000. Cross-language predictors of consonant-vowel syllables. *American Anthropologist* 101:730–742.

Emde, Robert, Robert Plomin, Jo Ann Robinson, Robin Corley, John DeFries, David Fulker, J. S. Resnick, J. Campos, J. Kagan, and C. Zahn-Waxler. 1992. Temperament, emotion and cognition at fourteen months: The MacArthur longitudinal twin study. *Child Development* 63:1437–55.

Emery, Nathan J. 2000. The eyes have it: The neuroethology, function and evolution of social gaze. *Neuroscience and Biobehavioral Reviews* 24:581–604.

Emlen, Stephen. 1982. The evolution of helping, part 1: An ecological constraints model. *American Naturalist* 119:29–39.

———. 1991. Evolution of cooperative breeding in birds and mammals. In *Behavioral Ecology,* 3rd ed., ed. J. R. Krebs and N. B. Davies, 301–337. Oxford: Blackwell Scientific.

———. 1995. An evolutionary theory of the family. *Proceedings of the National Academy of Sciences (USA)* 92:8090–99.

———. 1997. Predicting family dynamics in social vertebrates. In *Behavioural Ecology,* 4th ed., ed. J. R. Krebs and N. B. Davies, 228–253. Oxford: Blackwell Science.

Emlen, Stephen, Peter Wrege, and Natalie J. Demong. 1995. Making decisions in the family: An evolutionary perspective. *American Scientist* 83:148–157.

Engle, Patrice. 1995. Mother's money, father's money and maternal commitment: Guatemala and Nicaragua. In *Engendering wealth and well-being,* ed. R. Blumberg, C. A. Rawkowski, I. Tinker, and M. Monteon, 155–180. Boulder: Westview.

Engle, Patrice L., and Cynthia Breaux. 1998. Fathers' involvement with children: Perspectives from developing countries. *Social Policy Report* 12 (1):1–21.

Estrada, Alejandro. 1982. A case of adoption of a howler monkey infant (*Alouatta vilosa*) by a female spider monkey (*Ateles geoffroyi*). *Primates* 23:135–137.

Euler, H. A., and B. Weitzel. 1996. Discriminative grandparental solicitude as reproductive strategy. *Human Nature* 7:39–59.

Fairbanks, Lynn A. 1988. Vervet monkey grandmothers: Effects on mother-infant relationships. *Behaviour* 104:176–188.

———. 1993. What is a good mother? Adaptive variation in maternal behavior in primates. *Current Directions in Psychological Science* 2:179–183.

———. 2000. Maternal investment throughout the lifespan of Old World monkeys. In *Old world monkeys,* ed. P. F. Whitehead and C. Jolly, 341–367. Cambridge: Cambridge University Press.

Fairbanks, Lynn A., and M. McGuire. 1986. Age, reproductive value, and dominance-related behavior in vervet monkey females: Cross-generational influence on social relationships and reproduction. *Animal Behaviour* 34:1710–21.

Falk, Dean. 2004a. Prelinguistic evolution in early hominins: Whence motherese? *Behavioral and Brain Sciences* 27:491–503, 531–541.

———. 2004b. The "putting the baby down" hypothesis: Bipedalism, babbling and baby slings. Open peer commentary: Author's response. *Behavioral and Brain Sciences* 27:526–541.

Farmer, Penelope. 2000. *The Virago book of grandmothers: An autobiographical anthology.* London: Virago.

Farroni, Teresa, Gergely Csibra, Francesca Simion, and Mark H. Johnson. 2002. Eye contact detection in humans from birth. *Proceedings of the National Academy of Sciences* 99:9602–5.

Farroni, Teresa, S. Massaccesi, D. Pividori, and M. H. Johnson. 2004. Gaze-following in newborns. *Infancy* 5:39–60.

Fedigan, L. M., S. D. Carnegie, and K. M. Jack. 2007. Predictors of reproductive success in female white-faced capuchins (*Cebus capuchinus*). *American Journal of Physical Anthropology* 137:82–90.

Fehr, Ernst, and Urs Fischbacher. 2003. The nature of human altruism. *Nature* 425:785–791.

Feistner, A. T. C., and W. C. McGrew. 1989. Food-sharing in primates: A critical review. In *Primate biology,* vol. 3, ed. P. K. Seth, 21–36. New Delhi: Today and Tomorrow's Printers and Publishers.

Fernald, A., T. Taeschner, J. Dunn, M. Papousek, and B. De Boysson-Bardies. 1989. A cross-language study of prosodic modification in mothers' and fathers' speech to preverbal infants. *Journal of Child Language* 16:398–406.

Fernandez-Duque, E. 2007. Costs and benefits of paternal care in free-ranging owl monkeys (*Aotus azarai*). Abstract. Paper presented at the 76th annual meeting of the American Association of Physical Anthropologists, March 28–31, Philadelphia.

Ferrari, Pier F., E. Visalberghi, A. Paukner, L. Fogassi, A. Ruggiero, and S. J. Suomi. 2006. Neonatal imitation in rhesus macaques. *Public Library of Science* 4(9): e302.

Ferris, Craig F., Praveen Kulkarni, John M. Sullivan Jr., Josie A. Harder, and Marcelo Febo. 2005. Pup suckling is more rewarding than cocaine: Evidence from functional magnetic resonance imaging and three-dimensional computational analysis. *Journal of Neuroscience* 25:149–156.

Fite, Jeffrey, K. J. Patera, J. A. French, M. Rukstalis, E. C. Hopkins, and C. N. Ross. 2005. Opportunistic mothers: Female marmosets (*Callithrix kuhlii*) reduce their investment in offspring when they have to, and when they can. *Journal of Human Evolution* 49:122–142.

Fite, Jeffrey, J. A. French, K. J. Patera, E. C. Hopkins, M. Rukstalis, H. A. Jensen, and C. N. Ross. 2003. Nighttime wakefulness associated with infant rearing in *Callithrix kuhlii*. *International Journal of Primatology* 24:1267–80.

Fleming, Alison. 2005. Plasticity of innate behavior: Experiences throughout life affect maternal behavior and its neurobiology. In *Attachment and bonding: A new synthesis*, ed. C. S. Carter et al., 137–168. Dahlem Workshop Reports. Cambridge: MIT Press.

Fleming, Alison, and C. Corter. 1988. Factors influencing maternal responsiveness in humans: Usefulness of an animal model. *Psychoneuroendocrinology* 13:189–212.

Fleming, Alison, C. Corter, J. Stallings, and M. Steiner. 2002. Testosterone and prolactin are associated with emotional responses to infant cries in new fathers. *Hormones and Behavior* 42:399–413.

Fleming, Alison S., and Andrea Gonzalez. 2009. Neurobiology of human maternal care. In *Endocrinology of social relationships*, ed. Peter T. Ellison and Peter B. Gray, 294–318. Cambridge: Harvard University Press.

Fleming, Alison, M. Korsmit, and M. Deller. 1994. Rat pups are potent reinforcers to the maternal animal: Effects of experience, parity, hormones and dopamine function. *Psychobiology* 22:44–53.

Fleming, Alison, D. Ruble, H. Krieger, and P. Y. Wong. 1997. Hormonal and experiential correlates of maternal responsiveness during pregnancy and the puerperium in human mothers. *Hormones and Behavior* 31:145–158.

Flinn, Mark V. 1989. Household composition and female reproductive strategies in a Trinidadian village. In *The sociobiology of sexual and reproductive strategies*, ed. A. E. Rasa, C. Vogel, and E. Voland, 206–233. London: Chapman and Hall.

Flinn, Mark V., David C. Geary, and Carol V. Ward. 2005. Ecological dominance, social competition, and coalitionary arms races: Why humans evolved extraordinary intelligence. *Evolution and Human Behavior* 26:10–46.

Flinn, Mark V., and David V. Leone. 2006. Early family trauma and the ontogeny of glucocorticoid stress response in the human child: Grandmothers as a secure base. *Journal of Developmental Processes* 1:31–65.

Fonagy, Peter, György Gergely, Elliot Jurist, and Mary Target. 2002. *Affect regulation, mentalization, and the development of self.* New York: Other Press.

Fossey, Dian. 1979. Development of the mountain gorilla (*Gorilla gorilla beringei*): The first thirty-six months. In *The great apes,* ed. David Hamburg and Elizabeth McCown, 139–186. Menlo Park: Benjamin Cummings.

———. 1984. Infanticide in mountain gorillas (*Gorilla gorilla beringei*) with comparative notes on chimpanzees. In *Infanticide: Comparative and evolutionary perspectives,* ed. G. Hausfater and S. Hrdy, 217–236. Hawthorne, NY: Aldine.

Foster, Kevin R., and Francis L. W. Ratnieks. 2005. A new eusocial vertebrate? *Trends in Ecology and Evolution* 20:363–364.

Freeman, James M. 1979. *Untouchable: An Indian life history.* Stanford: Stanford University Press.

French, Jeffrey A. 2007. Lecture delivered at University of California–Davis, April 10, 2007.

French, Jeffrey A., Karen Bales, Andrew J. Baker, and James M. Dietz. 2003. Endocrine monitoring of wild dominant and subordinate female *Leontopithecus rosalia. International Journal of Primatology* 24:1281–1300.

Fruth, Barbara, and Gottfried Höhmann. 2006. Social grease for females? Same-sex genital contacts in wild bonobos. In *Homosexual behaviour in animals: An evolutionary perspective,* ed. Volker Sommer and Paul L. Vasey, 294–315. Cambridge: Cambridge University Press.

Fry, Douglas. 2007. *Beyond war: The human potential for peace.* Oxford: Oxford University Press.

Fu, Genyue, and Kang Lee. 2007. Social grooming in the kindergarten: The emergence of flattery behavior. *Developmental Science* 10:255–265.

Furstenberg, Frank. 1976. *Unplanned parenthood: The social consequences of teenage childbearing.* New York: Free Press.

Gadgil, Madhav, and P. Vijayakumaran Nair. 1984. Observations on the social behaviour of free ranging groups of tame Asiatic elephants (*Elephas maximus* Linn.). *Proceedings of the Indian Academy of Sciences* (Animal Science) 93:225–233.

Gagneux, Pascal. 1993. The behavioral development of wild chimpanzee infants: The acquisition and maternal influences on learning. M.A. thesis (Diplomarbeit). Zoologisches Institut, University of Basel.

Galdikas, Birute. 1982. Wild orangutan birth at Tanjung Putting Reserve. *Primates* 23:500–510.

Gallese, Vittorio, Pier Francesco Ferrari, and Maria Alessandra Umilta. 2002. The mirror matching system: A shared manifold for intersubjectivity. *Behavioral and Brain Sciences* 25:35–36.

Garber, Paul A. 1997. One for all and breeding for one: Cooperation and competition as a tamarin reproductive strategy. *Evolutionary Anthropology* 7:187–199.

Gaulin, S. J. C., D. H. McBurney, and S. L. Brakeman-Wartell. 1997. Matrilateral biases in the investment of aunts and uncles. *Human Nature* 8:661–688.

Gaulin, S. J. C., and A. Schlegel. 1980. Paternal confidence and paternal investment: A cross-cultural test of a sociobiological hypothesis. *Ethology and Sociobiology* 1:301–309.

Gerlach, G., and S. Bartmann. 2002. Reproductive skew, costs and benefits of cooperative breeding in female wood mice (*Apodemus sylvaticus*). *Behavioral Ecology* 13:408–418.

Ghiglieri, M. 1987. Sociobiology of the Great Apes and the hominid ancestor. *Journal of Human Evolution* 16:319–357.

Gibson, Mhairi A., and Ruth Mace. 2005. Helpful grandmothers in rural Ethiopia: A study of the effect of kin on child survival and growth. *Evolution and Human Behavior* 26:469–482.

Gilby, I. C., L. E. Egerly, L. Pintea, and A. E. Pusey. 2006. Ecological and social influences on the hunting behavior of wild chimpanzees. *Animal Behaviour* 71:169–180.

Gilligan, Carol. 1982. *In a different voice: Psychological theory and women's development.* Cambridge: Harvard University Press.

Gintis, Herbert. 2001. Foreword: Beyond selfishness in modeling human behavior. In *Evolution and the capacity for commitment,* ed. R. Nesse, xiiix–viii. New York: Russell Sage.

Gittleman, J. L. 1986. Carnivore life history patterns: Allometric, phylogenetic, and ecological association. *American Naturalist* 127:744–771.

Goleman, Daniel. 2006. *Social intelligence: The new science of human relationships.* New York: Bantam/Dell, Random House.

Golombok, Susan, Fiona Tasker, and Clare Murray. 1997. Children raised in fatherless families from infancy: Family relationships and the socioemotional development of children of lesbian and single heterosexual mothers. *Journal of Child Psychology and Psychiatry* 36:783–791.

Gomez, Juan Carlos. 2004. *Apes, monkeys, children, and the growth of mind.* Cambridge: Harvard University Press.

Goodale, Jane. 1971. *Tiwi wives: A study of the women of Melville Island, North Australia.* Seattle: University of Washington Press.

Goodall, Jane. 1969. Mother-offspring relationships in free-ranging chimpanzees. In *Primate ethology,* ed. Desmond Morris, 365–436. New York: Doubleday.

——. 1977. Infant-killing and cannibalism in free-living chimpanzees. *Folia Primatologica* 28:259–282.

——. 1986. *The chimpanzees of Gombe: Patterns of behavior.* Cambridge: Belknap Press of Harvard University Press.

Gottlieb, Alma. 2004. *The afterlife is where we come from: The culture of infancy in West Africa.* Chicago: University of Chicago Press.

Gowaty, Patricia Adair, ed. 1997. *Feminism and evolutionary biology: Boundaries, intersections and frontiers.* New York: Chapman and Hall.

Graglia, F. Carolyn. 1998. *Domestic tranquility: A brief against feminism.* Dallas: Spence.

Gray, Peter B., and Peter T. Ellison. 2009. Introduction: Endocrinology of social relationships. In *Endocrinology of social relationships,* ed. Peter T. Ellison and Peter B. Gray, 1–9. Cambridge: Harvard University Press.

Gray, Peter B., Sonya M. Kahlenberg, Emily S. Barrett, Susan Lipson, and Peter Ellison. 2002. Marriage and fatherhood are associated with lower testosterone in males. *Evolution and Human Behavior* 23:1–9.

Greene, Harry W., Peter G. May, David L. Hardy Sr., Jolie M. Sciturro, and Terence M. Farrell. 2002. Parental behavior by vipers. In *Biology of the vipers,* ed. Gordon W. Schuett, Mats Höggren, Michael E. Douglas, and Harry W. Greene, 179-205. Eagle Mountain, Utah: Eagle Mountain Publishing.

Greenhouse, Linda. 2005. Court lets stand Florida's ban on gay adoption. *San Francisco Chronicle,* January 11, 2005.

Gregg, Jennifer, and K. Wynne-Edwards. 2005. Placentophagia in naive adults, new fathers, and new mothers in the biparental dwarf hamster, *Phodopus cambelli. Psychobiology* 47(20):179-188.

Gregory, Elizabeth. 2007. *Ready: Why women are embracing the new later motherhood.* New York: Basic Books.

Griffin, A. S., and S. A. West. 2003. Kin discrimination and the benefits of helping in cooperatively breeding vertebrates. *Science* 302:634-636.

Grossmann, K. E., and K. Grossmann. 2005. Universality of human social attachment as an adaptive process. In *Attachment and bonding: A new synthesis,* ed. C. S. Carter et al., 199-228. Dahlem Workshop Reports. Cambridge: MIT Press.

Groves, C. 2001. *Primate taxonomy.* Washington, DC: Smithsonian Institution.

Gunnar, M., and M. Donahue. 1980. Sex differences in social responsiveness between six months and twelve months. *Child Development* 51:262-265.

Gurven, M., and H. Kaplan. 2007. Longevity among hunter-gatherers: A cross-cultural perspective. *Population and Development Review* 33:321-365.

Guyer, Jane. 1994. Lineal identities and lateral networks: The logic of polyandrous motherhood. In *Nuptiality in sub-Saharan Africa: Contemporary anthropological and demographic perspectives,* ed. C. Bledsoe and G. Pison, 231-252. Oxford: Clarendon/Oxford University Press.

Hagen, E. H., and H. C. Barrett. 2007. Perinatal sadness among Shuar women. *Medical Anthropology Quarterly* 21:22-40.

——. n.d. Cooperative breeding and adolescent siblings: Evidence for the ecological constraints model? Ms. submitted for publication.

Haig, David. 1999. What is a marmoset? *American Journal of Primatology* 49:285-296.

Hakansson, T. 1988. *Bridewealth, women and land: Social change among the Gusii of Kenya.* Uppsala Studies in Cultural Anthropology 10.

Hamai, M., T. Nishida, H. Takasaki, and L. A. Turner. 1992. New records of within-group infanticide and cannibalism in wild chimpanzees. *Primates* 33:151-162.

Hames, Raymond. 1988. The allocation of parental care among the Ye'kwana. In *Human reproductive behavior: A Darwinian perspective,* ed. Laura Betzig, Monique Borgerhoff Mulder, and Paul Turke, 237-251. Cambridge: Cambridge University Press.

Hames, Raymond, and Patricia Draper. 2004. Women's work, childcare and helpers at the nest in a hunter-gatherer society. *Human Nature* 15:319-341.

Hamilton, Annette. 1974. The role of women in aboriginal marriage arrangements. In *Women's role in Aboriginal society,* ed. Fay Gale, 28–35. Canberra: Australian Institute of Aboriginal Studies.

Hamilton, Grant, Mark Stoneking, and Laurent Excoffier. 2005. Molecular analysis reveals tighter social regulation of immigration in patrilocal than in matrilocal populations. *Proceedings of the National Academy of Sciences* 102(21): 7476–80.

Hamilton, W. D. 1964. The genetical evolution of social behavior. *Journal of Theoretical Biology* 7:1–52.

———. 1966. The molding of senescence by natural selection. *Journal of Theoretical Biology* 12:12–45.

Hamlin, J. Kiley, Karen Winn, and Paul Bloom. 2007. Social evaluation by preverbal brains. *Nature* 450:557–560.

Hammerstein, Peter, ed. 2003. *Genetic and cultural evolution of cooperation.* Dahlem Workshop Reports. Cambridge: MIT Press.

Hampson, Elizabeth, Sari M. van Anders, and Lucy I. Mullin. 2006. Female advantage in the recognition of emotional facial expressions: Test of an evolutionary hypothesis. *Evolution and Human Behavior* 27:401–416.

Harcourt, A. H. 1988. Alliances in contests and social intelligence. In *Machiavellian intelligence: Social expertise and the evolution of intellect in monkeys, apes, and humans,* ed. Richard W. Byrne and Andrew Whiten, 132–159. Oxford: Oxford University Press.

Harcourt, A., D. Fossey, and J. Sabatier-Pi. 1981. Demography of *Gorilla gorilla. Journal of the Zoological Society of London* 195:215–233.

Harcourt, A. H., and K. J. Stewart. 2007. *Gorilla society: Conflict, compromise and cooperation.* Chicago: University of Chicago Press.

Hare, Brian, Michelle Brown, Christina Williamson, and Michael Tomasello. 2002. The domestication of social cognition in dogs. *Science* 298:1634–36.

Hare, Brian, Alicia P. Melis, Vanessa Woods, Sara Hastings, and Richard Wrangham. 2007. Tolerance allows bonobos to outperform chimpanzees on a cooperative task. *Current Biology* 17:1–5.

Hare, Brian, and Michael Tomasello. 2004. Chimpanzees are more skillful in competitive than in cooperative cognitive tasks. *Animal Behaviour* 68:571–581.

Harlow, H. K., M. K. Harlow, R. O. Dodsworth, and G. L. Arling. 1966. Maternal behavior of rhesus monkeys deprived of mothering and peer association in infancy. *Proceedings of the American Philosophical Society* 110:58–66.

Harpending, Henry, M. A. Batzer, M. Gurven, L. B. Jourde, A. Rogers, and S. T. Sherry. 1996. Genetic traces of ancient demography. *Proceedings of the National Academy of Sciences (USA)* 95:1961–67.

Harpending, Henry, and Gregory Cochran. 2002. In our genes. Commentary. *Proceedings of the National Academy of Sciences (USA)* 99:10–12.

Harris, Paul. 2000. *The work of the imagination.* Oxford: Blackwell.

Hart, C. W. M., and A. R. Pilling. 1979. *The Tiwi of Northern Australia*. New York: Holt, Rinehart and Winston.

Hasegawa, T., and M. Hiraiwa. 1980. Social interactions of orphans reared in a free-ranging troop of Japanese monkeys. *Folia Primatologica* 33:129–158.

Hauber, M. E., and E. A. Lacey. 2005. Bateman's principle in cooperatively breeding vertebrates: The effects of non-breeding alloparents on variability in female and male reproductive success. *Integrative and Comparative Biology* 45:903–914.

Hauser, Marc D. 1992. Costs of deception: Cheaters are punished in rhesus monkeys (*Macaca mulatta*). *Proceedings of the National Academy of Sciences (USA)* 89:12137–39.

———. 1996. *The evolution of communication*. Cambridge: MIT Press/Bradford Books.

———. 2000. *Wild minds: What animals really think*. New York: Henry Holt.

———. 2006. *Moral minds: How nature designed our universal sense of right and wrong*. New York: Harper Collins.

Hauser, M. D., M. K. Chen, F. Chen, and Emmeline Chuang. 2003. Give unto others: Genetically unrelated cotton-top tamarin monkeys preferentially give food to those who altruistically give food back. *Proceedings of the Royal Society of London B* 270:2363–70.

Hauser, Marc D., Noam Chomsky, and W. Tecumseh Fitch. 2002. The faculty of language: What is it, who has it, and how did it evolve? *Science* 298:1569–79.

Hawkes, Kristen. 1991. Showing off: Test of an hypothesis about men's foraging goals. *Ethology and Sociobiology* 12:29–54.

———. 2001. Hunting and nuclear families. *Current Anthropology* 42:681–709.

———. 2004a. The grandmother effect. *Nature* 428:128–129.

———. 2004b. Mating, parenting and the evolution of human pair bonds. In *Kinship and behavior in primates*, ed. Bernard Chapais and Carol Berman, 443–473. Oxford: Oxford University Press.

———. 2006. Slow life histories. In *The evolution of human life history*, ed. Kristen Hawkes and Richard R. Paine, 95–126. Santa Fe: SAR Press.

Hawkes, K., and N. Blurton Jones. 2005. Human age structures, paleodemography, and the grandmother hypothesis. In *Grandmotherhood: The evolutionary significance of the second half of female life*, ed. E. Voland, A. Chasiotis, and W. Schiefenhövel, 118–142. New Brunswick, NJ: Rutgers University Press.

Hawkes, Kristen, J. F. O'Connell, and N. G. Blurton Jones. 1989. Hardworking Hadza grandmothers. In *Comparative socioecology: The behavioral ecology of humans and other mammals*, ed. V. Standen and R. A. Foley, 341–366. London: Basil Blackwell.

———. 1995. Hadza children's foraging: Juvenile dependency, social arrangements, and mobility among hunter-gatherers. *Current Anthropology* 36:688–700.

——. 1997. Hadza women's time allocation, offspring provisioning and the evolution of post-menopausal lifespans. *Current Anthropology* 38:551–577.

——. 2001. Hunting and nuclear families: Some lessons from the Hadza about men's work. *Current Anthropology* 42:681–709.

Hawkes, Kristen, J. F. O'Connell, N. G. Blurton Jones, H. Alvarez, and E. L. Charnov. 1998. Grandmothering, menopause and the evolution of human life histories. *Proceedings of the National Academy of Sciences* 95:1336–39.

Hawkes, Kristen, and Richard R. Paine, eds. 2006. *The evolution of human life history.* Santa Fe: SAR Press.

Hawks, John, Eric T. Wang, Gregory Cochran, Henry C. Harpending, and Robert K. Moyzis. 2007. Recent acceleration of human adaptive evolution. *Proceedings of the National Academy of Sciences (USA)* 104:20753–58.

Heinsohn, R. G. 1991. Kidnapping and reciprocity in cooperatively breeding white-winged choughs. *Animal Behaviour* 41:1097–1100.

Hennighausen, Katherine H., and Karlen Lyons-Ruth. 2005. Disorganization of behavioral and attentional strategies toward primary attachment figures: From biologic to dialogic processes. In *Attachment and bonding: The new synthesis,* ed. C. S. Carter et al., 269–299. Dahlem Workshop Reports. Cambridge: MIT Press.

Henning, Anne, Tricia Striano, and Elena V. M. Lieven. 2005. Maternal speech to infants at 1 and 3 months of age. *Infant Behavior and Development* 28:519–536.

Henrich, Joseph, Richard McElreath, A. Barr, J. Ensminger, C. Barrett, A. Bolyanatz, J. C. Carenas, M. Gurven, E. Gwako, N. Henrich, C. Lesorogol, F. Marlowe, D. Tracer, and J. Ziker. 2006. Costly punishment across societies. *Science* 312:1767–70.

Henzi, S. P., and Louise Barrett. 2002. Infants as commodity in a baboon market. *Animal Behaviour* 63:915–921.

Hernandez-Aguilar, R. Adriana, Jim Moore, and T. R. Pickering. 2007. Savanna chimpanzees use tools to harvest the underground storage organs of plants. *Proceedings of the National Academy of Sciences.*

Herrmann, Esther, J. Call, M. V. Hernández-Lloreda, B. Hare, and M. Tomasello. 2007. Humans have evolved specialized skills of social cognition: The cultural intelligence hypothesis. *Science* 317:1360–66.

Hewlett, Barry. 1988. Sexual selection and paternal investment among Aka pygmies. In *Human reproductive behaviour: A Darwinian perspective,* ed. L. Betzig, M. Borgerhoff Mulder, and P. Turke, 263–276. Cambridge: Cambridge University Press.

——. 1989a. *Diverse contexts of human infancy.* Englewood Cliffs, NJ: Prentice Hall.

——. 1989b. Multiple caretaking among African Pygmies. *American Anthropologist* 91:270–276.

——. 1991a. *Intimate fathers: The nature and context of Aka pygmy paternal infant care.* Ann Arbor: University of Michigan Press.

——. 1991b. Demography and childcare in preindustrial societies. *Journal of Anthropological Research* 47:1–37.

——. 1992. Husband-wife reciprocity and the father-infant relationship among Aka pygmies. In *Father-child relations: Cultural and biosocial contexts,* ed. Barry Hewlett, 153–176. Hawthorne, NY: Aldine de Gruyter.

——. 2001. The cultural nexus of Aka father-infant bonding. In *Gender in cross-cultural perspective,* 3rd ed., ed. Caroline Brettell and Carolyn Sargent, 45–56. Upper Saddle River, NJ: Prentice Hall.

——. 2007. Why sleep alone? An integrated evolutionary approach to intracultural and intercultural variability in Aka, Ngandu and Euro-American co-sleeping. Paper presented at the annual meeting of the Society for Cross-Cultural Research, February, San Antonio.

Hewlett, Barry, and D. Alster. n.d. Prolactin and infant holding among American fathers. Unpublished manuscript.

Hewlett, Barry, and Michael Lamb, eds. 2005. *Hunter-gatherer childhoods: Evolutionary, developmental and cultural perspectives.* New Brunswick, NJ: Aldine/Transaction.

——. 2005. Emerging issues in the study of hunter-gatherer childhoods. In *Hunter-gatherer childhoods,* ed. B. Hewlett and Michael Lamb, 3–18. Piscataway, NJ: Aldine/Transaction.

Hewlett, Barry, Michael Lamb, Birgit Leyendecker, and Axel Scholmerich. 2000. Internal working models, trust, and sharing among foragers. *Current Anthropology* 41:287–297.

Hewlett, Barry, Michael Lamb, Donald Shannon, Birgit Leyendecker, and Axel Scholmerich. 1998. Culture and early infancy among Central African foragers and farmers. *Developmental Psychology* 34:653–661.

Hewlett, Sylvia Ann, and Cornel West. 1998. *The war against parents.* Boston: Houghton Mifflin.

Hill, Kim. 2002. Altruistic cooperation during foraging by Ache, and the evolved predisposition to cooperate. *Human Nature* 13:105–128.

——. 2009. Are characteristics of human "culture" that account for human uniqueness missing from animal social traditions? In *The question of animal culture,* ed. Kevin N. Laland and Bennett G. Galef Jr., 269–287. Cambridge: Harvard University Press.

Hill, Kim, C. Boesch, J. Goodall, A. Pusey, J. Williams, and R. Wrangham. 2001. Mortality among wild chimpanzees. *Journal of Human Evolution* 39: 437–450.

Hill, Kim, and A. Magdalena Hurtado. 1989. Hunter-gatherers of the New World. *American Scientist* 77:437–443.

——. 1996. *Ache life history: The ecology and demography of a foraging people.* Hawthorne, NY: Aldine de Gruyter.

Hill, Kim, and Hillard Kaplan. 1988. Tradeoffs in male and female reproductive strategies among the Ache, Parts I and II. In *Human reproductive behaviour: A Darwinian perspective,* ed. L. Betzig, M. Borgerhoff Mulder, and P. Turke, 277–305. Cambridge: Cambridge University Press.

Hinde, Robert. 1982. Attachment: Some conceptual and biological issues. In *The place of attachment in human behavior,* ed. C. M. Parkes and J. Stevenson-Hinde, 60–70. New York: Basic Books.

Hobson, Peter. 1989. On sharing experiences. *Development and Psychopathology* 1:197–203.

———. 2004. *The cradle of thought: Exploring the origins of thinking.* Oxford: Oxford University Press.

Hodges, Sarah J., T. P. Flower, and T. H. Clutton-Brock. 2007. Offspring competition and helper associations in cooperative meerkats. *Animal Behaviour* 74:957–964.

Hoffman, Kurt A., S. Mendoza, M. Hennessey, and W. Mason. 1995. Responses of infant titi monkeys *Callicebus molloch* to removal of one or both parents: Evidence of paternal attachment. *Developmental Psychobiology* 28:399–407.

Höhmann, Gottfried. 2001. Association and social interactions between strangers and residents in bonobos (*Pan paniscus*). *Primates* 42:91–99.

Höhmann, Gottfried, and Barbara Fruth. 1996. Food sharing and status in unprovisioned bonobos. In *Food and the status quest,* ed. Polly Wiessner and Wulf Schiefenhövel, 48–67. Providence: Berghahn Books.

Holden, Constance. 2006. Eyes reveal our paleo-brain in action. *Science* 313:25.

Hölldobler, B. 1983. Territorial behavior in the green tree ant (*Oecophylla smaraagdina*). *Biotropica* 15:241–250.

Hölldobler, B., and E. O. Wilson. 1990. *The ants.* Cambridge: Harvard University Press.

Holmes, Melissa, Greta Rosen, Cynthia Jordan, Geert de Vries, Bruce Goldman, and Nancy Forger. 2007. Social control of brain morphology in a eusocial mammal. *Proceedings of the National Academy of Sciences (USA)* 104:10548–52.

Howell, Nancy. 1979. *Demography of the Dobe !Kung.* New York: Academic Press.

Hrdy, S. B. 1976. Care and exploitation of nonhuman primate infants by conspecifics other than the mother. *Advances in the Study of Behavior* 6:101–158. New York: Academic Press.

———. 1977a. *The langurs of Abu: Female and male strategies of reproduction.* Cambridge: Harvard University Press.

———. 1977b. Infanticide as a primate reproductive strategy. *American Scientist* 65:40–49.

———. 1979. Infanticide among animals: A review, classification and examination of the implications for the reproductive strategies of females. *Ethology and Sociobiology* 1:13–40.

———. 1981a. *The woman that never evolved.* Cambridge: Harvard University Press.

———. 1981b. Matriarchs and altruists: The behavior of senescent females in macaques and langur monkeys. In *Other ways of growing old*, ed. A. Amoss and S. Harrell, 59–76. Stanford: Stanford University Press.

———. 1992. Fitness tradeoffs in the history and evolution of delegated mothering with special reference to wet-nursing, abandonment, and infanticide. *Ethology and Sociobiology* 13:409–442.

———. 1997. Raising Darwin's consciousness: Female sexuality and the prehominid origins of patriarchy. *Human Nature* 8:1–49.

———. 1999. *Mother nature: A history of mothers, infants and natural selection.* New York: Pantheon.

———. 2000. The optimal number of fathers: Evolution, demography, and history in the shaping of female mate preferences. In *Evolutionary perspectives on human reproductive behavior*, ed. D. LeCroy and Peter Moller. *Annals of the New York Academy of Sciences* 907:75–96.

———. 2002. The past, present, and future of the human family, Parts one and two. In *The Tanner Lectures on Human Values* 23, ed. G. Peterson, 57–110. Salt Lake City: University of Utah Press.

———. 2005a. Evolutionary context of human development: The cooperative breeding model. In *Attachment and bonding: A new synthesis*, ed. C. S. Carter et al., 9–32. Dahlem Workshop Reports. Cambridge: MIT Press.

———. 2005b. Comes the child before man: How cooperative breeding and prolonged postweaning dependence shaped human potential. In *Hunter-gatherer childhoods*, ed. Barry S. Hewlett and Michael E. Lamb, 65–91. New Brunswick, NJ: Aldine/Transaction.

———. 2005c. Cooperative breeders with an ace in the hole. In *Grandmotherhood: The evolutionary significance of the second half of female life*, ed. E. Voland, A. Chasiotis, and W. Schiefenhövel, 295–318. New Brunswick, NJ: Rutgers University Press.

Hrdy, S. B., and William Bennett. 1981. Lucy's husband: What did he stand for? *Harvard Magazine*, July–August, pp. 7–9, 46.

Hrdy, S. B., and D. Hrdy. 1976. Hierarchical relationships among female Hanuman langurs (Primates: Colobinae, *Presbytis entellus*). *Science* 193:913–915.

Hrdy, S. B., and George C. Williams. 1983. Behavioral biology and the double standard. In *Social behavior of female vertebrates*, ed. Samuel K. Wasser, 3–17. New York: Academic Press.

Hua, Cai. 2001. *A society without fathers or husbands: The Na of China.* Trans. Asti Hustvedt. New York: Zone Books.

Hughes, W. O. H., and J. J. Boomsma. 2008. Genetic royal cheats in leaf-cutting ant societies. *Proceedings of the National Academy of Sciences* 105:5150–53.

Hurlburt, Anya, and Yazhu Ling. 2007. Biological components of sex differences in color preferences. *Current Biology* 17(16):R623–625.

Hurtado, A. M., K. Hill, H. Kaplan, and I. Hurtado. 1992. Tradeoffs between female food acquisition and childcare among Hiwi and Ache foragers. *Human Nature* 3:185–216.

Ingman, Max, H. Kaessmann, Svante Pääbo, and U. Gyllensten. 2000. Mitochondrial genome variation and the origin of modern humans. *Nature* 408:708–713.

Inoue, Sana, and Tetsuro Matsuzawa. 2007. Working memory of numerals in chimpanzees. *Current Biology* 17:R1004–1005.

Irons, William. 1988. Parental behaviour in humans. In *Human reproductive behavior: A Darwinian perspective,* ed. Laura Betzig, Monique Borgerhoff Mulder, and Paul Turke, 307–314. Cambridge: Cambridge University Press.

Isbell, Lynne. 2006. Snakes as agents of evolutionary change in primate brains. *Journal of Human Evolution* 51:1–35.

Isler, K., and C. van Schaik. 2008. Why are there so few smart mammals (but so many smart birds)? *Biology Letters.*

Ivey, Paula. 1993. *Life history theory perspectives on allocaretaking strategies among Efé foragers of the Ituri Forest of Zaire.* Ph.D. diss., University of New Mexico, Albuquerque.

——. 2000. Cooperative reproduction in Ituri forest hunter-gatherers: Who cares for Efé infants? *Current Anthropology* 41: 856–866.

Ivey Henry, Paula, Gilda A. Morelli, and Edward Z. Tronick. 2005. Child caretakers among Efe foragers of the Ituri forest. In *Hunter-gatherer childhoods,* ed. B. Hewlett and Michael Lamb, 191–213. Piscataway, NJ: Aldine/Transaction.

Jamieson, I. G. 1991. The unselected hypothesis for the evolution of helping behavior: Too much or too little emphasis on natural selection? *American Naturalist* 138:271–282.

Jamison, C. Sorenson, L. L. Cornell, P. L. Jamison, and H. Nakazato. 2002. Are all grandmothers equal? A review and a preliminary test of the "Grandmother Hypothesis" in Tokugawa Japan. *American Journal of Physical Anthropology* 119:67–76.

Jankowiak, William, ed. 1995. *Romantic passion: A universal experience?* New York: Columbia University Press.

Janson, C., and C. van Schaik. 1993. Ecological risk aversion in juvenile primates: Slow and steady wins the race. In *Juvenile primates: Life history, development and behavior,* ed. M. Pereira and L. Fairbanks, 57–74. Chicago: University of Chicago Press.

Jay, Phyllis. 1963. The female primate. In *The potential of women,* ed. S. Farber and R. Wilson, 3–47. New York: McGraw-Hill.

Jennions, Michael D., and David W. Macdonald. 1994. Cooperative breeding in mammals. *Trends in Evolutionary Ecology* 9(3):89–93.

Jensen, Keith, Josep Call, and M. Tomasello. 2007. Chimpanzees are vengeful but not spiteful. *Proceedings of the National Academy of Sciences* 104:13046–50.

Jensen, K., B. Hare, J. Call, and M. Tomasello. 2006. What's in it for me? Self-regard precludes altruism and spite in chimpanzees. *Proceedings of the Royal Society of London B* 273:1013–21.

Johnson, Allen W., and Timothy Earle. 2000. *The evolution of human societies.* Stanford: Stanford University Press.

Johnson, Lorna D., A. J. Petto, and P. K. Sehgal. 1991. Factors in the rejection and survival of cotton top tamarins (*Saguinus oedipus*). *American Journal of Primatology* 25:91–102.

Jones, Dan. 2008. Killer instincts. *Nature* 453:512–515

Jones, J. S., and K. Wynne-Edwards 2001. Paternal behavior in biparental hamsters, *Phodopus cambelli*, does not require contact with the pregnant female. *Animal Behaviour* 62:453–464.

Jones, K. P., L. C. Walker, D. Anderson, A. Lacreuse, S. L. Robson, and K. Hawkes. 2007. Depletion of ovarian follicles with age in chimpanzees: Similarities to humans. *Biology of Reproduction* 77:247–251.

Jones, Susan S. 2007. Imitation in infancy: The development of mimicry. *Psychological Science* 18:593–599.

Judge, D. S., and J. Carey. 2000. Postreproductive life predicted by primate patterns. *Journal of Gerontology: Biological Sciences* 55a:B201–209.

Judge, D. S., and S. B. Hrdy. 1992. Allocation of accumulated resources among close kin: Inheritance in Sacramento, CA, 1890–1984. *Ethology and Sociobiology* 13:495–522.

Kagan, J., and N. Snidman. 2004. *The long shadow of temperament.* Cambridge: Belknap Press of Harvard University Press.

Kaiser, Sylvia, M. Kirtzeck, G. Hornschuh, and Norbert Sachser. 2003. Sex-specific difference in social support: A study in female guinea pigs. *Physiology and Behavior* 79:297–303.

Kano, Takayoshi. 1992. *The last ape: Pygmy chimpanzee behavior and ecology.* Trans. E. Vineberg. Stanford: Stanford University Press.

Kaplan, H. 1994. Evolutionary and wealth flows theories of fertility: Empirical tests and new models. *Population and Development Review* 20:753–791.

Kaplan, H., K. Hill, and A. M. Hurtado. 1990. Risk, foraging and food sharing among the Ache. In *Risk and uncertainty in tribal and peasant economies,* ed. Elizabeth Cashdan, 107–144. Boulder: Westview.

Kaplan, H., K. Hill, A. M. Hurtado, and J. Lancaster. 2001. The embodied capital hypothesis. In *Reproduction and human evolution,* ed. P. T. Ellison, 293–317. Hawthorne, NY: Aldine de Gruyter.

Kaplan, H., K. Hill, J. Lancaster, and A. M. Hurtado. 2000. A theory of human life history evolution: Diet, intelligence and longevity. *Evolutionary Anthropology* 9:156–185.

Katz, M. M., and M. J. Konner. 1981. The role of father: An anthropological perspective. In *The role of the father in child development,* 2nd ed., ed. M. Lamb, 55–85. New York: John Wiley and Sons.

Kaye, K., and A. Fogel. 1980. The temporal structure of face-to-face communication between mothers and infants. *Developmental Psychology* 16:454–464.

Keeley, Lawrence. 1996. *War before civilization: The myth of the peaceful savage.* Oxford: Oxford University Press.

Keller, Heidi. 2004. Development as the interface between biology and culture: A conceptualization of early ontogenetic experiences. In *Between culture and development,* ed. H. Keller, Y. H. Poortinga, and A. Scholmerich, 215–240. Cambridge: Cambridge University Press.

Keller, Heidi, A. Scholmerich, and I. Eibl-Eibesfeldt. 1988. Communication patterns in adult-infant interactions in western and non-western cultures. *Journal of Cross-Cultural Psychology* 19:427–445.

Keller, L., and M. Genoud. 1997. Extraordinary lifespans in ants: A test of evolutionary theories of aging. *Nature* 389:958–960.

Kelly, Jay. 2004. Life history and cognitive evolution in the apes. In *The evolution of thought,* ed. Anne E. Russon and David R. Begun, 280–297. Cambridge: Cambridge University Press.

Kelly, Raymond C. 2005. The evolution of lethal intergroup violence. *Proceedings of the National Academy of Sciences (USA)* 102:15294–98.

Kermoian, Rosanne, and P. Herbert Leiderman. 1986. Infant attachment to mother and child caretaker in an East African community. *International Journal of Behavioral Development* 9:455–469.

Kertzer, David. 1993. *Sacrificed for honor: Italian infant abandonment and the politics of reproductive control.* Boston: Beacon.

Kessler, S. E., and L. T. Nash. 2008. Grandmothering in captive *Galago senegalensis braccatus.* Paper presented at the XXII Congress of the International Primatological Society, August 3–8, Edinburgh, UK.

Keverne, E. B. 2005. Neurobiological and molecular approaches to attachment and bonding. In *Attachment and bonding: A new synthesis,* ed. C. S. Carter et al., 101–117. Dahlem Workshop Reports. Cambridge: MIT Press.

Keverne, Eric B., Fran L. Martel, and Claire M. Nevison. 1996. Primate brain evolution: Genetic and functional consideration. *Proceedings of the Royal Society of London B* 263:689–696.

Kilner, Rebecca, and Rufus Johnstone. 1997. Begging the question: Are offspring solicitation behaviors signals of need? *Trends in Evolutionary Ecology* 12:11–15.

Kilner, Rebecca, D. G. Noble, and N. B. Davies. 1999. Signals of need in parent-offspring communication and their exploitation by the common cuckoo. *Nature* 397:667–672.

Kjellström, Rolf. 1973. *Eskimo marriage.* Trans. David Burton. Stockholm: Nordiska Mussetts.

Kleiman, D., and J. Malcolm. 1981. The evolution of male parental investment in mammals. *Quarterly Review of Biology* 52:39–68.

Klein, Richard G., with Blake Edgar. 2002. *The dawn of human culture: A bold new theory on what sparked the "big bang" of human consciousness.* New York: Wiley.

Knight, A., P. A. Underhill, H. M. Mortensen, L. A. Zhivotovsky, A. A. Lin, B. M.

Henn, D. Louis, M. Ruhlen, and J. L. Mountain. 2003. African Y chromosome and mtDNA divergence provides insight into the history of click languages. *Current Biology* 13:464–473.

Knight, Chris, and Camilla Power. 2005. Grandmothers, politics and getting back to science. In *Grandmotherhood: The evolutionary significance of the second half of female life,* ed. Eckart Voland, Athanasios Chasiotis, and Wulf Schiefenhövel, 81–98. New Brunswick, NJ: Rutgers University Press.

Knott, Cheryl. 2001. Female reproductive ecology of the apes: Implications for human evolution. In *Reproductive ecology and human evolution,* ed. P. Ellison, 429–463. Hawthorne, NY: Aldine de Gruyter.

Koenig, W. D., and J. Dickinson, eds. 2004. *Ecology and evolution of cooperative breeding in birds.* Cambridge: Cambridge University Press.

Koenig, W. D., and P. B. Stacey. 1990. Acorn woodpeckers: Group-living and food storage under contrasting ecological conditions. In *Cooperative breeding in birds,* ed. Peter B. Stacey and Walter D. Koenig, 415–453. Cambridge: Cambridge University Press.

Kojima, Shozo. 2001. Early vocal development in a chimpanzee infant. In *Primate origins of human cognition and behavior,* ed. T. Matsuzawa, 190–196. Tokyo: Springer Verlag.

Kokko, H., R. A. Johnstone, and J. Wright. 2002. The evolution of parental care and alloparental effort in cooperatively breeding groups: When should helpers pay to stay? *Behavioral Ecology* 13:291–300.

König, Barbara. 1994. Components of lifetime reproductive success in communally and solitarily nursing house mice—a laboratory study. *Behavioral Ecology and Sociobiology* 34:275–283.

Konner, Melvin. 1972. Aspects of the developmental ecology of a foraging people. In *Ethological studies of child behavior,* ed. N. Blurton Jones, 285–304. Cambridge: Cambridge University Press.

———. 1976. Maternal care, infant behavior and development among the !Kung. In *Kalahari hunter-gatherers,* ed. R. B. Lee and Irven DeVore, 218–245. Cambridge: Harvard University Press.

———. 1991. *Childhood.* Boston: Little Brown.

———. 2005. Hunter-gatherer infancy and childhood: The !Kung and others. In *Hunter-gatherer childhoods,* ed. Barry Hewlett and Michael Lamb, 19–64. New Brunswick, NJ: Aldine/Transaction.

Kosfeld, Michael, Markus Heinrichs, Paul Zak, Urs Fischbacher, and Ernst Fehr. 2005. Oxytocin increases trust in humans. *Nature* 435:673–676.

Kramer, Karen. 2005a. *Maya children: Helpers at the farm.* Cambridge: Harvard University Press.

———. 2005b. Children's help and the pace of reproduction in humans. *Evolutionary Anthropology* 14:224–237.

———. 2008. Early sexual maturity among Pume foragers of Venezuela: Fitness implications of teen motherhood. *American Journal of Physical Anthropology* 136:338–350.

Kringelbach, M., A. Lehtonen, S. Squire, A. G. Harvey, M. Craske, I. Holliday, A. Green, T. Aziz, P. Hansen, P. Cornelissen, and A. Stein. 2008. A specific and rapid neural signature for parental instinct. *PLOS* 3(2):e1664.

Krutzen, M., J. Mann, M. R. Heithaus, R. C. Connor, L. Bejder, and W. B. Sherwin. 2005. Cultural transmission of tool use in bottlenose dolphins. *Proceedings of the National Academy of Sciences (USA)* 102:8939–43.

Kurland, Jeffrey, and C. Sparks. 2003. Is there a Paleolithic demography? Implications for evolutionary psychology and sociobiology. Paper presented at 15th annual meeting of the Human Behavior and Evolution Society, June 6, Lincoln, Nebraska.

La Barre, Weston. 1954/1967. *The human animal.* Chicago: University of Chicago Press.

Lacey, Eileen A., and Paul W. Sherman. 1997. Cooperative breeding in naked mole-rats: Implications for vertebrate and invertebrate sociality. In *Cooperative breeding in mammals,* ed. N. Solomon and J. French, 267–301. Cambridge: Cambridge University Press.

——. 2005. Redefining eusociality: Concepts, goals and levels of analysis. *Annales Zoologic Fennici* 42:573–577.

Lacey, Marc. 2002. Five little oryxes and the big bad lioness of Kenya. *New York Times,* October 12, 2005.

Laden, G., and R. W. Wrangham. 2005. The rise of the hominids as an adaptive shift in fallback foods: Plant underground storage organs (USOs) and Australopith origins. *Journal of Human Evolution* 49:482–498.

Lahdenperä, Mirkka, Virpi Lummaa, Samuli Helle, Marc Tremblay, and Andrew F. Russell. 2004. Fitness benefits of prolonged post-reproductive lifespan in women. *Nature* 428:178–181.

Lahti, David C. 2005. Evolution of bird eggs in the absence of cuckoo parasitism. *Proceedings of the National Academy of Sciences (USA)* 102:18057–62.

Lakatos, K., I. Toth, Z. Nemoda, K. Ney, M. Sasvari-Szekely, and J. Gervai. 2000. Dopamine D4 receptor (DRD4) gene polymorphism is associated with attachment disorders in infancy. *Molecular Psychiatry* 5:633–637.

Lamb, Michael. 1977a. Father-infant and mother-infant interaction in the first year of life. *Child Development* 78:157–181.

——. 1977b. The development of infant-mother and father-infant attachment in the second year of life. *Developmental Psychology* 13:537–578.

——, ed. 1981. *The role of the father in child development,* 2nd ed. New York: John Wiley and Sons.

——. 2006. Non-parental care and emotional development. Background paper for a conference on Early Development, Attachment and Social Policy, December, University of Cambridge.

Lamb, Michael, J. H. Pleck, E. L. Charnov, and J. A. Levine. 1987. A biosocial perspective on paternal behavior and involvement. In *Parenting across the life span,* ed. by J. B. Lancaster, J. Altmann, A. Rossi, and L. Sherrod, 111–142. Hawthorne, NY: Aldine.

Lamb, Michael, R. Thompson, W. Gardner, and Eric Charnov, eds. 1985. *Infant-mother attachment: The origins and developmental significance of individual differences in strange situation behavior.* Hillsdale, NJ: Lawrence Erlbaum.

Lancaster, Jane. 1971. Play-mothering: The relations between juvenile females and young infants among free-ranging vervet monkeys (*Cercopithecus aethiops*). *Folia Primatologica* 15:161–182.

———. 1978. Carrying and sharing in human evolution. *Human Nature* 1 (2):82–89.

———. 1989. Evolutionary and cross-cultural perspectives on single-parenthood. In *Sociobiology and the social sciences,* ed. R. W. Bell and J. J. Bell, 63–72. Lubbock: Texas Tech University Press.

Lancaster, Jane B., and Chet Lancaster. 1987. The watershed: Changes in parental-investment and family formation strategies in the course of human evolution. In *Parenting across the life span,* ed. J. B. Lancaster, J. Altmann, A. Rossi, and L. Sherrod, 187–205. Hawthorne, NY: Aldine.

Langen, Tom A. 1996. Skill acquisition and timing of natal dispersal in the white-throated magpie jay, *Calocitta formosa. Animal Behaviour* 51:575–588.

———. 2000. Prolonged offspring dependence and cooperative breeding in birds. *Behavioral Ecology* 11:367–377.

Langergraber, Kevin E., John Mitani, and Linda Vigilant. 2007. The limited impact of kinship on cooperation in wild chimpanzees. *Proceedings of the National Academy of Sciences (USA)* 104:7786–90.

Langford, D. J., S. Crager, Z. Shehzad, S. B. Smith, S. G. Sotocinal, J. S. Levenstadt, M. L. Chanda, D. J. Levitin, and Jeffrey S. Mogil. 2006. Social modulation of pain as evidence for empathy in mice. *Science* 312:1967–70.

Langlois, J. H., L. A. Roggman, R. J. Casey, J. M. Ritter, L. A. Rieser-Danner, and V. Y. Jenkins. 1987. Infant preferences for attractive faces: Rudiments of a stereotype. *Developmental Psychology* 23:263–269.

Lavelli, M., and A. Fogel. 2002. Developmental changes in mother infant face-to-face communication. *Developmental Psychology* 38:288–305.

Lawrence, P. R., and N. Nohria. 2002. *Driven: How human nature shapes our choices.* Boston: Harvard Business School Press.

Leacock, Eleanor. 1980. Montagnais women and the program for Jesuit colonization. In *Women and colonization: Anthropological perspectives,* ed. Mona Etienne and Eleanor Leacock, 25–42. New York: Praeger.

Leakey, Richard. 2005. Our endangered siblings. *Boston Globe,* September 22, 2005.

Leavens, David A. 2004. Manual deixis in apes and humans. *Interaction Studies* 5:387–408.

———. 2006. It takes time and experience to learn to interpret gaze in mentalistic terms. *Infant and Child Development* 15:187–190.

Leavens, David A., W. D. Hopkins, and Kim A. Bard. 2008. The heterochronic origins of explicit reference. In *The shared mind: Perspectives on intersubjectivity,* ed. J. Slatev, T. P. Racine, C. Sinha, and E. Itkonen, 185–214. Amsterdam: John Benjamins.

Leckman, J. F., C. S. Carter, M. B. Hennessy, S. B. Hrdy, E. B. Keverne, G. Klann-Delius, C. Shradin, D. Todt, and D. von Holst. 2005. Biobehavioral processes in attachment and bonding. In *Attachment and bonding: A new synthesis,* ed. by C. S. Carter et al., 301–348. Dahlem Workshop Reports. Cambridge: MIT Press.

Leckman, J. F., L. C. Mayes, R. Feldman, D. W. Evans, R. A. King, and D. J. Cohen. 1999. Early parental preoccupations and behaviors and their possible relationship to the symptoms of obsessive-compulsive disorder. *Acta Psychiatrica Scandinavia* 396:1–26.

Lee, Phyllis. 1987. Allomothering among African elephants. *Animal Behaviour* 35:278–291.

Lee, Richard B. 1979. *The !Kung San: Men, Women and Work in a Foraging Society.* Cambridge: Cambridge University Press.

———. 2003. *The Dobe Ju/'hoansi.* Australia: Wadsworth/Thomson Learning.

Lee, Ronald D., and Karen Kramer. 2002. Children's economic roles in the Maya family life cycle: Cain, Caldwell and Chayanov revisited. *Population and Development Review* 28:475–499.

Leonetti, Donna, Dilip Nath, and Natabar S. Hemam. 2007. In-law conflict: Women's reproductive lives and the roles of their mothers and husbands among the matrilineal Khasi. *Current Anthropology* 48:861–888.

Leonetti, Donna L., Dilip C. Nath, Natabar S. Hemam, and Dawn B. Neill. 2005. Kinship organization and the impact of grandmothers on reproductive success among the matrilineal Khasi and patrilineal Bengali of Northeast India. In *Grandmotherhood: The evolutionary significance of the second half of female life,* ed. E. Voland, A. Chasiotis, and W. Schiefenhövel, 194–214. New Brunswick, NJ: Rutgers University Press.

LeVine, Robert, S. Dixon, S. LeVine, A. Richman, P. H. Leiderman, C. Kefer, and T. B. Brazelton. 1996. *Child care and culture: Lessons from Africa.* New York: Cambridge University Press.

Lévi-Strauss, Claude. 1949. *Les structures élémentaires de parenté.* Paris: Plon.

Lewis, Charlie, Norman H. Freeman, Chrystalla Kyriakidou, Katerina Maridaki-Kassotaki, and Damon M. Berridge. 1996. Social influences on false belief access: Specific sibling influences or general apprenticeship? *Child Development* 67:2930–47.

Lieberman, Philip. 2007. The evolution of speech: Its anatomical and neural bases. *Current Anthropology* 48:39–66.

Liesen, Laurette. 2007. Women, behavior, and evolution: Understanding the debate between feminist evolutionists and evolutionary psychologists. *Politics and Life Sciences* 26:51–70.

Ligon, J. David, and D. Brent Burt. 2004. Evolutionary origins. In *Ecology and evolution of cooperative breeding in birds,* ed. Walter Koenig and Janis Dickinson, 5–34. Cambridge: Cambridge University Press.

Little, Katherine, Volker Sommer, and Mike Bruford. 2002. Genetics and relatedness: A test of hypotheses using wild Hanuman langurs (*Presbytis entellus*). (Abstract) XIX Congress of the International Primatological Society, August 4–9, Beijing.

Locke, John. 1993. *The child's path to spoken language.* Cambridge: Harvard University Press.

Locke, John, and Barry Bogin. 2006. Language and life history: A new perspective on the development and evolution of human language. *Behavioral and Brain Sciences* 20:259–325.

Loeb, E. M. 1926. *Pomo folkways.* Berkeley: University of California Publications in American Archaeology and Ethnology 19(2).

Lorenz, Konrad. 1951/1971. Part and parcel in animal and human societies. In *Studies in animal behaviour,* vol. 2, 114–195. Trans. Robert Martin. Cambridge: Harvard University Press.

Lovejoy, O. 1981. The origin of man. *Science* 211:341–350.

Lyons-Ruth, K. 1996. Attachment relationships among children with aggressive behavior problems: The role of disorganized early attachment patterns. *Journal of Consulting and Clinical Psychology* 64:64–73.

Lyons-Ruth, Karlen, E. Bronfman, and E. Parsons. 1999. Frightened, frightening and atypical maternal behavior and disorganized attachment strategies. In *Atypical attachment in infancy and early childhood among children at developmental risk,* ed. Joan I. Vondra and Douglas Barnett, 67–96. Monographs of the Society for Research in Child Development 64(3).

Lyons-Ruth, Karlen, D. B. Cornell, and H. Grunebaum. 1990. Infants at social risk: Maternal depression and family support services as mediators of infant development and security of attachment. *Child Development* 61:85–98.

Lyons-Ruth, Karlen, and C. Zeanah. 1993. The family context of infant mental health, 1: Affective development in the primary caregiving relationship. In *Handbook of infant mental health,* ed. C. Zeanah, 14–37. New York: Guilford.

Macdonald, D. 1980. Social factors affecting reproduction among red foxes. In *The red fox,* ed. E. Zimen, 123–175. *Biogeographica* 18. The Hague: Junk.

Mace, Ruth, and Rebecca Sear. 2005. Are humans communal breeders? In *Grandmotherhood: The evolutionary significance of the second half of female life,* ed. Eckart Voland, Athanasios Chasiotis, and Wulf Schiefenhövel, 143–159. New Brunswick, NJ: Rutgers University Press.

MacLean, Paul D. 1985. Brain evolution related to family, play and the separation call. *Archives of General Psychiatry* 42:405–417.

Maestripieri, Dario. 2001. Biological bases of maternal attachment. *Current Directions in Psychological Science* 10:79–83.

Main, Mary. 1999. Epilogue: Attachment theory—eighteen points with suggestions for future studies. In *Handbook of attachment,* ed. Jude Cassidy and Phillip Shaver, 845–887. New York: Guilford.

Main, Mary, and Erik Hesse. 1990. Parents' unresolved traumatic experiences are related to infant disorganized attachment status: Is frightened and/or frightening parental behavior the linking mechanism? In *Attachment in the preschool years: Theory, research and intervention,* ed. M. Greenberg, D. Chiccheti, and E. M. Cummings, 161–184. Chicago: University of Chicago Press.

Malcolm, James R., and Ken Marten. 1982. Natural selection and the communal rearing of pups in African wild dogs (*Lycaon pictus*). *Behavioral Ecology and Sociobiology* 10:1–13.

Manson, Joseph. 1999. Infant handling in wild *Cebus capucinus:* Testing bonds between females. *Animal Behaviour* 57:911–921.

Marci, Carl D., Jacob Ham, Erin Moran, and Scott Orr. 2007. Physiological correlates of perceived therapist empathy and social-emotional process during psychotherapy. *Journal of Nervous and Mental Disease* 195:103–111.

Marech, Rona. 2004. Publicity-shy critic at center of storm. *San Francisco Chronicle,* August 7, 2004, A1.

Marlowe, Frank. 1999a. The patriarch hypothesis: An alternative explanation of menopause. *Human Nature* 11:27–42.

———. 1999b. Showoffs or providers? The parenting effort of Hadza men. *Evolution and Human Behavior* 20:391–404.

———. 2001. Male contributions to diet and female reproductive success among foragers. *Current Anthropology* 42(5):755–760.

———. 2004. Marital residence among foragers. *Current Anthropology* 45:277–284.

———. 2005a. Hunter-gatherers and human evolution. *Evolutionary Anthropology* 14:54–67.

———. 2005b. Who tends Hadza children? In *Hunter-gatherer childhoods,* ed. B. Hewlett and M. Lamb, 177–190. New Brunswick, NJ: Aldine/Transaction.

Marsh, Jason. 2004. The cost of apathy: An interview with Robert Reich. *Greater Good* 1 (2):4–5.

Marshall, Lorna. 1976. *The !Kung of Nyae Nyae.* Cambridge: Harvard University Press.

Martel, F. L., C. M. Nevison, M. D. A. Simpson, and E. B. Keverne. 1993. Effects of opioid receptor blockade on the social behaviour of rhesus monkeys living in large family groups. *Developmental Psychobiology* 28:71–84.

Martins, Waldney P., Vanessa de Oliveira Guimarães, and Karen B. Strier. 2007. A case of infant swapping by wild northern muriquis (*Brachyteles hypoxanthus*). *Primates* 48:324–326.

Marwick, Ben. 2003. Pleistocene exchange networks as evidence for the evolution of language. *Cambridge Archaeological Journal* 13:67–81.

Masataka, N. 1982. A field study on the vocalization of Goeldi's monkeys (*Callimico goeldi*). *Primates* 23:206–219.

Mason, William. 1966. Social organization of the South American monkey, *Callicebus moloch:* A preliminary report. *Tulane Studies in Zoology* 13:23–28.

Masserman, J. H., S. Wechkin, and W. Terris. 1964. "Altruistic" behavior in rhesus monkeys. *American Journal of Psychiatry* 121:584–585.

Matsuzawa, Tetsuro. 1996. Chimpanzee intelligence in nature and in captivity: Isomorphism of symbol use and tool use. In *Great ape societies,* ed. W. C. McGrew, Linda Marchant, and T. Nishida, 196–209. Cambridge: Cambridge University Press.

——. 2001. Primate foundations of human intelligence: A view of tool use in nonhuman primates and fossil hominids. In *Primate origins of human cognition and behavior,* ed. T. Matsuzawa, 3–25. Tokyo: Springer Verlag.

——. 2003. The Ai project: Historical and ecological contexts. *Animal Cognition* 6:199–211.

——. 2006. Evolutionary origins of the human mother-infant relationships. In *Cognitive development in chimpanzees,* ed. T. Matsuzawa, M. Tomonaga, and M. Tanaga, 27–141. Tokyo: Springer.

Mauss, Marcel. 1867/1925. *The Gift* (or, *Essai sur le don*). Trans. Ian Cunnison. New York: W. W. Norton.

McAdoo, Harriet Pipes. 1986. Strategies used by single black mothers against stress. In *Slipping through the cracks,* ed. M. Simms and J. Malveaux, 153–166. New Brunswick, NJ: Transaction.

McAuliffe, Katherine, and Hal Whitehead. 2005. Eusociality, menopause and information in matrilineal whales. *Trends in Ecology and Evolution* 20:650.

McBrearty, S., and A. S. Brooks. 2000. The revolution that wasn't: A new interpretation of the origin of modern human behavior. *Journal of Human Evolution* 39:453–463.

McBurney, Donald H., Jessica Simon, Steven J. Gaulin, and Allan Giliebter. 2001. Matrilateral biases in the investment of aunts and uncles: Replication in a population presumed to have high certainty of paternity. *Human Nature* 13:391–402.

McCartney, Kathleen. 2004. Current research on child care effects. In *Encyclopedia for early childhood development,* ed. R. E. Tremblay, R. G. Barr, and R. de V. Peters. Montreal: Centre of Excellence for Early Childhood Development.

McDade, T. W., V. Reyes-Garcia, P. Blackinton, S. Tanner, T. Huanca, and W. R.

Leonard. 2007. Ethnobotanical knowledge is associated with indices of child health in the Bolivian Amazon. *Proceedings of the National Academy of Sciences (USA)* 104:6134–39.

McGrew, W. 1987. Helpers at the nest-box, or, are cotton-top tamarins really Florida scrub jays? *Primate Report* 18:21–26.

———. 1992. *Chimpanzee material culture: Implications for human evolution.* Cambridge: Cambridge University Press.

———. 2007a. It takes a community to raise a child, or does it? Socialization in wild chimpanzees (*Pan troglodytes*). Abstract. Paper presented at the 76th Annual Meeting of the American Association of Physical Anthropologists, March 28–31, Philadelphia.

———. 2007b. Savanna chimpanzees dig for food. *Proceedings of the National Academy of Sciences (USA)* 104 (49):19167–68.

McGrew, W. C., and J. Barnett. 2008. Lifetime reproductive success in a female common marmoset (*Callithrix jacchus*): A case study (Abstract). *American Journal of Physical Anthropology* Supplement 46:152.

McHenry, H. 1992. How big were early hominids? *Evolutionary Anthropology* 1 (1):15–20.

———. 1996. Sexual dimorphism in fossil hominids and its socioecological implications. In *Power, sex and tradition,* ed. James Steele and Stephan Shennan, 91–109. London: Routledge.

———. 2009. Human evolution. In *Evolution: The first four billion years,* ed. M. Ruse and J. Travis, 256–280. Cambridge: The Belknap Press of Harvard University Press.

McKenna, James, E. B. Thoman, T. F. Anders, A. Sadeh, V. Schechtman, and S. F. Glotzbach. 1993. Infant-parent cosleeping in an evolutionary perspective: Implications for understanding infant sleep development and the Sudden Infant Death Syndrome. *Sleep* 16:263–282.

Mead, Margaret. 1966. A cultural anthropologist's approach to maternal deprivation. In *Deprivation of maternal care: A reassessment of its effects,* ed. Mary D. S. Ainsworth, 235–254. New York: Schocken Books.

Meehan, Courtney. 2005. The effects of residential locality on parental and alloparental investment among the Aka foragers of the Central African Republic. *Human Nature* 16:58–80.

———. 2008. Allomaternal investment and relational uncertainty among Ngandu farmers of the Central African Republic. *Human Nature* 19:211–226.

Meins, Elizabeth, Charles Fernyhough, Rachel Wainwright, Mani Das Gupta, Emma Fradley, and Michelle Tuckey. 2002. Maternal-mindedness and attachment security as predictors of theory of mind understanding. *Child Development* 73:1715–26.

Mekel-Bobrov, Nitzan, S. L. Gilbert, P. D. Evans, E. J. Vallender, J. R. Anderson,

R. R. Hudson, S. A. Tishkoff, and Bruce T. Lahn. 2005. Ongoing adaptive evolution of ASPM, a brain size determinant in *Homo sapiens. Science* 309:1720–22.

Melis, Alicia, Brian Hare, and Michael Tomasello. 2006a. Engineering cooperation in chimpanzees: Tolerance constraints on cooperation. *Animal Behaviour* 72:275–286.

———. 2006b. Chimpanzees recruit the best collaborators. *Science* 311:1297–1300.

Meltzoff, A. N. 2002. Imitation as a mechanism of social cognition. Origins of empathy, theory of mind, and the representation of action. In *Handbook of childhood cognitive development*, ed. U. Goswami, 6–25. Oxford: Blackwell.

Meltzoff, A. N., and M. K. Moore. 1977. Imitation of facial and manual gestures by human neonates. *Science* 198:75–78.

Menges, Maria, and Wulf Schiefenhövel. 2007. Evolutional and biological aspects of placentophagia (in German). *Anthropologischer Anzeiger* 65:97–108.

Mercader, Julio, H. Barton, J. Gillespie, J. Harris, S. Kuhn, R. Tyler, and C. Boesch. 2007. 4,300-year-old chimpanzee sites and the origins of percussive stone technology. *Proceedings of the National Academy of Sciences (USA)* 104: 3043–48.

Merkin, Daphne. 2002. The close reader: Bloomsbury becomes me, and vice versa. *New York Times Book Review,* June 30, 2002, 23.

Miller, Jean Baker. 1976. *Toward a new psychology of women.* Boston: Beacon.

Miller, Laura J. 2002. Postpartum depression. *Journal of the American Medical Association* 287:762–765.

Mills, M. G. L. 1990. *Kalahari hyenas.* London: Unwin/Hyman.

Mitani, J., C. Merriwether, and C. Zhang. 2000. Male affiliation, cooperation and kinship in wild chimpanzees. *Animal Behaviour* 59:885–893.

Mitani, J., and David Watts. 1997. The evolution of non-maternal caretaking among anthropoid primates: Do helpers help? *Behavioral Ecology and Sociobiology* 40:213–220.

Moehlman, P. D. 1983. Socioecology of silverbacked and golden jackals (*Canis mesomelas* and *Canis aureus*). In *Recent advances in the study of mammalian behavior,* ed. J. Eisenberg and D. Kleiman, 423–453. Lawrence, KS: American Society of Mammalogists.

Moore, James. 1984. The evolution of reciprocal sharing. *Ethology and Sociobiology* 5:5–15.

Morell, Virginia. 2007. The Discover interview: Jane Goodall. *Discover Magazine* (February):50–53.

Morelli, G. A., and E. Z. Tronick. 1991. Efe multiple caretaking and attachment. In *Intersections with attachment,* ed. J. L. Gewirtz and W. M. Kurtines, 41–51. Hillsdale, NJ: Erlbaum.

Moses, R. A., and J. S. Millar. 1994. Philopatry and mother-daughter associations in bushy-tailed wood rats: Space use and reproductive success. *Behavioral Ecology and Sociobiology* 35:131–140.

Mota, M. T., and M. B. C. Sousa. 2000. Prolactin levels in fathers and helpers related to alloparental care in common marmosets, *Callithrix jacchus*. *Folia Primatologica* 71:22–26.

Moynihan, Daniel Patrick. 1986. *Family and nation: The Godkin Lectures, Harvard University.* San Diego: Harcourt Brace Jovanovich.

Mulcahy, Nicholas, and Josep Call. 2006. Apes save tools for future use. *Science* 312:1038–40.

Mulder, R. A., P. O. Dunn, A. Cockburn, K. A. Lazenby-Cohen, and M. J. Howell. 1994. Helpers liberate female fairy-wrens from constraints on extra-pair mate choice. *Proceedings of the Royal Society of London B* 255:223–229.

Mulder, R. A., and N. E. Langmore. 1993. Dominant males punish helpers for temporary defection in superb fairy wren. *Animal Behaviour* 45:830–833.

Murdock, G. P. 1967. *Ethnographic atlas.* Pittsburgh: University of Pittsburgh Press.

Murray, L., and C. Trevarthen. 1986. The infant's role in mother-infant communication. *Journal of Child Language* 13:15–29.

Myowa, Masako. 1996. Imitation of facial gestures by an infant chimpanzee. *Primates* 37:207–213.

Myowa-Yamakoshi, Masako, Masaki Tomonaga, Tanaka Masayuki, and Tetsuro Matsuzawa. 2004. Imitation in neonatal chimpanzees (*Pan troglodytes*). *Developmental Science* 7:437–442.

Nakamichi, Masayuki, A. Silldorff, C. Bringham, and P. Sexton. 2004. Baby-transfer and other interactions between its mother and grandmother in a captive social group of lowland gorillas. *Primates* 45:73–77.

Nesse, Randolph M. 2001. Natural selection and the capacity for subjective commitment. In *Evolution and the capacity for commitment,* ed. Randolph M. Nesse, 1–44. New York: Russell Sage Foundation.

———. 2007. Runaway social selection for displays of partner value and altruism. *Biological Theory* 2 (2):143–155.

Nettelbeck, Anouchka Rebekka. 1998. Brief report: Observations on food sharing in wild lar gibbons (*Hylobates lar*). *Folia Primatologica* 69:386–91.

NICHD Early Child Care Research Network. 1997. The effects of child care on infant-mother attachment security: Results of the NICHD study of early child care. *Child Development* 68:860–879.

Nicolson, Nancy. 1987. Infants, mothers and other females. In *Primate societies,* ed. B. B. Smuts, D. L. Cheney, R. M. Seyfarth, R. W. Wrangham, and T. T. Struhsaker, 330–342. Chicago: University of Chicago Press.

Nishida, T. 1983. Alloparental behavior in wild chimpanzees of the Mahale Mountains, Tanzania. *Folia Primatologica* 41:1–33.

Nishida, T., M. Hiraiwa-Hasegawa, and Y. Takahata. 1985. Group extinction and female transfers in wild chimpanzees in the Mahale National Park, Tanzania. *Zeitschrift für Tierpsychologie* 67:284–301.

Nishimura, T. 2006. Descent of the larynx in chimpanzees: Mosaic and multiple-step evolution of the foundations for human speech. In *Cognitive development in chimpanzees,* ed. T. Matsuzawa, M. Tomonaga, and M. Tanaka, 75–95. Tokyo: Springer.

Nosaka, Akiko, and Athanasios Chasiotis. 2005. Exploring the variation in intergenerational relationships among Germans and Turkish immigrants: An evolutionary perspective on behavior in a modern social setting. In *Grandmotherhood: The evolutionary significance of the second half of female life,* ed. E. Voland, A. Chasiotis, and W. Schiefenhövel, 256–276. New Brunswick, NJ: Rutgers University Press.

Numan, Michael. 1988. Maternal behavior. In *The physiology of reproduction,* vol. 2, ed. E. Knobil and J. D. Neill, 1569–1645. New York: Raven.

O'Brien, Tim. 1998. Parasitic nursing behavior in the wedge-capped capuchin monkey (*Cebus olivaceus*). *American Journal of Primatology* 16:341–344.

O'Connell, James F., K. Hawkes, and N. G. Blurton Jones. 1999. Grandmothering and the evolution of *Homo erectus. Journal of Human Evolution* 36:461–485.

O'Connell, James F., K. Hawkes, K. D. Lupo, and N. G. Blurton Jones. 2002. Male strategies and Plio-Pleistocene archeology. *Journal of Human Evolution* 43:831–872.

O'Connor, D., and R. Shine. 2002. Lizards in "nuclear families": A novel reptilian social system in *Egernia saxatilis* (Scincidae). *Molecular Ecology* 12 (March):743–752.

O'Connor, T. G., M. Rutter, and the English and Romanian Adoptees Study Team. 2000. Attachment disorders following early severe deprivation: Extension and longitudinal follow-up. *Journal of the American Academy of Child Adolescent Psychology* 39:703–712.

Olazábal, D. E., and L. J. Young. 2006. Oxytocin receptors in the nucleus accumbens facilitate "spontaneous" maternal behavior in adult female prairie voles. *Neuroscience* 141:559–568.

Olds, David L., C. R. Henderson, R. Chamberlin, and R. Tatelbaum. 1986. Preventing child abuse and neglect: A randomized trial of nurse home visitation. *Pediatrics* 78:65–78.

Olds, David L., J. Robinson, Ruth O'Brien, D. Luckey, L. Pettitt, C. R. Henderson, R. K. Ng, K. L. Sheff, J. Korfmacher, S. Hiatt, and A. Talmi. 2002. Home visiting by paraprofessionals and by nurses: A randomized control trial. *Pediatrics* 110:486–496.

Olds, David L., Lois Sadler, and Harriet Kitzman. 2007. Programs for parents of infants and toddlers: Recent evidence from randomized trials. *Journal of Child Psychology and Psychiatry* 48:355–391.

Onishi, Norimitsu. 2007. Japan welfare: A slow death, a harsh light. *New York Times,* October 12, 2007.

Oppenheim, D., A. Sagi, and M. E. Lamb. 1990. Infant-adult attachments on the kibbutz and their relation to socioemotional development four years later. In *Annual progress in child psychiatry and child development* 1989, ed. S. Chess and M. E. Hertzig, 92–106. New York: Brunner/Mazel.

O'Riain, M. J., J. U. M. Jarvis, R. Alexander, R. Buffenstein, and C. Peters. 2000. Morphological castes in a vertebrate. *Proceedings of the National Academy of Sciences (USA)* 97:13194–97.

Ostrom, Elinor. 1998. A behavioral approach to the rational choice theory of collective action: Presidential address, American Political Science Association, 1997. *American Political Science Review* 92:1–22.

Otterbein, Keith. 1968. Marquesan polyandry. In *Marriage, family and residence,* ed. John Bohannan and Paul Middleton, 287–296. Garden City: Natural History Press.

Packer, Craig, Susan Lewis, and Anne Pusey. 1992. A comparative analysis of non-offspring nursing. *Animal Behaviour* 43:265–281.

Page, R., and C. Peng. 2001. Aging and development in social insects with emphasis on the honeybee, *Apis mellifera* L. *Experimental Gerontology* 36:695–711.

Palombit, Ryne. 1999. Infanticide and the evolution of pair bonds in nonhuman primates. *Evolutionary Anthropology* 7:117–129.

———. 2001. Infanticide and the evolution of male-female bonds in animals. In *Infanticide by males and its implications,* ed. Carel P. van Schaik and Charles H. Janson, 239–268. Cambridge: Cambridge University Press.

Palombit, Ryne, D. L. Cheney, and R. M. Seyfarth. 2001. Female-female competition for male "friends" in wild chacma baboons (*Papio cynocephalus ursinus*). *Animal Behaviour* 61:1159–71.

Panksepp, J. 2000. *Affective neuroscience: The foundations of human and animal emotions.* Oxford: Oxford University Press.

Papousek, Hanus, and M. Papousek. 1977. Mothering and the cognitive head start: Psychobiological considerations. In *Studies in mother-infant interactions,* ed. H. R. Shaffer, 63–85. New York: Academic Press.

Papousek, Hanus, M. Papousek, S. Suomi, and C. W. Rahn. 1991. Preverbal communication and attachment: Comparative views. In *Intersections with attachment,* ed. J. L. Gewirtz and W. M. Kurtines, 97–122. Hillsdale, NJ: Lawrence Erlbaum Associates.

Parish, Amy. 1994. Sex and food control in the "uncommon chimpanzee": How bonobo females overcome a phylogenetic legacy of male dominance. *Ethology and Sociobiology* 15:157–179.

———. 1998. Reciprocity and other forms of food sharing among foragers. Paper presented at the symposium on Cooperation, Reciprocity and Food Sharing in Human Groups, at the 18th annual meeting of the Politics and Life Sciences Association, Boston.

Parish, Amy, and F. B. de Waal. 1992. Bonobos fish for sweets: The female sex-for-food connection. Paper presented at the XIVth Congress of the International Primatological Society, August 16–21, Strasbourg, France.

———. 2000. The other "closest living relative": How bonobos (*Pan paniscus*) challenge traditional assumptions about females, dominance, intra- and inter-sexual interactions, and hominid evolution. *Annals of the New York Academy of Sciences* 907:97–113.

Partridge, Linda, David Gems, and Dominic J. Withers. 2005. Sex and death: What is the connection? *Cell* 120:461–472.

Pashos, A. 2000. Does paternal uncertainty explain discriminative grandparental solicitude? A cross-cultural study in Greece and Germany. *Evolution and Human Behavior* 21:97–109.

Pashos, A., and D. H. McBurney. 2008. Kin relationships and the caregiving biases of grandparents, aunts and uncles: A two-generational questionnaire study. *Human Nature* 19:311–330.

Paul, A. 2005. Primate predispositions. In *Grandmotherhood: The evolutionary significance of the second half of female life,* ed. E. Voland, A. Chasiotis, and W. Schiefenhövel, 21–37. New Brunswick, NJ: Rutgers University Press.

Paul, Andreas, Jutta Kuester, and Doris Podzuweit. 1993. Reproductive senescence and terminal investment in female Barbary macaques (*Macaca sylvanus*) at Salem. *International Journal of Primatology* 14:105–124.

Paul, A., Signe Preuschoft, and Carel P. van Schaik. 2000. The other side of the coin: Infanticide and the evolution of affiliative male-infant interactions in Old World primates. In *Infanticide by males and its implications,* ed. Carel P. van Schaik and Charles H. Janson, 269–292. Cambridge: Cambridge University Press.

Pavelka, M. L. 1990. Do old females have specific role? *Primates* 31:363–373.

Pavelka, M. L., and Linda M. Fedigan. 1991. Menopause: A comparative life history perspective. *Yearbook of Physical Anthropology* 34:13–38.

Pavelka, M., L. Fedigan, and M. Zohar. 2002. Availability and adaptive value of reproductive and post-reproductive Japanese macaque mothers and grandmothers. *Animal Behaviour* 64:407–414.

Payne, Katy. 2003. Source of social complexity in three elephant species. In *Animal social complexity: Intelligence, culture, and individualized societies,* ed. Frans de Waal and Peter Tyack, 57–85. Cambridge: Harvard University Press.

Pearse, Emma. 2005. Germany in angst over low birthrate. *Women's eNews,* April 4, 2005. Berlin.

Penn, Derek C., and Daniel J. Povinelli. 2007. On the lack of evidence that nonhuman animals possess anything remotely resembling a "theory of mind." *Philosophical Transactions of the Royal Society B* 362:731–734.

Penn, Dustin J., and Ken R. Smith. 2007. Differential fitness costs of reproduction between the sexes. *Proceedings of the National Academy of Sciences (USA)* 104:553–558.

Pereira, Michael, and Lynn Fairbanks, eds. 1993. *Juvenile primates: Life history, development and behavior.* Chicago: University of Chicago Press.

Pereira, Michael, and M. Kay Izard. 1989. Lactation and care for unrelated infants in forest-living ring-tail lemurs. *American Journal of Primatology* 18:101–108.

Pereira, Michael E., Annette Klepper, and E. L. Symons. 1987. Tactics of care for young infants by forest-living ruffed lemurs (*Varecia variegata variegata*): Ground nests, parking, and biparental guarding. *American Journal of Primatology* 13:129–144.

Perner, Josef, T. Ruffman, and Susan R. Leekam. 1994. Theory of mind is contagious: You catch it from your sibs. *Child Development* 65:1228–35.

Perry, George, Nathaniel Dominy, K. G. Claw, A. S. Lee, H. Fiegler, R. Redon, J. Werner, F. A Villanea, J. L. Mountain, R. Misra, N. Carter, C. Lee, and A. C. Stone. 2007. Diet and the evolution of human amylase gene copy number variations. *Nature Genetics* 39:1256–60.

Perry, Susan. 1996. Female-female social relationships in wild white-faced capuchin monkeys, *Cebus capucinus. American Journal of Primatology* 40:167–182.

Peters, J. F. 1982. Polyandry among the Yanomana Shirishana, revisited. *Journal of Comparative Family Studies* 13:89–95.

Peters, John F., and Chester L. Hunt. 1975. Polyandry among the Yanomama Shirishana. *Journal of Comparative Family Studies* 6:197–207.

Peterson, Jean T. 1978. *The ecology of social boundaries: Agta foragers of the Philippines.* Urbana: University of Illinois Press.

Pinker, Steven. 1997. *How the mind works.* New York: Norton.

———. 2002. *The blank slate: The modern denial of human nature.* New York: Viking.

Pollick, Amy S., and Frans B. M. de Waal. 2007. Ape gesture and language evolution. *Proceedings of the National Academy of Sciences (USA)* 104:8184–89.

Pollock, Donald. 2002. Partible paternity and multiple paternity among the Kulina. In *Cultures of multiple fathers: The culture and practice of partible paternity in lowland South America,* ed. Stephen Beckerman and Paul Valentine, 42–61. Gainesville: University Press of Florida.

Pope, S. K., L. Whiteside, J. Brooks-Gunn, K. J. Kelleher, V. I. Rickert, R. H. Bradley, and P. H. Casey. 1993. Low-birth-weight infants born to adolescent mothers: Effects of co-residency with grandmother on child development. *Journal of American Medical Association* 269:1396–1400.

Popenoe, David. 1996. *Life without father: Compelling new evidence that fatherhood and marriage are indispensable for the good of children and society.* Cambridge: Harvard University Press.

Porter, L. M., and P. A. Garber. 2008. Limited dispersal and cooperative breeding in *Callimico goeldii.* Paper presented at the XXII Congress of the International Primatological Society, August 3–8, Edinburgh, UK.

Porter, Richard. 1999. Olfaction and human kin recognition. *Genetics* 104:259–263.

Premack, David. 2004. Is language the key to human intelligence? *Science* 303:318–320.

Premack, David, and G. Woodruff. 1978. Does the chimpanzee have a theory of mind? *Behavioral and Brain Sciences* 1:515–526.

Preston, Stephanie D., and Frans B. de Waal. 2002. Empathy: Its ultimate and proximate bases. *Behavioral and Brain Sciences* 25:1–72.

Prince, Peter. 1963. *A study of polyandry.* The Hague: Mouton.

Prudom, S. L., C. A. Broz, N. Schultz-Darken, C. T. Ferris, C. Snowdon, and T. Ziegler. 2008. Exposure to infant scent lowers serum testosterone in father common marmosets (*Callithrix jacchus*): *Biology Letters* 4(6):603–605.

Pruett-Jones, Stephen. 2004. Summary. In *Ecology and evolution of cooperative breeding in birds,* ed. Walter Koenig and Janis Dickinson, 228–238. Cambridge: Cambridge University Press.

Pruetz, Jill D., and Paco Bertolani. 2007. Savanna chimpanzees, *Pan troglodytes verus,* hunt with tools. *Current Biology* 17:412–417.

Pusey, A., C. Murray, W. Wallauer, M. Wilson, E. Wroblewski, and J. Goodall. 2008. Severe aggression among female *Pan troglodytes schweinfurthii* at Gombe National Park, Tanzania. *International Journal of Primatology.*

Pusey, A., and C. Packer. 1987. Dispersal and philopatry. In *Primate societies,* ed. B. Smuts, et al., 250–266. Chicago: University of Chicago Press.

Pusey, Anne, J. Williams, and J. Goodall. 1997. The influence of dominance rank on reproductive success of female chimpanzees. *Science* 277:828–831.

Putnam, Robert D. 2000. *Bowling alone: The collapse and revival of American community.* New York: Simon and Schuster.

Queller, David C. 2006. To work or not to work. *Nature* 444:42–43.

Quinlan, R. J., and M. V. Flinn. 2005. Kinship and reproduction in a Caribbean community. *Human Nature* 16:32–57.

Quinlan, R. J., and M. B. Quinlan. 2008. Human lactation, pair bonds, and alloparents: A cross-cultural analysis. *Human Nature* 19:87–102.

Quinn, P. C., J. Yarr, A. Kuhn, A. M. Slater, and O. Pascalis. 2002. Representation of the gender of human faces by infants: A preference for female. *Perception* 31:1109–21.

Raby, C. R., D. M. Alexis, A. Dickinson, and N. S. Clayton. 2007. Planning for the future by western scrub-jays. *Nature* 445:919–921.

Radhakrishna, Sindhu, and Mewa Singh. 2004. Infant development in the slender loris (*Loris lydekkerianus lydekkerianus*). *Current Science* 86:1121–27.

Radke-Yarrow, M., C. Zahn-Waxler, D. Richardson, A. Susman, and P. Martinez. 1994. Caring behavior in children of clinically depressed and well mothers. *Child Development* 65:1405–14.

Rajecki, D. W., Michael E. Lamb, and P. Obsmascher. 1978. Towards a general theory of infantile attachment: A comparative review of aspects of the social bond. *Behavioral and Brain Sciences* 3:417–464.

Ramalingaswami, V., U. Jonsson, and J. Rodhe. 1996. The Asian enigma. In *The progress of nations,* 10–17. New York: UNICEF.

Rapaport, L. G. 2006. Parenting and behavior: Babbling bird teachers? *Current Biology* 16(17):R675–677.

Rapaport, L. G., and G. R. Brown. 2008. Social influences on foraging behavior in young primates: Learning what, where, and how to eat. *Evolutionary Anthropology* 17:189–201.

Rapaport, L. G., and C. R. Ruiz-Miranda. 2002. Tutoring in wild golden lion tamarins. *International Journal of Primatology* 23:1063–70.

Reddy, Vasudevi. 2003. On being the object of attention: Implications for self-other consciousness. *Trends in Cognitive Sciences* 7:397–402.

———. 2007. Getting back to the "rough" ground: Deception and social living. *Philosophical Transactions of the Royal Society B* 362:621–637.

Reed, D. L., J. E. Light, J. M. Allen, and J. J. Kirchman. 2007. Pair of lice lost or parasites regained: The evolutionary history of anthropoid primate lice. *BMC Biology* 5(7).

Reeve, H. K. 1992. Queen activation of lazy workers in colonies of the eusocial naked mole-rat. *Nature* 358:147–149.

Reeve, H. K., and G. J. Gamboa. 1987. Queen regulation of worker foraging in paper wasps: A social feedback-control system (*Polistes fuscatus,* Hymenoptera, Vespidae). *Behaviour* 102:147–167.

Rendall, D., and A. Di Fiore. 2007. Homoplasy, homology, and the perceived special status of behavior in evolution. *Journal of Human Evolution* 52:504–521.

Richards, M., C. Rengo, Fulvio Cruciano, F. Gratrix, J. F. Wilson, R. Cozzari, V. Macaulay, and A. Torroni. 2003. Extensive female-mediated gene flow from sub-Saharan Africa into Near Eastern Arab populations. *American Journal of Human Genetics* 72:1058–64.

Ricklefs, R. E. 1984. The optimization of growth rate in altricial birds. *Ecology* 65:1602–16.

Riddell, F. A. 1978. Maidu and Konkow. In *Handbook of North American Indians,* vol. 8: *California,* gen. ed. W. C. Sturtevant, 370–386. Washington, DC: Smithsonian.

Ridley, Matt. 1996. *The origins of virtue: Human instincts and the evolution of coopera-*
tion. New York: Penguin.

Rilling, J. K. 2006. Human and nonhuman primate brains: Are they allometri-
cally scaled versions of the same design? *Evolutionary Anthropology*
15:65–77.

Rilling, J. K., D. A. Gutman, T. R. Zeh, G. Pagnoni, G. S. Berns, and C. D. Kilts.
2002. A neural basis for social cooperation. *Neuron* 35:395–405.

Rilling, J. K., A. G. Sanfey, J. A. Aronson, L. E. Nystrom, and J. D. Cohen. 2004a.
The neural correlates of theory of mind within interpersonal interactions.
NeuroImage 22:1694–1703.

———. 2004b. Opposing BOLD responses to reciprocated and unreciprocated altruism in putative reward pathways. *Neuroreport* 15(116): 2539–43.

Rizzolatti, G., L. Fadiga, L. Fogassi, and V. Gallese. 1996. Premotor cortex and the
recognition of motor actions. *Cognitive Brain Research* 3:131–141.

Rizzolatti, G., L. Fogassi, and V. Gallese. 2006. Mirrors in the mind. *Scientific*
American 295(5):54–61.

Roberts, R. Lucille, A. K. Miller, S. E. Taymans, and C. Sue Carter. 1998. Role of
social and endocrine factors in alloparental behavior of prairie voles (*Mi-*
crotus ochrogaster). *Canadian Journal of Zoology* 76:1862–68.

Robson, S. L. 2004. Breast milk, diet and large human brains. *Current Anthropol-*
ogy 45:419–424.

Robson, S. L., C. P. van Schaik, and K. Hawkes. 2006. The derived features of human life history. In *The evolution of human life history*, ed. K. Hawkes and
R. R. Paine, 17–44. Santa Fe: SAR Press.

Rodseth, Lars, and Richard Wrangham. 2004. Human kinship: A continuation
of politics by other means? In *Kinship and behavior among primates,* ed. Bernard Chapais and Carol Berman, 389–419. Oxford: Oxford University
Press.

Rodseth, Lars, R. Wrangham, A. Harrington, and B. Smuts. 1991. The human
community as a primate society. *Current Anthropology* 32:221–254.

Roscoe, Paul. 2007. Intelligence, coalitional killing, and the antecedents of war.
American Anthropologist 109:485–495.

Rose, L. 1997. Vertebrate predation and food sharing in *Cebus* and *Pan*. *Interna-*
tional Journal of Primatology 18:727–765.

Rosenberg, Karen, and Wenda Trevathan. 1996. Bipedalism and human birth:
The obstetrical dilemma revisited. *Evolutionary Anthropology* 4:161–168.

Rosenbloom, Stephanie. 2006. Here come the great-grandparents: Families include more generations, fewer gaps. *New York Times,* November 2, 2006.

Ross, Caroline, and Ann MacLarnon. 2000. The evolution of non-maternal care
in anthropoid primates: A test of hypotheses. *Folia Primatologica*
71:93–113.

Ross, Corinna N., J. A. French, and Guillermo Orti. 2007. Germ-line chimerism and paternal care in marmosets (*Callithrix kuhlii*). *Proceedings of the National Academy of Sciences (USA)* 104:6278–82.

Rothschild, Babette. 2004. Mirror, mirror: Our brains are hardwired for empathy. Published at http://home.webuniverse.net/babette/Mirror.html.

Rowe, Noel. 1996. *The pictorial guide to the living primates.* East Hampton, NY: Pogonias.

Rowley, Ian. 1978. Communal activities among white-winged choughs *Corcorax melanorhamphus. Ibis* 120:178–197.

Rowley, I., and E. Russell. 1990. Splendid fairy wrens: Demonstrating the importance of longevity. In *Cooperative breeding in birds,* ed. P. Stacey and W. Koenig, 3–30. Cambridge: Cambridge University Press.

Rubenstein, Dustin. 2007. Female extrapair mate choice in a cooperative breeder: Trading sex for help and increasing offspring heterozygosity. *Proceedings of the Royal Society B* 274:1895–1903.

Rubenstein, Dustin R., and I. J. Lovette. 2007. Temporal environmental variability drives the evolution of cooperative breeding in birds. *Current Biology* 17:1414–19.

Ruffman, T., J. Perner, M. Naito, L. Parkin, and W. Clements. 1998. Older (but not younger) siblings facilitate false belief understanding. *Developmental Psychology* 34(10):161–174.

Russell, Andrew F. 2004. Mammals: Comparisons and contrasts. In *Ecology and evolution of cooperative breeding in birds,* ed. W. Koenig and J. Dickinson, 210–227. Cambridge: Cambridge University Press.

Russell, Andrew F., Anne A. Carlson, Grant M. McIlrath, Neil R. Jordan, and Tim Clutton-Brock. 2004. Adaptive size modification by dominant female meerkats. *Evolution* 58:1600–7.

Russell, Andrew F., N. E. Langmore, A. Cockburn, L. B. Astheimer, and R. M. Kilner. 2007. Reduced egg investment can conceal helper effects in cooperatively breeding birds. *Science* 317:941–943.

Russell, Andrew F., L. L. Sharpe, P. N. M. Brotherton, and T. H. Clutton-Brock. 2003. Cost minimization by helpers in cooperative vertebrates. *Proceedings of the National Academy of Sciences (USA)* 100:3333–38.

Russell, Eleanor M. 2000. Avian life histories: Is extended parental care the Southern secret? *Emu* 100:377–399.

Rutter, Michael. 1974. *The qualities of mothering: Maternal deprivation reassessed.* New York: Jason.

Rutter, Michael, and Thomas O'Connor. 1999. Implications of attachment theory for child care policies. In *Handbook of attachment,* ed. J. Cassidy and P. Shaver, 823–844. New York: Guilford.

Sachser, Norbert, D. Hierzel, and M. Durschlag. 1998. Social relationships and the management of stress. *Psychoneuroendocrinology* 23:891–904.

Sagi, A., M. Lamb, K. Lewkowicz, R. Shoham, R. Dvir, and D. Estes. 1985. Security of infant-mother, -father, and -*metapelet* attachments among kibbutz-reared Israeli children. In *Growing points of attachment theory and research,* ed. I. Bretherton and E. Waters, 257–275. Monographs of the Society for Research in Child Development, 50.

Sagi, Abraham, Marinus H. van IJzendoorn, Ora Aviezer, Frank Donnell, Nina Koren-Karie, Tirtsa Joels, and Yael Harel. 1995. Attachments in a multiple-caregiver and multiple-infant environment: The case of the Israeli kibbutzim. In *Caregiving, cultural, and cognitive perspectives on secure-base behavior,* ed. Everett Waters, et al., 71–91. Monographs of the Society for Research in Child Development, 60.

Saltzman, Wendy, and David H. Abbott. 2005. Diminished maternal responsiveness during pregnancy in multiparous female common marmosets. *Hormones and Behavior* 47:151–163.

Saltzman, Wendy, K. J. Liedl, O. J. Salper, R. R. Pick, and D. H. Abbott. 2008. Post-conception reproductive competition in cooperatively breeding common marmosets. *Hormones and Behavior* 53:274–286.

Sangree, W. H. 1980. The persistence of polyandry in Irigwe, Nigeria. *Journal of Comparative Family Studies* 11:335–343.

Sapolsky, R. M., S. C. Alberts, and J. Altmann. 1997. Hypercortisolism is associated with social subordination and social isolation among wild baboons. *Archives of General Psychiatry* 54:1137–43.

Savage-Rumbaugh, Sue, and Kelly McDonald. 1988. Deception and social manipulation in symbol-using apes. In *Machiavellian intelligence: Social expertise and the evolution of intellect in monkeys, apes, and humans,* ed. Richard W. Byrne and Andrew Whiten, 224–237. Oxford: Oxford University Press.

Sayer, Liana C., Suzanne M. Bianchi, and John P. Robinson. 2004. Are parents investing less in children? Trends in mothers' and fathers' time with children. *American Journal of Sociology* 110:1–43.

Scelza, Brooke, and Rebecca Bliege Bird. 2008. Group structure and female comparative networks in Australia's Western Desert. *Human Nature* 19:231–248.

Schaller, George. 1972. *The Serengeti lion: A study of predator-prey relations.* Chicago: University of Chicago Press.

Schiefenhövel, W. 1989. Reproduction and sex-ratio manipulation through preferential female infanticide among the Eipo, in the western Highlands of New Guinea. In *The sociobiology of sexual and reproductive strategies,* ed. A. Rasa, C. Vogel, and E. Voland, 170–193. London: Chapman and Hall.

Schiefenhövel, W., and Paul Blum. n.d. Insects: Forgotten and rediscovered as food. Entomophagy among the Eipo, Highlands of West-New Guinea and in other traditional societies. Unpublished report from Max-Planck Institute (Human Ethology), Andechs, Germany.

Schiefenhövel, W., and A. Grabolle. 2005. The role of maternal grandmothers in

Trobriand adoptions. In *Grandmotherhood: The evolutionary significance of the second half of female life,* ed. Eckart Voland, Athanasios Chasiotis, and Wulf Schiefenhövel, 177–193. New Brunswick, NJ: Rutgers University Press.

Schoesch, Stephan J. 1998. Physiology of helping in Florida scrub jays. *American Scientist* 86:70–77.

Schoesch, Stephan J., S. J. Reynolds, and Raoul K. Boughton. 2004. Endocrinology. In *Ecology and evolution of cooperative breeding in birds,* ed. W. Koenig and J. Dickinson, 128–141. Cambridge: Cambridge University Press.

Schölmerich, Axel, B. Leyendecker, B. Citlak, A. Miller, and R. Harwood. 2005. Variability in grandmothers' roles. In *Grandmotherhood: The evolutionary significance of the second half of female life,* ed. Eckart Voland, Athanasios Chasiotis, and Wulf Schiefenhövel, 277–292. New Brunswick, NJ: Rutgers University Press.

Schradin, Carsten, and Gustl Anzenberger. 1999. Prolactin, the hormone of paternity. *News in Physiological Sciences* 14:223–231.

Schradin, Carsten, Dee Ann M. Reeder, Sally P. Mendoza, and Gustl Anzenberger. 2003. Prolactin and paternal care: Comparisons of three species of New World monkeys (*Callicebus cupreus, Callithrix jacchus* and *Callimico goldii*). *Journal of Comparative Psychology* 117:166–175.

Sealy, Judith. 2006. Diet, mobility, and settlement pattern among Holocene hunter-gatherers in southernmost Africa. *Current Anthropology* 47: 569–595.

Sear, Rebecca. 2008. Kin and child survival in rural Malawi: Are matrilineal kin always beneficial in a matrilineal society? *Human Nature* 19:277–293.

Sear, Rebecca, and Ruth Mace. 2008. Who keeps children alive? A review of the effects of kin on child survival. *Evolution and Human Behavior* 29:1–18.

Sear, Rebecca, R. Mace, and Ian A. McGregor. 2000. Maternal grandmothers improve the nutritional status and survival of children in rural Gambia. *Proceedings of the Royal Society of London B* 267:461–467.

Sear, Rebecca, Fiona Steele, Ian A. McGregor, and Ruth Mace. 2002. The effects of kin on child mortality in rural Gambia. *Demography* 39:43–63.

Seay, B. 1966. Maternal behavior in primiparous and multiparous rhesus monkeys. *Folia Primatologica* 4:146–168.

Seelye, Katherine Q. 2007. Decision to have baby isn't political, Mary Cheney says. *New York Times,* February 1, 2007.

Seger, Jon. 1977. Appendix 3: A numerical method for estimating coefficients of relationship in a langur troop. In *The langurs of Abu,* by Sarah B. Hrdy, 317–326. Cambridge: Harvard University Press.

Seilstad, M. T., E. Minch, and L. Cavalli-Sforza. 1998. Genetic evidence for a higher female migration rate in humans. *Nature Genetics* 20:278–280.

Shaver, P. R., and K. A. Brennan. 1992. Attachment styles and the "Big Five" personality traits: Their connections with each other and with romantic relationship outcomes. *Personality and Social Psychology Bulletin* 18:536–545.

Sherman, Paul, Eileen Lacey, Hudson Reeve, and Laurent Keller. 1995. Forum: The eusociality continuum. *Behavioral Ecology* 6:102–108.

Shostak, M. 1976. A !Kung woman's memories of childhood. In *Kalahari hunter-gatherers: Studies of the !Kung San and their neighbors,* ed. R. B. Lee and I. DeVore, 246–278. Cambridge: Harvard University Press.

Shur, M. D., R. Palombit, and P. Whitten. 2008. Association between male testosterone and friendship formation with lactating females in wild olive baboons (*Papio hamadryas anubis*). Abstract. *American Journal of Physical Anthropology* Supplement 46:193.

Silk, Joan. 1978. Patterns of food sharing among mother and infant chimpanzees at Gombe National Park, Tanzania. *Folia Primatologica* 29:129–141.

———. 1990. Human adoption in evolutionary perspective. *Human Nature* 1:25–52.

———. 1999. Why are infants so attractive to others? The form and function of infant handling in bonnet macaques. *Animal Behaviour* 57:1021–32.

———. 2002. Females, food, family, and friendship. *Evolutionary Anthropology* 11:85–87.

———. 2003. Cooperation without counting: The puzzle of friendship. In *The genetic and cultural evolution of cooperation,* ed. Peter Hammerstein, 37–54. Dahlem Workshop Reports. Cambridge: MIT Press.

———. 2005. Who are more helpful, humans or chimpanzees? *Science* 311:1248–49.

———. 2007. The adaptive value of sociality in mammalian groups. *Proceedings of the Royal Society of London B* 362:539–559.

Silk, Joan B., S. Alberts, and J. Altmann. 2003. Social bonds of female baboons enhance infant survival. *Science* 302:1231–34.

Silk, Joan B., Sarah Brosnan, Jennifer Vonk, Joseph Henrich, Daniel Povinelli, Amanda S. Richardson, Susan P. Lambeth, Jenny Mascaro, and Steven J. Schapiro. 2005. Chimpanzees are indifferent to the welfare of unrelated group members. *Nature* 437:1357–59.

Singer, Stephen. 2007. Mother cat adopts newborn rottweiler. *Boston Globe,* February 15, 2007.

Skinner, G. W. 2004. Grandparental effects on reproductive strategizing: Nobi villagers in early modern Japan. *Demographic Research* 11(5):112–147.

Skutch, Alexander F. 1935. Helpers at the nest. *Auk* 52:257–273.

Slater, Kathy Y., C. M. Shaffner, and F. Aureli. 2007. Embraces for infant handling in spider monkeys: Evidence for a biological market? *Animal Behaviour* 74:455–461.

Smail, Daniel. 2007. *On deep history and the brain.* Berkeley: University of California Press.

Small, Meredith. 1990. Promiscuity in barbary macaques (*Macaca sylvana*). *American Journal of Primatology* 20:267–282.

———. 1998. *Our babies, ourselves.* New York: Anchor Books.

Smith, Adam. 1759/1984. *The theory of moral sentiments,* ed. D. D. Raphael and A. L. Macfie. Indianapolis: Liberty Classics.

Smith, A. C., E. R. Tirado Herrera, H. M. Buchanan-Smith, and Eckhard W. Heymann. 2001. Multiple breeding females and allo-nursing in a wild group of moustached tamarins (*Saguinus mystax*). *Neotropical Primates* 9:67–69.

Smith, David Livingstone. 2007. *The most dangerous animal: Human nature and the origins of war.* New York: St. Martin's.

Smith, E. A. 2003. Human cooperation: Perspectives from behavioral ecology. In *Genetic and cultural evolution of cooperation,* ed. Peter Hammerstein, 401–427. Dahlem Workshop Reports. Cambridge: MIT Press.

Smith, Holly, and Robert L. Tompkins. 1995. Toward a life history of the Hominidae. *Annual Review of Anthropology* 24:257–279.

Smith, J., S. C. Alberts, and J. Altmann. 2003. Wild female baboons bias their social behaviour towards paternal half-sisters. *Proceedings of the Royal Society of London B* 270:503–510.

Smith, M. S. 1991. An evolutionary perspective on grandparent-grandchild relationships. In *The psychology of grandparenthood: An international perspective,* ed. P. K. Smith, 157–176. London: Routledge.

Smuts, Barbara. 1985. *Sex and friendship in baboons.* New York: Aldine.

Snowdon, C. 1984. Social development during the first twenty weeks in the cottontop tamarin (*Saguinus oedipus*). *Animal Behaviour* 32:432–444.

———. 1996. Infant care in cooperatively breeding species. *Advances in the Study of Behavior* 25:643–689.

Snowdon, C. T., and K. A. Cronin. 2007. Cooperative breeders do cooperate. *Behavioural Processes* 76:138–141.

Sober, E., and David Sloane Wilson. 1998. *Unto others: The evolution and psychology of unselfish behavior.* Cambridge: Harvard University Press.

Solomon, J., and C. George, eds. 1999. *Attachment disorganization.* New York: Guilford.

Solomon, Nancy G., and Jeffrey A. French. 1997. The study of mammalian cooperative breeding. In *Cooperative breeding in mammals,* ed. Nancy G. Solomon and Jeffrey A. French, 1–10. Cambridge: Cambridge University Press.

———, eds. 1997. *Cooperative breeding in mammals.* Cambridge: Cambridge University Press.

Soltis, Joseph. 2004. The signal functions of early infant crying. *Behavioral and Brain Sciences* 27:443–490.

Sommer, Matthew H. 2005. Making sex work: Polyandry as a survival strategy in Qing Dynasty China. In *Gender in motion: Divisions of labor and cultural change in late imperial and modern China,* ed. Bryna Goodman and Wendy Larson, 29–54. Lanham, MD: Rowman and Littlefield.

Sommer, Volker. 1994. Infanticide among the langurs of Jodhpur: Testing the sexual selection hypothesis with a long-term record. In *Infanticide and parental care,* ed. Stefano Parmigiani and F. vom Saal, 155–198. Langhorne, PA: Harwood Academic.

Spangler, Gottfried, and Karin Grossmann. 1999. Individual and physiological correlates of attachment disorder in infancy. In *Attachment disorganization,* ed. J. Solomon and C. George, 95–124. New York: Guilford.

Spencer-Booth, Yvette, and R. A. Hinde. 1971a. Effects of brief separation from mother on rhesus monkeys. *Science* 173:111–118.

——. 1971b. Effects of 6 days' separation from mother in 18- to 32-week-old rhesus monkeys. *Animal Behaviour* 19:174–191.

Spieker, S. J., and L. Bensley. 1994. Roles of living arrangements and grandmother social support in adolescent mothering and infant attachment. *Developmental Psychology* 30:102–111.

Spier, R. E. 2002. Towards a new human species. Review of *Redesigning animals and our posthuman future. Science* 296:1807–8.

Stack, Carol. 1974. *All our kin: Strategies for survival in a black community.* New York: Harper and Row.

Stallings, Joy, Alison Fleming, C. Corter, C. Worthman, and M. Steiner. 2001. The effects of infant cries and odors on sympathy, cortisol, and autonomic responses, I: New mothers and nonpostpartum women. *Parenting: Science and Practice* 1:71–100.

Stanford, Craig. 1999. *The hunting apes.* Princeton: Princeton University Press.

——. 2003. *Upright: The evolutionary key to becoming human.* Boston: Houghton Mifflin.

Starr, Alexandra. 2003. Washington's $1 billion lecture to the poor: Why a "pro-marriage" bill isn't likely to help much. *BusinessWeek,* October 20, 2003, 116.

Stern, Daniel. 2002. Lecture at a conference on Attachment: Early Childhood through the Lifespan, March 9–10, UCLA. Audio tape/cd version available at www.lifespanlearn.org.

Stern, Daniel, S. Spieker, R. Barnett, and K. Mackain. 1983. The prosody of maternal speech: Infant age and context related change. *Journal of Child Language* 10:1–15.

Stewart, Kelly J. 2001. Social relationships of immature gorillas and silverbacks. In *Mountain gorillas: Three decades of research at Karisoke,* ed. M. M. Robbins, P. Sicotte, and K. J. Stewart, 183–213. Cambridge: Cambridge University Press.

Stiner, Mary, N. D. Munro, T. Surovell, E. Tchernov, and O. Bar-Yosef. 1999. Paleolithic population growth pulses evidenced by small animal exploitation. *Science* 283:190–194.

Stoll, Andrew L. 2001. *The omega-3 connection.* New York: Simon and Schuster.

Stone, Lawrence. 1977. *The family, sex and marriage in England, 1500–1800.* London: Weidenfeld and Nicolson.

Storey, Anne E., Krista M. Delahunty, D. W. McKay, C. J. Walsh, and S. I. Wilhelm. 2006. Social and hormonal bases of individual differences in the parental behaviour of birds and mammals. *Canadian Journal of Experimental Psychology* 60:237–245.

Storey, Anne E., Carolyn J. Walsh, Roma L. Quinton, and Katherine E. Wynne-Edwards. 2000. Hormonal correlates of paternal responsiveness in new and expectant fathers. *Evolution and Human Behavior* 21:79–95.

Strassmann, B. 1993. Menstrual hut visits by Dogon women: A hormonal test distinguishes deceit from honest signaling. *Behavioral Ecology* 7 (3):304–315.

———. 1997. Polygyny as a risk factor for child mortality among the Dogon. *Current Anthropology* 38:688–695.

Strassmann, B., and B. Gillespie. 2007. Life-history theory, fertility and reproductive success in humans. *Proceedings of the Royal Society of London, Series B: Biological Sciences* 269:552–569.

Strassmann, B., and K. Hunley. 1996. Polygyny, sorcery and child mortality among the Dogon of Mali. Paper presented at the 95th annual meeting of the American Anthropological Association, November 20–24, San Francisco.

Strathearn, Lane, Jian Li, Peter Fonagy, and P. Read Montague. 2007. Infant affect modulates maternal brain reward activation. (Abstract.) Paper presented at the Parental Brain Conference, Tufts University, June 7–10, Boston.

Strier, Karen B. 1992. *Faces in the forest: The endangered muriqui monkeys of Brazil.* Oxford: Oxford University Press.

Struhsaker, Thomas. 1975. *The red colobus monkey.* Chicago: University of Chicago Press.

Sugiyama, Lawrence, and Richard Chacon. 2005. Juvenile responses to household ecology among the Yora of Peruvian Amazonia. In *Hunter-gatherer childhoods,* ed. B. Hewlett and M. Lamb, 237–261. Piscataway, NJ: Aldine/Transaction.

Sugiyama, Lawrence S., J. Tooby, and L. Cosmides. 2002. Cross-cultural evidence of cognitive adaptations for social exchange among the Shiwiar of the Ecuadorian Amazonia. *Proceedings of the National Academy of Sciences (USA)* 99:11537–42.

Sumner, Petroc, and J. D. Mellon. 2003. Colors of primate pelage and skin: Objective assessment of conspicuousness. *American Journal of Primatology* 59:67–91.

Symons, Don. 1979. *The evolution of human sexuality.* Oxford: Oxford University Press.

———. 1982. Another woman that never existed. *Quarterly Review of Biology* 57:297–300.

Tardieu, C. 1998. Short adolescence in early hominids: Infantile and adolescent growth in the human femur. *American Journal of Physical Anthropology* 107:163–178.

Taub, David. 1984. *Primate paternalism.* New York: Van Nostrand Reinhold.

Taylor, Shelley. 2002. *The tending instinct: How nurturing is essential to who we are and how we live.* New York: Henry Holt.

Thierry, Bernard. 2007. Unity in diversity: Lessons from macaque societies. *Evolutionary Anthropology* 16:224–238.

Thiessen, Del, and Yoko Umezawa. 1998. The sociobiology of everyday life. *Human Nature* 9:293–320.

Thomas, Elizabeth Marshall. 2006. *The old way: A story of the first people.* New York: Farrar, Straus and Giraux.

Thompson, Ross A. 2006. The development of the person: Social understanding, relationships, self, conscience. In *Handbook of child psychology,* 6th ed., vol. 3: *Social, emotional, and personality development,* ed. N. Eisenberg, 24–98. New York: Wiley.

Thompson, Ross A., K. E. Grossmann, M. R. Gunnar, M. Heinrichs, H. Keller, T. G. O'Connor, G. Spangler, E. Voland, and S. Wang. 2005. Early social attachment and its consequences. In *Attachment and bonding: A new synthesis,* ed. C. S. Carter et al., 349–383. Dahlem Workshop Reports. Cambridge: MIT Press.

Thornton, Alex, and Katherine McAuliffe. 2006. Teaching in wild meerkats. *Science* 313:227–229.

Tiger, Lionel. 1970. *Men in groups.* New York: Vintage.

Tomasello, Michael. 1999. *The cultural origins of human cognition.* Cambridge: Harvard University Press.

———. 2007. For human eyes only. *New York Times,* January 13, 2007.

Tomasello, Michael, Josep Call, and Brian Hare. 2003. Chimpanzees understand psychological states—the question is, which ones and to what extent? *Trends in Cognitive Science* 7:153–156.

Tomasello, Michael, Malinda Carpenter, Josep Call, Tanya Behne, and Henrike Moll. 2005. Understanding and sharing intentions: The origins of cultural cognition. *Behavioral and Brain Sciences* 28:675–691.

Tomonaga, Masaki, Mayasuki Tanaka, Tetsoro Matsuzawa, M. Myowa-Yamakoshi, Daisuke Kosugi, Yuu Mizuno, Sanae Okamoto, Masami Yamaguchi, and Kim Bard. 2004. Development of social cognition in infant chimpanzees (*Pan troglodytes*): Face recognition, smiling, gaze, and the lack of triadic interactions. *Japanese Psychological Research* 46:227–235.

Toth, Amy L., K. Varala, T. C. Newman, F. E. Miguez, S. K. Hutchison, D. A. Willoughby, J. F. Simons, M. Egholm, J. H. Hunt, M. E. Hudson, and G. E.

Robinson. 2007. Wasp gene expression supports an evolutionary link between maternal behavior and eusociality. *Science* 318:441–444.

Townsend, Simon W., K. E. Slocombe, Melissa E. Thompson, and Klaus Zuberbühler. 2007. Female-led infanticide in wild chimpanzees. *Current Biology* 17(10):R355–356.

Trevarthen, C. 2005. Stepping away from the mirror: Pride and shame in adventures of companionship: Reflections on the nature and emotional needs of infant intersubjectivity. *Attachment and bonding: A new synthesis,* ed. C. S. Carter et al., 55–84. Dahlem Workshop Reports. Cambridge: MIT Press.

Trevarthen, C., and K. J. Aitken. 2001. Infant intersubjectivity: Research, theory, and clinical applications. *Journal of Child Psychology and Psychiatry* 42:3–48.

Trevarthen, Colwyn, and K. Logotheti. 1989. Child and culture: Genesis of co-operative knowing. In *Cognition and social worlds,* ed. A. Gellatly, D. Rogers, and J. Sloboda, 37–56. Oxford: Clarendon University Press.

Trivers, R. L. 1971. The evolution of reciprocal altruism. *Quarterly Review of Biology* 46:35–57.

———. 1972. Parental investment and sexual selection. In *Sexual selection and the descent of man, 1871–1971,* ed. B. Campbell, 136–179. Chicago: Aldine.

———. 1974. Parent-offspring conflict. *American Zoologist* 14:249–264.

———. 2006. Reciprocal altruism—30 years later. In *Cooperation in primates and humans,* ed. P. M. Kappeler and C. P. van Schaik, 67–83. Berlin: Springer.

Tronick, Edward, H. Als, L. B. Adamson, S. Wise, and T. B. Brazelton. 1978. The infant's response to entrapment by contradictory messages in face-to-face interaction. *Journal of the American Academy of Child Psychiatry* 17:1–13.

Tronick, Edward Z., Gilda A. Morelli, and Paula K. Ivey. 1992. The Efe forager infant and toddler's pattern of social relationships: Multiple and simultaneous. *Developmental Psychology* 28:568–577.

Tronick, E. Z., G. Morelli, and S. Winn. 1987. Multiple caretaking of Efe (Pygmy) infants. *American Anthropologist* 89:96–106.

Tsao, Doris Y., Winrich A. Freiwald, Roger B. H. Tootell, and Margaret S. Livingstone. 2006. A cortical region consisting entirely of face-selective cells. *Science* 311:670–74.

Tucker, Bram, and A. G. Young. 2005. Growing up Mikea: Children's time allocation and tuber foraging in southwestern Madagascar. In *Hunter-gatherer childhoods,* ed. B. Hewlett and M. Lamb, 147–171. Piscataway, NJ: Aldine/Transaction.

Turke, Paul. 1988. "Helpers at the nest": Childcare networks on Ifaluk. In *Human reproductive behaviour: A Darwinian perspective,* ed. L. Betzig, M. Borgerhoff Mulder, and P. Turke, 173–188. Cambridge: Cambridge University Press.

Turnbull, Colin M. 1965. *The Mbuti pygmies: An ethnographic survey.* New York: American Museum of Natural History.

———. 1978. The politics of non-aggression. In *Learning non-aggression,* ed. A. Montagu, 161–221. Oxford: Oxford University Press.

Turner, Sarah E., Lisa Gould, and David A. Duffus. 2005. Maternal behavior and infant congenital limb malformation in a free-ranging group of *Macaca fuscata* on Awaji Island, Japan. *International Journal of Primatology* 26:1435–57.

Tyre, Peg, and Daniel McGinn. 2003. She works, he doesn't. *Newsweek,* May 12, 2003, 44–52.

Ueno, Ari. 2006. Food sharing and referencing behavior in chimpanzee mother and infant. In *Cognitive development in chimpanzees,* ed. T. Matsuzawa, M. Tomonaga, and M. Tanaka, 172–181. Berlin: Springer-Verlag.

Valeggia, Claudia. 2009. Changing times: Who cares for the baby now? In *Substitute parents: Alloparenting in human societies,* ed. G. Bentley and R. Mace. New York: Berghahn Books.

Valenzuela, Marta. 1990. Attachment in chronically underweight young children. *Child Development* 61:1984–96.

Van der Dennen, J. 1995. *The origin of war,* 2 vols. Groningen: Origin Press.

Van IJzendoorn, Marinus, and Abraham Sagi. 1999. Cross-cultural patterns of attachment. In *Handbook of attachment,* ed. Jude Cassidy and Phillip Shaver, 713–734. New York: Guilford.

Van IJzendoorn, Marinus, Abraham Sagi, and Mirjam Lambermon. 1992. The multiple caretaker paradox: Data from Holland and Israel. In *Beyond the parents: The role of other adults in children's lives,* ed. R. C. Pianta, 5–24. New Directions for Child Development 57. San Francisco: Jossey Bass.

Van IJzendoorn, Marinus, C. Schuengel, and M. Bakermans-Kranenburg. 1999. Disorganized attachment in early childhood: Meta-analysis of precursors, concomitants and sequelae. *Development and Psychopathology* 11:225–250.

Van Noordwijk, Maria, and Carel van Schaik. 2005. Development of ecological competence in Sumatran orangutans. *American Journal of Physical Anthropology* 127:79–94.

Van Schaik, Carel P. 2004. *Among orangutans: Red apes and the rise of human culture.* Cambridge: Harvard University Press.

Van Schaik, Carel, M. Ancrenaz, G. Borgen, B. Galdikas, C. D. Knott, I. Singleton, A. Suzuki, S. Utami, and M. Merrill. 2003. Orangutan cultures and the evolution of material culture. *Science* 299:102–105.

Van Schaik, C. P., and R. Dunbar. 1990. The evolution of monogamy in large primates: A new hypothesis and some crucial tests. *Behavior* 115:30–62.

Van Schaik, C. P., J. K. Hodges, and C. L. Nunn. 2000. Paternity confusion and the ovarian cycles of female primates. In *Infanticide by males and its implications,* ed. C. P. van Schaik and C. Janson, 361–387. Cambridge: Cambridge University Press.

Van Schaik, C. P., and C. Janson, eds. 2000. *Infanticide by males and its implications.* Cambridge: Cambridge University Press.

Van Schaik, C. P., and A. Paul. 1996. Male care in primates: Does it ever reflect paternity? *Evolutionary Anthropology* 5:152–156.

Varki, Ajit, and Tasha K. Altheide. 2005. Comparing the human and chimpanzee genomes: Searching for needles in a haystack. *Genome Research* 15:1746–58.

Vasey, Natalie. 2008. Alloparenting in red ruffed lemurs (*Varecia rubra*) of the Masoala Peninsula, Madagascar. Paper presented at the XXII Congress of the International Primatological Society, August 3–8, Edinburgh, UK.

Vaughn, Brian E., Muriel R. Azria, Lisa Krzysik, Lisa R. Caya, Kelly K. Bost, Wanda Newell, and Kerry L. Kazura. 2000. Friendship and social competence in a sample of preschool children attending Head Start. *Developmental Psychology* 36:326–338.

Vigilant, L., M. Hofreiter, H. Siedel, and C. Boesch. 2001. Paternity and relatedness in wild chimpanzee communities. *Proceedings of the National Academy of Sciences (USA)* 98:12890–95.

Voland, Eckart, and Jan Beise. 2002. Opposite effects of maternal and paternal grandmothers on infant survival in historical Krummhörn. *Behavioral Ecology and Sociobiology* 52:435–443.

———. 2005. "The husband's mother is the devil in the house": Data on the impact of the mother-in-law on stillbirth mortality in historical Krummhörn (1850–1874) and some thoughts on the evolution of postgenerative female life. In *Grandmotherhood: The evolutionary significance of the second half of female life,* ed. E. Voland, A. Chasiotis, and W. Schiefenhövel, 239–255. New Brunswick, NJ: Rutgers University Press.

Voland, Eckart, Athanasios Chasiotis, and Wulf Schiefenhövel, eds. 2005. *Grandmotherhood: The evolutionary significance of the second half of female life.* New Brunswick, NJ: Rutgers University Press.

———. 2005. A short overview of three fields of research on the evolutionary significance of postgenerative female life. In *Grandmotherhood: The evolutionary significance of the second half of female life,* ed. Eckart Voland, Athanasios Chasiotis, and Wulf Schiefenhövel, 1–17. New Brunswick, NJ: Rutgers University Press.

Vonk, J., S. F. Brosnan, J. B. Silk, J. Henrich, A. S. Richardson, S. P. Lambeth, S. J. Schapiro, and D. Povinelli. 2008. Chimpanzees do not take advantage of very low cost opportunities to deliver food to unrelated group members. *Animal Behaviour* 75:1757–70.

Wade, Nicholas. 2006. *Before the dawn: Recovering the lost history of our ancestors.* New York: Penguin Books.

Walker, Alan, and Pat Shipman. 1996. *The wisdom of the bones: In search of human origins.* New York: Alfred Knopf.

Walker, Marcus. 2006. In Estonia, paying women to have babies is paying off. *Wall Street Journal,* October 20, 2006, 1.

Wall-Scheffler, C. M., K. Geiger, and K. L. Steudel-Number. 2007. Infant carrying:

The role of increased locomotory costs in early tool development. *American Journal of Physical Anthropology* 133:841–846.

Want, Stephen C., and Paul L. Harris. 2001. Learning from other people's mistakes: Causal understanding in learning to use a tool. *Child Development* 72:421–443.

———. 2002. How do children ape? Applying concepts from the study of nonhuman primates to the developmental study of "imitation" in children. *Developmental Science* 5:1–41.

Warneken, Felix, F. Chen, and Michael Tomasello. 2006. Co-operative activities in young children and chimpanzees. *Child Development* 77:640–663.

Warneken, Felix, and Brian Hare. 2007. Altruistic helping in human infants and young chimpanzees. *PLOS* 5(7):1414–20.

Warneken, Felix, and Michael Tomasello. 2006. Altruistic helping in human infants and young chimpanzees. *Science* 311:1301–3.

Washburn, Sherwood, and David Hamburg. 1965. Implications of primate research. In *Primate behavior,* ed. I. DeVore, 293–303. New York: Holt, Rinehart and Winston.

———. 1968. Aggressive behavior in Old World monkeys and apes. In *Primate societies,* ed. Phyllis C. Jay, 458–478. New York: Holt, Rinehart and Winston.

Washburn, S., and C. Lancaster. 1968. The evolution of hunting. In *Man the hunter,* ed. R. Lee and I. DeVore, 293–303. Chicago: Aldine.

Watson, John. 1928. *Psychological care of infant and child.* New York: W. W. Norton.

Watts, D., and J. C. Mitani. 2000. Infanticide and cannibalism by male chimpanzees at Ngogo, Kibale National Park, Uganda. *Primates* 41:357–365.

Wcislo, W. T., and B. N. Danforth. 1997. Secondarily solitary: The evolutionary loss of social behaviour. *Trends in Ecology and Evolution* 12:468–474.

Weinberger-Thomas, Catherine. 1999. *Ashes of immortality: Widow-burning in India.* Trans. Jeffrey Mehlman and David Gordon White. Chicago: University of Chicago Press.

Weisner, T., and R. Gallimore. 1977. My brother's keeper: Child and sibling caretaking. *Current Anthropology* 18:169–190.

Welty, Joel Carl, and Luis Baptista. 1990. *The life of birds,* 4th ed. Fort Worth: Harcourt College Publishers.

Wenseleers, Tom, and Francis L. W. Ratnieks. 2006. Enforced altruism in insect societies. *Nature* 444:50.

Werner, Emmy. 1984. *Child care: Kith and kin and hired hands.* Baltimore: University Park Press.

Werner, Emmy E., and Ruth Smith. 1992. *Overcoming the odds: High risk children from birth to adulthood.* Ithaca: Cornell University Press.

West, M. M., and M. Konner. 1976. The role of the father in cross-cultural perspective. In *The role of the father in child development,* ed. Michael E. Lamb, 185–216. New York: John Wiley.

West-Eberhard, Mary Jane. 1975. The evolution of social behavior by kin selection. *Quarterly Review of Biology* 50:1–53.

———. 1978. Polygyny and the evolution of social behavior in wasps. *Journal of the Kansas Entomological Society* 51:832–856.

———. 1979. Sexual selection, social selection and evolution. *Proceedings of the American Philosophical Society* 123:222–234.

———. 1986. Dominance relations in *Polistes canadensis* (L.), a tropical social wasp. *Monitore Zoologico Italiano* (n.s.) 20:263–281.

———. 1988a. Flexible strategy and social evolution. In *Animal societies: Theories and facts,* ed. Y. Ito, J. L. Brown, and L. Kikkawa, 35–51. Tokyo: Japan Scientific Societies Press.

———. 1988b. Phenotypic plasticity and "genetic" theories of insect sociality. In *Evolution of social behavior and integrative levels,* vol. 3, ed. G. Greenberg and Ethel Tobach, 123–133. Mahwah, NJ: Lawrence Erlbaum Associates.

———. 2003. *Developmental plasticity and evolution.* Oxford: Oxford University Press.

Westman, M. 2001. Stress and strain crossover. *Human Relations* 54:557–591.

Whalen, Paul J., Jerome Kagan, R. G. Cook, F. C. Davis, H. Kim, S. Polis, D. G. McLaren, L. H. Somerville, A. A. McLean, J. S. Maxwell, and T. Johnstone. 2004. Human amygdala responsivity to masked fearful eye whites. *Science* 306:2061–62.

White, Edmund. 2001. It all adds up. Review of Gilla Lustiger's *The Inventory. New York Times Book Review,* January 7, 2001, 14.

White, Frances J. 1994. Food sharing in wild pygmy chimpanzees, *Pan paniscus.* In *Current primatology,* vol. 2: *Social development, learning and behavior,* ed. J. J. Roeder, B. Thierry, J. R. Anderson, and N. Herrenschmidt, 1–10. Strasbourg, France: Université Louis Pasteur.

Whitehead, Hal, and Janet Mann. 2000. Female reproductive strategies of cetaceans: Life histories and calf care. In *Cetacean societies,* ed. J. Mann, R. C. Connor, P. L. Tyack, and H. Whitehead, 219–247. Chicago: University of Chicago Press.

Whiten, Andrew, and Richard W. Byrne, eds. 1997. *Machiavellian intelligence II: Extensions and evaluations.* Oxford: Oxford University Press.

Whiten, A., J. Goodall, W. McGrew, T. Nishida, V. Reynolds, Y. Sugiyama, C. Tutin, R. Wrangham, and C. Boesch. 1999. Cultures in chimpanzees. *Nature* 399:682–685.

Whiting, Beatrice, and Carolyn Pope Edwards. 1988. *Children of different worlds: The formation of social behavior.* Cambridge: Harvard University Press.

Whitten, Patricia L. 1983. Diet and dominance among female vervet monkeys (*Cercopithecus aethiops*). *American Journal of Primatology* 5:139–159.

Wiessner, Polly. 1977. *Hxaro: A Regional System of Reciprocity for Reducing Risk among the !Kung San.* Ann Arbor: University Microfilms.

———. 1982. Risk, reciprocity and social influences on !Kung San economics. In

Politics and history in band societies, ed. Eleanor Leacock and Richard Lee, 61–86. Cambridge: Cambridge University Press.

———. 1996. Leveling the hunter: Constraints on the status quest in foraging societies. In *Food and the status quest,* ed. P. Wiessner and W. Schiefenhövel, 171–191. Oxford: Berghahn Books.

———. 2002a. Taking the risk out of risky transactions: A forager's dilemma. In *Risky transactions: Trust, kinship and ethnicity,* ed. Frank K. Salter, 21–43. New York: Berghahn Books.

———. 2002b. Hunting, healing, and *hxaro* exchange: A long-term perspective on !Kung (Ju/'hoansi) large-game hunting. *Evolution and Human Behavior* 23:407–436.

———. 2005. Norm enforcement among the Ju/'hoansi bushmen. *Human Nature* 16:115–145.

———. 2006. From spears to M-16s: Testing the imbalance of power hypothesis among the Enga. *Journal of Anthropological Research* 62:165–191.

Wile, J., et al. 1999. Sociocultural aspects of postpartum depression. In *Postpartum mood disorders,* ed. Linda Miller, 83–89. Washington, DC: American Psychiatric Press.

Williams, George C. 1957. Pleiotropy, natural selection and the evolution of senescence. *Evolution* 11:398–411.

Wilson, David Sloane. 2003. *Darwin's cathedral: Evolution, religion and the nature of society.* Chicago: University of Chicago Press.

Wilson, Edward O. 1971a. *The insect societies.* Cambridge: Harvard University Press.

———. 1971b. Competitive and aggressive behavior. In *Man and beast: Comparative social behavior,* ed. J. F. Eisenberg and W. S. Dillon, 183–217. Washington, DC: Smithsonian Institution Press.

———. 1975. *Sociobiology: The new synthesis.* Cambridge: Harvard University Press.

Wilson, Edward O., and Bert Hölldobler. 2005. Eusociality: Origins and consequences. *Proceedings of the National Academy of Sciences (USA)* 102:13367–71.

Winking, J., and M. Gurven. 2007. Effects of paternal care among Tsimane forager-horticulturalists. (Abstract.) Paper presented at the 76th Annual Meeting of the American Association of Physical Anthropologists, March 28–31, Philadelphia.

Winn, Steve, Gilda Morelli, and Ed Tronick. 1989. The infant and the group: A look at Efe caretaking practices. In *The cultural context of infancy,* ed. J. K. Nugent, B. M. Lester, and T. B. Brazelton. Norwood, NJ: Ablex.

Wisenden, B. D., and M. H. A. Keenleyside. 1992. Intraspecific brood adoption in convict cichlids: A mutual benefit. *Behavioral Ecology and Sociobiology* 31:263–269.

Wolovich, C. K., J. P. Perea-Rodriguez, and E. Fernandez-Duque. 2007. Food transfers to young and mates in wild owl monkeys (*Aotus azarai*). *American Journal of Primatology* 69:1–16.

Wood, B., and B. G. Richmond. 2000. Human evolution: Taxonomy and paleobiology. *Journal of Anatomy* 196:19–60.

Wood, Brian. 2006. Prestige or provisioning? A test of foraging goals among the Hadza. *Current Anthropology* 47:383–387.

Wood, Justin, D. D. Glynn, B. C. Phillips, and M. D. Hauser. 2007. The perception of rational goal-directed action in nonhuman primates. *Science* 317:1402–5.

Wrangham, Richard. 1987. The significance of African apes for reconstructing human social evolution. In *The evolution of human behavior: Primate models*, ed. Warren Kinzey, 55–71. Albany: SUNY Press.

———. 1999. The evolution of coalitionary killing. *Yearbook of Physical Anthropology* 42:1–30.

Wrangham, Richard, J. H. Jones, G. Laden, D. Pilbeam, and N. Conklin-Brittain. 1999. The raw and the stolen: Cooking and the ecology of human origins. *Current Anthropology* 40:567–594.

Wrangham, Richard, and Dale Peterson. 1996. *Demonic males: Apes and the origins of human violence.* New York: Houghton Mifflin.

Wright, Patricia. 1984. Biparental care in *Aotus trivirgatus* and *Callicebus molloch*. In *Female primates: Studies by women primatologists*, ed. Meredith Small, 59–75. New York: Alan Liss.

———. 2008. Alloparenting in primates: What have we learned? Presentation at XXII Congress of the International Primatological Society, Edinburgh, Aug. 3–8, 2008.

Wroblewski, Emily E. 2008. An unusual incident of adoption in a wild chimpanzee (*Pan troglodytes*) population at Gombe National Park. *American Journal of Primatology* 70:1–4.

Wyckoff, G. J., W. Wan, and Chung-I Wu. 2000. Rapid evolution of male reproductive genes in the descent of man. *Nature* 401:304–309.

Wynne-Edwards, Katherine. 2001. Hormonal changes in mammalian fathers. *Hormones and Behavior* 40:139–145.

Wynne-Edwards, Katherine E., and Catharine Reburn. 2000. Behavioral endocrinology of mammalian fatherhood. *Trends in Evolutionary Ecology* 15:464–468.

Wynne-Edwards, Katherine, and Mary E. Timonin. 2007. Paternal care in rodents: Weakening support for hormonal regulation of the transition to behavioral fatherhood in rodent animal models of biparental care. *Hormones and Behavior* 53:114–121.

Yeakel, J. D., N. C. Bennett, P. L. Koch, and N. J. Dominy. 2007. The isotopic ecology of African mole-rats informs hypotheses on the evolution of human diet. *Proceedings of the Royal Society of London B* 274:1723–30.

Young, Andrew J., and Tim Clutton-Brock. 2006. Infanticide by subordinates influences reproductive sharing in cooperatively breeding meerkats. *Biology Letters,* 2(3):385–387.

Young, Liane, Fiery Cushman, Marc Hauser, and Rebecca Saxe. 2007. The neural basis of the interaction between theory of mind and moral judgment. *Proceedings of the National Academy of Sciences (USA)* 104:8235–40.

Zahed, S. R., Prudom, S. L., Snowdon, C. T., and Ziegler, T. E. 2007. Male parenting and response to infant stimuli in the common marmoset (*Callithrix jacchus*). *American Journal of Primatology* 69:1–15.

Zahn-Waxler, C. 2000. The early development of empathy, guilt and internalization of distress: Implications for gender differences in internalizing and externalizing problems. In *Anxiety, depression and emotions,* ed. R. Davison, 222–265. Oxford: Oxford University Press.

Zahn-Waxler, C., M. Radke-Yarrow, E. Wagner, and M. Chapman. 1992. Development of concern for others. *Developmental Psychology* 28:126–136.

Zahn-Waxler, C., J. Robinson, and R. Emde. 1992. The development of empathy in twins. *Developmental Psychology* 28:1038–47.

Zak, Paul, and Lori Uber-Zak. 2006. The neurobiology of trust. Abstract. *Neurology* 66(5):A206.

Zerjal, T., Y. Xue, B. Bertorelle, R. S. Wells, W. Bao, S. Zhu, R. Qamar, Q. Ayub, et al. 2003. The genetic legacy of the Mongols. *American Journal of Human Genetics* 72:717–721.

Ziegler, Toni E. 2000. Hormones associated with non-maternal infant care: A review of mammalian and avian studies. *Folia Primatologica* 71:6–21.

Ziegler, Toni E., Shelley L. Prudom, Nancy Schultz-Dacken, A. V. Kurlan, and C. T. Snowdon. 2006. Pregnancy weight gain: Marmoset and tamarin dads show it too. *Biology Letters* 2:181–183.

Ziegler, Toni E., and Charles T. Snowdon. 2000. Preparental hormone levels and parenting in male cottontop tamarins, *Saguinus oedipus. Hormones and Behavior* 38:159–167.

Ziegler, Toni E., Kate F. Washabaugh, and Charles T. Snowdon. 2004. Responsiveness of expectant male cottontop tamarins, *Saguinus oedipus,* to mate's pregnancy. *Hormones and Behavior* 45:84–92.

Zihlman, Adrienne, Debra Bolter, and Christophe Boesch. 2004. Wild chimpanzee dentition and its implications for assessing life history in immature hominin fossils. *Proceedings of the National Academy of Sciences (USA)* 101:10541–43.

Zimmer, Carl. 2006. Chimps display a hallmark of human behavior: Cooperation. *New York Times,* March 3, 2006.

Zinn, Howard. 2003. *A people's history of the United States,* new ed. New York: Perennial Classics.

ACKNOWLEDGMENTS

Over the years, many colleagues nurtured the development of this book. Without my being aware of it, the underlying ideas were conceived in 1971 when Neil Chalmers made it possible for me to observe allomaternal behavior among patas monkeys at the Tigoni Primate Center in Kenya. I was surprised to learn how much allomaternal care goes on. The following year, as a beginning graduate student, I wrote about the "care and exploitation of nonhuman primate infants by conspecifics other than the mother" in what was possibly the world's first seminar on sociobiology, co-taught by Edward O. Wilson. With Wilson's encouragement, and help from Robert Hinde of Cambridge University, that course paper grew into my first scientific publication. I owe a profound debt to these generous and inspiring mentors.

In writing this book I was fortunate to have had access to the photographic archives housed at the Max Planck Institute in Andechs, Germany. These images represent a world treasure, and I am grateful to Irenäus Eibl-Eibesfeldt for making them available. I owe a special debt to Polly Wiessner, whose observations and ideas are central to this book, and to her talented son, Niko Larsen. Early in the project, they helped me test a few ideas using the photo archives at Max Planck Institute and led me to discard some wrong starting assumptions. The images Niko provided and his insightful descriptions of the behaviors depicted convinced me that allomaternal provisioning begins earlier than I had realized. I also owe huge intellectual debts to Mary Jane West-Eberhard for illuminating the role that development plays in evolution; to Kristen Hawkes and Barry Hewlett for their insights into how children are cared for and provisioned among hunter-gatherers; and to Marc Hauser for opening my eyes to what behavioral ecologists can (and cannot) learn from laboratory experiments.

In the course of writing an earlier book, *Mother Nature,* I recognized how critical alloparental input must have been for child survival in the Pleistocene, but only later did I begin to consider *how* cooperative breeding evolved in the hominin line and what the implications were for human nature. Invitations to deliver the 2001 Tanner Lectures at the University of Utah and to participate in Barry Hewlett and Michael Lamb's conference on *Hunter Gatherer Childhoods* and Eckart Voland and colleagues' conference on *Grandmotherhood* provided opportunities to work out my ideas. Then and subsequently, I turned for advice to Sue Carter, who urged me to participate in the 2003 Dahlem Workshop on Attachment and Bonding that she and Lieselotte Ahnert were organizing. This book grew out of the position paper I wrote for the Dahlem volume. Through Sue, I met Karlen Lyons-Ruth, whose thinking about intersubjectivity became a central focus of this book.

Topics covered here often took me far afield from my own areas of expertise. Fortunately, generous guides took me by the hand. They read and reread particular sections of my draft and, in the case of Marc Hauser, Kristen Hawkes, Polly Wiessner, and Bill Zimmerman provided detailed criticisms of the entire manuscript. Many colleagues answered questions or provided preprints of work in progress. These included Jeanne Altmann, Karen Bales, Kim Bard, Monique Borgerhoff Mulder, Judith Burkart, Jim Chisholm, Janice Chism, Jose Diaz Rossello, Pat Draper, Melissa Emory-Thompson, Linda Fedigan, John Fleagle, Alison Fleming, Jeff French, Pascal Gagneux, Patricia Adair Gowaty, Ray Hames, Sandy Harcourt, Peter Hobson, Dan Hrdy, William Irons, Lynne Isbell, Paula Henry Ivey, David Joffe, Susan Jones, Cheryl Knott, Michael Lamb, Tetsuro Matsuzawa, Courtney Meehan, Jim Moore, James O'Connell, Ryne Palombit, Amy Parish, Noel Rowe, Joan Silk, Meredith Small, Chuck Snowdon, Kelly Stewart, Anne Storey, Frank Sulloway, Bernard Thierry, Ross Thompson, Michael Tomasello, Sarah Turner, Carel van Schaik, Ajit Varki, Bernard von Bothmer, Mary Wister Rawlins, and Katherine Wynne-Edwards.

I also thank members of the Center for Academic Research and Training in Anthropogeny at the University of California, San Diego;

participants of the Parental Brain Conference organized by Robert Bridges, Daniel Smail, and other participants at the workshop on Deep History at the Radcliffe Institute for Advanced Study; and especially Jim Chisholm, Ian Rowley, Eleanor Russell, and Ant and Mary Lou Simpson, my hosts and guides who made it possible for me to watch splendid fairy wrens and some of the other cooperative breeders from Down Under, including those "thuggish" noisy miners.

From the time this book was no more than a glimmer in my eye, I benefited from the advice of the talented and ever-sympathetic Elizabeth Knoll at Harvard University Press. I also thank Dan Frank and my agent, Peter Ginsberg, for wise counsel and for understanding the special needs of this project. Another old friend, Susan Wallace Boehmer, shepherded the manuscript through its final maturation. The ever-resourceful June-el Piper arranged for photographic permissions, formatted the manuscript, and with the greatest good humor imposed discipline on an awkward and unwieldy process. I cannot thank these supremely gifted literary allomothers enough. I am also grateful to Nancy and Claire DeVore at AnthroPhoto and the wonderful staff at the Peabody Museum's Photographic Archives.

On the home front, Gene Miner, office manager of Citrona Farms, offered steadfast technical assistance. Throughout, and as always, my husband, Dan, provided intellectual, emotional, and practical support, remaining the best choice this female ever made. Meanwhile, my co-mother, Guadalupe de la Concha, helped keep our family's work and lives in balance. With this book I also had a new recruit, my scholar-daughter Sasha, whose pointed critiques of early drafts were among the most valuable I received. And finally, Katrinka and Niko deserve special thanks for keeping me abreast of the way we live now, and for constantly reminding their mother that the "Pleistocene is not the only scene."

68–70, 80, 101, 112, 114, 120–123, 138, 225, 234–235; imitation by, 58–59; fathers, 160; female migration, 197, 239, 271; adoption among, 236; breeding system of, 243, 249, 267, 271; self-medicating by, 257

China, 18, 153, 205

Choughs, 179, 191, 195

Christianity, 15, 146, 157, 262

Chuckchee, 12

Cichlid fish, 176, 192–193

Climate fluctuations, 5, 19, 230

Clinical psychology, 48

Clutton-Brock, Tim, 193–194

Cockburn, Andrew, 189

Code of Hammurabi, 206

Coercion of allomothers, 204–205

Cognitive abilities, 2, 8–9, 28–29, 39, 47, 50, 54–56, 58, 103–105, 116, 131, 136, 172, 231, 279–280, 292

Cognitive psychology, 2, 32, 138

Colobus monkeys, 3, 46, 86, 90–91, 102, 222–223

Columbus, Christopher, 27

Comfort suckling, 178

Commitment: maternal, 104, 112–114, 118–120, 139, 283–286, 290; paternal, 150–153, 161–162, 166–167, 174

Co-mothers, 204, 238

Comparative infant development, 32, 53

Comparative psychology, 8, 52

Compassion, 4–5, 28, 37, 132, 293

Competition, 7, 11, 19, 26, 31, 34, 45, 52, 231, 270–271, 277, 279; between infants, 5, 160, 220, 222; between mating males, 5; between mothers, 5, 204–205, 214, 246, 267, 287; between groups, 19–21, 27, 30, 37, 288; social, 46, 62; between alloparents, 204, 219; sperm, 248–249

Congo, 25

Continuous care and contact, 68–70, 72, 74, 83–85, 91, 113–114, 118, 123–124

Cook, James, 27

Coontz, Stephanie, 103

Cooperation, 4–5, 7, 9, 22, 28, 34, 175, 187, 293; evolutionary basis of, 6, 11–12, 52, 65–67, 283; by chimpanzees, 10, 35–36, 46, 231, 279; within-group, 19–20, 30–31, 230–231; and mind reading, 29, 37, 279–280, 286; in feeding young, 95–96

Cooperative breeding, 30, 32, 105, 212, 224, 264, 272, 275; defined, 30; evolution of, 31, 107, 124, 156, 164, 167, 176, 197–199, 230–231, 245, 276–280; role of alloparents, 80; in marmosets/tamarins, 92–101, 122, 156, 173–174; and attachment theory, 113, 285; effect on males, 168–169, 172, 174; early studies of, 177–180; critical importance of sharing food, 180–184; and eusociality, 184–186; Hamilton's rule, 186–190; costliness of not caring, 190–193; need for good help, 193–195; benefits of group membership, 195–197; and ecology, 197–199; and behavior, 199–203; and sterile castes, 203–207; possible candidates for, 227–231; flexible matings in, 249. *See also* Provisioning; Shared care

Cormorants, 25

Cortisol, 71, 170, 261

Costly young, 21, 100–102, 146–148, 151, 153, 162, 180, 250, 273

Cost/benefit components of altruism, 190–193, 197, 254

Cotton-top tamarins, 100

Cousins, 26, 79, 90, 112, 134, 245, 265, 269

Couvade symptoms, 98, 170

Co-wives, 246

Coyotes, 181

Cree, 133

Crittenden, Alyssa, 165, 204–205

Crocodiles, 39

Crows, 198

Ethiopia, 259

Ethnography, 20, 32, 72, 75, 204, 240, 244–245, 249, 268, 282

Ethology, 24, 34, 76, 81, 106, 221, 290

Eusociality, 184–187, 191, 202, 206–207, 264, 276

Euthanasia, 270

Evolution, 11, 26, 43, 85, 146, 174, 179, 212, 283, 285–286, 292–293; of genus *Homo*, 16–21, 28–29, 32, 62, 66–67, 138, 140, 147, 249, 275–280; natural selection, 29–30, 40, 42, 47, 66–67, 82, 119–121, 131, 156, 180, 192, 200–201, 203, 209, 212, 219–220, 223–224, 231, 238, 248, 254–255, 258, 276–277, 284, 292–293; adaptive behaviors, 37, 39–40, 53, 82, 111, 126, 147, 225–226, 231, 240; role of postreproductive women, 106, 109, 252; of cooperative breeding, 107, 124, 156, 164, 167, 176, 197–199, 230–231, 245, 276–280; and attachment theory, 113–114, 118–119, 124, 126; role of alloparents, 146, 164, 180, 215, 220; and male behavior, 157, 164, 167–168; of shared care, 202, 207, 230–231, 279–280; and residence patterns, 238–241; cultural, 281–282

Evolutionary anthropology, 17, 19, 67

Evolutionary biology, 101, 187, 207, 242, 293

Evolutionary ecology, 282

Evolutionary psychiatry, 133

Evolutionary psychology, 7, 19–20, 240, 271

Exchange networks, 12, 14–16, 26, 29

Exchange partnerships, 14–15

Extended families, 6, 14–16, 20, 65, 103, 105, 131–132, 136, 164, 166, 288

Extinction, 29, 87

"Extra" fathers, 153–156, 165, 272, 287

Eye contact, 47–56, 60, 62, 83, 112, 115, 119–121, 139

Facial expressions, 2, 6–7, 22, 24, 40, 42, 47–59, 62, 83, 114, 120–121, 285

Facultative fathering, 159–164, 167

Fairy wrens, 188–190, 202

Falk, Dean, 123

False-belief experiments, 135–136

False facts, 53

Families: extended (networks), 6, 14–16, 20, 65, 103, 105, 131–132, 136, 164, 166, 288; nuclear, 144–146, 166, 239; single-parent, 145, 150. *See also* Kinship

Farming-herding societies, 13, 27–28, 72, 75, 101, 107–108, 128, 151, 154, 161, 239, 246–249, 259, 269, 287

Fathers, 42, 76, 79–80, 93–94, 108–109, 112, 117, 145, 148, 265; as caregivers, 87–89; and lactation, 98, 169–170, 172; attachment to infants, 127–129; provisioning by, 148–149, 151–152, 160–163, 178; commitment by, 150–153, 161–163, 166–167, 174; stepfathers, 152, 165; "extra," 153–156, 165, 272, 287; facultative, 159–164, 167; chimpanzee, 160; emotional needs of, 162; and strategic flexibility, 165–167; and cads, 167–171; in residence patterns, 238–250, 254

Fear, 38

Fecal pellets, 182

Fertility, and food availability, 152–153

Fifi (chimp), 234, 243

Finland, 259

Fire, 249, 256

Fish. *See individual genera and species*

Fishing, 10

Fledging, 182–183, 195

Fleming, Alison, 42, 170–171

Flexibility, strategic, 165–167

Flinn, Mark, 105–107, 261

Flint (chimp), 234

Flo (chimp), 234, 243

Florida, 146

Fogel, Alan, 120

Food: caloric needs, 14, 31, 43, 75, 101, 147, 149, 152, 256; shortages, 14, 276; nuts, 43–44, 77, 256, 269; availability, and fertility, 152–153; regurgitated, 182, 185; fire-cooked, 249, 256; as evolutionary factor, 254–257, 278–279; tubers, 255–256, 269, 278. *See also* Provisioning

Food sharing, 23, 25, 35, 79–81, 92, 116, 180–181, 202, 207, 238, 256, 275, 278–279, 283. *See also* Provisioning

Foraging societies. *See* Hunting-gathering societies

Foresight, 8–9, 46, 171–172, 175

Fossils, 8, 18, 65, 87, 275, 277–278, 280, 284

Foster, Kevin, 207

Foster parents, 79, 195, 200–201, 211, 228–229, 259, 290–291

Foxes, 179, 181

France, 205, 281

French, Jeffrey, 93–94, 173, 216

French Guiana, 154

Freud, Sigmund, 179

G/wi San, 24

Gaia (chimp), 235–236, 243

Galagos, 86–87, 275

Gambia, 108–109

Games, 4–5, 54, 101, 112, 115, 133, 135–136

Gathering societies. *See* Hunting-gathering societies

Gaze direction, 51–52

Gazing, 47–56, 60, 62, 112, 115, 120–121, 139

Gender, "wrong," 70–72

Generosity, 5–6, 12, 14, 25–27, 80, 116, 133

Genetics, 9, 12–13, 21, 28, 66, 72, 157, 186–187, 202–203, 247–250, 276, 280, 291–292

Genghis Khan, 248

Genocide, 28

Georgia, 18, 284

Germany, 103, 150, 262–263

Germ line, 93

Gestures, 22, 24, 40, 112

Gibbon monkeys, 86

Gift giving, 4, 12, 14–16, 20, 23–25, 27, 29, 272

Giving impulses, 4, 12, 14–16, 21–26, 36, 66, 96–97, 175, 254, 293

Globalization, 150, 153

Golden lion tamarins, 98, 172–173, 222–223

Gombe reserve, 35, 235–237, 243

Goodall, Jane, 37, 234, 243, 279

Good manners, 4

Goodwill, 14–15

Gorillas, 9, 33, 43, 53, 62, 65, 68–70, 72, 84, 86, 91, 101, 114, 160, 216, 233, 236–237, 239, 243–244, 249, 266, 275

Gottlieb, Alma, 225–227

Grandfathers, 265–267

Grandmother hypothesis, 241–243, 255

Grandmothers, 79–80, 103, 107, 130, 165, 194, 233, 245, 253, 272, 279; maternal, 16, 76, 87–90, 103–104, 108, 241, 247; morphing of, 257–260; kinds of help from, 260–261; maternal versus paternal, 261–264; demographic considerations, 267–269; end of usefulness, 270. *See also* Alloparents; Postreproductive women

Grasping reflex, 72

Great Apes, 3, 8–11, 17, 21–23, 25, 27, 29–31, 33, 43, 62, 68–70, 83, 86, 101, 161, 196–197, 216, 229–230, 234, 236, 238–240, 243, 249, 254, 275, 280, 283. *See also* Bonobos; Chimpanzees; Gorillas; Orangutans

Great aunts, 76, 80, 107, 247, 253

Greeting ceremonies, 8

Gremlin (chimp), 236, 243

Grenada, 150

Grooming protocols, 8, 55, 218, 272

Ground squirrels, 93

Growth rates, 101–102, 107–108, 166, 278

Guatemala, 150

Guenon monkeys, 86

Gurche, John, 144

Gusii, 131

Hadza, 66, 76, 78, 106–107, 109, 149–150, 152, 157–158, 165, 171, 188, 204–205, 241, 245, 256, 259, 265

Haida, 12

Hamadryas baboons, 257

Hamilton, William D., 177, 186–188, 190, 197, 242–243

Hamlin, Kiley, 116

Hamsters, 162, 169, 214–216

Handbook of Attachment Theory, 83

Hanse Institute for Advanced Study, 258

Hanuman langurs, 3, 90

Harcourt, Alexander H., 45, 160

Harlow, Harry, 115, 118

Harpending, Henry, 292

Harvard Business School, 15

Harvard University, 96, 148, 191

Hauser, Marc, 96–97

Hawaii, 27, 205

Hawkes, Kristen, 106–107, 152, 241, 243, 255, 258, 268, 276

Hawks, John, 292

Helping, 4, 7, 25, 34, 36, 65, 116, 133, 197, 206, 254

Hennighausen, Katherine, 285

Henry, Paula Ivey, 107, 205, 256

Henzi, Peter, 218

Hewlett, Barry, 79, 112, 128–130, 132, 134–135, 163, 167–169

Hill, Kim, 270, 282

Himba, 24, 26, 50, 81

Hinde, Robert, 118

Hobson, Peter, 33–34, 38, 56

Holding of infants, 43, 69–79, 84, 123, 128, 134–135, 165, 168–169

Hölldobler, Bert, 175

Homicide, 3–4, 19–21, 27, 46, 154, 270

Hominin, formerly hominid, 17. *See also specific members of Genus* homo

Homo erectus, 16–18, 148–149, 249, 255–256, 276, 278, 283–284

Homo ergaster, 17–18, 149

Homo floresiensis, 17–18

Homo genus, 9, 11, 17, 28, 60, 62, 66, 102, 114, 207, 227, 231, 257, 275–276, 278

Homo georgicus, 284

Homo habilis, 17, 254–255

Homo heidelbergensis, 17

Homo neanderthalensis, 9, 17

Homo rudolfensis, 17

Homo sapiens, 17–18, 23, 28–30, 32, 109, 162, 176, 242, 254, 278, 283–284

Homosexuality, 146

Honeybees, 35, 179, 185–187, 271, 276

Hormones, 39–40, 71–72, 98, 169–173, 212–214, 236–238

Hospitality, 4, 23

Households, female-headed, 150

House mice, 181

Howell, Nancy, 166

Howler monkeys, 86, 228

Hrdy, Sarah Blaffer, 91, 127; *Mother Nature,* 120, 167

Hughes, T. H., 3

Human genome project, 248

Human Relations Area Files, 77, 240

Hunter hypothesis, 147–149, 239

Hunting-gathering societies, 11, 32, 62, 70, 78, 83, 85, 101, 105, 121, 123, 132, 135, 143–144, 147, 151, 154, 161, 198, 205–206, 236, 240, 244–247, 250, 254, 256, 260, 263, 266, 270, 279; African foragers, 12–16, 23, 44, 72, 75, 79, 106–107, 113, 124, 128–129, 133–134, 149–150, 163, 166–168, 171, 199, 204, 241–243, 265, 273; Pleistocene, 13, 19–20, 28, 67, 73, 109, 148, 166, 238–239, 249; Pliocene, 148, 255

Hxaro, 14–15, 23, 266

Hyenas, 82, 135, 181, 188, 194
Hypersocial attributes, 4, 9, 19–21, 29–30

Ifaluk atoll, 105, 107
Imitation, 48–50, 52–61, 66
Inbreeding, 196, 240
Inclusive fitness, 187–188
India, 3, 78, 87, 90, 133, 153, 251,
    258–259, 263–264
Indignation, 3
Individualism, 5, 286
Indonesia, 18, 222
Indris, 86
Infanticide, 46, 89, 99–100, 152, 158,
    193–194, 204, 229, 233–236, 250
Infants: reaction to facial expressions,
    6–7, 40, 42, 47–50, 52–59, 62, 83,
    114, 120–121; vocalizations of, 6,
    40–41, 60–61, 76, 112–113, 115,
    121–124; mortality rates, 16, 19,
    31, 67, 89, 102, 105–109, 112, 121,
    140, 152, 163, 166, 218–219, 226,
    233, 258–264, 268, 286, 288–289;
    protection of, 18, 31, 140, 151–152,
    159–161, 179, 187, 290; provisioning
    of, 18, 31, 92, 95–97, 99, 102, 109,
    122, 140, 151–152, 158, 160–163,
    166, 177–188, 198–199, 203, 220,
    273, 275, 277, 279; costliness of, 21,
    100–102, 146–148, 151, 153, 162,
    180, 250, 270; maturation rates, 21,
    29, 100–102, 140, 146–147, 151, 180,
    230, 250, 270, 276–277, 287; signal-
    ing by, 37–38, 52, 117, 220, 230,
    267; sensitivity of, 40, 112, 117–118;
    crying by, 42, 82–83, 170–171;
    holding of, 43, 69–79, 84, 123, 128,
    134–135, 165, 168–169; weaning of,
    43, 102, 116, 178, 182–183, 260, 273,
    275, 280, 283; gazing by, 47–56, 60,
    62, 112, 115, 119–121, 139; mind
    reading by, 47, 57, 131, 135–137,
    139, 231; imitation by, 48–50, 52–61,
    66; chimpanzee, 53–59, 61–62,
    68–70, 80, 101, 112, 114, 120–123,
    138, 225, 234–235; while sleeping,
    53, 55, 130–131; smiling by, 55,
    60–61, 76, 112; emotional needs
    of, 68, 79, 82–83, 115, 128, 132,
    289–290; abandonment of, 70–73,
    99–100, 103, 120; and foster care,
    79, 195, 200–201, 211, 228–229, 259,
    290–291; growth rates, 101–102,
    108, 166, 278; need for physical
    contact, 112, 114–115, 118–122, 235,
    285–286; separation from mothers,
    114, 117–118, 120–122; assessment
    of others, 115–119, 121, 135–137;
    teething of, 122; in daycare, 124–126,
    130–132, 288; empathy development
    in, 132, 286, 292; feelings about
    their environment, 132–135; innate
    responsiveness to, 212–215. *See also*
    Children
Infant sharing, 76–79, 84, 91, 117, 220,
    222, 225, 238–239, 246, 250
Inheritance systems, 16, 265–266, 287
Insects. *See individual genera and species*
Institute for Genomic Biology, 202
Intersubjectivity, 2, 11, 26, 28, 32,
    34, 37, 43, 47, 58, 60, 66–67, 117,
    131, 137–138, 176, 230–231, 275,
    280–283, 285
Interventions, supportive, 104
Irrationality, 7
Israel, 128–132
Italy, 205

Jackals, 181
Japan, 54, 153, 205, 259, 263, 270
Japanese macaques, 70–71, 253
Jarvis, Jennifer, 186
Java, 18, 222
Jays, 169, 176–177, 181, 183, 198
Jealousy, 3, 19, 155, 157, 260
Jesuits, 157
Johns, Chris, 182
Johnson, Allen, 151
Johnstone, Rufus, 207
Jones, Susan, 58–59

Ju/'hoansi, 12–16, 23, 27, 44, 72, 74–78, 109, 112–113, 115, 124, 127, 137, 147, 149, 165–168, 204, 242, 245, 260, 266, 274

Kalahari desert, 12–14, 77
Kamuniak (lion), 209–212
Kaplan, Hillard, 101
Kayapó, 10
Kenya, 131, 150, 158, 209–210
Keverne, Eric, 213
Khasi, 258, 263–264
Khoisan, 12
Kibbutzim, 130–131
Kidnapping, 195, 218, 237
Killing. See Homicide; Infanticide
Kin selection, 186, 212
Kinship: networks (extended families), 6, 14–16, 20, 65, 103, 105, 131–132, 136, 164, 166, 288; and caregiving, 186–190, 197, 239–243; manufactured, 270–272. See also Families
Kiss-feeding, 79, 81, 116
Kissing, 76, 79
Klein, Richard, 17
Konner, Mel, 74–76
Koryak, 12
Kramer, Karen, 101
Kuikuru, 154
Kula ring, 12
Kulina, 154–156
!Kung. See Ju/'hoansi
Kuni (bonobo), 34
Kurland, Jeffrey, 268
Kwakiutl, 12

Lactation, 104, 126, 160, 213, 279; hormonal basis, 39–40, 72, 98, 169, 172; and bonding with infant, 73; nursing by mothers who carry infants, 75, 77; by allomothers, 76, 78, 80, 92, 135, 180–181, 226; and fathers, 98, 169–170; comfort suckling, 178; by wet nurses, 181, 194, 206; end of, 259–260. See also Weaning

Lamb, Michael, 126, 128, 132, 134
Lamoko site, 25
Langen, Tom, 182–183
Language, 22, 24, 171–172, 272, 282; capacity for, 9, 37–38, 175, 280; development in humans, 11, 66, 123–124, 249, 280–281, 283; learned by child, 104, 116, 271. See also Vocalizations
Langur monkeys, 3, 41, 71, 86, 90–91, 117, 213–214, 217–219, 222, 246, 250–253
Larsen, Niko, 50
Laughing, 60–61
Lavelli, Manuela, 120
Leaf-cutting ants, 191–192
Leaf monkeys, 86, 91, 222
Leakey, Richard, 33–34
Leckman, James, 73
Lee, Richard, 75
Lemmons, Paul, 201
Lemurs, 3, 86–87, 275
Leonetti, Donna, 258, 263
Leopards, 82, 135
Lethal raiding, 19, 21, 46
Leyendecker, Birgit, 134
Life expectancy. See Longevity
Life history theory, 101
Life-history traits, 275–276
Ligon, David, 199
Lions, 93, 177–179, 181, 183, 209–212
Locomotion, 8–9, 121
Longevity, 16, 194, 197, 207, 241–243, 250, 254–255, 257, 267–268, 275–277
Lorenz, Konrad, 221
Lorises, 86–87
Love, 68, 112–113, 116, 120
Lusi, 153
Lyons-Ruth, Karlen, 281, 285, 291

Macaques, 35, 45, 47, 58–59, 68–71, 84, 86, 88–90, 213, 218, 220, 236–237, 253
Mace, Ruth, 107–108, 258–259, 265, 267